TARGETS FOR CHANGE: PERSPECTIVES ON AN ACTIVE SOCIOLOGY

EDITED BY NILS I. BATEMAN University of Maryland

Xerox
College
Publishing

Waltham, Massachusetts / Toronto

Targets for Change: Perspectives on an Active Sociology

DAVID M. PETERSEN   Ohio State University

Preface

This book for use in Basic Sociology is a collection of previously published articles and essays dealing with the general theme of social relevance. The selections have been chosen to provide the student with an overview of significant issues in contemporary American society. It is our intention that these readings will bring a sense of vitality and personal involvement into those courses in introductory sociology where it might be used as a pedagogical adjunct.

There is considerable evidence that a sizable number of students today find their college courses irrelevant and unrelated to the problems of the "contemporary scene." Many of the articles in anthologies currently available deal with obscure, abstract, and technically difficult material. All too frequently these materials "turn off" the student. While we are committed to an approach that presents the student with the basic rudiments of the sociological approach, it is our contention that the introductory course can be made more exciting by illustrating sociological concepts with issues and aspects of contemporary society. At the same time, we have attempted to include selections which have intrinsic interest for the student. There are many competent scholars conducting research in areas such as sexual behavior and the youth culture that elicit considerable student interest.

While this anthology includes papers directed toward social concern and increased student interest, we have adhered to a basic requirement that the material included be sociologically sound. By this we do not mean to imply the use of sophisticated methodology or esoteric statistical analysis. We do mean that the content of those materials selected had to be logical and consistent in terms of the larger body of theory and research which sociology has developed.

The reader will note that the table of contents has been based upon a traditional classification system—the use of major conceptual areas. The selections could have been divided into a number of parts or fields, such as a social problems approach or a delineation based upon organizational setting. However, in order to facilitate the use of *Targets for Change* we have elected to divide the subject matter into ten divisions which approximate the structure of many introductory texts currently in use.

N.I.B.
College Park, Maryland

D.M.P.
Columbus, Ohio

Contents

PART ONE / INTRODUCTION

1. *Sociology as an Individual Pastime*   PETER L. BERGER   3

PART TWO / CULTURE

2. *Body Ritual Among the Nacirema*   HORACE MINER   21
3. *The Flowering of the Hippie Movement*   JOHN ROBERT HOWARD   26
4. *The Subculture of Violence*   CLAUDE BROWN   39

PART THREE / SOCIALIZATION

5. *Becoming a Marijuana User*   HOWARD S. BECKER   47
6. *The Changing American Child—A Speculative Analysis*
   URIE BRONFENBRENNER   56
7. *The Fate of Idealism in Medical School*
   HOWARD S. BECKER AND BLANCHE GEER   66

PART FOUR / SOCIAL STRATIFICATION

8. *On Class in America*   CHRISTOPHER JENCKS AND DAVID RIESMAN   77
9. *The Invisible Poor*   MICHAEL HARRINGTON   94
10. *The Merchants and the Low-Income Consumer*   DAVID CAPLOVITZ   105

PART FIVE / COLLECTIVE BEHAVIOR

11. *Action in Chicago*   THE WALKER COMMISSION REPORT   119
12. *Internal Colonialism and Ghetto Revolt*   ROBERT BLAUNER   138
13. *Confrontation at Cornell*   WILLIAM H. FRIEDLAND AND HARRY EDWARDS   153

PART SIX / SOCIAL ORGANIZATION

14. *Work Behavior in a Service Industry*   DEAN HARPER AND FREDERICK EMMERT   167

15. *The College Sorority as a Social System*   WALTER M. GERSON   179
16. *The Cocktail Lounge: A Study of Heterosexual Relations in a Public Organization*   JULIAN ROEBUCK AND S. LEE SPRAY   186

PART SEVEN / SOCIAL CHANGE

17. *"The Times They Are A-Changing": The Music of Protest*
    ROBERT A. ROSENSTONE   197
18. *Changing Sexual Standards*   IRA L. REISS   211
19. *The Study of the Future*   DANIEL BELL   222

PART EIGHT / MINORITIES

20. *The Status of Women in Modern Patterns of Culture*   JESSIE BERNARD   237
21. *Seminole Girl*   MERWYN S. GARBARINO   249
22. *Nightmare in Mississippi*   PETER WEISS   260

PART NINE / POPULATION

23. *Too Many People*   PAUL EHRLICH   269
24. *Population Policy: Will Current Programs Succeed?*   KINGSLEY DAVIS   278

PART TEN / DEVIANCE AND CRIME

25. *Is Criminal Behavior Deviant Behavior?*   RICHARD QUINNEY   301
26. *What Looting in Civil Disturbances Really Means*
    RUSSELL DYNES AND E. L. QUARANTELLI   309
27. *The Social Organization of Armed Robbery*   WERNER J. EINSTADTER   317

Further Readings   337

TARGETS FOR CHANGE: PERSPECTIVES ON AN ACTIVE SOCIOLOGY

PART ONE Introduction

It is often very difficult for students exposed to their first course in sociology to understand what the discipline is all about. Traditionally, we inform the student that as one of the social sciences, sociology is concerned with the study of human behavior in a group setting, and that the distinguishing feature of sociology is its focus on human interaction. In order that the student may better handle such an abstraction, we identify some of the key concepts that provide a frame of reference for our field, such as society, culture, and socialization. In brief, we attempt to point out the major concerns of the discipline—the topics of sociological inquiry.

For purposes of introduction, we have chosen a selection from Peter Berger's Invitation to Sociology to illustrate what is meant by the sociological approach. Berger describes sociology as "an individual pastime"; a pastime that fascinates some men and bores others. To Berger, the sociological perspective is an all-consuming passion. Those persons who have made it their business to be concerned about understanding human society are persons "intensively, endlessly, shamelessly interested in the doings of men." In this essay, Berger points out the role of the professional sociologist and, in so doing, aptly illustrates the domain of the field of sociology.

1

Sociology as an Individual Pastime

PETER L. BERGER

There are very few jokes about sociologists. This is frustrating for the sociologists, especially if they compare themselves with their more favored second cousins, the psychologists, who have pretty much taken over that sector of American humor that used to be occupied by clergymen. A psychologist, introduced as such at a party, at once finds himself the object of considerable attention and uncomfortable mirth. A sociologist in the same circumstance is likely to meet with no more of a reaction than if he had been announced as an insurance salesman. He will have to win his attention the hard way, just like everyone else. This is annoying and unfair, but it may also be instructive. The dearth of jokes about sociologists indicates, of course, that they are not as much part of the popular imagination as psychologists have become. But it probably also indicates that there is a certain ambiguity in the images that people do have of them. It may thus be a good starting point for our considerations to take a closer look at some of these images.

If one asks undergraduate students why they are taking sociology as a major, one often gets the reply, "because I like to work with people." If one then goes on to ask such students about their occupational future, as they envisage it, one often hears that they intend to go into social work. Of this more in a moment. Other answers are more vague and general, but all indicate that the student in question would rather deal with people than with things. Occupations mentioned in this connection include personnel work, human relations in industry, public relations, advertising, community planning or religious work of the unordained variety. The common assumption is that in all these lines of endeavor one might "do something for people," "help people," "do work that is useful for the community." The image of the sociologist involved here could be described as a secularized version of the liberal Protestant ministry, with the YMCA secretary perhaps furnishing the connecting link between sacred and profane benevolence. Sociology is seen as an up-to-date variation on the classic American theme of "uplift." The sociologist is understood as one professionally concerned with edifying activities on behalf of individuals and of the community at large.

One of these days a great American novel will have to be written on the savage disappointment this sort of motivation is bound to suffer in most of the occupations just mentioned. There is moving pathos in the fate of these likers of people who go into personnel work and come up for the first time against the human realities of a strike that they must fight on one side of the savagely drawn battle lines, or who go into public relations and discover just what it is that they are expected to put over in what experts in the field have called "the en-

SOURCE: Reprinted from *Invitation to Sociology: A Humanistic Perspective* by Peter L. Berger, by permission of Doubleday and Company, Inc., and Penguin Books Ltd. Copyright © 1963 by Peter L. Berger.

gineering of consent," or who go into community agencies to begin a brutal education in the politics of real estate speculation. But our concern here is not with the despoiling of innocence. It is rather with a particular image of the sociologist, an image that is inaccurate and misleading.

It is, of course, true that some Boy Scout types have become sociologists. It is also true that a benevolent interest in people could be the biographical starting point for sociological studies. But it is important to point out that a malevolent and misanthropic outlook could serve just as well. Sociological insights are valuable to anyone concerned with action in society. But this action need not be particularly humanitarian. Some American sociologists today are employed by governmental agencies seeking to plan more livable communities for the nation. Other American sociologists are employed by governmental agencies concerned with wiping communities of hostile nations off the map, if and when the necessity should arise. Whatever the moral implications of these respective activities may be, there is no reason why interesting sociological studies could not be carried on in both. Similarly, criminology, as a special field within sociology, has uncovered valuable information about processes of crime in modern society. This information is equally valuable for those seeking to fight crime as it would be for those interested in promoting it. The fact that more criminologists have been employed by the police than by gangsters can be ascribed to the ethical bias of the criminologists themselves, the public relations of the police and perhaps the lack of scientific sophistication of the gangsters. It has nothing to do with the character of the information itself. In sum, "working with people" can mean getting them out of slums or getting them into jail, selling them propaganda or robbing them of their money (be it legally or illegally), making them produce better automobiles or making them better bomber pilots. As an image of the sociologist, then, the phrase leaves something to be desired, even though it may serve to describe at least the initial impulse as a result of which some people turn to the study of sociology.

Some additional comments are called for in connection with a closely related image of the sociologist as a sort of theoretician for social work. This image is understandable in view of the development of sociology in America. At least one of the roots of American sociology is to be found in the worries of social workers confronted with the massive problems following in the wake of the industrial revolution—the rapid growth of cities and of slums within them, mass immigration, mass movements of people, the disruption of traditional ways of life and the resulting disorientation of individuals caught in these processes. Much sociological research has been spurred by this sort of concern. And so it is still quite customary for undergraduate students planning to go into social work to major in sociology.

Actually, American social work has been far more influenced by psychology than by sociology in the development of its "theory." Very probably this fact is not unrelated to what was previously said about the relative status of sociology and psychology in the popular imagination. Social workers have had to fight an uphill battle for a long time to be recognized as "professionals," and to get the prestige, power and (not least) pay that such recognition entails. Looking around for a "professional" model to emulate, they found that of the psychiatrist to be the most natural. And so contemporary social workers receive their "clients" in an office, conduct fifty-minute "clinical interviews" with them, record the interviews in quadruplicate and discuss them with a hierarchy of "supervisors." Having adopted the outward paraphernalia of the psychiatrist, they naturally also adopted his ideology. Thus contemporary American social work "theory" consists very largely of a somewhat bowdlerized version of psychoanalytic psychology, a sort of poor man's Freudianism that serves to legitimate the social worker's claim to help people in a "scientific" way. We are not interested here in investigating the "scientific" validity of this synthetic doctrine. Our point is that not only does it have very little to do with sociology, but it is marked, indeed, by a singular obtuseness with regard to social reality. The identification of sociology with social work in the minds of many people is somewhat a phenomenon of "cultural lag," dating from the period when as yet pre-"professional" social workers dealt with poverty rather than with libidinal frustration, and did so without the benefit of a dictaphone.

But even if American social work had not jumped on the bandwagon of popular psychologism the image of the sociologist as the social worker's theoretical mentor would be misleading. Social work, whatever its theoretical rationalization, is a certain *practice* in society. Sociology is not a practice, but an *attempt to understand*. Certainly this understanding may have use for the practitioner. For that matter, we would contend that a more profound grasp of sociology would be of great use to the social worker and that such grasp would obviate the necessity of his descending into the mythological depths of the "subconscious" to explain matters that are typically quite conscious, much more simple and,

indeed, *social* in nature. But there is nothing inherent in the sociological enterprise of trying to understand society that necessarily leads to this practice, or to any other. Sociological understanding can be recommended to social workers, but also to salesmen, nurses, evangelists and politicians— in fact, to anyone whose goals involve the manipulation of men, for whatever purpose and with whatever moral justification.

This conception of the sociological enterprise is implied in the classic statement by Max Weber, one of the most important figures in the development of the field, to the effect that sociology is "value-free." Since it will be necessary to return to this a number of times later, it may be well to explicate it a little further at this point. Certainly the statement does *not* mean that the sociologist has or should have no values. In any case, it is just about impossible for a human being to exist without any values at all, though, of course, there can be tremendous variation in the values one may hold. The sociologist will normally have many values as a citizen, a private person, a member of a religious group or as an adherent of some other association of people. But within the limits of his activities as a sociologist there is one fundamental value only—that of scientific integrity. Even there, of course, the sociologist, being human, will have to reckon with his convictions, emotions and prejudices. But it is part of his intellectual training that he tries to understand and control these as *bias* that ought to be eliminated, as far as possible, from his work. It goes without saying that this is not always easy to do, but it is not impossible. The sociologist tries to see what is there. He may have hopes or fears concerning what he may find. But he will try to see regardless of his hopes or fears. It is thus an act of pure perception, as pure as humanly limited means allow, toward which sociology strives.

An analogy may serve to clarify this a little more. In any political or military conflict it is of advantage to capture the information used by the intelligence organs of the opposing side. But this is so only because good intelligence consists of information free of bias. If a spy does his reporting in terms of the ideology and ambitions of his superiors, his reports are useless not only to the enemy, if the latter should capture them, but also to the spy's own side. It has been claimed that one of the weaknesses of the espionage apparatus of totalitarian states is that spies report not what they find but what their superiors want to hear. This, quite evidently, is bad espionage. The good spy reports what is there. Others decide what should be done as a result of his information. The sociologist is a spy in very much the same way. His job is to report as accurately as he can about a certain social terrain. Others, or he himself in a role other than that of sociologist, will have to decide what moves ought to be made in that terrain. We would stress strongly that saying this does *not* imply that the sociologist has no responsibility to ask about the goals of his employers or the use to which they will put his work. But this asking is not sociological asking. It is asking the same questions that any man ought to ask himself about his actions in society. Again, in the same way, biological knowledge can be employed to heal or to kill. This does not mean that the biologist is free of responsibility as to which use he serves. But when he asks himself about this responsibility, he is not asking a biological question.

Another image of the sociologist, related to the two already discussed, is that of social reformer. Again, this image has historical roots, not only in America but also in Europe. Auguste Comte, the early nineteenth century French philosopher who invented the name of the discipline, thought of sociology as the doctrine of progress, a secularized successor to theology as the mistress of the sciences. The sociologist in this view plays the role of arbiter of all branches of knowledge for the welfare of men. This notion, even when stripped of its more fantastic pretensions, died especially hard in the development of French sociology. But it had its repercussions in America too, as when, in the early days of American sociology, some transatlantic disciples of Comte seriously suggested in a memorandum to the president of Brown University that all the departments of the latter should be reorganized under the department of sociology. Very few sociologists today, and probably none in this country, would think of their role in this way. But something of this conception survives when sociologists are expected to come up with blueprints for reform on any number of social issues.

It is gratifying from certain value positions (including some of this writer's) that sociological insights have served in a number of instances to improve the lot of groups of human beings by uncovering morally shocking conditions or by clearing away collective illusions or by showing that socially desired results could be obtained in more humane fashion. One might point, for example, to some applications of sociological knowledge in the penological practice of Western countries. Or one might cite the use made of sociological studies in the Supreme Court decision of 1954 on racial segregation in the public schools. Or one could look at the applications of other sociological studies to the humane planning of urban redevelopment. Certainly the sociologist who is morally and politically sensitive will derive gratification from such instances. But, once more, it will be well to keep in mind that what is at issue here is not sociological understanding as such but certain applications of this understanding. It is not difficult to see how the same understanding could be applied with opposite intentions. Thus the sociological understanding of the dynamics of racial prejudice can be applied effectively by those promoting intragroup hatred as well as by those wanting to spread tolerance. And the sociological understanding of the nature of human solidarity can be employed in the service of both totalitarian and democratic regimes. It is sobering to realize that the same processes that generate consensus can be manipulated by a social group worker in a summer camp in the Adirondacks and by a Communist brainwasher in a prisoner camp in China. One may readily grant that the sociologist can sometimes be called upon to give advice when it comes to changing certain social conditions deemed undesirable. But the image of the sociologist as social reformer suffers from the same confusion as the image of him as social worker.

If these images of the sociologist all have an element of "cultural lag" about them, we can now turn to some other images that are of more recent date and refer themselves to more recent developments in the discipline. One such image is that of the sociologist as a gatherer of statistics about human behavior. The sociologist is here seen essentially as an aide-de-camp to an IBM machine. He goes out with a questionnaire, interviews people selected at random, then goes home, enters his tabulations onto innumerable punch cards, which are then fed into a machine. In all of this, of course, he is supported by a large staff and a very large budget. Included in this image is the implication that the results of all this effort are picayune, a pedantic restatement of what everybody knows anyway. As one observer remarked pithily, a sociologist is a fellow who spends $100,000 to find his way to a house of ill repute.

This image of the sociologist has been strengthened in the public mind by the activities of many agencies that might well be called parasociological, mainly agencies concerned with public opinion and market trends. The pollster has become a well-known figure in American life, inopportuning people about their views from foreign policy to toilet paper. Since the methods used in the pollster business bear close resemblance to sociological research, the growth of this image of the sociologist is understandable. The Kinsey studies of American sexual behavior have probably greatly augmented the impact of this image. The fundamental sociological question, whether concerned with premarital petting or with Republican votes or with the incidence of gang knifings, is always presumed to be "how often?" or "how many?" Incidentally the very few jokes current about sociologists usually relate to this statistical image (which jokes had better be left to the imagination of the reader).

Now it must be admitted, albeit regretfully, that this image of the sociologist and his trade is not altogether a product of fantasy. Beginning shortly after World War I, American sociology turned rather resolutely away from theory to an intensive preoccupation with narrowly circumscribed empirical studies. In connection with this turn, sociologists increasingly refined their research techniques. Among these, very naturally, statistical techniques figured prominently. Since about the mid-1940's there has been a revival of interest in sociological theory, and there are good indications that this tendency away from a narrow empiricism is continuing to gather momentum. It remains true, however, that a goodly part of the sociological enterprise in this country continues to consist of little studies of obscure fragments of social life, irrelevant to any broader theoretical concern. One glance at the table of contents of the major sociological journals or at the list of papers read at sociological conventions will confirm this statement.

The political and economic structure of American academic life encourages this pattern, and not only in sociology. Colleges and universities are normally administered by very busy people with little time or inclination to delve into the esoterica produced by their scholarly employees. Yet these administrators are called upon to make decisions concerning the hiring and firing, promotion and tenure of their faculty personnel. What criteria should they use in these decisions? They cannot be expected to read what their professors write, having no time for such activities and, especially in the more technical disciplines, lacking the necessary qualifications to judge the material. The opinions of immediate colleagues of the professors in question are suspect *a priori,* the normal academic institution being a jungle of bitter warfare between faculty factions, none of which can be relied upon for an objective judgment of members of either his own or an opposing group. To ask the views of students would be even more uncertain procedure. Thus the administrators are left with a number of equally unsatisfactory options. They can go on the principle that the institution is one happy family, in which every member advances steadily up the status ladder regardless of merit. This has been tried often enough, but becomes ever more difficult in an age of competition for the favor of the public and the funds of foundations. Another option is to rely on the advice of one clique, chosen on some more or less rational basis. This creates obvious political difficulties for the administrator of a group chronically defensive about its independence. The third option, the one most common today, is to fall back on the criterion of productivity as used in the business world. Since it is very difficult indeed to judge the productivity of a scholar with whose field one is not well acquainted, one must somehow try to find out how acceptable the scholar is to unprejudiced colleagues in his field. It is then assumed that such acceptability can be deduced from the number of books or articles that publishers or editors of professional publications are willing to accept from the man in question. This forces scholars to concentrate on work that can easily and speedily be converted into a respectable little article likely to be accepted for publication in a professional journal. For sociologists this means some little empirical study of a narrowly confined topic. In most instances such studies will require the application of statistical techniques. Since most professional journals in the field are suspicious of articles that do not contain at least some statistical material, this tendency is further strengthened. And so eager young sociologists stranded somewhere in hinterland institutions, yearning for the richer pastures of the better universities, supply us with a steady stream of little statistical studies of the dating habits of their students, the political opinions of the surrounding natives or the class system of some hamlet within commuting distance of their campus. It might be added here that this system is not quite so terrible as it may seem to the newcomer to the field, since its ritual requirements are well known to all concerned.

As a result, the sensible person reads the sociological journals mainly for the book reviews and the obituaries, and goes to sociological meetings only if he is looking for a job or has other intrigues to carry on.

The prominence of statistical techniques in American sociology today has, then, certain ritual functions that are readily understandable in view of the power system within which most sociologists have to make a career. In fact, most sociologists have little more than a cookbook knowledge of statistics, treating it with about the same mixture of awe, ignorance and timid manipulation as a poor village priest would the mighty Latin cadences of Thomist theology. Once one has realized these things, however, it should be clear that sociology ought not to be judged by these aberrations. One then becomes, as it were, sociologically sophisticated about sociology, and enabled to look beyond the outward signs to whatever inward grace may be hidden behind them.

Statistical data by themselves do not make sociology. They become sociology only when they are sociologically interpreted, put within a theoretical frame of reference that is sociological. Simple counting, or even correlating different items that one counts, is not sociology. There is almost no sociology in the Kinsey reports. This does not mean that the data in these studies are not true or that they cannot be relevant to sociological understanding. They are, taken by themselves, raw materials that can be used in sociological interpretation. The interpretation, however, must be broader than the data themselves. So the sociologist cannot arrest himself at the frequency tables of premarital petting or extramarital pederasty. These enumerations are meaningful to him only in terms of their much broader implications for an understanding of institutions and values in our society. To arrive at such understanding the sociologist will often have to apply statistical techniques, especially when he is dealing with the mass phenomena of modern social life. But sociology consists of statistics as little as philology consists of conjugating irregular verbs or chemistry of making nasty smells in test tubes.

Another image of the sociologist current today and rather closely related to that of statistician is the one that sees him as a man mainly concerned in developing a scientific methodology that he can then impose on human phenomena. This image is frequently held by people in the humanities and presented as proof that sociology is a form of intellectual barbarism. One part of this criticism of sociology by the *littérateurs* is often a scathing commentary on the outlandish jargon in which much sociological writing is couched. By contrast, of course, the one who makes these criticisms offers himself as a guardian of the classical traditions of humane learning.

It would be quite possible to meet such criticism by an argument *ad hominem*. Intellectual barbarism seems to be fairly evenly distributed in the main scholarly disciplines dealing with the phenomenon "man." However, it is undignified to argue *ad hominem,* so we shall readily admit that, indeed, there is much that passes today under the heading of sociology that is justly called barbarian, if that word is intended to denote an ignorance of history and philosophy, narrow expertise without wider horizons, a preoccupation with technical skills, and total insensitivity to the uses of language. Once more, these elements can themselves be understood sociologically in terms of certain characteristics of contemporary academic life. The competition for prestige and jobs in fields rapidly becoming more and more complex forces specialization that all too frequently leads to a depressing parochialism of interests. But it would again be inaccurate to identify sociology with this much more pervasive intellectual trend.

Sociology has, from its beginnings, understood itself as a science. There has been much controversy about the precise meaning of this self-definition. For instance, German sociologists have emphasized the difference between the social and the natural sciences much more strongly than their French or American colleagues. But the allegiance of sociologists to the scientific ethos has meant everywhere a willingness to be bound by certain scientific canons of procedure. If the sociologist remains faithful to his calling, his statements must be arrived at through the observation of certain rules of evidence that allow others to check on or to repeat or to develop his findings further. It is this scientific discipline that often supplies the motive for reading a sociological work as against, say, a novel on the same topic that might describe matters in much more impressive and convincing language. As sociologists tried to develop their scientific rules of evidence, they were compelled to reflect upon methodological problems. This is why methodology is a necessary and valid part of the sociological enterprise.

At the same time it is quite true that some sociologists, especially in America, have become so preoccupied with methodological questions that they have ceased to be interested in society at all. As a result, they have found out nothing of significance about any aspect of social life, since in science as in love a concentration on technique is quite likely to lead to impotence. Much of this fixation on methodology

can be explained in terms of the urge of a relatively new discipline to find acceptance on the academic scene. Since science is an almost sacred entity among Americans in general and American academicians in particular, the desire to emulate the procedures of the older natural sciences is very strong among the newcomers in the marketplace of erudition. Giving in to this desire, the experimental psychologists, for instance, have succeeded to such an extent that their studies have commonly nothing more to do with anything that human beings are or do. The irony of this process lies in the fact that natural scientists themselves have been giving up the very positivistic dogmatism that their emulators are still straining to adopt. But this is not our concern here. Suffice it to say that sociologists have succeeded in avoiding some of the more grotesque exaggerations of this "methodism," as compared with some fields close by. As they become more secure in their academic status, it may be expected that this methodological inferiority complex will diminish even further.

The charge that many sociologists write in a barbaric dialect must also be admitted with similar reservations. Any scientific discipline must develop a terminology. This is self-evident for a discipline such as, say, nuclear physics that deals with matters unknown to most people and for which no words exist in common speech. However, terminology is possibly even more important for the social sciences, just because their subject matter *is* familiar and just because words *do* exist to denote it. Because we are well acquainted with the social institutions that surround us, our perception of them is imprecise and often erroneous. In very much the same way most of us will have considerable difficulty giving an accurate description of our parents, husbands or wives, children or close friends. Also, our language is often (and perhaps blessedly) vague and confusing in its references to social reality. Take for an example the concept of *class,* a very important one in sociology. There must be dozens of meanings that this term may have in common speech—income brackets, races, ethnic groups, power cliques, intelligence ratings, and many others. It is obvious that the sociologist must have a precise, unambiguous definition of the concept if his work is to proceed with any degree of scientific rigor. In view of these facts, one can understand that some sociologists have been tempted to invent altogether new words to avoid the semantic traps of the vernacular usage. We would contend, then, that some of these neologisms have been necessary. We would also contend, however, that most sociology can be presented in intelligible English with but a little effort and that a good deal of contemporary "sociologese" can be understood as a self-conscious mystification. Here again, however, we are confronted with an intellectual phenomenon that affects other fields as well. There may be a connection with the strong influence of German academic life in a formative period in the development of American universities. Scientific profundity was gauged by the ponderousness of scientific language. If scientific prose was unintelligible to any but the narrow circle of initiates to the field in question, this was *ipso facto* proof of its intellectual respectability. Much American scholarly writing still reads like a translation from the German. This is certainly regrettable. It has little to do, however, with the legitimacy of the sociological enterprise as such.

Finally, we would look at an image of the sociologist not so much in his profes-sional role as in his being, supposedly, a certain kind of person. This is the image of the sociologist as a detached, sardonic observer, and a cold manipulator of men. Where this image prevails, it may represent an ironic triumph of the sociologist's own efforts to be accepted as a genuine scientist. The sociologist here becomes the self-appointed superior man, standing off from the warm vitality of common existence, finding his satisfactions not in living but in coolly appraising the lives of others, filing them away in little categories, and thus presumably missing the real significance of what he is observing. Further, there is the notion that, when he involves himself in social processes at all, the sociologist does so as an uncommitted technician, putting his manipulative skills at the disposal of the powers that be.

This last image is probably not very widely held. It is mainly held by people concerned for political reasons with actual or possible misuses of sociology in modern societies. There is not very much to say about this image by way of refutation. As a general portrait of the contemporary sociologist it is certainly a gross distortion. It fits very few individuals that anyone is likely to meet in this country today. The problem of the political role of the social scientist is, nevertheless, a very genuine one. For instance, the employment of sociologists by certain branches of industry and government raises moral questions that ought to be faced more widely than they have been so far. These are, however, moral questions that concern all men in positions of responsibility in modern society. The image of the sociologist as an observer without compassion and a manipulator without conscience need not detain us further here. By and large, history produces very few Talleyrands. As for contemporary sociologists, most of them would lack the emotional equipment for such a role, even if they should aspire to it in moments of feverish fantasy.

How then are we to conceive of the sociologist? In discussing the various images of him that abound in the popular mind we have already brought out certain elements that would have to go into our conception. We can now put them together. In doing so, we shall construct what sociologists themselves call an "ideal type." This means that what we delineate will not be found in reality in its pure form. Instead, one will find approximations to it and deviations from it, in varying degrees. Nor is it to be understood as an empirical average. We would not even claim that all individuals who now call themselves sociologists will recognize themselves without reservations in our conception, nor would we dispute the right of those who do not so recognize themselves to use the appellation. Our business is not excommunication. We would, however, contend that our "ideal type" corresponds to the self-conception of most sociologists in the mainstream of the discipline, both historically (at least in this century) and today.

The sociologist, then, is someone concerned with understanding society in a disciplined way. The nature of this discipline is scientific. This means that what the sociologist finds and says about the social phenomena he studies occurs within a certain rather strictly defined frame of reference. One of the main characteristics of this scientific frame of reference is that operations are bound by certain rules of evidence. As a scientist, the sociologist tries to be objective, to control his personal preferences and prejudices, to perceive clearly rather than to judge normatively.

This restraint, of course, does not embrace the totality of the sociologist's existence as a human being, but it limited to his operations *qua* sociologist. Nor does the sociologist claim that his frame of reference is the only one within which society can be looked at. For that matter, very few scientists in any field would claim today that one should look at the world only scientifically. The botanist looking at a daffodil has no reason to dispute the right of the poet to look at the same object in a very different manner. There are many ways of playing. The point is not that one denies other people's games but that one is clear about the rules of one's own. The game of the sociologist, then, uses scientific rules. As a result, the sociologist must be clear in his own mind as to the meaning of these rules. That is, he must concern himself with methodological questions. Methodology does not constitute his goal. The latter, let us recall once more, is the attempt to understand society. Methodology helps in reaching this goal. In order to understand society, or that segment of it that he is studying at the moment, the sociologist will use a variety of means. Among these are statistical techniques. Statistics can be very useful in answering certain sociological questions. But statistics does not constitute sociology. As a scientist, the sociologist will have to be concerned with the exact significance of the terms he is using. That is, he will have to be careful about terminology. This does not have to mean that he must invent a new language of his own, but it does mean that he cannot naively use the language of everyday discourse. Finally, the interest of the sociologist is primarily theoretical. That is, he is interested in understanding for its own sake. He may be aware of or even concerned with the practical applicability and consequences of his findings, but at that point he leaves the sociological frame of reference as such and moves into realms of values, beliefs and ideas that he shares with other men who are not sociologists.

We daresay that this conception of the sociologist would meet with very wide consensus within the discipline today. But we would like to go a little bit further here and ask a somewhat more personal (and therefore, no doubt, more controversial) question. We would like to ask not only what it is that the sociologist is doing but also what it is that drives him to it. Or, to use the phrase Max Weber used in a similar connection, we want to inquire a little into the nature of the sociologist's demon. In doing so, we shall evoke an image that is not so much ideal-typical in the above sense but more confessional in the sense of personal commitment. Again, we are not interested in excommunicating anyone. The game of sociology goes on in a spacious playground. We are just describing a little more closely those we would like to tempt to join our game.

We would say then that the sociologist (that is, the one we would really like to invite to our game) is a person intensively, endlessly, shamelessly interested in the doings of men. His natural habitat is all the human gathering places of the world, wherever men come together. The sociologist may be interested in many other things. But his consuming interest remains in the world of men, their institutions, their history, their passions. And since he is interested in men, nothing that men do can be altogether tedious for him. He will naturally be interested in the events that engage men's ultimate beliefs, their

moments of tragedy and grandeur and ecstasy. But he will also be fascinated by the commonplace, the everyday. He will know reverence, but this reverence will not prevent him from wanting to see and to understand. He may sometimes feel revulsion or contempt. But this also will not deter him from wanting to have his questions answered. The sociologist, in his quest for understanding, moves through the world of men without respect for the usual lines of demarcation. Nobility and degradation, power and obscurity, intelligence and folly—these are equally *interesting* to him, however unequal they may be in his personal values or tastes. Thus his questions may lead him to all possible levels of society, the best and the least known places, the most respected and the most despised. And, if he is a good sociologist, he will find himself in all these places because his own questions have so taken possession of him that he has little choice but to seek for answers.

It would be possible to say the same things in a lower key. We could say that the sociologist, but for the grace of his academic title, is the man who must listen to gossip despite himself, who is tempted to look through keyholes, to read other people's mail, to open closed cabinets. Before some otherwise unoccupied psychologist sets out now to construct an aptitude test for sociologists on the basis of sublimated voyeurism, let us quickly say that we are speaking merely by way of analogy. Perhaps some little boys consumed with curiosity to watch their maiden aunts in the bathroom later become inveterate sociologists. This is quite uninteresting. What interests us is the curiosity that grips any sociologist in front of a closed door behind which there are human voices. If he is a good sociologist, he will want to open that door, to understand these voices. Behind each closed door he will anticipate some new facet of human life not yet perceived and understood.

The sociologist will occupy himself with matters that others regard as too sacred or as too distasteful for dispassionate investigation. He will find rewarding the company of priests or of prostitutes, depending not on his personal preferences but on the questions he happens to be asking at the moment. He will also concern himself with matters that others may find much too boring. He will be interested in the human interaction that goes with warfare or with great intellectual discoveries, but also in the relations between people employed in a restaurant or between a group of little girls playing with their dolls. His main focus of attention is not the ultimate significance of what men do, but the action in itself, as another example of the infinite richness of human conduct. So much for the image of our playmate.

In these journeys through the world of men the sociologist will inevitably encounter other professional Peeping Toms. Sometimes these will resent his presence, feeling that he is poaching on their preserves. In some places the sociologist will meet up with the economist, in others with the political scientist, in yet others with the psychologist or the ethnologist. Yet chances are that the questions that have brought him to these same places are different from the ones that propelled his fellow-trespassers. The sociologist's questions always remain essentially the same: "What are people doing with each other here?" "What are their relationships to each other?" "How are these relationships organized in institutions?" "What are the collective ideas that move men and insti-

tutions?" In trying to answer these questions in specific instances, the sociologist will, of course, have to deal with economic or political matters, but he will do so in a way rather different from that of the economist or the political scientist. The scene that he contemplates is the same human scene that these other scientists concern themselves with. But the sociologist's angle of vision is different. When this is understood, it becomes clear that it makes little sense to try to stake out a special enclave within which the sociologist will carry on business in his own right. Like Wesley the sociologist will have to confess that his parish is the world. But unlike some latter-day Wesleyans he will gladly share this parish with others. There is, however, one traveler whose path the sociologist will cross more often than anyone else's on his journeys. This is the historian. Indeed, as soon as the sociologist turns from the present to the past, his preoccupations are very hard indeed to distinguish from those of the historian. However, we shall leave this relationship to a later part of our considerations. Suffice it to say here that the sociological journey will be much impoverished unless it is punctuated frequently by conversation with that other particular traveler.

Any intellectual activity derives excitement from the moment it becomes a trail of discovery. In some fields of learning this is the discovery of worlds previously unthought and unthinkable. This is the excitement of the astronomer or of the nuclear physicist on the antipodal boundaries of the realities that man is capable of conceiving. But it can also be the excitement of bacteriology or geology. In a different way it can be the excitement of the linguist discovering new realms of human expression or of the anthropologist exploring human customs in faraway countries. In such discovery, when undertaken with passion, a widening of awareness, sometimes a veritable transformation of consciousness, occurs. The universe turns out to be much more wonder-full than one had ever dreamed. The excitement of sociology is usually of a different sort. Sometimes, it is true, the sociologist penetrates into worlds that had previously been quite unknown to him—for instance, the world of crime, or the world of some bizarre religious sect, or the world fashioned by the exclusive concerns of some group such as medical specialists or military leaders or advertising executives. However, much of the time the sociologist moves in sectors of experience that are familiar to him and to most people in his society. He investigates communities, institutions and activities that one can read about every day in the newspapers. Yet there is another excitement of discovery beckoning in his investigations. It is not the excitement of coming upon the totally unfamiliar, but rather the excitement of finding the familiar becoming transformed in its meaning. The fascination of sociology lies in the fact that its perspective makes us see in a new light the very world in which we have lived all our lives. This also constitutes a transformation of consciousness. Moreover, this transformation is more relevant existentially than that of many other intellectual disciplines, because it is more difficult to segregate in some special compartment of the mind. The astronomer does not live in the remote galaxies, and the nuclear physicist can, outside his laboratory, eat and laugh and marry and vote without thinking about the insides of the atom. The geologist looks at rocks only at appropriate times, and the linguist speaks English with his wife. The sociologist lives in society, on the job and off it. His own life, inevitably, is part of his subject matter. Men being what they are, sociologists too manage to segregate their professional insights from their everyday affairs. But it is a rather difficult feat to perform in good faith.

The sociologist moves in the common world of men, close to what most of them would call real. The categories he employs in his analyses are only refinements of the categories by which other men live—power, class, status, race, ethnicity. As a result, there is a deceptive simplicity and obviousness about some sociological investigations. One reads them, nods at the familiar scene, remarks that one has heard all this before and don't people have better things to do than to waste their time on truisms—until one is suddenly brought up against an insight that radically questions everything one had previously assumed about this familiar scene. This is the point at which one begins to sense the excitement of sociology.

Let us take a specific example. Imagine a sociology class in a Southern college where almost all the students are white Southerners. Imagine a lecture on the subject of the racial system of the South. The lecturer is talking here of matters that have been familiar to his students from the time of their infancy. Indeed, it may be that they are much more familiar with the minutiae of this system than he is. They are quite bored as a result. It seems to them that he is only using more pretentious words to describe what they already know. Thus he may use the term "caste," one commonly used now by American sociologists to describe the Southern racial system. But in explaining the term he shifts to traditional Hindu society, to make it clearer. He then goes on to analyze the magical beliefs inherent in caste tabus, the social dynamics of commensalism and connubium, the economic interests concealed within the system, the way in which religious beliefs relate to the tabus, the effects of the caste system upon the industrial development of the society and vice versa—all in India. But suddenly India is not very far away at all. The lecture then goes back to its Southern theme. The familiar now seems not quite so familiar any more. Questions are raised that are new, perhaps raised angrily, but raised all the same. And at least some of the students have begun to understand that there are functions involved in this business of race that they have not read about in the newspapers (at least not those in their hometowns) and that their parents have not told them—partly, at least, because neither the newspapers nor the parents knew about them.

It can be said that the first wisdom of sociology is this—things are not what they seem. This too is a deceptively simple statement. It ceases to be simple after a while. Social reality turns out to have many layers of meaning. The discovery of each new layer changes the perception of the whole.

Anthropologists use the term "culture shock" to describe the impact of a totally new culture upon a newcomer. In an extreme instance such shock will be experienced by the Western explorer who is told, halfway through dinner, that he is eating the nice old lady he had been chatting with the previous day—a shock with predictable physiological if not moral consequences. Most exploers no longer encounter cannibalism in their travels today. However, the first encounters with polygamy or with puberty rites or even with the way some nations drive their automobiles can be quite a shock to an American visitor. With the shock may go not only disapproval or disgust but a sense of excitement that things can *really* be that different from what they are at home. To some extent, at least, this is the excitement of any first travel abroad. The experience of sociological discovery could be described as "culture shock" minus geographical displacement. In other words, the sociologist travels at home—with shocking results. He is unlikely to find that he is eating a nice old lady for dinner. But the discovery, for instance, that his own church has considerable money invested in the missile industry or that a few blocks from his home there are people who engage in cultic orgies may not be drastically different in emotional impact. Yet we would not want to imply that sociological discoveries are always or even usually outrageous to moral sentiment. Not at all. What they have in common with exploration in distant lands, however, is the sudden illumination of new and unsuspected facets of human existence in society. This is the excitement and, as we shall try to show later, the humanistic justification of sociology.

People who like to avoid shocking discoveries, who prefer to believe that society is just what they were taught in Sunday School, who like the safety of the rules and the maxims of what Alfred Schuetz has called the "world-taken-for-granted," should stay away from sociology. People who feel no temptation before closed doors, who have no curiosity about human beings, who are content to admire scenery without wondering about the people who live in those houses on the other side of that river, should probably also stay away from sociology. They will find it unpleasant or, at any rate, unrewarding. People who are interested in human beings only if they can change, convert or reform them should also be warned, for they will find sociology much less useful than they hoped. And people whose interest is mainly in their own conceptual constructions will do just as well to turn to the study of little white mice. Sociology will be satisfying, in the long run, only to those who can think of nothing more entrancing than to watch men and to understand things human.

It may now be clear that we have, albeit deliberately, understated the case in the title of this chapter. To be sure, sociology is an individual pastime in the sense that it interests some men and bores others. Some like to observe human beings, others to experiment with mice. The world is big enough to hold all kinds and there is no logical priority for one interest as against another. But the word "pastime" is weak in describing what we mean. Sociology is more like a passion. The sociological perspective is more like a demon that possesses one, that drives one compellingly, again and again, to the questions that are its own. An introduction to sociology is, therefore, an invitation to a very special kind of passion. No passion is without its dangers. The sociologist who sells his wares should make sure that he clearly pronounces a *caveat emptor* quite early in the transaction.

PART TWO Culture

Culture as it has been traditionally defined in sociology refers to the social heritage of a society. This definition usually includes the norms, beliefs, values, customs, and skills which have become a part of the life style of the group. Each individual is born into a culture which defines and limits his perceptions, behavior and outlook. Culture as a concept is usually applied to a total society and the process by which it is passed from one generation to another is emphasized. However, in any complex society there are segments of the population which develop distinctive styles of their own. In the United States, for example, factors such as religion, economics, race, age, and geography create distinctive groups which develop unique life styles. These distinctive segments of the population, which accept and reject various aspects of the more general culture, may be defined as subculture.

Culture is often illustrated through studies of primitive societies or esoteric religious groups. Our selections have been chosen to emphasize aspects of the contemporary scene. The first selection is the now classic piece by Horace Miner, "Body Ritual Among the Nacirema." This tongue-in-cheek description of American culture should help jar a few of our ethnocentric biases. The remaining two articles are descriptions of two modern American subcultures, the "hippie" movement and the Black ghetto. John Howard, in "The Flowering of the Hippie Movement," attempts to delineate structure and types in the hippie movement. Claude Brown's autobiography of life in Harlem shows how the tradition of violence is passed from one generation to the next.

2

Body Ritual Among the Nacirema

HORACE MINER

The anthropologist has become so familiar with the diversity of ways in which different peoples behave in similar situations that he is not apt to be surprised by even the most exotic customs. In fact, if all of the logically possible combinations of behavior have not been found somewhere in the world, he is apt to suspect that they must be present in some yet undescribed tribe. This point has, in fact, been expressed with respect to clan organization by Murdock.[1] In this light, the magical beliefs and practices of the Nacirema present such unusual aspects that it seems desirable to describe them as an example of the extremes to which human behavior can go.

Professor Linton first brought the ritual of the Nacirema to the attention of anthropologists twenty years ago,[2] but the culture of this people is still very poorly understood. They are a North American group living in the territory between the Canadian Cree, the Yaqui and Tarahumare of Mexico, and the Carib and Arawak of the Antilles. Little is known of their origin, although tradition states that they came from the east. According to Nacirema mythology, their nation was originated by a culture hero, Notgnihsaw, who is otherwise known for two great feats of strength—the throwing of a piece of wampum across the river Pa-To-Mac and the chopping down of a cherry tree in which the Spirit of Truth resided.

Nacirema culture is characterized by a highly developed market economy which has evolved in a rich natural habitat. While much of the people's time is devoted to economic pursuits, a large part of the fruits of these labors and a considerable portion of the day are spent in ritual activity. The focus of this activity is the human body, the appearance and health of which loom as a dominant concern in the ethos of the people. While such a concern is certainly not unusual, its ceremonial aspects and associated philosophy are unique.

The fundamental belief underlying the whole system appears to be that the human body is ugly and that its natural tendency is to debility and disease. Incarcerated in such a body, man's only hope is to avert these characteristics through the use of the powerful influences of ritual and ceremony. Every household has one or more shrines devoted to this purpose. The more powerful individuals in the society have several shrines in their houses and, in fact, the opulence of a house is often referred to in terms of the number of such ritual centers it possesses. Most houses are of wattle and daub construction, but the shrine rooms of the more wealthy are walled with stone. Poorer families imitate the rich by applying pottery plaques to their shrine walls.

While each family has at least one such shrine, the rituals associated with it are

SOURCE: Reprinted from *The American Anthropologist*, June, 1956, 58:503–507, by permission of the author and the American Anthropological Association.

not family ceremonies but are private and secret. The rites are normally only discussed with children, and then only during the period when they are being initiated into these mysteries. I was able, however, to establish sufficient rapport with the natives to examine these shrines and to have the rituals described to me.

The focal point of the shrine is a box or chest which is built into the wall. In this chest are kept the many charms and magical potions without which no native believes he could live. These preparations are secured from a variety of specialized practitioners. The most powerful of these are the medicine men, whose assistance must be rewarded with substantial gifts. However, the medicine men do not provide the curative potions for their clients, but decide what the ingredients should be and then write them down in an ancient and secret language. This writing is understood only by the medicine men and by the herbalists who, for another gift, provide the required charm.

The charm is not disposed of after it has served its purpose, but is placed in the charm-box of the household shrine. As these magical materials are specific for certain ills, and the real or imagined maladies of the people are many, the charm-box is usually full to overflowing. The magical packets are so numerous that people forget what their purposes were and fear to use them again. While the natives are very vague on this point, we can only assume that the idea in retaining all the old magical materials is that their presence in the charm-box, before which the body rituals are conducted, will in some way protect the worshipper.

Beneath the charm-box is a small font. Each day every member of the family, in succession, enters the shrine room, bows

his head before the charm-box, mingles different sorts of holy water in the font, and proceeds with a brief rite of ablution. The holy waters are secured from the Water Temple of the community, where the priests conduct elaborate ceremonies to make the liquid ritually pure.

In the hierarchy of magical practitioners, and below the medicine men in prestige, are specialists whose designation is best translated "holy-mouth-men." The Nacirema have an almost pathological horror of and fascination with the mouth, the condition of which is believed to have a supernatural influence on all social relationships. Were it not for the rituals of the mouth, they believe that their teeth would fall out, their gums bleed, their jaws shrink, their friends desert them, and their lovers reject them. They also believe that a strong relationship exists between oral and moral characteristics. For example, there is a ritual ablution of the mouth for children which is supposed to improve their moral fiber.

The daily body ritual performed by everyone includes a mouth-rite. Despite the fact that these people are so punctillious about care of the mouth, this rite involves a practice which strikes the uninitiated stranger as revolting. It was reported to me that the ritual consists of inserting a small bundle of hog hairs into the mouth, along with certain magical powders, and then moving the bundle in a highly formalized series of gestures.

In addition to the private mouth-rite, the people seek out a holy-mouth-man once or twice a year. These practitioners have an impressive set of paraphernalia, consisting of a variety of augers, awls, probes, and prods. The use of these objects in the exorcism of the evils of the mouth involves almost unbelievable ritual torture of the client. The holy-mouth-man opens the client's mouth and, using the above mentioned tools, enlarges any holes which decay may have created in the teeth. Magical materials are put into these holes. If there are no naturally occuring holes in the teeth, large sections of one or more teeth are gouged out so that the supernatural substance can be applied. In the client's view, the purpose of these ministrations is to arrest decay and to draw friends. The extremely sacred and traditional character of the rite is evident in the fact that the natives return to the holy-mouth-men year after year, despite the fact that their teeth continue to decay.

It is hoped that, when a thorough study of the Nacirema is made, there will be careful inquiry into the personality structure of these people. One has but to watch the gleam in the eye of a holy-mouth-man, as he jabs an awl into an exposed nerve, to suspect that a certain amount of sadism is involved. If this can be established, a very interesting pattern emerges, for most of the population shows definite masochistic tendencies. It was to these that Professor Linton referred in discussing a distinctive part of the daily body ritual which is performed only by men. This part of the rite involves scraping and lacerating the surface of the face with a sharp instrument. Special women's rites are performed only four times during each lunar month, but what they lack in frequency is made up in barbarity. As part of this ceremony, women bake their heads in small ovens for about an hour. The theoretically interesting point is that what seems to be a preponderantly masochistic people have developed sadistic specialists.

The medicine men have an imposing temple, or *latipso,* in every community of any size. The more elaborate ceremonies required to treat very sick patients can only be performed at this temple. These ceremonies involve not only the thaumaturge but a permanent group of vestal maidens who move sedately about the temple chambers in distinctive costume and headdress.

The *latipso* ceremonies are so harsh that it is phenomenal that a fair proportion of the really sick natives who enter the temple ever recover. Small children whose indoctrination is still incomplete have been known to resist attempts to take them to the temple because "that is where you go to die." Despite this fact, sick adults are not only willing but eager to undergo the protracted ritual purification, if they can afford to do so. No matter how ill the supplicant or how grave the emergency, the guardians of many temples will not admit a client if he cannot give a rich gift to the custodian. Even after one has gained admission and survived the ceremonies, the guardians will not permit the neophyte to leave until he makes still another gift.

The supplicant entering the temple is first stripped of all his or her clothes. In every-day life the Nacirema avoids exposure of his body and its natural functions. Bathing and excretory acts are performed only in the secrecy of the household shrine, where they are ritualized as part of the body-rites. Psychological shock results from the fact that body secrecy is suddenly lost upon entry into the *latipso.* A man, whose own wife has never seen him in an excretory act, suddenly finds himself naked and assisted by a vestal maiden while he performs his natural functions into a sacred vessel. This sort of ceremonial treatment is necessitated by the fact that the excreta are used by a diviner to ascertain the course and nature of the client's sickness. Female clients, on the other hand, find their naked bodies are subjected to the scrutiny, manipulation and prodding of the medicine men.

Few supplicants in the temple are well enough to do anything but lie on their hard beds. The daily ceremonies, like the rites of the holy-mouth-men, involve discomfort and torture. With ritual precision, the vestals awaken their miserable charges each dawn and roll them about on their beds of pain while performing ablutions, in the formal movements of which the maidens are highly trained. At other times they insert magic wands in the supplicant's mouth or force him to eat substances which are supposed to be healing. From time to time the medicine men come to their clients and jab magically treated needles into their flesh. The fact that these temple ceremonies may not cure, and may even kill the neophyte, in no way decreases the people's faith in the medicine men.

There remains one other kind of practitioner, known as a "listener." This witch-doctor has the power to exorcise the devils that lodge in the heads of people who have been bewitched. The Nacirema believe that parents bewitch their own children. Mothers are particularly suspected of putting a curse on children while teaching them the secret body rituals. The counter-magic of the witch-doctor is unusual in its lack of ritual. The patient simply tells the "listener" all his troubles and fears, beginning with the earliest difficulties he can remember. The memory displayed by the Nacirema in these exorcism sessions is truly remarkable. It is not uncommon for the patient to bemoan the rejection he felt upon being weaned as a babe, and a few individuals even see their troubles going back to the traumatic effects of their own birth.

In conclusion, mention must be made of certain practices which have their base in native esthetics but which depend upon the pervasive aversion to the natural body and its functions. There are ritual fasts to make fat people thin and ceremonial feasts to make thin people fat. Still other rites are used to make women's breasts larger if they are small, and smaller if they are large. General dissatisfaction with breast shape is symbolized in the fact that the ideal form is virtually outside the range of human variation. A few women afflicted with almost inhuman hypermammary development are so idolized that they make a handsome living by simply going from village to village and permitting the natives to stare at them for a fee.

Reference has already been made to the fact that excretory functions are ritualized, routinized, and relegated to secrecy. Natural reproductive functions are similarly distorted. Intercourse is taboo as a topic and scheduled as an act. Efforts are made to avoid pregnancy by the use of magical materials or by limiting intercourse to certain phases of the moon. Conception is actually very infrequent. When pregnant, women dress so as to hide their condition. Parturition takes place in secret, without friends or relatives to assist, and the majority of women do not nurse their infants.

Our review of the ritual life of the Nacirema has certainly shown them to be a magic-ridden people. It is hard to understand how they have managed to exist so long under the burdens which they have imposed upon themselves. But even such exotic customs as these take on real meaning when they are viewed with the insight provided by Malinowski when he wrote:

Looking from far and above, from our high places of safety in the developed civilization, it is easy to see all the crudity and irrelevance of magic. But without its power and guidance early man could not have mastered his practical difficulties as he has done, nor could man have advanced to the higher stages of civilization.[3]

Footnotes

[1] George P. Murdock, *Social Structure*, New York: The Macmillan Co., 1949, p. 71.

[2] Ralph Linton, *The Study of Man*, New York: D. Appleton-Century Co., 1936, p. 326.

[3] Bronislaw Malinowski, *Magic, Science, and Religion*, Glencoe: The Free Press, 1948, p. 70.

3

The Flowering of the Hippie Movement

JOHN ROBERT HOWARD

The greatest fool in history was Christ. This great fool was crucified by the commercial pharisees, by the authority of the respectable, and by the mediocre official culture of the philistines. And has not the church crucified Christ more deeply and subtly by its hypocrisy than any pagan? This Divine Fool, whose immortal compassion and holy folly placed a light in the dark hands of the world.*
The Vision of the Fool, CECIL COLLINS

This article is written for people who, in future years, may want to understand something of the hippie movement. To that end, I have (1) described the hippie scene as an anthropologist might describe the culture of a South Sea island tribe, (2) reviewed some of the more prominent "explanations" for the movement, and (3) advanced what seems to me to be a useful theory of the hippie phenomenon.

The data for this article were drawn from literature by and about hippies and other Bohemians in American society, and from extensive informal participation in the hippie movement.

The Hippie Scene

I first heard the term "hippie" in the Fall of 1966. I had gone to the Fillmore Auditorium in San Francisco to hear a rock musical group, one of a number which had formed as a result of the smashing impact of the Beatles upon youth culture. The Fillmore previously had presented mostly black performers, but, increasingly, white rock groups were being featured.

A new cultural style was evolving and was on display that evening. The rock group blasted its sound out through multiple amplifiers, the decibels beating in on the room like angry waves. Above and behind them, a melange of colors and images played upon a huge movie screen. Muted reds and somber blues spilled across the screen, shifting and blending, suddenly exploding like a burst of sunlight let into a dark room, then receding slowly like a gentle tide. Bright images and jagged shapes leaped out from the screen, only to be washed away by the colors before appearing again. Image and color fused and swirled, then melted apart. Film-clips of old serials played on two smaller screens suspended high on the walls of either side of the hall, while shifting multicolored lights illuminated the dancers, the shafts of yellow and blue and red seeming to leap and bounce off the frenetic dance floor. The total effect was that sought by the Dadaists in the early 1920's, a breaking up of traditional linear habits of thought, a disconnection of the sensory apparatus from traditional categories of perception.

Late in the evening, I fell into conversation with a gaily dressed couple, and, in

SOURCE: Reprinted from *The Annals*, March, 1969, 382:44–55, by permission of the author and The American Academy of Political and Social Science.
* Cecil Collins, *The Vision of the Fool*, London, Grey Walls Press, n.d.

the course of an exchange of remarks, the girl referred to the persons at the dance as "hippies." I had not heard the term before and asked them of its derivation but they had no idea how it had originated.[1] As we parted, neither they nor I realized that within nine months, there would be no hamlet or haven in the United States that would not have heard of hippies. Within a year, young people by the thousands were to stream to San Francisco—hippie heaven —while little old ladies in Des Moines trembled at this new evidence that the foundations of the Republic were crumbling.

The Life and Death of Haight-Asbury

Before the rise of Haight-Asbury, the aspiring writer or artist from the Midwest fled to Greenwich Village. By the summer of 1967, Haight-Asbury had replaced the Village as the place to go, and, indeed, people were leaving the Village to move to San Francisco. The words of Horace Greeley, "Go west, young man," had rarely been so diligently heeded.

The Haight-Asbury area was for many years an upper-middle-class neighborhood. Haight Street was named for Henry Haight, a conservative former governor of California, who would be appalled could he have foreseen that his name was to be associated with the "love generation."

As the city grew and the residents of the area prospered, they moved out and rented their property. Eventually, the expanding black population began to move in and, in the late 1950's and early 1960's, were joined by beatnik refugees from the North Beach area of the city. Eventually, in this relatively tolerant community, a small homosexual colony formed. Even

before the hippies appeared, then, Haight-Asbury had become a kind of quiet Bohemia.

"Hippie" is a generic term. It refers to a general orientation of which there are a number of somewhat different manifestations. In the following section, I shall discuss four character types commonly found on the hippie scene: (1) the visionaries, (2) the freaks and heads, (3) the midnight hippies, and (4) the plastic hippies.

The Visionaries

The visionaries gave birth to the movement. It lived and died with them in Haight-Asbury. Let us attempt here to understand what happened.

The hippies offered, in 1966 and 1967, a serious, though not well-articulated, alternative to the conventional social system. To the extent that there was theory of change implicit in their actions, it might be summed up by the phrase "transformation by example." [2] Unlike political revolutionaries, they attempted no seizure of power. Rather, they asked for the freedom to "do their thing," that is, to create their own social system. They assumed, implicitly, that what they created would be so joyous, so dazzling, so "groovy" that the "straight" [3] would abandon his own "up-tight" life and come over to their side. A kind of anti-intellectualism pervades hippie thinking; thus, their theory of change was never made explicit.

The essential elements in the hippie ethic are based on some very old notions— the mind-body dichotomy, condemnation of the worship of "things," the estrangement of people from each other, and so on. Drastically collapsed, the hippie critique of society runs roughly as follows: Success in this society is defined largely in terms of having money and a certain standard of living. The work roles which yield the income and the standard of living are, for the most part, either meaningless or intrinsically demeaning. Paul Goodman, a favored writer among the young estranged, has caught the essence of this indictment.

Consider the men and women in TV advertisements demonstrating the product and singing the jingle. They are clowns and mannequins, in grimace, speech, and action. . . . What I want to call to attention in this advertising is not the economic problem of synthetic demand . . . but the human problem that these are human beings working as clowns; and the writers and designers of it are human beings thinking like idiots. . . .

> "Juicily glubbily
> Blubber is dubbily
> delicious and nutritious
> —eat it, kitty, it's good." [4]

Further, the rewards of the system, the accouterments of the standard of living, are not intrinsically satisfying. Once one has the split-level ranch-type house, the swimming pool, the barbecue, and the color television set—then what? Does one, then, measure his progress in life by moving from a twenty-one-inch set to a twenty-four-inch set? The American tragedy, according to the hippies, is that the "normal" American evaluates himself and others in terms of these dehumanizing standards.

The hippies, in a sense, invert traditional values. Rather than making "good" use of their time, they "waste" it; rather than striving for upward mobility, they live in voluntary poverty.

The dimensions of the experiment first came to public attention in terms of a number of hippie actions which ran directly counter to some of the most cherished values of the society. A group called the Diggers came into existence and began to feed people free in Golden Gate Park in San Francisco and in Constitution Park in Berkeley. They themselves begged for the food that they prepared. They repudiated the notion that the right of people to satisfy their basic needs must be mediated by money. If they had food, one could share it with them, no questions asked. Unlike the Salvation Army, they did not require prayers as a condition of being fed; unlike the Welfare Department, they did not demand proof of being without means. If a person needed lodgings, they attempted to make space available. They repudiated the cash nexus and sought to relate to people in terms of their needs.

Free stores were opened in Berkeley and San Francisco, stores where a person could come and take what he needed. Rock groups such as Country Joe and the Fish gave free concerts in the park.

On the personal level, a rejection of the conventional social system involved dropping out. Given the logic of the hippie ethic, dropping out made sense. The school system prepares a person for an occupational role. The occupational role yields money and allows the person to buy the things which society says are necessary for the "good life." If society's definition of the good life is rejected, then dropping out becomes a sensible action, in that one does not want the money with which to purchase such a life. By dropping out, a person can "do his own thing." And that might entail making beads or sandals, or exploring various levels of consciousness, or working in the soil to raise the food that he eats.

They had a vision of people grooving together, and they attempted to remove those things which posed barriers—property, prejudice, and preconceptions about what is moral and immoral.

By the summer of 1968, it was generally felt by those who remained that Haight-Asbury was no longer a good place. "It's pretty heavy out there on the street," a former methedrine addict remarked to me as we talked of changes in the community, and his sentiments were echoed in one of the underground newspapers, *The San Francisco Express Times*: "For at least a year now . . . the community as a common commitment of its parts, has deteriorated steadily. Most of the old crowd is gone. Some say they haven't actually left but are staying away from the street because of bad vibrations."

In those streets, in the summer of 1968, one sensed despair. Significantly, the agencies and facilities dealing with problems and disasters were still very much in evidence, while those which had expressed the *élan* and hope of the community either no longer existed, or were difficult to find. The Free Clinic was still there, as was the shelter for runaways, and the refuge for persons on bad trips; but free food was no longer served in the parks, and I looked for several days before finding the Diggers.

Both external pressures (coercion from the police and various agencies of city government) and internal contradictions brought about the disintegration of the experiment. Toward the end of this paper, I shall discuss external pressures and why they were mounted. At this point, I am analyzing only the internal contradictions of the hippie ethic.

Stated simply, the argument is as follows. The hippies assumed that voluntarism (every man doing his thing) was com-patible with satisfying essential group and individual needs and with the maintenance of a social system in which there was an absence of power differentials and invidious distinctions based on, for example, wealth, sex, or race. That assumption is open to question. Voluntarism can work only where the participants in a social system have a sufficient understanding of the needs of the system to be willing to do things which they do not want to do in order for the system to persist. Put somewhat differently, every system has its own needs, and where voluntarism prevails, one must assume that the participants will both understand what needs to be done and be willing to do it.

Let me clarify by way of illustration. I asked one of the Diggers why they were no longer distributing food in the park.

Well, man, it took a lot of organization to get that done. We had to scuffle to get the food. Then the chicks or somebody had to prepare it. Then we got to serve it. A lot of people got to do a lot of things at the right time or it doesn't come off. Well, it got so that people weren't doing it. I mean a cat wouldn't let us have his truck when we needed it or some chick is grooving somewhere and can't help out. Now you hate to get into a power bag and start telling people what to do but without that, man, well.

By refusing to introduce explicit rules designed to prevent invidious power distinctions from arising, such distinctions inevitably began to appear. Don S., a former student of mine who had moved to Haight-Asbury, commented on the decline of the communal house in which he had lived.

We had all kinds of people there at first and anybody could stay if there was room.

Anybody could crash out there. Some of the motorcycle types began to congregate in the kitchen. That became *their* room, and if you wanted to get something to eat or a beer you had to step over them. Pretty soon, in a way, people were cut off from the food. I don't mean that they wouldn't give it to you, but you had to go on their "turf" to get it. It was like they had begun, in some very quiet and subtle way, to run things.

In the absence of external pressures, the internal contradictions of the hippie ethic would probably have led to a splintering of the experiment. Significantly, many of the visionaries are trying it again outside the city. There are rural communes throughout California. In at least some of them, allocation of task and responsibility is fairly specific. There is the attempt within the framework of their core values —freedom from hang-ups about property, status, sex, race, and the other furies which pursue the normal American—to establish the degree of order necessary to ensure the persistence of the system within which these values are expressed.

The visionaries used drugs, but that was not at the core of their behavior. For that reason, a distinction between them and more heavily drug-oriented hippies is legitimate. The public stereotype of the hippie is actually a composite of these two somewhat different types.

Let us now discuss the heavy drug users.

Freaks and Heads

Drugs are a common element on the hip scene. The most frequently used are marijuana and hashish, which are derived from plants, and Lysergic Acid Diethylamine (LSD) and methedrine, which are chemical derivatives. Much less commonly used are opium and heroin. The plant derivatives are smoked, while the chemicals are taken orally, "mainlined" (shot into a vein), or "skin-popped" (injected under the skin). To account for the use of drugs among hippies, one must understand something of the mythology and ideology surrounding their use.

Marijuana is almost universally used by the hip and by hippies.[5] For some, it is simply a matter of being "in"; others find it a mild euphoriant. A sub-group places the use of drugs within a religious or ideological context.

Both freaks and heads are frequent users of one or more psychedelic agents; the term "freak," however, has negative connotations, suggesting either that the user is compulsive in his drug-taking, and therefore in a "bag," or that his behavior has become odd and vaguely objectionable as a result of sustained drug use. The mild nature of marijuana is suggested by the fact that, among drug users, one hears frequent mention of "pot heads" but never of "pot freaks." LSD and methedrine, on the other hand, seem to have the capacity to induce freakiness, the "acid freak" and the "speed freak" being frequently mentioned.

In 1966 and 1967 in Haigh-Asbury, the drug of choice for those who wanted to go beyond marijuana was LSD. An elaborate ideology surrounded its use, and something of a cult developed around the figure of Dr. Timothy Leary, the former Harvard professor who advocated it as the answer to the world's problems.

The LSD Ideology

The major tenets of the ideology may be summed up as follows.

(1) LSD introduces the user to levels

of reality which are ordinarily not perceived.

The straight might speak of "hallucinations," suggesting that the "acid" user is seeing things which are not real. The user admits that part of his trip consists of images and visions, but insists that part also consists of an appreciation of new and more basic levels of reality. To make the straight understand, some users argue that if a microscope had been placed under the eyes of a person during the Middle Ages, that person would have seen a level of reality for which there was no accounting within the framework of his belief system. He possibly would have spoken of "hallucinations" and demanded that microscopes be banned as dangerous.

Some users speak of being able, while on a trip, to feel the rhythm and pulse of the earth and to see the life within a tree. They contend that the trip leaves them with a capacity to experience reality with greater intensity and greater subtlety even when not high.

(2) LSD develops a certain sense of fusion with all living things.

The tripper speaks of the "collapse of ego," by which he means a breakdown of the fears, anxieties, rationalizations, and phobias which have kept him from relating to others in a human way. He also speaks of sensing the life process in leaves, in flowers, in the earth, in himself. This process links all things, makes all things one.

The ideology can be expanded, but these are some of its essential elements.

Three things account for the decline of "acid" use in Haight-Asbury: (1) personal disillusionment on the part of many people with Timothy Leary, (2) a rise in the frequency of "acid burns" (the sale of fake LSD), and (3) the rise of methedrine use.

Let us deal with the decline and fall of Timothy Leary. Leary was, in a sense, the Johnny Appleseed of LSD. He was hailed by some as a new Christ. When the unbelievers began to persecute him, however, he had need of money to fight various charges of violation of drug laws which carried the possibility of up to thirty years in jail. Possibly for that reason, he embarked upon what was, in essence, a theatrical tour. His show (billed as a religious celebration) was intended to simulate the LSD experience. It was bad theater, however, and consisted mostly of Leary sitting cross-legged on the stage in front of candles and imploring his audience, which might have had to pay up to $4.00 apiece, to commune with the billion-year-old wisdom in their cells. Leary's tour coincided in time with the beginning of his decline among hippies, and probably contributed to it. Additionally, the increased demand for LSD brought on traffic in fake "acid," the unsuspecting would-be tripper possibly getting only baking soda or powdered milk for his money.

In 1967 methedrine replaced LSD as the major drug in Haight-Asbury. There is no evidence that marijuana is physically harmful. The evidence on LSD is open to either interpretation. Methedrine, on the other hand, is a dangerous drug. It is a type of amphetamine or "pep" pill and is most commonly referred to as "speed." Taken orally, it has the effect of a very powerful amphetamine. "It uses up body energy as a furnace does wood. . . . When it is shot [taken in the blood stream] it is said to produce an effect of watching the sun come up from one hundred miles away. And the user is bursting with energy." In an interview which I conducted in July 1968, a former "speed freak" discussed the effects of the drug.

You're really going. You know you can do anything when you're high on speed. You seem to be able to think clearer and really understand things. You feel powerful. And the more you drop the stuff the more you feel like that. It kills the appetite so, over time, malnutrition sets in. You're in a weakened state and become susceptible to all kinds of diseases. I caught pneumonia when I was on speed. But I couldn't stop. I was falling apart, but it was like I was running so fast I couldn't hit the ground. It was a kind of dynamic collapse.

The use of methedrine seemed to have leveled off in mid-1968 and was even possibly in decline.

From 1966 through 1968, there was a discernible pattern in drug use in Haight-Asbury, a pattern which has relevance in terms of the effectiveness of drug laws. I would advance as a proposition that the volume of use of a drug is determined not by the laws, but by the effects of the drug. If a drug is relatively harmless (as with marijuana), its use will spread, irrespective of severe laws. If it is harmful, its use will be limited, despite more lenient laws (as with methedrine). That heroin, cocaine, and the like have not penetrated Haight-Asbury can probably be explained in terms of the fact that their deleterious effects are well known. Methedrine was an unknown, was tried, and was found to be dangerous; thus, one frequently hears in Haight-Asbury the admonition that "speed kills."

In summary, then, the pattern of use probably reflects the effects of each drug. Marijuana, being relatively mild, is widely used. LSD is much more powerful; a person may have a good trip or a very bad one; thus, its pattern of use is checkered. Methedrine is dangerous; consequently, powerful sentiment against it has begun to form. Hippies, then, are very much pre-disposed to go beyond tobacco and alcohol in terms of drug use, and if what has been said here is correct, the pattern of use should be seen as a realistic response to the effects of the drugs available to them.

The Plastic Hippie

Everybody is familiar with the story of King Midas who turned whatever he touched into gold. Ironically, this faculty eventually brings tragedy to his life and, with it, some insight into the nature of love. In a strange kind of way, the story of Midas is relevant in terms of the hippie movement. The hippies repudiate the values of conventional society, particularly as these relate to work and commerce. They decry the consumption mania—the ethic and passion which compels people to buy more and more. They grieve that so many people are locked into the system, making or selling things which other people do not need, and buying from them equally useless things. The system is such that every man is both victim and victimizer.

Their repudiation of conventional society brought notoriety to the hippies, and, ironically, they themselves became a marketable item, another product to be hawked in the market place. And the more they defamed the commercial process, the more they became a "hot" commercial item.

Those who used the hippie phenomenon to make money appealed in part to an audience which wanted to be titillated and outraged by revelations about sex orgies and drug parties, and in part to adolescents and young people who were not inclined to drop out, but who viewed wearing the paraphernalia of the hippie—love beads, headbands, Benjamin Franklin eyeglasses, leather shirts, and the like—as daring and exciting. These were the plastic hippies.

Any movement runs the risk of becoming merely a fad, of being divested of substance and becoming mostly style. Symbols which might at one time have powerfully expressed outrage at society's oppression and absurdity become merely fashionable and decadent. By the spring of 1968, the plastic hippie was common in the land, and leather shirts and trousers sold in Haight-Asbury shops for more than $100. Some of the suits at Brooks Brothers did not cost as much.

In April of 1968, I interviewed Deans of Students at four Bay Area colleges—San José State College, Stanford University, Foothill Junior College, and the College of San Mateo. The research, financed by the United States Office of Education, focused on students who dropped out of school to live the hippie life. Uniformly, the deans indicated that, despite appearances, there were very few hippies on campus. Despite long hair and beads, most of their students were as career-oriented and grade-conscious as ever. They wore the paraphernalia of the outsider, but were not themselves outsiders.

The plastic hippies have, unintentionally, had an impact on the hippie movement. First, in one important respect, their behavior overlaps with the core behavior of the true hippie—many are users of marijuana. By the summer of 1968, the demand for "grass" had become so great that there was a severe shortage in the Haight-Asbury area. Beyond the obvious consideration of price, the shortage had two consequences. The number of "burns" increased, a "burn" being the sale of some fraudulent substance—alfalfa, oregano, ordinary tobacco, and the like—as genuine marijuana. And a synthetic marijuana was put on the market.

The "pot squeeze" and the resulting burns, along with persistent but unsubstantiated rumors that "the Mob" (organized crime) had moved in and taken over the lucrative trade, contributed to what was, by the summer of 1968, an accelerating sense of demoralization in the Haight-Asbury community.

The Midnight Hippie

Most hippies are in their teens or early twenties. There are a significant number of people, however, who share a whole complex of values with hippies, but who are integrated into the straight world to the extent of having families and careers. Most of these people are in their thirties. They were in college during the 1950's and were nonconformists by the standards of the time. Journalists and commentators of the 1950's decried the apathy of youth and spoke of a "silent generation." These people were part of that minority of youth who were not silent. They were involved, even then, in civil rights and peace and the other issues which were to engage the passions of youth in the 1960's.

There was no hippie scene into which these people could move. They could have dropped out of school, but there was no Haight-Asbury for them to drop into. Consequently, they finished school and moved on into the job world. Significantly, many are in professions which can accommodate a certain amount of Bohemianism. They teach in colleges and universities and thus avoid working the conventional nine-to-five day, or work as book salesmen on the college and university circuit. Relatively few are in straight occupations such as engineering or insurance or banking. They are in jobs in which there is some tolerance for new ideas and which facilitate trying out various styles of life.

The midnight hippie provides an important link between straight society and the hippie world. The straight finds hippies strange, weird, or disgusting. Therefore, he views any action taken against them as justified. The midnight hippie, on the other hand, looks straight. He has a straight job, and does not evoke the same immediate hostility from the straight that the hippie does. The midnight hippie's relative social acceptance allows him to articulate and justify the hippie point of view with at least some possibility of being listened to and believed.

Hippies, Beats, and the "Lost Generation"

How may we account for the hippie phenomenon? Is it simply the traditional rebellion of youth against parental authority, or does it have more profound implications for the society and greater consequences for those who take part in it?

I am inclined to view it as more significant than previous youth movements. Hippies differ in important ways from the beats of the 1950's or the "lost generation" of the 1920's, two groups with whom they have often been compared. In attempting to account for the movement, I have developed a theory of social deviance which identifies its unique features and yields certain predictions with regard to its future.

Vertical and Lateral Deviance

The literature of sociology is rich in theories of deviance. Some focus on "cause," as, for example, the delinquency theories of Cloward and Ohlin which suggest that lower-class boys, in the face of inadequate opportunities to realize middle-class goals,

resort to various forms of unlawful behavior. Others deal with the process whereby a person learns to be a deviant, Howard Becker's paper "Becoming a Marijuana User" being a major example.

In the approach taken here, neither cause nor process is the focus. Rather, I identify two types of deviance: vertical and lateral. The dimensions of each type seem to be useful in differentiating the hippies from earlier Bohemians, and in reaching conclusions about their future.

Vertical and lateral deviance occur in the context of social systems in which differentiations according to rank exist, that is, officer-recruit, teacher-student, adult-child, boss-employee, or guard-convict. Inevitably, certain privileges and prerogatives attach to the superior ranks. That is one of the things which makes them superior. Adults can smoke, consume alcoholic beverages, obtain drivers' licenses, vote, and do a host of other things which are denied to children or teenagers.

Vertical deviance occurs when persons in a subordinate rank attempt to enjoy the privileges and prerogatives of those in a superior rank. Thus, the ten-year-old who sneaks behind the garage to smoke is engaging in a form of vertical deviance, as is the fourteen-year-old who drives a car despite being too young to get a license and the sixteen-year-old who bribes a twenty-two-year-old to buy him a six-pack of beer. They are attempting to indulge themselves in ways deemed not appropriate for persons of their rank.

Lateral deviance occurs when persons in a subordinate rank develop their own standards and norms apart from and opposed to those of persons in a superior rank. Thus, the teenager who smokes pot rather than tobacco is engaging in lateral deviance, as is the seventeen-year-old girl who runs away to live in a commune, rather than eloping with the boy next door. Lateral deviance occurs in a context in which the values of the nondeviant are rejected. The pot-smoking seventeen-year-old, wearing Benjamin Franklin eyeglasses and an earring, does not share his parents' definition of the good life. Whereas value consensus characterizes vertical deviance, there is a certain kind of value dissensus involved in lateral deviance.

Let us explore the implications of these two types of deviance.

Where vertical deviance occurs, power ultimately remains with the privileged. The rule-breaker wants what they have. They can control him by gradually extending prerogatives to him in return for conforming behavior. They have the power to offer conditional rewards and, in that way, can control and shape the deviant's behavior. The sixteen-year-old is told that he can take the car if he behaves himself at home. Where lateral deviance occurs, the possibility of conditional rewards being used to induce conformity disappears. The deviant does not want what the privileged have; therefore, they cannot control him by promising to let him "have a little taste." From the standpoint of the privileged, the situation becomes an extremely difficult one to handle. Value dissensus removes a powerful lever for inducing conformity. The impotent, incoherent rage so often expressed by adults towards hippies possibly derives from this source. A letter to the Editor of the *Portland Oregonian* exemplifies this barely controlled anger.

Why condone this rot and filth that is "hippie" in this beautiful city of ours? Those who desecrate our flag, refuse to work, flaunt their sexual freedom, spread their filthy diseases and their garbage in public parks are

due no charitable consideration. The already overloaded taxpayer picks up the bill.

If every city so afflicted would give them a bum's rush out of town, eventually with no place to light, they might just wake up to find how stupid and disgusting they are. Their feeling of being so clever and original might fade into reality. They might wake up and change their tactics.[6]

The second implication follows from the first. Being unable to maintain control via conditional rewards, the parent, adult or other representative of authority is forced to adopt more coercive tactics. This, of course, has the consequence of further estranging the deviant. What constitutes coercion varies with the situation, and can range all the way from locking a teenage girl in her room to setting the police on anyone with long hair and love beads. Lateral deviance has a certain potential for polarization built into it. To the extent that polarization takes place, the deviant becomes more committed to his deviance.

The third implication follows from the first two and allows us to differentiate hippies from earlier Bohemians. Bennett Berger, the sociologist, contends that the Bohemians of the 1920's and the hippies of the 1960's are similar as regards ideology. Borrowing from Malcolm Cowley's *Exile's Return,* he identifies a number of seemingly common elements in the thinking of the two groups, and, following Cowley, suggests that Bohemians since the mid-nineteenth century have tended to subscribe to the same set of ideas. The ideology of Bohemianism includes: the idea of salvation by the child, an emphasis on self-expression, the notion that the body is a temple where there is nothing unclean, a belief in living for the moment, in female equality, in liberty, and in the possibility of perceiving new levels of reality. There is also a love of the people and places presumably still unspoiled by the corrupt values of society. The noble savages may be Negroes or Indians or Mexicans. The exotic places may be Paris or Tangier or Tahiti or Big Sur.[7]

I would dispute Bennett Berger's analysis and contend that the differences between the hippies and the lost generation are quite profound. The deviant youth of the 1920's simply lived out what many "squares" of the time considered the exciting life—the life of the "swinger." Theirs was a kind of deviance which largely accepted society's definitions of the bad and the beautiful. Lawrence Lipton contrasted values of the lost generation with those of the beatniks, but his remarks are even more appropriate in terms of the differences between the lost generation and the hippies.

Ours was not the dedicated poverty of the present-day beat. We coveted expensive illustrated editions and bought them when we had the ready cash, even if it meant going without other things. We wanted to attend operas and symphony concerts, even if it meant a seat up under the roof in the last gallery or ushering the rich to their seats in the "diamond horseshoe." . . . We had disaffiliated ourselves from the rat race . . . but we had not rejected the rewards of the rat race. We had expensive tastes and we meant to indulge them, even if we had to steal books from the bookstores where we worked, or shoplift, or run up bills on charge accounts that we never intended to pay, or borrow money from banks and leave our co-signers to pay it back with interest. We were no sandal and sweatshirt set. We liked to dress well, if unconventionally, and sometimes exotically, especially the girls. We lived perforce on crackers and cheese most of the time but we talked like gourmets, and if we had a windfall we spent the money in the best restaurants in town, treating our friends in a show of princely largess.[8]

Could they have been more unlike the hippies? The lost generation was engaging in vertical deviance. They wanted the perquisites of the good life but did not want to do the things necessary to get them. They were a generation which had seen its ranks severely decimated in World War I and, having some sense of the temporal nature of existence, possibly did not want to wait their turn to live the beautiful life. Their deviance was at least comprehensible to their elders. They wanted what any "normal" person would want.

From 1957 through 1960, the beat movement flourished, its major centers being the North Beach section of San Francisco and Greenwich Village in New York. The beat movement and the hippie movement are sufficiently close in time for the same individual to have participated in both. Ned Polsky, writing about the Greenwich Village beat scene in 1960, indicated that "the attitudes of beats in their thirties have spread rapidly downward all the way to the very young teenagers (13–15)." [9] It is not unlikely, then, that some hippies began as beats. There are several reasons for suggesting beat influence on the hippie movement. The beat indictment of society is very much like that of the hippies. Lipton recounted Kenneth Rexroth's observations on the social system and its values:

As Kenneth Rexroth has put it, you can't fill the heads of young lovers with "buy me the new five-hundred-dollar deep-freeze and I'll love you" advertising propaganda without poisoning the very act of love itself; you can't hop up your young people with sadism in the movies and television and train them to commando tactics in the army camps, to say nothing of brutalizing them in wars, and then expect to "untense" them with Coca-Cola and Y.M.C.A. hymn sings. Because underneath . . . the New Capitalism . . . and Prosperity Unlimited—lies the ugly fact of an economy geared to war production, a design, not for living, but for death.[10]

Like the hippie a decade later, the beat dropped out. He disaffiliated himself, disaffiliation being "a voluntary self-alienation from the family cult, from moneytheism and all its works and ways." He spoke of a New Poverty as the answer to the New Prosperity, indicating that "it is important to make a living but it is even more important to make a life."

Both the hippie and the beat engage in lateral deviance. Their behavior is incomprehensible to the square. Why would anyone want to live in poverty? Given the nature of their deviance, they cannot be seduced back into squareness. Lipton recounts the remarks of a beat writer to the square who offered him an advertising job: "I'll scrub your floors and carry your slops to make a living, but I will not lie for you, pimp for you, stool for you, or rat for you." [11]

The values of beats and hippies are virtually identical: the two movements differ principally with regard to social organization. Hippies have attempted to form a community. There were beat enclaves in San Francisco and New York, but no beat community. The difference between a ghetto and a community is relevant in terms of understanding the difference between the two movements. In a ghetto, there is rarely any sense of common purpose or common identity. Every man is prey to every other man. In a community, certain shared goals and values generate personal involvement for the common good. Haight-Asbury was a community in the

beginning but degenerated into a ghetto. Significantly, however, more viable rural communities have been established by hippies in response to the failure of urban experiment. The beats had neither any concept of community nor any dream of transforming society.

Given their attempt to establish a viable community, the hippies will probably survive longer than the beats, and should have a more profound impact upon the society. As has been indicated, if a society fails to seduce the lateral deviant away from his deviance it may move to cruder methods (police harassment, barely veiled incitements to hoodlums to attack the deviants, and the like). A functioning community can both render assistance to the deviant in the face of these assaults and sustain his commitment to the values which justify and explain his deviance.

The beats, then, have influenced the hippies. Their beliefs are very similar, and there is probably an overlap in membership. The hippies' efforts to establish self-supporting communities suggest, however, that their movement will survive longer than did that of the beats.

In summary, the hippies have commented powerfully on some of the absurdities and irrationalities of the society. It is unlikely that the straight will throw away his credit cards and move to a rural commune, but it is equally unlikely that he will very soon again wear the emblems of his straightness with quite so much self-satisfaction.

Footnotes

[1] During the 1950's the term "hipster" was used by beatniks and those familiar with the beat scene. It had several meanings. The hipster was an individual whose attitude toward the square world (a steady job, material acquisitions, and the like) was one of contempt. He shared with beats an appreci-

ation of jazz-cum-poetry, drugs, and casual sex. The hipster might also be a kind of confidence man, sustaining his participation in the beat scene by some hustle practiced on squares. The word "hip" identified these orientations. "Hip" and "hep" were common words in the jive-talk of the 1940's; both indicated familiarity with the world of jazz musicians, hustlers, and other colorful but often disreputable types. I suspect that the word "hippie" derives from "hipster" which, in turn, probably derived from "hip" or "hep."

[2] Interestingly, Martin Buber, in *Paths in Utopia,* suggested that the example of the *kibbutz* might transform the rest of society. The values of the *kibbutzim* and those of the hippie movement are not dissimilar.

[3] We shall have occasion to speak frequently of "straights." The derivation of the word is even more obscure than that of "hippie." At one time, it had positive connotations, meaning a person who was honest or forthright. "He's straight, man" meant that the referent was a person to be trusted. As used in the hippie world, "straight" has a variety of mildly to strongly negative connotations. In its mildest form, it simply means an individual who does not partake of the behavior of a given subculture (such as that of homosexuals or marijuana users). In its strongest form, it refers to the individual who does not participate and who is also very hostile to the subculture.

[4] Paul Goodman, *Growing Up Absurd,* New York: Vintage Books, 1960, pp. 25–26.

[5] Marijuana, also known as "weed," "pot," "grass," "maryjane," and "reefers," has not been proven to be physically addictive. It is one of a number of "natural" hallucinogens, some of which are found growing around any home: Jimson weed, Hawaiian wood roses, common sage and nutmeg, and morning-glory seeds. There are claims in Haight-Asbury that the dried seeds of the bluebonnet, the state flower of Texas, have the same property. In California, the bluebonnet is called "Lupin" and grows wild along the highways, as does the Scotch broom, another highly praised drug source.

[6] Letter to the Editor, *Portland Oregonian,* July 31, 1968, p. 22.

[7] Bennett Berger, "Hippie Morality—More Old Than New," *Trans-action,* Vol. 5, No. 2, December 1967, pp. 19–20.

[8] Lawrence Lipton, *The Holy Barbarians,* New York: Grove Press, 1959, p. 284.

[9] Ned Polsky, "The Village Beat Scene: Summer 1960," *Dissent,* Vol. 3, No. 3, Summer 1960, p. 341.

[10] Lipton, *op. cit.,* p. 150.

[11] *Ibid.*

4

The Subculture of Violence

CLAUDE BROWN

If anyone had asked me around the latter part of 1957 just what I thought had made the greatest impression on my generation in Harlem, I would have said, "Drugs." I don't think too many people would have contested this. About ten years earlier, in 1947, or just eight years earlier, in 1949, this wouldn't have been true.

In 1949, I would have answered that same question with the answer, "The knife." Perhaps all this could have been summed up in saying, "The bad mother-fucker." Throughout my childhood in Harlem, nothing was more strongly impressed upon me than the fact that you had to fight and that you should fight. Everybody would accept it if a person was scared to fight, but not if he was so scared that he didn't fight.

As I saw it in my childhood, most of the cats I swung with were more afraid of not fighting than they were of fighting. This was how it was supposed to be, because this was what we had come up under. The adults in the neighorhood practiced this. They lived by the concept that a man was supposed to fight. When two little boys got into a fight in the neighborhood, the men around would encourage them and egg them on. They'd never think about stopping the fight.

There were some little boys, like myself, who when we got into a fight—even though we weren't ten years old yet— all the young men, the street-corner cats, they would come out of the bars or the numbers joints or anyplace they were and watch. Somebody would say, "Little Sonny Boy is on the street fightin' again," and everybody had to see this.

Down on 146th Street, they'd put money on street fights. If there were two little boys on one block who were good with their hands, or one around the corner and one on Eighth Avenue, men on the corner would try and egg them into a fight.

I remember Big Bill, one of the street-corner hustlers before he went to jail for killing a bartender. When I was about seven or eight years old, I remember being on the street and Bill telling me one day, "Sonny Boy, I know you can kick this little boy's ass on 146th Street, and I'll give you a dollar to do it."

I knew I couldn't say no, couldn't be afraid. He was telling all these other men around there on the street that I could beat this boy's ass. There was another man, a numbers hustler, who said, "No. They ain't got nobody here on Eighth Avenue who could beat little Rip's ass on 146th Street."

Bill said, "Sonny Boy, can you do it?" And he'd already promised me the dollar.

I said, "Yeah." I was scared, because I'd seen Rip and heard of him.

He was a mean-looking little boy. He was real dark-skinned, had big lips and bulgy eyes, and looked like he was always mad. One time I had seen him go at somebody with a knife. A woman had taken the knife out of his hand, but she cut her hand getting it. I knew he would have messed up the cat if he could have held on to that knife.

He knew me too, and he had never messed with me. I remember one time he told me that he was going to kick my ass. I said, "Well, here it is. Start kickin'." He never did. I don't think he was too anxious to mess with me. I didn't want to mess with him either, but since Big Bill had given me this dollar and kept pushing me, I couldn't have said no. They would have said I was scared of him, and if that had gotten back to him, I know he would have messed with me.

I fought him for three days. I beat him one day, and he beat me the next day. On the third day, we fought three fights. I had a black eye, and he had a bloody lip. He had a bloody nose, and I had a bloody nose. By the end of the day, we had become good friends. Somebody took us to the candy store and bought us ice cream cones.

Rip and I got real tight. If anybody messed with him and I heard about it, I wanted to fight them. And it was the same with him if anybody messed with me.

This was something that took place in all the poor colored neighborhoods throughout New York City. Every place I went, it was the same way, at least with the colored guys. You had to fight, and everybody respected people for fighting. I guess if you were used to it and were good at it, there was nothing else you could do. I guess that was why Turk became a fighter. He had fought so long and had been so preoccupied with fighting that he couldn't do anything else. He had to get this fighting out of his system.

With cats like Turk and many others who came up on the Harlem streets, the first day they came out of the house by themselves, at about five or six years old, the prizefight ring beckoned to them. It beckoned to them in the form of the cat around the corner who had the reputation or the cat who wanted to mess with your little brother or your little sister. If you went to school and somebody said, "I'm gon kick your ass if you don't bring me some money tomorrow to buy my lunch," it was the prizefight ring beckoning to you.

I remember they used to say on the streets, "Don't mess with a man's money, his woman, or his manhood." This was the thing when I was about twelve or thirteen. This was what the gang fights were all about. If somebody messed with your brother, you could just punch him in his mouth, and this was all right. But if anybody was to mess with your sister, you had to really fuck him up—break his leg or stab him in the eye with an ice pick, something vicious.

I suppose the main things were the women in the family and the money. This was something we learned very early. If you went to the store and lost some money or if you let somebody gorilla you out of some money that your mother or your father had given you, you got your ass beaten when you came back home. You couldn't go upstairs and say, "Well, Daddy, that big boy down there took the money that you gave me to buy some cigars." Shit, you didn't have any business letting anybody take your money. You got your ass whipped for that, and you were supposed to.

You were supposed to go to war about your money. Maybe this was why the cats on the corner were killing each other over a two dollar crap game or a petty debt. People were always shooting, cutting, or killing somebody over three dollars.

I remember going to the store for my father on a Sunday morning. He'd given me a quarter to get him some chewing tobacco. I had to walk up to 149th Street, because no place else was open. I went up to the drugstore on 149th Street, and there were some cats standing around there. I was about eight, and they were about ten or eleven.

One of them said, "Hey, boy, come here," one of those things. I was scared to run, because I knew I wouldn't be able to outrun them all. I figured that if I acted kind of bad, they might not be so quick to mess with me. So I walked right up to them. One cat said, "You got any money?"

I said, "No, I ain't got no money."

I guess I shouldn't have said that. He kept looking at me real mean, trying to scare me. He said, "Jump up and down." I knew what this was all about, because I used to do it myself. If you jumped up and down and the cat who was shaking you down heard some change jingling, he was supposed to try to beat your ass and take the money.

I said, "No, man. I ain't jumpin' up and down."

He grabbed me by my collar. Somebody said, "He's got something in his hand." That was Dad's quarter. One cat grabbed my hand. I'd forgotten all about the guy who had my collar. I hit the boy who had my hand. Then the cat who had me by the collar started punching me in the jaw. I wasn't even thinking about him. I was still fighting the other cat to keep that quarter.

A woman came out a door and said, "You all stop beatin' that boy!"

I had a bloody nose; they'd kicked my ass good, but I didn't mind, because they hadn't taken my quarter. It wasn't the value of money. It couldn't have been. It was just these things symbolized a man's manhood or principles. That's what Johnny Wilkes used to like to call it, a man's principles. You don't mess with a man's money; you don't mess with a man's woman; you don't mess with a man's family or his manhood—these were a man's principles, according to Johnny Wilkes.

Most girls in Harlem could fight pretty well themselves, and if other girls bothered them, they could take care of themselves. You couldn't let other cats bother your sisters. In the bebopping days in Harlem, if the girls had brothers who were scared to fight, everybody would mess with them and treat them like they wanted to. Cats would come up and say things like, "You better meet me up on the roof," or "You better meet me in the park."

It went deep. It went very deep—until drugs came. Fighting was the thing that people concentrated on. In our childhood, we all had to make our reputations in the neighborhood. Then we'd spend the rest of our lives living up to them. A man was respected on the basis of his reputation. The people in the neighborhood whom everybody looked up to were the cats who'd killed somebody. The little boys in the neighborhood whom the adults respected were the little boys who didn't let anybody mess with them.

Dad once saw me run away from a fight. He was looking out the window one day, and the Morris brothers were messing with me. I didn't think I could beat both of them, so I ran in the house. Dad was at the door when I got there. He said, "Where are you runnin' to, boy?"

I said, "Dad, these boys are out there, and they messin' with me."

He said, "Well, if you come in here, I'm

gon mess with you too. You ain't got no business runnin' from nobody."

I said, "Yeah, Dad, I know that. But there's two of 'em, and they're both bigger than me. They can hit harder than I can hit."

Dad said, "You think they can hit harder than I can hit?"

I said. "No, Dad. I know they can't hit harder than you." I was wondering what was behind this remark, because I knew he wasn't going to go out there on the street and fight some boys for me. He wasn't going to fight anybody for me.

He said, "Well, damn right I can hit harder than they can. And if you come in here you got to get hit by me."

He stood on the side of the door and held on to the knob with one hand. I knew I couldn't go in there. If I went downstairs, the Morris brothers were going to kick my ass. I just stood there looking at Dad, and he stood there for a while looking at me and mumbling about me running from somebody like some little girl, all that kind of shit.

Dad had a complex about his size, I think. He was real short. Maybe that's why he played that bad mother-fucker part so strong. That's probably why he always had his knife. This was what used to scare me about him more than anything—the scar on the neck and his knife. I used to associate the two of them together.

Every night when Dad went to bed, he'd put his watch, his money, his wallet, and his knife under his pillow. When he got up, he would wind his watch, but he would take more time with his knife. He had a switchblade, and he would try it a couple of times. Sometimes he would oil it. He never went out without his knife. He never went to church, but I don't think

Dad would have even gone to church without his knife. I guess it was because of that scar on his neck; he never was going to get caught without it again.

The Morris brothers were hollering, "Sonny, you ain't comin' down? Man, you better not come down here any more, 'cause I'm gon kick your ass."

They would take turns hollering up and telling me all this. Dad was standing there in the doorway, and I had a headache. I had a real bad headache, but I knew that wasn't going to help. Dad started telling me about running from somebody who was bigger than me. He said, "You'll probably be short all your life, and little too. But that don't mean you got to run from anybody. If you gon start runnin' this early, you better be good at it, 'cause you probably gon be runnin' all your life."

I just sat down there on the cold hallway tile, my head hurting.

Dad said, "Get up off that floor, boy."

Mama came to the door and said, "Boy, what's wrong with you?"

Dad said, "There ain't nothin' wrong with him. He just scared, that's all. That's what's wrong with him. The thing that's wrong is you try and pamper him too much. You stay away from that boy."

Mama said, "That boy looks like he sick. Don't be botherin' him now. What you gettin' ready to beat him for?"

Dad said, "Ain't nobody gettin' ready to beat him. I'm just gon beat him if he come in this house."

Mama came in the hallway and put her arms around me and said, "Come on in the house and lay down."

I went in and I laid down. I just got sicker until I went downstairs. They really did kick my ass. But it was all right. I didn't feel sick any more.

I remember one time I hit a boy in the face with a bottle of Pepsi Cola. I did it because I knew the older cats on 146th Street were watching me. The boy had messed with Carole. He had taken her candy from her and thrown it on the ground.

I came up to him and said, "Man, what you mess with my sister for?"

All the older guys were saying, "That's that little boy who lives on Eighth Avenue. They call him Sonny Boy. We gon see somethin' good out here now."

There was a Pepsi Cola truck there; they were unloading some crates. They were stacking up the crates to roll them inside. The boy who had hit Carole was kind of big and acted kind of mean. He had a stick in his hand, and he said, "Yeah, I did it, so what you gon do about it?"

I looked at him for a while, and he looked big. He was holding that stick like he meant to use it, so I snatched a Pepsi Cola bottle and hit him right in the face. He grabbed his face and started crying. He fell down, and I started to hit him again, but the man who was unloading the Pepsi Cola bottles grabbed me. He took the bottle away from me and shook me. He asked me if I was crazy or something.

All the guys on the corner started saying, "You better leave that boy alone," and "Let go of that kid." I guess he got kind of scared. He was white, and here were all these mean-looking colored cats talking about "Let go that kid" and looking at him. They weren't asking him to let me go; they were telling him. He let me go.

Afterward, if I came by, they'd start saying, "Hey, Sonny Boy, how you doin'?" They'd ask me, "You kick anybody's ass today?" I knew that they admired me for this, and I knew that I had to keep on doing it. This was the reputation I was making, and I had to keep living up to it every day that I came out of the house. Every day, there was a greater demand on me. I couldn't beat the same little boys every day. They got bigger and bigger. I had to get more vicious as the cats got bigger. When the bigger guys started messing with you, you couldn't hit them or give them a black eye or a bloody nose. You had to get a bottle or a stick or a knife. All the other cats out there on the streets expected this of me, and they gave me encouragement.

When I was about ten years old, the Forty Thieves—part of the Buccaneers—adopted me. Danny and Butch and Kid were already in it. Johnny Wilkes was older than Butch, and Butch was older than Danny and Kid. Johnny was an old Buccaneer. He had to be. When he came out on the streets in the early forties, it must have been twice as hard as it was a few years later. Harlem became less vicious from year to year, and it was hard when I first started coming out of the house, in 1944 and 1945, and raising all kinds of hell. It was something terrible out there on the streets.

Being one of the older Buccaneers, Johnny took Butch, Danny, and Kid as his fellows. He adopted them. I guess he liked the fact that they all admired him. They adopted me because I was a thief. I don't know why or how I first started stealing. I remember it was Danny and Butch who were the first ones who took me up on the hill to the white stores and downtown. I had already started stealing in Harlem. It was before I started going to school, so it must have been about 1943. Danny used to steal money, and he used to take me to the show with him and buy me popcorn and potato chips. After a while,

I stole money too. Stealing became something good. It was exciting. I don't know what made it so exciting, but I liked it. I liked stealing more than I liked fighting.

I didn't like fighting at first. But after a while, it got me a lot of praise and respect in the street. It was the fighting and the stealing that made me somebody. If I hadn't fought or stolen, I would have been just another kid in the street. I put bandages on cats, and people would ask, "Who did that?" The older cats didn't believe that a little boy had broke somebody's arm by hitting him with a pipe or had hit somebody in the face with a bottle or had hit somebody in the head with a door hinge and put that big patch on his head. They didn't believe things like this at first, but my name got around and they believed it.

I became the mascot of the Buccaneers. They adopted me, and they started teaching me things. At that time, they were just the street-corner hoodlums, the delinquents, the little teen-age gangsters of the future. They were outside of things, but they knew the people who were into things, all the older hustlers and the prostitutes, the bootleggers, the pimps, the numbers runners. They knew the professional thieves, the people who dealt the guns, the stickup artists, the people who sold reefers. I was learning how to make homemades and how to steal things and what reefers were. I was learning all the things that you needed to know in the streets. The main thing I was learning was our code.

We looked upon ourselves as the aristocracy of the community. We felt that we were the hippest people and that the other people didn't know anything. When I was in the street with these people, we all had to live for one another. We had to live in a way that we would be respected by one another. We couldn't let our friends think anything terrible of us, and we didn't want to think anything bad about our friends.

PART THREE Socialization

Socialization in a broad sense may be thought of as the means *by which culture is transmitted from one generation to another. This definition includes not only the way in which a child learns a general culture, or a subculture, but also the process by which an individual learns to adjust to new roles and situations. Socialization includes both the learning of behavior and the internalization of appropriate patterns, values, and feelings. That is, one not only learns what is expected of him and behaves accordingly, but he also feels that this is the proper way to think and behave. The process of socialization is not limited simply to childhood, but continues throughout life as the individual interacts with new groups and adjusts to different roles.*

Howard Becker's study of marijuana users illustrates that even in such things as marijuana smoking there is a socialization process which takes place. Evidently for many, smoking satisfaction is a step by step progression which is strongly influenced by group factors. The second article in this section, written by Urie Bronfenbrenner, focuses on the more traditional area—childhood. This article, admittedly speculative, concentrates on changing child rearing practices and the possible effects of these changes on family structure and personality development. The third selection, by Howard Becker and Blanche Geer, is primarily concerned with socialization into a professional role. The process by which the idealism of beginning medical students is transformed into a more objective appraisal of the role of the physician, offers an excellent example of the ongoing process of socialization in adult life.

5

Becoming a Marijuana User

HOWARD S. BECKER

The use of marijuana is and has been the focus of a good deal of attention on the part of both scientists and laymen. One of the major problems students of the practice have addressed themselves to has been the identification of those individual psychological traits which differentiate marijuana users from nonusers and which are assumed to account for the use of the drug. That approach, common in the study of behavior categorized as deviant, is based on the premise that the presence of a given kind of behavior in an individual can best be explained as the result of some trait which predisposes or motivates him to engage in the behavior.

This study is likewise concerned with accounting for the presence or absence of marijuana use in an individual's behavior. It starts, however, from a different premise: that the presence of a given kind of behavior is the result of a sequence of social experiences during which the person acquires a conception of the meaning of the behavior, and perceptions and judgments of objects and situations, all of which make the activity possible and desirable. Thus, the motivation or disposition to engage in the activity is built up in the course of learning to engage in it and does not antedate this learning process. For such a view it is not necessary to identify those "traits" which "cause" the behavior. Instead, the problem becomes one of describing the set of changes in the person's

conception of the activity and of the experience it provides for him.[1]

This paper seeks to describe the sequence of changes in attitude and experience which lead to *the use of marijuana for pleasure*. Marijuana does not produce addiction, as do alcohol and the opiate drugs; there is no withdrawal sickness and no ineradicable craving for the drug. The most frequent pattern of use might be termed "recreational." The drug is used occasionally for the pleasure the user finds in it, a relatively casual kind of behavior in comparison with that connected with the use of addicting drugs. The term "use for pleasure" is meant to emphasize the noncompulsive and casual character of the behavior. It is also meant to eliminate from consideration here those few cases in which marijuana is used for its prestige value only, as a symbol that one is a certain kind of person, with no pleasure at all being derived from its use.

The analysis presented here is conceived of as demonstrating the greater explanatory usefulness of the kind of theory outlined above as opposed to the predispositional theories now current. This may be seen in two ways: (1) predispositional theories cannot account for that group of users (whose existence is admitted) who do not exhibit the trait or traits considered to cause the behavior, and (2) such theories cannot account for the great variability over time of a given individual's behavior with

SOURCE: Reprinted from *American Journal of Sociology,* November, 1953, 59:235–242, by permission of the author and the University of Chicago Press. Copyright 1953 by the University of Chicago.

reference to the drug. The same person will at one stage be unable to use the drug for pleasure, at a later stage be able and willing to do so, and, still later, again be unable to use it in this way. These changes, difficult to explain from a predispositional or motivational theory, are readily understandable in terms of changes in the individual's conception of the drug as is the existence of "normal" users.

The study attempted to arrive at a general statement of the sequence of changes in individual attitude and experience which have always occurred when the individual has become willing and able to use marijuana for pleasure and which have not occurred or not been permanently maintained when this is not the case. This generalization is stated in universal terms in order that negative cases may be discovered and used to revise the explanatory hypothesis.[2]

Fifty interviews with marijuana users from a variety of social backgrounds and present positions in society constitute the data from which the generalization was constructed and against which it was tested.[3] The interviews focused on the history of the person's experience with the drug, seeking major changes in his attitude toward it and in his actual use of it and the reasons for these changes. The final generalization is a statement of that sequence of changes in attitude which occurred in every case known to me in which the person came to use marijuana for pleasure. Until a negative case is found, it may be considered as an explanation of all cases of marijuana use for pleasure. In addition, changes from use to nonuse are shown to be related to similar changes in conception, and in each case it is possible to explain variations in the individual's behavior in these terms.

This paper covers only a portion of the natural history of an individual's use of marijuana, starting with the person having arrived at the point of willingness to try marijuana. He knows that others use it to "get high," but he does not know what this means in concrete terms. He is curious about the experience, ignorant of what it may turn out to be, and afraid that it may be more than he has bargained for. The steps outlined below, if he undergoes them all and maintains the attitudes developed in them, leave him willing and able to use the drug for pleasure when the opportunity presents itself.

I

The novice does not ordinarily get high the first time he smokes marijuana, and several attempts are usually necessary to induce this state. One explanation of this may be that the drug is not smoked "properly," that is, in a way that insures sufficient dosage to produce real symptoms of intoxication. Most users agree that it cannot be smoked like tobacco if one is to get high:

Take in a lot of air, you know, and . . . I don't know how to describe it, you don't smoke it like a cigarette, you draw in a lot of air and get it deep down in your system and then keep it there. Keep it there as long as you can.

Without the use of some such technique[4] the drug will produce no effects, and the user will be unable to get high:

The trouble with people like that [who are not able to get high] is that they're just not smoking it right, that's all there is to it. Either they're not holding it down long enough, or they're getting too much air and not enough smoke, or the other way around or something like that. A lot of people just don't smoke it right, so naturally nothing's gonna happen.

If nothing happens, it is manifestly impossible for the user to develop a conception of the drug as an object which can be used for pleasure, and use will therefore not continue. The first step in the sequence of events that must occur if the person is to become a user is that he must learn to use the proper smoking technique in order that his use of the drug will produce some effects in terms of which his conception of it can change.

Such a change is, as might be expected, a result of the individual's participation in groups in which marijuana is used. In them the individual learns the proper way to smoke the drug. This may occur through direct teaching:

I was smoking like I did an ordinary cigarette. He said, "No, don't do it like that." He said, "Suck it, you know, draw in and hold it in your lungs till you . . . for a period of time."
I said, "Is there any limit of time to hold it?"
He said, "No, just till you feel that you want to let it out, let it out." So I did that three or four times.

Many new users are ashamed to admit ignorance and, pretending to know already, must learn through the more indirect means of observation and imitation:

I came on like I had turned on [smoked marijuana] many times before, you know. I didn't want to seem like a punk to this cat. See, like I didn't know the first thing about it—how to smoke it, or what was going to happen, or what. I just watched him like a hawk—I didn't take my eyes off him for a second, because I wanted to do everything just

as he did it. I watched how he held it, how he smoked it, and everything. Then when he gave it to me I just came on cool, as though I knew exactly what the score was. I held it like he did and took a poke just the way he did.

No person continued marijuana use for pleasure without learning a technique that supplied sufficient dosage for the effects of the drug to appear. Only when this was learned was it possible for a conception of the drug as an object which could be used for pleasure to emerge. Without such a conception marijuana use was considered meaningless and did not continue.

II

Even after he learns the proper smoking technique, the new user may not get high and thus not form a conception of the drug as something which can be used for pleasure. A remark made by a user suggested the reason for this difficulty in getting high and pointed to the next necessary step on the road to being a user:

I was told during an interview, "As a matter of fact, I've seen a guy who was high out of his mind and didn't know it."
I expressed disbelief: "How can that be, man?"
The interviewee said, "Well, it's pretty strange, I'll grant you that, but I've seen it. This guy got on with me, claiming that he'd never got high, one of those guys, and he got completely stoned. And he kept insisting that he wasn't high. So I had to prove to him that he was."

What does this mean? It suggests that being high consists of two elements: the presence of symptoms caused by marijuana use and the recognition of these symptoms and their connection by the user with his use of the drug. It is not enough, that is, that the effects be present; they alone do not automatically provide the experience of being high. The user must be able to point them out to himself and consciously connect them with his having smoked marijuana before he can have this experience. Otherwise, regardless of the actual effects produced, he considers that the drug has had no effect on him: "I figured it either had no effect on me or other people were exaggerating its effect on them, you know. I thought it was probably psychological, see." Such persons believe that the whole thing is an illusion and that the wish to be high leads the user to deceive himself into believing that something is happening when, in fact, nothing is. They do not continue marijuana use, feeling that "it does nothing" for them.

Typically, however, the novice has faith (developed from his observation of users who do get high) that the drug actually will produce some new experience and continues to experiment with it until it does. His failure to get high worries him, and he is likely to ask more experienced users or provoke comments from them about it. In such conversations he is made aware of specific details of his experience which he may not have noticed or may have noticed but failed to identify as symptoms of being high:

I didn't get high the first time. . . . I don't think I held it in long enough. I probably let it out, you know, you're a little afraid. The second time I wasn't sure, and he [smoking companion] told me, like I asked him for some of the symptoms or something, how would I know, you know. . . . So he told me to sit on a stool. I sat on—I think I sat on a bar stool—and he said, "Let your feet hang," and then when I got down my feet were real cold, you know.

And I started feeling it, you know. That was the first time. And then about a week after that, something pretty close to it, I really got on. That was the first time I got on a big laughing kick, you know. Then I really knew I was on.

One symptom of being high is an intense hunger. In the next case the novice becomes aware of this and gets high for the first time:

They were just laughing the hell out of me because like I was eating so much. I just scoffed [ate] so much food, and they were just laughing at me, you know. Sometimes I'd be looking at them, you know, wondering why they're laughing, you know, not knowing what I was doing. [Well, did they tell you why they were laughing eventually?] Yeah, yeah, I come back, "Hey, man, what's happening?" Like, you know, like I'd ask, "What's happening?" and all of a sudden I feel weird, you know. "Man, you're on, you know. You're on pot [high on marijuana]." I said, "No, am I?" Like I don't know what's happening.

The learning may occur in more indirect ways:

I heard little remarks that were made by other people. Somebody said, "My legs are rubbery," and I can't remember all the remarks that were made because I was very attentively listening for all these cues for what I was supposed to feel like.

The novice, then, eager to have this feeling, picks up from other users some concrete referents of the term "high" and applies these notions to his own experience. The new concepts make it possible for him to locate these symptoms among his own sensations and to point out to himself a "something different" in his experience that he connects with drug use. It is only when

he can do this that he is high. In the
next case, the contrast between two successive experiences of a user makes clear
the crucial importance of the awareness of
the symptoms in being high and re-empha-
sizes the important role of interaction with
other users in acquiring the concepts that
make this awareness possible:

[Did you get high the first time you turned
on?] Yeah, sure. Although, come to think of
it, I guess I really didn't. I mean, like that
first time it was more or less of a mild drunk.
I was happy, I guess, you know what I mean.
But I didn't really know I was high, you
know what I mean. It was only after the
second time I got high that I realized I was
high the first time. Then I knew that something different was happening.

[How did you know that?] How did I
know? If what happened to me that night
would of happened to you, you would've
known, believe me. We played the first tune
for almost two hours—one tune! Imagine,
man! We got on the stand and played this
one tune, we started at nine o'clock. When we
got finished I looked at my watch, it's a quarter
to eleven. Almost two hours on one tune. And
it didn't seem like anything.

I mean, you know, it does that to you. It's
like you have much more time or something.
Anyway, when I saw that, man, it was too
much. I knew I must really be high or something if anything like that could happen. See,
and then they explained to me that that's what
it did to you, you had a different sense of
time and everything. So I realized that that's
what it was. I knew then. Like the first time,
I probably felt that way, you know, but I
didn't know what's happening.

It is only when the novice becomes able
to get high in this sense that he will
continue to use marijuana for pleasure.
In every case in which use continued, the
user had acquired the necessary concepts
with which to express to himself the fact
that he was experiencing new sensations

caused by the drug. That is, for use to
continue, it is necessary not only to use
the drug so as to produce effects but also
to learn to perceive these effects when they
occur. In this way marijuana acquires
meaning for the user as an object which can
be used for pleasure.

With increasing experience the user
develops a greater appreciation of the
drug's effects; he continues to learn to get
high. He examines succeeding experiences
closely, looking for new effects, making
sure the old ones are still there. Out of
this there grows a stable set of categories
for experiencing the drug's effects whose
presence enables the user to get high
with ease.

The ability to perceive the drug's effects
must be maintained if use is to continue;
if it is lost, marijuana use ceases. Two
kinds of evidence support this statement.
First, people who become heavy users of
alcohol, barbiturates, or opiates do not
continue to smoke marijuana, largely because they lose the ability to distinguish
between its effects and those of the other
drugs.[5] They no longer know whether the
marijuana gets them high. Second, in
those few cases in which an individual uses
marijuana in such quantities that he is
always high, he is apt to get this same
feeling that the drug has no effect on him,
since the essential element of a noticeable
difference between feeling high and feeling
normal is missing. In such a situation, use
is likely to be given up completely, but
temporarily, in order that the user may
once again be able to perceive the
difference.

III

One more step is necessary if the user who
has now learned to get high is to continue

use. He must learn to enjoy the effects he has just learned to experience. Marijuana-produced sensations are not automatically or necessarily pleasurable. The taste for such experience is a socially acquired one, not different in kind from acquired tastes for oysters or dry martinis. The user feels dizzy, thirsty; his scalp tingles; he misjudges time and distances; and so on. Are these things pleasurable? He isn't sure. If he is to continue marijuana use, he must decide that they are. Otherwise, getting high, while a real enough experience, will be an unpleasant one he would rather avoid.

The effects of the drug, when first perceived, may be physically unpleasant or at least ambiguous:

It started taking effect, and I didn't know what was happening, you know, what it was, and I was very sick. I walked around the room, walking around the room trying to get off, you know; it just scared me at first, you know. I wasn't used to that kind of feeling.

In addition, the novice's naïve interpretation of what is happening to him may further confuse and frighten him, particularly if he decides, as many do, that he is going insane:

I felt I was insane, you know. Everything people done to me just wigged me. I couldn't hold a conversation, and my mind would be wandering, and I was always thinking, oh, I don't know, weird things, like hearing music different. . . . I get the feeling that I can't talk to anyone. I'll goof completely.

Given these typically frightening and unpleasant first experiences, the beginner will not continue use unless he learns to redefine the sensations as pleasurable:

It was offered to me, and I tried it. I'll tell you one thing. I never did enjoy it at all. I mean it was just nothing that I could enjoy. [Well, did you get high when you turned on?] Oh, yeah, I got definite feelings from it. But I didn't enjoy them. I mean I got plenty of reactions, but they were mostly reactions of fear. [You were frightened?] Yes. I didn't enjoy it. I couldn't seem to relax with it, you know. If you can't relax with a thing, you can't enjoy it, I don't think.

In other cases the first experiences were also definitely unpleasant, but the person did become a marijuana user. This occurred, however, only after a later experience enabled him to redefine the sensations as pleasurable:

[This man's first experience was extremely unpleasant, involving distortion of spatial relationships and sounds, violent thirst, and panic produced by these symptoms.] After the first time I didn't turn on for about, I'd say, ten months to a year. . . . It wasn't a moral thing; it was because I'd gotten so frightened, bein' so high. An' I didn't want to go through that again, I mean, my reaction was, "Well, if this is what they call bein' high, I don't dig [like] it." . . . So I didn't turn on for a year almost, accounta that. . . .

Well, my friends started, an' consequently I started again. But I didn't have any more, I didn't have that same initial reaction, after I started turning on again.

[In interaction with his friends he became able to find pleasure in the effects of the drug and eventually became a regular user.]

In no case will use continue without such a redefinition of the effects as enjoyable.

This redefinition occurs, typically, in interaction with more experienced users who, in a number of ways, teach the novice to find pleasure in this experience which is at first so frightening. They may reassure him as to the temporary character of the unpleasant sensations and minimize their seriousness, at the same time calling attention to the more enjoyable aspects. An experienced user describes how he handles newcomers to marijuana use:

Well, they get pretty high sometimes. The average person isn't ready for that, and it is a little frightening to them sometimes. I mean, they've been high on lush [alcohol], and they get higher that way than they've ever been before, and they don't know what's happening to them. Because they think they're going to keep going up, up, up till they lose their minds or begin doing weird things or something. You have to like reassure them, explain to them that they're not really flipping or anything, that they're gonna be all right. You have to just talk them out of being afraid. Keep talking to them, reassuring, telling them it's all right. And come on with your own story, you know: "The same thing happened to me. You'll get to like that after a while." Keep coming on like that; pretty soon you talk them out of being scared. And besides they see you doing it and nothing horrible is happening to you, so that gives them more confidence.

The more experienced user may also teach the novice to regulate the amount he smokes more carefully, so as to avoid any severely uncomfortable symptoms while retaining the pleasant ones. Finally, he teaches the new user that he can "get to like it after a while." He teaches him to regard those ambiguous experiences formerly defined as unpleasant as enjoyable. The older user in the following incident is a person whose tastes have shifted in this way, and his remarks have the effect of helping others to make a similar redefinition:

A new user had her first experience of the effects of marijuana and became frightened and hysterical. She "felt like she was half in and half out of the room" and experienced a number of alarming physical symptoms. One of the more experienced users present said, "She's dragged because she's high like that. I'd give anything to get that high myself. I haven't been that high in years."

In short, what was once frightening and distasteful becomes, after a taste for it is built up, pleasant, desired, and sought after. Enjoyment is introduced by the favorable definition of the experience that one acquires from others. Without this, use will not continue, for marijuana will not be for the user an object he can use for pleasure.

In addition to being a necessary step in becoming a user, this represents an important condition for continued use. It is quite common for experienced users suddenly to have an unpleasant or frightening experience, which they cannot define as pleasurable, either because they have used a larger amount of marijuana than usual or because it turns out to be a higher-quality marijuana than they expected. The user has sensations which go beyond any conception he has of what being high is and is in much the same situation as the novice, uncomfortable and frightened. He may blame it on an overdose and simply be more careful in the future. But he may make this the occasion for a rethinking of his attitude toward the drug and decide that it no longer can give him pleasure. When this occurs and is not followed by a redefinition of the drug as capable of producing pleasure, use will cease.

The likelihood of such a redefinition occurring depends on the degree of the individual's participation with other users. Where this participation is intensive, the individual is quickly talked out of his feeling against marijuana use. In the next case, on the other hand, the experience was very disturbing, and the aftermath of the incident cut the person's participation with other users to almost zero. Use stopped for three years and began again only when a combination of circumstances, important among which was a resumption of ties with users, made possible a redefinition of the nature of the drug:

It was too much, like I only made about four pokes, and I couldn't even get it out of my mouth, I was so high, and I got real flipped. In the basement, you know, I just couldn't stay in there anymore. My heart was pounding real hard, you know, and I was going out of my mind; I thought I was losing my mind completely. So I cut out of this basement, and this other guy, he's out of his mind, told me, "Don't, don't leave me, man. Stay here." And I couldn't.

I walked outside, and it was five below zero, and I thought I was dying, and I had my coat open; I was sweating, I was perspiring. My whole insides were all . . . , and I walked about two blocks away, and I fainted behind a bush. I don't know how long I laid there. I woke up, and I was feeling the worst, I can't describe it at all, so I made it to a bowling alley, man, and I was trying to act normal, I was trying to shoot pool, you know, trying to act real normal, and I couldn't lay and I couldn't stand up and I couldn't sit down, and I went up and laid down where some guys that spot pins lay down, and that didn't help me, and I went down to a doctor's office. I was going to go in there and tell the doctor to put me out of my misery . . . because my heart was pounding so hard, you know. . . . So then all weekend I started flipping, seeing things there and going through hell, you know, all kinds of abnormal things. . . . I just quit for a long time then.

[He went to a doctor who defined the symptoms for him as those of a nervous breakdown caused by "nerves" and "worries."

Although he was no longer using marijuana, he had some recurrences of the symptoms which led him to suspect that "it was all his nerves."] So I just stopped worrying, you know; so it was about thirty-six months later I started making it again. I'd just take a few pokes, you know. [He first resumed use in the company of the same user-friend with whom he had been involved in the original incident.]

A person, then, cannot begin to use marijuana for pleasure, or continue its use for pleasure, unless he learns to define its effects as enjoyable, unless it becomes and remains an object which he conceives of as capable of producing pleasure.

IV

In summary, an individual will be able to use marijuana for pleasure only when he goes through a process of learning to conceive of it as an object which can be used in this way. No one becomes a user without (1) learning to smoke the drug in a way which will produce real effects; (2) learning to recognize the effects and connect them with drug use (learning, in other words, to get high); and (3) learning to enjoy the sensations he perceives. In the course of this process he develops a disposition or motivation to use marijuana which was not and could not have been present when he began use, for it involves and depends on conceptions of the drug which could only grow out of the kind of actual experience detailed above. On completion of this process he is willing and able to use marijuana for pleasure.

He has learned, in short, to answer "Yes" to the question: "Is it fun?" The direction his further use of the drug takes depends on his being able to continue to answer "Yes" to this question and, in addition, on his being able to answer "Yes" to other questions which arise as he becomes aware of the implications of the fact that the society as a whole disapproves of the practice: "Is it expedient?" "Is it moral?" Once he has acquired the ability to get enjoyment out of the drug, use will continue to be possible for him. Considerations of morality and expediency, occasioned by the reactions of society, may interfere and inhibit use, but use continues to be a possibility in terms of his conception of the drug. The act becomes impossible only when the ability to enjoy the experience of being high is lost, through a change in the user's conception of the drug occasioned by certain kinds of experience with it.

In comparing this theory with those which ascribe marijuana use to motives or predispositions rooted deep in individual behavior, the evidence makes it clear that marijuana use for pleasure can occur only when the process described above is undergone and cannot occur without it. This is apparently so without reference to the nature of the individual's personal makeup or psychic problems. Such theories assume that people have stable modes of response which predetermine the way they will act in relation to any particular situation or object and that, when they come in contact with the given object or situation, they act in the way in which their makeup predisposes them.

This analysis of the genesis of marijuana use shows that the individuals who come in contact with a given object may respond to it at first in a great variety of ways. If a stable form of new behavior toward the object is to emerge, a transformation of meanings must occur, in which the person develops a new conception of the nature of the object. This happens in a series of communicative acts in which others point out new aspects of his experience to him, present him with new interpretations of events, and help him achieve a new conceptual organization of his world, without which the new behavior is not possible. Persons who do not achieve the proper kind of conceptualization are unable to engage in the given behavior and turn off in the direction of some other relationship to the object or activity.

This suggests that behavior of any kind might fruitfully be studied developmentally, in terms of changes in meanings and concepts, their organization and reorganization, and the way they channel behavior, making some acts possible while excluding others.

Footnotes

[1] This approach stems from George Herbert Mead's discussion of objects in *Mind, Self, and Society*, Chicago: University of Chicago Press, 1934, pp. 277–280.

[2] The method used is that described by Alfred R. Lindesmith in his *Opiate Addiction*, Bloomington: Principia Press, 1947, Chap. I. I would like also to acknowledge the important role Lindesmith's work played in shaping my thinking about the genesis of marijuana use.

[3] Most of the interviews were done by the author. I am grateful to Solomon Kobrin and Harold Finestone for allowing me to make use of interviews done by them.

[4] A pharmacologist notes that this ritual is in fact an extremely efficient way of getting the drug into the blood stream (R. P. Walton, *Marijuana: America's New Drug Problem*, Philadelphia: J. B. Lippincott, 1938, p. 48).

[5] "Smokers have repeatedly stated that the consumption of whiskey while smoking negates the potency of the drug. They find it very difficult to get 'high' while drinking whiskey and because of that smokers will not drink while using the 'weed' " (cf. New York City Mayor's Committee on Marijuana, *The Marijuana Problem in the City of New York*, Lancaster, Pa.: Jacques Cattell Press, 1944, p. 13).

6

The Changing American Child—A Speculative Analysis

URIE BRONFENBRENNER

A Question of Moment

It is now a matter of scientific record that patterns of child rearing in the United States have changed appreciably over the past twenty-five years.[1] Middle class parents especially have moved away from the more rigid and strict styles of care and discipline advocated in the early Twenties and Thirties toward modes of response involving greater tolerance of the child's impulses and desires, freer expression of affection, and increased reliance on "psychological" methods of discipline, such as reasoning and appeals to guilt, as distinguished from more direct techniques like physical punishment. At the same time, the gap between the social classes in their goals and methods of child rearing appears to be narrowing, with working class parents beginning to adopt both the values and techniques of the middle class. Finally, there is dramatic correspondence between these observed shifts in parental values and behavior and the changing character of the attitudes and practices advocated in successive editions of such widely read manuals as the Children's Bureau bulletin on *Infant Care* and Spock's *Baby and Child Care*. Such correspondence should not be taken to mean that the expert has now become the principal instigator and instrument of social change, since the ideas of scientists and professional workers themselves reflect in part the operation of deep-rooted cultural

processes. Nevertheless, the fact remains that changes in values and practices advocated by prestigeful professional figures can be substantially accelerated by rapid and widespread dissemination through the press, mass media of communication, and public discussion.

Given these facts, it becomes especially important to gauge the effect of the changes that are advocated and adapted. Nowhere is this issue more significant, both scientifically and socially, than in the sphere of familial values and behavior. It is certainly no trivial matter to ask whether the changes that have occurred in the attitudes and actions of parents over the past twenty-five years have been such as to affect the personality development of their children, so that the boys and girls of today are somewhat different in character structure from those of a decade or more ago. Or, to put the question more succinctly: has the changing American parent produced a changing American child?

A Strategy of Inference

Do we have any basis for answering this intriguing question? To begin with, do we have any evidence of changes in the behavior of children in successive decades analogous to those we have already been able to find for parents? If so, we could take an important first step toward a

SOURCE: Reprinted from *The Journal of Social Issues,* Vol. XVII, No. 7:6–18, by permission of the author and the Society for the Psychological Study of Social Issues.

solution of the problem. Unfortunately, in contrast to his gratifying experience in seeking and finding appropriate data on parents, the present writer has, to date, been unable to locate enough instances in which comparable methods of behavioral assessment have been employed with different groups of children of similar ages over an extended period of time. Although the absence of such material precludes any direct and unequivocal approach to the question at hand, it is nevertheless possible, through a series of inferences from facts already known, to arrive at some estimate of what the answer might be. Specifically, although as yet we have no comparable data on the relation between parental and child behavior for different families at successive points in time, we do have facts on the influence of parental treatment on child behavior at a given point in time; that is, we know that certain variations in parental behavior tend to be accompanied by systematic differences in the personality characteristics of children. If we are willing to assume that these same relationships obtained not only at a given moment but across different points in time, we are in a position to infer the possible effects on children of changing patterns of child rearing over the years. It is this strategy that we propose to follow.

The Changing American Parent

We have already noted the major changes in parental behavior discerned in a recent analysis of data reported over a twenty-five year period. These secular trends may be summarized as follows:

1. Greater permissiveness toward the child's spontaneous desires

2. Freer expression of affection

3. Increased reliance on indirect "psychological" techniques of discipline (such as reasoning or appeals to guilt) vs. direct methods (like physical punishment, scolding, or threats)

4. In consequence of the above shifts in the direction of what are predominantly middle class values and techniques, a narrowing of the gap between social classes in their patterns of child rearing.

Since the above analysis was published, a new study has documented an additional trend. Bronson, Katten, and Livson have compared patterns of paternal and maternal authority and affection in two generations of families from the California Guidance Study.[2] Unfortunately, the time span surveyed overlaps only partially with the twenty-five year period covered in our own analysis, the first California generation having been raised in the early 1900's and the second in the late '20's and early '30's. Accordingly, if we are to consider the California results along with the others cited above, we must make the somewhat risky assumption that a trend discerned in the first three decades of the century has continued in the same direction through the early 1950's. With this important qualification, an examination of the data cited by Bronson et al.[3] points to still another, secular trend—a shift over the years in the pattern of parental role differentiation within the family. Specifically:

5. In succeeding generations the relative position of the father vis-à-vis the mother is shifting with the former becoming increasingly more affectionate and less authoritarian, and the latter becoming relatively more important as the agent of discipline, especially for boys.

"Psychological" Techniques of Discipline and Their Effects

In pursuing our analytic strategy, we next seek evidence of the effects on the behavior of children of variations in parental treatment of the type noted in our inventory. We may begin by noting that the variables involved in the first three secular trends constitute a complex that has received considerable attention in recent research in parent-child relationships. Within the last three years, two sets of investigators, working independently, have called attention to the greater efficacy of "love-oriented" or "psychological" techniques in bringing about desired behavior in the child.[4] The present writer, noting that such methods are especially favored by middle class parents, offered the following analysis of the nature of these techniques and the reasons for their effectiveness.

Such parents are, in the first place, more likely to overlook offenses, and when they do punish, they are less likely to ridicule or inflict physical pain. Instead, they reason with the youngster, isolate him, appeal to guilt, show disappointment—in short, convey in a variety of ways, on the one hand, the kind of behavior that is expected of the child; on the other, the realization that transgression means the interruption of a mutually valued relationship. . . .

These findings [of greater efficacy] mean that middle class parents, though in one sense more lenient in their discipline techniques, are using methods that are actually more compelling. Moreover, the compelling power of these practices is probably enhanced by the more permissive treatment accorded to middle class children in the early years of life. The successful use of withdrawal of love as a discipline technique implies the prior existence of a gratifying relationship; the more love present in the first instance,

the greater the threat implied in its withdrawal.[5]

It is now a well established fact that children from middle class families tend to excel those from lower class in many characteristics ordinarily regarded as desirable, such as self-control, achievement, responsibility, leadership, popularity, and adjustment in general.[6] If, as seems plausible, such differences in behavior are attributable at least in part to class-linked variations in parental treatment, the strategy of inference we have adopted would appear on first blush to lead to a rather optimistic conclusion. Since, over the years, increasing numbers of parents have been adopting the more effective socialization techniques typically employed by the middle class, does it not follow that successive generations of children should show gains in the development of effective behavior and desirable personality characteristics?

Unfortunately, this welcome conclusion, however logical, is premature, for it fails to take into account all of the available facts.

Sex, Socialization, and Social Class

To begin with, the parental behaviors we have been discussing are differentially distributed not only by socio-economic status but also by sex. As we have pointed out elsewhere,[7] girls are exposed to more affection and less punishment than boys, but at the same time are more likely to be subjected to "love-oriented" discipline of the type which encourages the development of internalized controls. And, consistent with our line of reasoning, girls are found repeatedly to be "more obedient, cooperative, and in general better socialized than boys at comparable age levels." But this is not the whole story.

. . . At the same time, the research results indicate that girls tend to be more anxious, timid, dependent, and sensitive to rejection. If these differences are a function of differential treatment by parents, then it would seem that the more "efficient" methods of child rearing employed with girls involve some risk of what might be called "oversocialization."

One could argue, of course, that the contrasting behaviors of boys and girls have less to do with differential parental treatment than with genetically-based maturational influences. Nevertheless, two independent lines of evidence suggest that socialization techniques do contribute to individual differences, *within the same sex,* precisely in the types of personality characteristics noted above. In the first place, variations in child behavior and parental treatment strikingly similar to those we have cited for the two sexes are reported in a recent comprehensive study of differences between first and later born children.[8] Like girls, first children receive more attention, are more likely to be exposed to "psychological" discipline, and end up more anxious and dependent, whereas later children, like boys, are more aggressive and self-confident.

A second line of evidence comes from our own current research. We have been concerned with the role of parents in the development of such "constructive" personality characteristics as responsibility and leadership among adolescent boys and girls. Our findings reveal not only the usual differences in adolescents' and parents' behaviors associated with the sex of the child, but also a striking contrast in the relationship between parental and child behaviors for the two sexes. To start on firm and

familiar ground, girls are rated by their teachers as more responsible than boys, whereas the latter obtain higher scores on leadership. Expected differences similarly appear in the realm of parental behavior: girls receive more affection, praise, and companionship; boys are subjected to more physical punishment and achievement demands. Quite unanticipated, however, at least by us, was the finding that both parental affection and discipline appeared to facilitate effective psychological functioning in boys, but to impede the development of such constructive behavior in girls. Closer examination of our data indicated that both extremes of either affection or discipline were deleterious for all children, but that the process of socialization entailed somewhat different risks for the two sexes. Girls were especially susceptible to the detrimental influence of overprotection; boys to the ill effects of insufficient parental discipline and support. Or, to put it in more colloquial terms: boys suffered more often from too little taming, girls from too much.

In an attempt to account for this contrasting pattern of relationships, we proposed the notion of differential optimal levels of affection and authority for the two sexes.

The qualities of independence, initiative, and self-sufficiency, which are especially valued for boys in our culture, apparently require for their development a somewhat different balance of authority and affection than is found in the "love-oriented" strategy characteristically applied with girls. While an affectional context is important for the socialization of boys, it must evidently be accompanied by and be compatible with a strong component of parental discipline. Otherwise, the boy finds himself in the same situation as the girl, who, having received greater affection, is more sensitive to its withdrawal, with the result that a little discipline goes a long way and strong authority is constricting rather than constructive.[9]

What is more, available data suggest that this very process may already be operating for boys from upper middle class homes. To begin with, differential treatment of the sexes is at a minimum for these families. Contrasting parental attitudes and behaviors toward boys and girls are pronounced only at lower class levels, and decrease as one moves up the socio-economic scale.[10] Thus our own results show that it is primarily at lower middle class levels that boys get more punishment than girls, and the latter receive greater warmth and attention. With an increase in the family's social position, direct discipline drops off, especially for boys, and indulgence and protectiveness decrease for girls. As a result, patterns of parental treatment for the two sexes begin to converge. In like manner, we find that the differential effects of parental behavior on the two sexes are marked only in the lower middle class. It is here that girls especially risk being over-protected and boys not receiving sufficient discipline and support. In upper middle class the picture changes. Girls are not as readily debilitated by parental affection and power; nor is parental discipline as effective in fostering the development of responsibility and leadership in boys.

All these trends point to the conclusion that the "risks" experienced by each sex during the process of socialization tend to be somewhat different at different social class levels. Thus the danger of overprotection for girls is especially great in lower class families, but lower in upper middle class because of the decreased likelihood of overprotection. Analogously, boys are in

greater danger of suffering from inadequate discipline and support in lower middle than in upper middle class. But the upper middle class boy, unlike the girl, exchanges one hazard for another. Since at this upper level the more potent "psychological" techniques of discipline are likely to be employed with both sexes, the boy presumably now too runs the risk of being "oversocialized," of losing some of his capacity for independent aggressive accomplishment.

Accordingly, if our line of reasoning is correct, we should expect a changing pattern of sex differences at successive socio-economic levels. Specifically, aspects of effective psychological functioning favoring girls should be most pronounced in the upper middle class; those favoring boys in the lower middle. A recent analysis of some of our data bears out this expectation. Girls excel boys on such variables as *responsibility* and *social acceptance* primarily at the higher socio-economic levels. In contrast, boys surpass girls on such traits as *leadership, level of aspiration,* and *competitiveness* almost exclusively in lower middle class. Indeed, with a rise in a family's social position, the differences tend to reverse themselves with girls now excelling boys.[11]

Trends in Personality Development: A First Approximation

The implications for our original line of inquiry are clear. We are suggesting that the "love-oriented" socialization techniques, which over the past twenty-five years have been employed in increasing degree by American middle class families, may have negative as well as constructive aspects. While fostering the internalization of adult standards and the development of socialized behavior, they may also have the effect of undermining capacities for initiative and independence, particularly in boys. Males exposed to this "modern" pattern of child rearing might be expected to differ from their counterparts of a quarter century ago in being somewhat more conforming and anxious, less enterprising and self-sufficient, and, in general, possessing more of the virtues and liabilities commonly associated with feminine character structure.[12]

At long last, then, our strategy of inference has led us to a first major conclusion. The term "major" is appropriate since the conclusion takes as its points of departure and return four of the secular trends which served as the impetus for our inquiry. Specifically, through a series of empirical links and theoretical extrapolations, we have arrived at an estimate of the effects on children of the tendency of successive generations of parents to become progressively more permissive, to express affection more freely, to utilize "psychological" techniques of discipline, and, by moving in these directions to narrow the gap between the social classes in their patterns of child rearing.

Family Structure and Personality Development

But one other secular trend remains to be considered: what of the changing pattern of parental role differentiation during the first three decades of the century? If our extrapolation is correct, the balance of power within the family has continued to shift with fathers yielding parental authority to mothers and taking on some of the nurturant and affectional functions traditionally associated with the maternal role. Again we have no direct evidence of the effects of such secular changes on successive generations of children, and must look for leads to analogous data on contemporaneous relationships.

We may begin by considering the contribution of each parent to the socialization processes we have examined thus far. Our data indicate that it is primarily mothers who tend to employ "love-oriented" techniques of discipline and fathers who rely on more direct methods like physical punishment. The above statement must be qualified, however, by reference to the sex of the child, for it is only in relation to boys that fathers use direct punishment more than mothers. More generally, . . . the results reveal a tendency for each parent to be somewhat more active, firm, and demanding with a child of the same sex, more lenient and indulgent with a child of the opposite sex. . . . The reversal is most complete with respect to discipline, with fathers being stricter with boys, mothers with girls. In the spheres of affection and protectiveness, there is no actual shift in preference, but the tendency to be especially warm and solicitous with girls is much more pronounced among fathers than among mothers. In fact, generally speaking, it is the father who is more likely to treat children of the two sexes differently.[13]

Consistent with this pattern of results, it is primarily the behavior of fathers that accounts for the differential effects of parental behavior on the two sexes and for the individual differences within each sex. In other words, it is paternal authority and affection that tend especially to be salutary for sons but detrimental for daughters. But as might be anticipated from what we already know, these trends are pronounced only in the lower middle class; with a rise in the family's social status, both parents tend to have similar effects on their children, both within and across sexes. Such a trend is entirely to be expected since parental role differentiation tends to decrease markedly as one ascends the socio-economic ladder. It is almost exclusively in lower middle class homes that fathers are more strict with boys and mothers with girls. To the extent that direct discipline is employed in upper middle classs families, it tends to be exercised by both parents equally. Here again we see a parallelism between shifts in parental behavior across time and social class in the direction of forms (in this instance of family structure) favored by the upper middle class group.

What kinds of children, then, can we expect to develop in families in which the father plays a predominantly affectionate role, and a relatively low level of discipline is exercised equally by both parents? A tentative answer to this question is supplied by a preliminary analysis of our data in which the relation between parental role structure and adolescent behavior was examined with controls for the family's social class position. The results of this analysis are summarized as follows: . . . Both responsibility and leadership are fostered by the relatively greater salience of the parent of the same sex. . . . Boys tend to be more responsible when the father rather than the mother is the principal disciplinarian; girls are more dependable when the mother is the major authority figure. . . . In short, boys thrive in a patriarchal context, girls in a matriarchal. . . . The most dependent and least dependable adolescents describe family arrangements that are neither patriarchal nor matriarchal, but equalitarian. To state the issue in more provocative form, our data suggest that the democratic family, which for so many years has been held up and aspired to as a model by professionals

and enlightened laymen, tends to produce young people who "do not take initiative," "look to others for direction and decision," and "cannot be counted on to fulfill obligations." [14]

In the wake of so sweeping a conclusion, it is important to call attention to the tentative, if not tenuous character of our findings. The results were based on a single study employing crude questionnaire methods and rating scales. Also, our interpretation is limited by the somewhat "attenuated" character of most of the families classified as patriarchal or matriarchal in our sample. Extreme concentrations of power in one or another parent were comparatively rare. Had they been more frequent, we suspect the data would have shown that such extreme asymmetrical patterns of authority were detrimental rather than salutary for effective psychological development, perhaps even more disorganizing than equalitarian forms.

Nevertheless, our findings do find some peripheral support in the work of others. A number of investigations, for example, point to the special importance of the father in the socialization of boys.[15] Further corroborative evidence appears in the growing series of studies of effects of paternal absence.[16] The absence of the father apparently not only affects the behavior of the child directly but also influences the mother in the direction of greater overprotectiveness. The effect of both these tendencies is especially critical for male children; boys from father-absent homes tend to be markedly more submissive and dependent. Studies dealing explicitly with the influence of parental role structure in intact families are few and far between. Papanek, in an unpublished doctoral dissertation,[17] reports greater sex-role differentiation among children from homes in which the parental roles were differentiated. And in a carefully controlled study, Kohn and Clausen find that "schizophrenic patients more frequently than normal persons report that their mothers played a very strong authority role and the father a very weak authority role."[18] Finally, what might best be called complementary evidence for our inferences regarding trends in family structure and their effects comes from the work of Miller, Swanson, and their associates[19] on the differing patterns of behavior exhibited by families from *bureaucratic* and *entrepreneurial* work settings. These investigators argue that the entrepreneurial-bureaucratic dichotomy represents a new cleavage in American social structure that cuts across and overrides social class influences and carries with it its own characteristic patterns of family structure and socialization. Thus one investigation[20] contrasts the exercise of power in families of husbands employed in two kinds of job situations: a) those working in large organizations with three or more levels of supervision; b) those self-employed or working in small organizations with few levels of supervision. With appropriate controls for social class, equalitarian families were found more frequently in the bureaucratic groups; patriarchal and, to a lesser extent, matriarchal in the entrepreneurial setting. Another study[21] shows that, in line with Miller and Swanson's hypotheses, parents from these same two groups tend to favor rather different ends and means of socialization, with entrepreneurial families putting considerably more emphasis on the development of independence and mastery and on the use of "psychological" techniques of discipline. These differences appear at both upper and lower middle class levels but are less pronounced in higher socio-economic strata. It is Miller and Swanson's belief, however, that the trend is toward the bureaucratic way of life, with its less structured patterns of family organization and child rearing. The evidence we have cited on secular changes in family structure and the inferences we have drawn regarding their possible effects on personality development are on the whole consistent with their views.

Looking Forward

If Miller and Swanson are correct in the prediction that America is moving toward a bureaucratic society that emphasizes, to put it colloquially, "getting along" rather than "getting ahead," then presumably we can look forward to ever increasing numbers of equalitarian families who, in turn, will produce successive generations of ever more adaptable but unaggressive "organization men." But recent signs do not all point in this direction. In our review of secular trends in child rearing practices we detected in the data from the more recent studies a slowing up in the headlong rush toward greater permissiveness and toward reliance on indirect methods of discipline. We pointed out also that if the most recent editions of well-thumbed guidebooks on child care are as reliable harbingers of the future as they have been in the past, we can anticipate something of a return to the more explicit discipline techniques of an earlier era. Perhaps the most important forces, however, acting to redirect both the aims and methods of child rearing in America emanate from behind the Iron Curtain. With the firing of the first Sputnik, Achievement began to replace Adjustment as the highest goal of the American way of life. We have become concerned—perhaps even obsessed

—with "education for excellence" and the maximal utilization of our intellectual resources. Already, ability grouping, and the guidance counsellor who is its prophet, have moved down from the junior high to the elementary school, and parents can be counted on to do their part in preparing their youngsters for survival in the new competitive world of applications and achievement tests.

But if a new trend in parental behavior is to develop, it must do so in the context of changes already under way. And if the focus of parental authority is shifting from husband to wife, then perhaps we should anticipate that pressures for achievement will be imposed primarily by mothers rather than fathers. Moreover, the mother's comtinuing strong emotional investment in the child should provide her with a powerful lever for evoking desired performance. It is noteworthy in this connection that recent studies of the familial origins of need-achievement point to the matriarchy as the optimal context for development of the motive to excel.[22]

The prospect of a society in which socialization techniques are directed toward maximizing achievement drive is not altogether a pleasant one. As a number of investigators have shown,[23] high achievement motivation appears to flourish in a family atmosphere of "cold democracy" in which initial high levels of maternal involvement are followed by pressures for independence and accomplishment.[24] Nor does the product of this process give ground for reassurance. True, children from achievement-oriented homes excel in planfulness and performance, but they are also more aggressive, tense, domineering, and cruel.[25] It would appear that education for excellence if pursued single-mindedly may entail some sobering social costs.

But by now we are in danger of having stretched our chain of inference beyond the strength of its weakest link. Our speculative analysis has become far more speculative than analytic and to pursue it further would bring us past the bounds of science into the realms of science fiction. In concluding our discussion, we would re-emphasize that speculations should, by their very nature, be held suspect. It is for good reason that, like "damn Yankees" they too carry their almost inseparable sobriquets: speculations are either "idle" or "wild." Given the scientific and social importance of the issues we have raised, we would dismiss the first of these labels out of hand, but the second cannot be disposed of so easily. Like the impetuous child, the "wild" speculation responds best to the sobering influence of friendly but firm discipline, in this instance from the hand of the behavioral scientist. As we look ahead to the next twenty-five years of human socialization, let us hope that the "optimal levels" of involvement and discipline can be achieved not only by the parent who is unavoidably engaged in the process, but also by the scientist who attempts to understand its working, and who—also unavoidably—contributes to shaping its course.

Footnotes

[1] U. Bronfenbrenner, "Socialization and Social Class Through Time and Space," *Readings in Social Psychology*, ed. E. Maccoby *et al.*, New York: Henry Holt, 1958, pp. 400–425.

[2] W. C. Bronson, E. S. Katten, and N. Livson, "Patterns of Authority and Affection in Two Generations," *Journal of Abnormal and Social Psychology*, 58, 1959, pp. 143–152.

[3] *Ibid*.

[4] See: R. R. Sears, E. Maccoby, and M. Levin, *Patterns of Child Rearing*, Evanston: Row, Peterson, 1957; D. R. Miller and G. E. Swanson, *The Changing American Parent*, New York: John Wiley,

1958; Miller and Swanson, *Inner Conflict and Defense,* New York: Henry Holt, 1960.

[5] Bronfenbrenner, 1958.

[6] For a summary of findings on social class differences in children's behavior and personality characteristics, see P. H. Mussen, and J. J. Conger, *Child Development and Personality,* New York: Harper, 1956.

[7] U. Bronfenbrenner, "Some Familial Antecedents of Responsibility and Leadership in Adolescents," *Leadership and Interpersonal Behavior,* ed. L. Petrullo, *et al.,* New York: Holt, Rinehart, and Winston, 1961.

[8] S. Schachter, *The Psychology of Affiliation,* Stanford: Stanford University Press, 1959.

[9] Bronfenbrenner, 1961.

[10] See: Bronfenbrenner, 1961; M. L. Kohn, "Social Class and Parental Values, *"American Journal of Sociology,* 44, 1959, pp. 337–351.

[11] These shifts in sex difference with a rise in class status are significant at the 5% level of confidence (one-tailed test).

[12] Strikingly similar conclusions were reached almost fifteen years ago in a provocative essay by Arnold Green ("The Middle Class Male Child and Neurosis," *American Sociological Review,* 11, 1946, 31–41). With little to go on beyond scattered clinical observations and impressions, Green was able to detect many of the same trends which we have begun to discern in more recent systematic empirical data.

[13] Bronfenbrenner, 1961.

[14] *Ibid.*

[15] See: A. Bandura and R. H. Walters, *Adolescent Aggression,* New York: Ronald Press, 1959; P. Mussen and L. Distler, "Masculinity, Identification, and Father-Son Relationships," *Journal of Abnormal and Social Psychology,* 59, 1959, pp. 350–356.

[16] See: G. R. Bach, "Father-Fantasies and Father-Typing in Father-Separated Children," *Child Development,* 17, 1946, pp. 63–79; R. R. Sears, M. H. Pintler, and P. S. Sears, "Effects of Father-Separation on Preschool Children's Doll Play Aggression, *"Child Development,* 17, 1946, pp. 219–243; D. B. Lynn and W. L. Sawrey, "The Effects of Father-Absence on Norwegian Boys and Girls," *Journal of Abnormal and Social Psychology,* 59, 1959, pp. 258–262; P. O. Tiller, "Father-Absence and Personality Development of Children in Sailor Families," *Nordisk Psykologis Monograph Series,* 9, 1958.

[17] M. Papanek, *Authority and Interpersonal Relations in the Family,* unpub. Ph.D. dissertation, Radcliffe College Library, 1957.

[18] M. L. Kohn and J. A. Clausen, "Parental Authority Behavior and Schizophrenia," *American Journal of Orthopsychiatry,* 26, 1956, pp. 297–313.

[19] Miller and Swanson, 1958, 1960.

[20] M. Gold and C. Slater, "Office, Factory, Store—and Family: A Study of Integration Setting," *American Sociological Review,* 23, 1959, pp. 64–74.

[21] Miller and Swanson, 1958.

[22] See: F. L. Strodtbeck, "Family Interaction, Values, and Achievement," *Talents and Society,* ed. D. C. McClelland *et al.,* Princeton: Van Nostrand, 1958, pp. 135–194; B. L. Rosen and R. D'Andrade, "The Psychological Origins of Achievement Motivation," *Sociometry,* 22, 1959, pp. 185–217.

[23] See: A. L. Baldwin, J. Kalhorn, and F. H. Breese, "The Appraisal of Parent Behavior," *Psychological Monographs,* 58, 1945, No. 3 (Whole No. 268); A. L. Baldwin, "Socialization and the Parent-Child Relationship," *Child Development,* 19, 1948, pp. 127–136; E. A. Haggard, "Socialization, Personality, and Academic Achievement in Gifted Children," *The School Review,* 65, 1957, pp. 388–414; M. R. Winterbottom, "The Relation of Need Achievement to Learning Experiences in Independence and Mastery," *Motives in Fantasy, Action, and Society,* ed. J. W. Atkinson, Princeton: Van Nostrand, 1958, pp. 453–494; Rosen and D'Andrade, 1959.

[24] Cold democracy under female administration appears to foster the development of achievement not only in the home but in the classroom as well. In a review of research on teaching effectiveness, Ackerman reports that teachers most successful in bringing about gains in achievement score for their pupils were judged "least considerate," while those thought friendly and congenial were least effective. W. I. Ackerman, "Teacher Competence and Pupil Change," *Harvard Educational Review,* 24, 1954, 273–289.

[25] See: Baldwin, Kalhorn, and Breese, 1945; Baldwin, 1948; Haggard, 1957.

7

The Fate of Idealism in Medical School

HOWARD S. BECKER AND BLANCHE GEER

It makes some difference in a man's performance of his work whether he believes wholeheartedly in what he is doing or feels that in important respects it is a fraud, whether he feels convinced that it is a good thing or believes that it is not really of much use after all. The distinction we are making is the one people have in mind when they refer, for example, to their calling as a "noble profession" on the one hand or a "racket" on the other. In the one case they idealistically proclaim that their work is all that it claims on the surface to be; in the other they cynically concede that it is first and foremost a way of making a living and that its surface pretensions are just that and nothing more. Presumably, different modes of behavior are associated with these perspectives when wholeheartedly embraced. The cynic cuts corners with a feeling of inevitability while the idealist goes down fighting. *The Blackboard Jungle* and *Not as a Stranger* are only the most recent in a long tradition of fictional portrayals of the importance of this aspect of a man's adjustment to his work.

Professional schools often receive a major share of the blame for producing this kind of cynicism—and none more than the medical school. The idealistic young freshman changes into a tough, hardened, unfeeling doctor; or so the popular view has it. Teachers of medicine sometimes rephrase the distinction between the clinical and pre-clinical years into one between the "cynical" and "pre-cynical" years. Psychological research supports this view, presenting attitude surveys which show medical students year by year scoring lower on "idealism" and higher on "cynicism." [1] Typically, this cynicism is seen as developing in response to the shattering of ideals consequent on coming face-to-face with the realities of professional practice.

In this paper, we attempt to describe the kind of idealism that characterizes the medical freshmen and to trace both the development of cynicism and the vicissitudes of that idealism in the course of the four years of medical training. Our main themes are that though they develop cynical feelings in specific situations directly associated with their medical school experience, the medical students never lose their original idealism about the practice of medicine; that the growth of both cynicism and idealism are not simple developments, but are instead complex transformations; and that the very notions "idealism" and "cynicism" need further analysis, and must be seen as situational in their expressions rather than as stable traits possessed by individuals in greater or lesser degree. Finally, we see the greater portion of these feelings as being collective rather than individual phenomena.

Our discussion is based on a study we are now conducting at a state medical school,[2] in which we have carried on par-

SOURCE: Reprinted from *American Sociological Review*, February, 1958, 23:50–56, by permission of the authors and the publisher.

ticipant observation with students of all four years in all of the courses and clinical work to which they are exposed. We joined the students in their activities in school and after school and watched them at work in labs, on the hospital wards, and in the clinic. Often spending as much as a month with a small group of from five to fifteen students assigned to a particular activity, we came to know them well and were able to gather information in informal interviews and by overhearing the ordinary daily conversation of the group.[3] In the course of our observation and interviewing we have gathered much information on the subject of idealism. Of necessity, we shall have to present the very briefest statement of our findings with little or no supporting evidence.[4] The problem of idealism is, of course, many-faceted and complex and we have dealt with it in a simplified way, describing only some of its grosser features.[5]

The Freshmen

The medical students enter school with what we may think of as the idealistic notion, implicit in lay culture, that the practice of medicine is a wonderful thing and that they are going to devote their lives to service to mankind. They believe that medicine is made up of a great body of well-established facts that they will be taught from the first day on and that these facts will be of immediate practical use to them as physicians. They enter school expecting to work industriously and expecting that if they work hard enough they will be able to master this body of fact and thus become good doctors.

In several ways the first year of medical school does not live up to their expectations. They are disillusioned when they find they will not be near patients at all, that the first year will be just like another year of college. In fact, some feel that it is not even as good as college because their work in certain areas is not as thorough as courses in the same fields in undergraduate school. They come to think that their courses (with the exception of anatomy) are not worth much because, in the first place, the faculty (being Ph.D.'s) know nothing about the practice of medicine, and, in the second place, the subject matter itself is irrelevant, or as the students say, "ancient history."

The freshmen are further disillusioned when the faculty tells them in a variety of ways that there is more to medicine than they can possibly learn. They realize it may be impossible for them to learn all they need to know in order to practice medicine properly. Their disillusionment becomes more profound when they discover that this statement of the faculty is literally true.[6] Experience in trying to master the details of the anatomy of the extremities convinces them that they cannot do so in the time they have. Their expectation of hard work is not disappointed; they put in an eight-hour day of classes and laboratories, and study four or five hours a night and most of the weekend as well.

Some of the students, the brightest, continue to attempt to learn it all, but succeed only in getting more and more worried about their work. The majority decide that, since they can't learn it all, they must select from among all the facts presented to them those they will attempt to learn. There are two ways of making this selection. On the one hand, the student may decide on the basis of his own uninformed notions about the nature of medical practice that many facts are not important, since they relate to things which seldom come up in the actual practice of medicine; therefore, he reasons, it is useless to learn them. On the other hand, the student can decide that the important thing is to pass his examinations and, therefore, that the important facts are those which are likely to be asked on an examination; he uses this as a basis for selecting both facts to memorize and courses for intensive study. For example, the work in physiology is dismissed on both of these grounds, being considered neither relevant to the facts of medical life nor important in terms of the amount of time the faculty devotes to it and the number of examinations in the subject.

A student may use either or both of these bases of selection at the beginning of the year, before many tests have been given. But after a few tests have been taken, the student makes "what the faculty wants" the chief basis of his selection of what to learn, for he now has a better idea of what this is and also has become aware that it is possible to fail examinations and that he therefore must learn the expectations of the faculty if he wishes to stay in school. The fact that one group of students, that with the highest prestige in the class, took this view early and did well on examinations was decisive in swinging the whole class around to this position. The students were equally influenced to become "test-wise" by the fact that, although they had all been in the upper range in their colleges, the class average on the first examination was frighteningly low.

In becoming test-wise, the students begin to develop systems for discovering the faculty wishes and learning them. These systems are both methods for studying their texts and short-cuts that can be taken in laboratory work. For instance, they begin to select facts for memorization by looking over the files of old examinations maintained in each of the medical fraternity houses. They share tip-offs from the lectures and offhand remarks of the faculty as to what will be on the examinations. In anatomy, they agree not to bother to dissect out subcutaneous nerves, reasoning that it is both difficult and time-consuming and the information can be secured from books with less effort. The interaction involved in the development of such systems and short-cuts helps to create a social group of a class which had previously been only an aggregation of smaller and less organized groups.

In this medical school, the students learn in this way to distinguish between the activities of the first year and their original view that everything that happens to them in medical school will be important. Thus they become cynical about the value of their activities in the first year. They feel that the real thing—learning which will help them to help mankind—has been postponed, perhaps until the second year, or perhaps even farther, at which time they will be able again to act on idealistic premises. They believe that what they do in their later years in school under supervision will be about the same thing they will do, as physicians, on their own; the first year had disappointed this expectation.

There is one matter, however, about which the students are not disappointed during the first year: the so-called trauma of dealing with the cadaver. But this experience, rather than producing cynicism, reinforces the student's attachment to his idealistic view of medicine by making him feel that he is experiencing at least some of the necessary unpleasantness of the doctor's. Such difficulties, however, do not loom as large for the student as those of solving the problem of just what the faculty wants.

On this and other points, a working consensus develops in the new consolidated group about the interpretation of their experience in medical school and its norms of conduct. This consensus, which we call *student culture*,[7] focuses their attention almost completely on their day-to-day activities in school and obscures or sidetracks their earlier idealistic preoccupations. Cynicism, griping, and minor cheating become endemic, but the cynicism is specific to the educational situation, to the first year, and to only parts of it. Thus the students keep their cynicism separate from their idealistic feelings and by postponement protect their belief that medicine is a wonderful thing, that their school is a fine one, and that they will become good doctors.

Later Years

The sophomore year does not differ greatly from the freshman year. Both the work load and anxiety over examinations probably increase. Though they begin some medical activities, as in their attendance at autopsies and particularly in their introductory course in physical diagnosis, most of what they do continues to repeat the pattern of the college science curriculum. Their attention still centers on the problem of getting through school by doing well in examinations.

During the third and fourth, or clinical years, teaching takes a new form. In place of lectures and laboratories, the students' work now consists of the study of actual patients admitted to the hospital or seen in the clinic. Each patient who enters the hospital is assigned to a student who interviews him about his illnesses, past and present, and performs a physical examination. He writes this up for the patient's chart, and appends the diagnosis and the treatment that he would use were he allowed actually to treat the patient. During conferences with faculty physicians, often held at the patient's bedside, the student is quizzed about items of his report and called upon to defend them or to explain their significance. Most of the teaching in the clinical years is of this order.

Contact with patients brings a new set of circumstances with which the student must deal. He no longer feels the great pressure created by tests, for he is told by the faculty, and this is confirmed by his daily experience, that examinations are now less important. His problems now become those of coping with a steady stream of patients in a way that will please the staff man under whom he is working, and of handling what is sometimes a tremendous load of clinical work so as to allow himself time for studying diseases and treatments that interest him and for play and family life.

The students earlier have expected that once they reach the clinical years they will be able to realize their idealistic ambitions to help people and to learn those things immediately useful in aiding people who are ill. But they find themselves working to understand cases as medical problems rather than working to help the sick and memorizing the relevant available facts so that these can be produced immediately for a questioning staff man. When they make ward rounds with a faculty member they are likely to be quizzed about any of the seemingly countless facts possibly related to the condition of the patient for whom they are "caring."

Observers speak of the cynicism that overtakes the student and the lack of concern for his patients as human beings. This change does take place, but it is not produced solely by "the anxiety brought about by the presence of death and suffering." [8] The student becomes preoccupied with the technical aspects of the cases with which he deals because the faculty requires him to do so. He is questioned about so many technical details that he must spend most of his time learning them.

The frustrations created by his position in the teaching hospital further divert the student from idealistic concerns. He finds himself low man in a hierarchy based on clinical experience, so that he is allowed very little of the medical responsibility he would like to assume. Because of his lack of experience, he cannot write orders, and he receives permission to perform medical and surgical procedures (if at all) at a rate he considers far too slow. He usually must content himself with "mere" vicarious participation in the drama of danger, life, and death that he sees as the core of medical practice. The student culture accents these difficulties so that events (and especially those involving patients) are interpreted and reacted to as they push him toward or hold him back from further participation in this drama. He does not think in terms the layman might use.

As a result of the increasingly technical emphasis of his thinking the student appears cynical to the non-medical outsider, though from his own point of view he is simply seeing what is "really important." Instead of reacting with the layman's horror and sympathy for the patient to the sight of a cancerous organ that has been surgically removed, the student is more likely to regret that he was not allowed to close the incision at the completion of the operation, and to rue the hours that he must spend searching in the fatty flesh for the lymph nodes that will reveal how far the disease has spread. As in other lines of work, he drops lay attitudes for those more relevant to the way the event affects someone in his position.

This is not to say that the students lose their original idealism. When issues of idealism are openly raised in a situation they define as appropriate, they respond as they might have when they were freshmen. But the influence of the student culture is such that questions which might bring forth this idealism are not brought up. Students are often assigned patients for examination and follow-up whose conditions might be expected to provoke idealistic crises. Students discuss such patients, however, with reference to the problems they create for the *student*. Patients with terminal diseases who are a long time dying, and patients with chronic diseases who show little change from week to week, are more likely to be viewed as creating extra work without extra compensation in knowledge or the opportunity to practice new skills than as examples of illness which raise questions about euthanasia. Such cases require the student to spend time every day checking on progress which he feels will probably not take place and to write long "progress" notes in the patient's chart although little progress has occurred.

This apparent cynicism is a collective matter. Group activities are built around this kind of workaday perspective, constraining the students in two ways. First, they do not openly express the lay idealistic notions they may hold, for their culture does not sanction such expression; second, they are less likely to have thoughts of this deviant kind when they are engaged in group activity. The collective nature of this "cynicism" is indicated by the fact that students become more openly idealistic whenever they are removed from the influence of student culture—when they are alone with a sociologist as they near the finish of school and sense the approaching end of student life, for example, or when they are isolated from their classmates and therefore are less influenced by this culture.[9]

They still feel, as advanced students, though much less so than before, that school is irrelevant to actual medical practice. Many of their tasks, like running laboratory tests on patients newly admitted to the hospital or examining surgical specimens in the pathology laboratory, seem to them to have nothing to do with their visions of their future activity as doctors. As in their freshman year, they believe that perhaps they must obtain the knowledge they will need in spite of the school. They still conceive of medicine as a huge body of proven facts, but no longer believe that they will ever be able to master it all. They now say that they are going to try to apply the solution of the practicing M.D. to their own dilemma: learn a few things that they are interested in very well and know enough about other things to pass examinations while in school and, later on in practice, to know to which specialist to send difficult patients.

Their original medical idealism reasserts itself as the end of school approaches. Seniors show more interest than students in earlier years in serious ethical dilemmas of the kind they expect to face in practice. They have become aware of ethical problems laymen often see as crucial for the physician—whether it is right to keep pa-

tients with fatal diseases alive as long as possible, or what should be done if an influential patient demands an abortion—and worry about them. As they near graduation and student culture begins to break down as the soon-to-be doctors are about to go their separate ways, these questions are more and more openly discussed.

While in school, they have added to their earlier idealism a new and peculiarly professional idealism. Even though they know that few doctors live up to the standards they have been taught, they intend always to examine their patients thoroughly and to give treatment based on firm diagnosis rather than merely to relieve symptoms. This expansion and transformation of idealism appear most explicitly in their consideration of alternative careers, concerning both specialization and the kind of arrangements to be made for setting up practice. Many of their hypothetical choices aim at making it possible for them to be the kind of doctors their original idealism pictured. Many seniors consider specialty training so that they will be able to work in a limited field in which it will be more nearly possible to know all there is to know, thus avoiding the necessity of dealing in a more ignorant way with the wider range of problems general practice would present. In the same manner, they think of schemes to establish partnerships or other arrangements making it easier to avoid a work load which would prevent them from giving each patient the thorough examination and care they now see as ideal.

In other words, as school comes to an end, the cynicism specific to the school situation also comes to an end and their original and more general idealism about medicine comes to the fore again, though within a framework of more realistic alternatives. Their idealism is now more informed although no less selfless.

Discussion

We have used the words "idealism" and "cynicism" loosely in our description of the changeable state of mind of the medical student, playing on ambiguities we can now attempt to clear up. Retaining a core of common meaning, the dictionary definition, in our reference to the person's belief in the worth of his activity and the claims made for it, we have seen that this is not a generalized trait of the students we studied but rather an attitude which varies greatly, depending on the particular activity the worth of which is questioned and the situation in which the attitude is expressed.

This variability of the idealistic attitude suggests that in using such an element of personal perspective in sociological analysis one should not treat it as homogeneous but should make a determined search for subtypes which may arise under different conditions and have differing consequences. Such subtypes presumably can be constructed along many dimensions. There might, for instance, be consistent variations in the medical students' idealism through the four years of school that are related to their social class backgrounds. We have stressed in this report the subtypes that can be constructed according to variations in the object of the idealistic attitude and variations in the audience the person has in mind when he adopts the attitude. The medical students can be viewed as both idealistic and cynical, depending on whether one has in mind their view of their school activities or the future they envision for themselves as doctors. Further, they might take one or another of these positions de-

pending on whether their implied audience is made up of other students, their instructors, or the lay public.

A final complication arises because cynicism and idealism are not merely attributes of the actor, but are as dependent on the person doing the attributing as they are on the qualities of the individual to whom they are attributed.[10] Though the student may see his own disregard of the unique personal troubles of a particular patient as proper scientific objectivity, the layman may view this objectivity as heartless cynicism.[11]

Having made these analytic distinctions, we can now summarize the transformations of these characteristics as we have seen them occurring among medical students. Some of the students' determined idealism at the outset is reaction against the lay notion, of which they are uncomfortably aware, that doctors are money-hungry cynics; they counter this with an idealism of similar lay origin stressing the doctor's devotion to service. But this idealism soon meets a setback, as students find that it will not be relevant for awhile, since medical school has, it seems, little relation to the practice of medicine, as they see it. As it has not been refuted, but only shown to be temporarily beside the point, the students "agree" to set this idealism aside in favor of a realistic approach to the problem of getting through school. This approach, which we have labeled as the cynicism specific to the school experience, serves as protection for the earlier grandiose feelings about medicine by postponing their exposure to reality to a distant future. As that future approaches near the end of the four years and its possible mistreatment of their ideals moves closer, the students again worry about maintaining their integrity, this time in actual medical practice.

They use some of the knowledge they have gained to plan careers which, it is hoped, can best bring their ideals to realization.

We can put this in propositional form by saying that when a man's ideals are challenged by outsiders and then further strained by reality, he may salvage them by postponing their application to a future time when conditions are expected to be more propitious.

Footnotes

[1] Leonard D. Eron, "Effect of Medical Education on Medical Students," *Journal of Medical Education,* 10, October, 1955, pp. 559–566.

[2] This study is sponsored by Community Studies, Inc., of Kansas City, Missouri, and is being carried on at the University of Kansas Medical School, to whose dean, staff, and students we are indebted for their wholehearted cooperation. Professor Everett C. Hughes of the University of Chicago is director of the project.

[3] The technique of participant observation has not been fully systematized, but some approaches to this have been made. See, for example, Florence R. Kluckhohn, "The Participant Observer Technique in Small Communities," *American Journal of Sociology,* 45, November, 1940, pp. 331–343; Arthur Vidich, "Participant Observation and the Collection and Interpretation of Data," *ibid.,* 60, January, 1955, pp. 354–360; William Foote Whyte, "Observational Field-Work Methods," in Maria Jahoda, Morton Deutsch, and Stuart W. Cook (editors), *Research Methods in the Social Sciences,* New York: Dryden Press, 1951, II, pp. 393–514; and *Street Corner Society* (Enlarged Edition), Chicago: University of Chicago Press, 1955, pp. 279–358; Rosalie Hankey Wax, "Twelve Years Later: An Analysis of Field Experience," *American Journal of Sociology,* 63, September, 1957, pp. 133–142; Morris S. Schwartz and Charlotte Green Schwartz, "Problems in Participant Observation,"

ibid., 60, January, 1955, pp. 343–353; and Howard S. Becker and Blanche Geer, "Participant Observation and Interviewing: A Comparison," *Human Organization* (forthcoming). The last item represents the first of a projected series of papers attempting to make explicit the operations involved in this method. For a short description of some techniques used in this study, see Howard S. Becker, "Interviewing Medical Students," *American Journal of Sociology,* 62, September, 1956, pp. 199–201.

[4] A fuller analysis and presentation of evidence will be contained in a volume on this study now being prepared by the authors in collaboration with Everett C. Hughes and Anselm L. Strauss.

[5] Renee Fox has shown how complex one aspect of this whole subject is in her analysis of the way medical students at Cornell become aware of and adjust to both their own failure to master all available knowledge and the gaps in current knowledge in many fields. See her "Training for Uncertainty," in Robert K. Merton, George G. Reader, and Patricia L. Kendall, *The Student Physician: Introductory Studies in the Sociology of Medical Education,* Cambridge: Harvard University Press, 1957, pp. 207–241.

[6] Compare Fox' description of student reaction to this problem at Cornell (*op. cit.,* pp. 209–221).

[7] The concept of student culture is analyzed in some detail in Howard S. Becker and Blanche Geer, "Student Culture in Medical School," *Harvard Educational Review* (forthcoming).

[8] Dana L. Farnsworth, "Some Observations on the Attitudes and Motivations of the Harvard Medical Student," *Harvard Medical Alumni Bulletin,* January, 1956, p. 34.

[9] See the discussion in Howard S. Becker, "Interviewing Medical Students," *op. cit.*

[10] See Philip Selznick's related discussion of fanaticism in *TVA and the Grass Roots,* Berkeley: University of California Press, 1953, pp. 205–213.

[11] George Orwell gives the layman's side in his essay, "How the Poor Die" in *Shooting an Elephant and Other Essays,* London: Secker and Warburg, 1950, pp. 18–32.

PART FOUR   Social Stratification

Social stratification in one form or another has been found in every society of which we are aware. Utopian systems or societies yet undiscovered might exist without social stratification, but as of now even the most loosely structured primitive society has some minimal forms of stratification. Social stratification appears to have three major aspects: class, status, and power. Class may be considered the economic wealth dimension. Status refers, in this sense, to the personal prestige of an individual, and power is the degree to which an individual has the ability to enforce his will upon others. These dimensions are typically associated together, although there are notable exceptions.

Stratification may also be analyzed in terms of the relative ease or difficulty with which one may move within the system. Following this line of thought, stratification systems may be placed on a continuum anchored at one end by a theoretical system with absolutely no vertical mobility and anchored at the other end by a system, though nonexistent as yet, in which stratification is determined completely by the individuals' accomplishments. Given this continuum, what is the position of the United States? Do we have greater or lesser social mobility than other societies? Is mobility increasing or decreasing in this country?

The articles in this section address themselves to these types of questions. The first selection, by Christopher Jencks and David Riesman, provides an analysis of the current class structure in the United States. Michael Harrington's essay, "The Invisible Poor," is from his book The Other America which was largely responsible for making this country aware of the extent of our poverty. This essay provides information concerning the large number of people in this country undergoing severe deprivations. The final article is taken from David Caplovitz's book The Poor Pay More. This essay attempts to analyze the factors that frequently put the poor at a disadvantage and force them to pay more money for inferior goods.

8

On Class in America

CHRISTOPHER JENCKS AND DAVID RIESMAN

Until relatively recently, most Americans were allergic to discussions of social class in this country. In part, this was because they assumed social classes were by definition hereditary. Admitting their existence, would, therefore, undermine the idea that America rewarded diligence and competence no matter what their ancestry. But the desire to believe that America was a classless society had other roots, too. The New World's great achievement was said to be its respect for regional, religious, and ethnic variety, as well as for groups that the Old World looked upon as less equal than others: for women as well as men, for the young as well as the old, for manual as well as cerebral work, for the culture of the populace as well as of the palace. Diversity was thus portrayed as the product of egalitarian pluralism rather than of invidious hierarchies. Talk of social classes seemed to deny this.

There were, of course, skeptics. Many 19th-century observers noted, for example, that the elimination of traditional social hierarchies had forced Americans to rely on the one surviving measure of power and prestige: money. Cash was by no means evenly distributed, even in pre-industrial America. Those who had less than their share almost always envied those who had more, while those who had more reciprocated by looking down on those who had

less. In this respect, then, America was never really a classless society. Wealth and poverty in America allegedly depended on individual merit more than on ancestry, but few denied that they were a source of inequality, just as in Europe.

Despite all the talk about "respect for honest labor," moreover, Americans were stratified in terms of their jobs as well as their incomes. So long as the majority of men lived on farms, manual labor was nearly universal. Nonetheless, there were probably very few young men, even in pre-industrial America, who would not have chosen a job which required them to use only their head over a job which required them to use only their back. Urbanization, industrialization, and the increasingly complex division of labor intensified and complicated these concerns. Not only was there a division between blue collar and white collar workers, but there were further divisions within these two broad classifications. Some white collar workers, such as plant managers and higher government officials, exercised a good deal of power over other people; others, such as self-employed professionals and businessmen, had less direct power over others, but they had more control over their own lives. Clerical and sales workers usually had neither. Just as with money, so too with power: those with less envied those with

SOURCE: Reprinted from *The Public Interest,* Winter, 1968, 10:65–85, by permission of the authors and the publisher. Copyright © 1968 by National Affairs, Inc. This article also appeared in *The Academic Revolution* by Christopher Jencks and David Riesman, Copyright © 1968, 1969 by Christopher Jencks and David Riesman, and is reprinted with the permission of the publisher, Doubleday & Co., Inc., New York.

more, while those with more felt superior to those with less. The result was another system of stratification, based on occupation, parallel to that based on income.

As a general rule, the economic and occupational hierarchies reinforce each other. Most jobs of high prestige and power also pay well, and most jobs which pay well give their holder both prestige and power. Those with "upper-middle" jobs are therefore likely to have "upper-middle" incomes, and those with "lower" incomes are likely to have "lower" jobs. In the discussion which follows we will therefore collapse *economic* and *occupational* class into a single concept, which we will call *social class*. When we speak of the upper-middle class, for example, we will mean families headed by someone with a professional or managerial job, usually making at least twice as much as the average American family. When we speak of the lower-middle class we will mean families headed by clerical or sales workers, or small businessmen, usually earning fairly close to the median national income. When we speak of the working class we will mean families headed by a blue-collar worker, again with incomes close to the national average. When we speak of the lower class we will mean families whose head is frequently unemployed and often a woman, with average incomes around half the national average.

A Lack of Perfect Congruence

It is important to emphasize that these categories are by no means perfectly descriptive. Occupational power and prestige do not always correlate perfectly with income, even in principle. A judge, for example, usually has more power and prestige than an attorney, but he usually makes less money on the bench than he would in private practice. The result is that some men prefer to remain attorneys even when offered a judgeship, while others will spend large sums to become judges. Similarly, clergymen usually have more power and prestige than undertakers serving the same parishioners, but usually make considerably less money. The result is a certain degree of dissonance. There is an additional problem. The most powerful and prestigious jobs in America are mostly "professional" or "managerial." But these two categories also include many jobs which nobody regards as prestigious. The Census category, "managers, officials, and proprietors," for example, includes self-employed peanut vendors as well as the President of the United States, while the category "professional, technical, and kindred" includes stripteasers and baseball umpires as well as prosperous Wall Street lawyers and atomic physicists.

Under these circumstances it is not surprising to find that many of those who hold nominally professional or managerial jobs do not have income anything like double the national average. In 1960, for example, about 10 percent of the male labor force held professional jobs, and another 10 percent held managerial jobs. Within this crudely defined "top fifth" of the occupational distribution, only 46 percent also had incomes which put them in the top fifth of economic distribution. A more detailed, and therefore more sensitive, selection of those in the top fifth of the occupational distribution would undoubtedly increase the proportion falling in the income elite, but it would by no means make the two synonymous.

Another way to describe this lack of congruence between the two distributions is to start with an economic elite and look at its occupational distribution. Table 1 shows the broad occupational categories of the heads of the richest 5 percent of all American families in 1959. While the majority with "upper" incomes have "upper" jobs, there are plainly a lot of deviant cases. This is equally true of those with "upper-middle," "lower-middle," and even "lower" incomes.

Defining Social Class

Despite these difficulties, there is certainly enough parallelism between the income hierarchy and the job hierarchy to justify talking about social stratification. Indeed, stratification, while perhaps not absolutely necessary, is found in all societies actually extant or readily foreseeable. Yet to say that social classes are traditional and universal does not mean that they are everywhere and always the same. It is therefore important to say something about the changing character and size of social classes.

TABLE 1. *Occupations of Heads of Families with Incomes over $15,000 in 1959*

Occupation	
Self-Employed Professional	12
Salaried Professional	14
Self-Employed Businessman	15
Salaried Businessman	23
Clerical or Sales Worker	14
Blue Collar Worker	16
Farmers	3
Unknown	3
Total	100

Source: *1960 Census*, I (1), Table 230. In 1959, 5.1 percent of all families reported incomes over $15,000. The distribution for unrelated individuals was considerably lower.

In a sense, this is a matter of definition. Some people, for example, define class in strictly relativistic terms. One can, for example, define the "upper middle class" as

the richest and most powerful fifth of the population. It is clearly impossible for an upper-middle class defined in this way to grow proportionally larger or smaller over time. Conversely, one might define those whose jobs put them in the bottom fifth of the occupational distribution as a lower class. Having assumed this, no research is needed to show that the size of this lower class is fixed and cannot be reduced by, e.g., an anti-poverty program. This sort of definition may capture a good deal of the truth about life in a competitive society. But it has the disadvantage of concealing change even when it takes place.

Other people therefore define class in absolute terms, saying that anyone who can afford two cars is middle class, or that anyone who has a nonmanual job is middle class, or some such thing. This sort of definition obviously makes the size of classes very responsive to technological innovations. During the past sixty years, for example, productivity has more than doubled. The increase in real per capita GNP between 1909 and 1966 was between 150 and 175 percent. If one had defined the "lower class" in absolute terms in 1909 as any family with $750 a year or less, the term would have subsumed half the population. If this same absolute standard were again used in 1966 (with inflation taken into account), it would embrace only about one family in eight.

Does this sort of definition help us understand society better than the strictly relative one just discussed? What does it mean to say that the "lower class" has now shrunk to a quarter its size in 1909? It seems fairly clear that such a proposition greatly exaggerates the character and rate of social and cultural change. The real incomes of the poorest fifth of the American population today, for example, approximate those of the second fifth during the 1930's. Yet this does not mean that the poorest fifth of today's American population resembles the second fifth of the 1930's in other important respects. The fact of being at the bottom seems to be at least as important as absolute purchasing power in defining families' life styles. Families in the poorest fifth of the population today may have twice the real income their grandparents had, but they have so much less than today's typical family that they still *feel* very poor. But competitive, subjective feelings aside, families with the lowest incomes have great difficulty getting along because the changing economic and social arrangements of an industrial society presume a certain level of affluence, and this is always more than the poorest families have. When the median income was $750, for example, public transportation was essential for the majority of the population and was available to it. Today, on the other hand, 80 percent of all families can afford an automobile. Public transportation has therefore deteriorated, and the minority which still cannot afford a car may be, in this respect, worse off than before.

Similar ambiguities mark the history of the occupational distribution. The occupational structure has been significantly upgraded over the past hundred years. The typical job today requires more brain-power and less muscle than it did a century ago. In 1900, for example, 42 percent of all men worked on farms; by 1960 it was 9 percent. Similarly, one man in seven was an unskilled laborer in 1900; by 1960 it was one in fourteen. Conversely, the proportion of men doing what the Census calls professional work has risen from one in thirty to one in nine since 1900, most of the increase coming since 1940. The proportion classified as "managers, officials, and pro-

prietors" has risen from one in fifteen to one in nine, and the rise would be even greater if one looked solely at managers and officials and excluded small businessmen. But this does not tell us whether the typical worker has more or less control over his own job situation than in the past, or whether modern economic institutions diffuse power or concentrate it.

Room at the Top?

Very little is known about the distribution of power in the occupational structure. Sociologists have chronicled the movement of workers from manual to nonmanual jobs, from farm to city, and from job to job. Some have concluded that since the fastest growing groups are those which have traditionally exercised the most power over society, there is more "room at the top" today than in the past. This conclusion is, however, probably premature. True, there are more people in jobs traditionally defined as "professional" and "managerial" in 1967 than in 1900, and fewer people chopping cotton or digging ditches. But changes of this kind do not necessarily mean any basic change in the distribution of power, prestige, or even self-respect. A janitor is still at the bottom of the heap even if he throws the switch on an oil furnace instead of stoking a coal furnace, and a farm-owner's son is still in the middle of the heap if he becomes a school teacher, even though he has nominally risen into the "professional class."

Noting all this, some observers have jumped to the opposite conclusion. Economists, for example, have noted the declining number of small businesses, both farm and nonfarm, and the increasing concentration of corporate power as a result of mergers. Some radicals have taken this as prima facie evidence that power is today concentrated in fewer hands than a generation or two ago. This implies that there is less and less room at the top. Actual ownership of large corporations has, however, grown more diverse as their domination of the economy has increased. Ownership, moreover, may be less important than radicals assume. It is far from clear, for example, that the owner of a corner grocery store has more power vis à vis his creditors, suppliers, and customers than the salaried manager of a supermarket. Nor is it obvious that a 19th-century farmer had more freedom of action in his confrontations with the weather, the railroads, the banks, and the market than his teacher grandson in his confrontations with school principals, boards of education, parents, and students.

Under these circumstances we cannot assume that the relative size of various social classes is changing just because the overall standard of living and the overall level of occupational competence are rising. Instead, we must regard the size of social classes as a researchable question, albeit one to which definitive answers are never likely to be available, the idea of social class itself being so imprecise. One way to investigate this question is to look at the distribution of occupational power and family income among various strata. If, for example, the most powerful 5 percent of the work force could be shown to exercise less control over the economy than fifty years ago, and the next most powerful 15 percent could be shown to exercise more, we could conclude that the relative size of the upper and upper-middle classes had changed. If, correspondingly, the poorest fifth of all families once consumed 10 percent of the nation's goods and services, and if the same slice of the pie

were now divided among the poorest quarter of the population, we could conclude that the lower class had grown.

Fortunately for society, but unfortunately for social scientists, the power or influence of a given job is had to quantify. The closest approximation is probably pay. Despite the exceptions noted earlier, jobs which give the incumbent what is usually called responsibility tend to pay well, while those which involve little power usually pay badly. Hence if the amount of room at the top of the occupational structure were increasing, we would expect more people to be sharing in the slice of the pie traditionally reserved for the elite. Conversely, if the number of menial and expendable jobs were diminishing, we would expect to find fewer people dividing the (much smaller) slice of the pie that is traditionally available for society's castoffs.

In point of fact, however, Table 2 indicates that there has been no significant change in the distribution of income since 1945. This makes it hard to believe that there has been much change in the distribution of occupational power and prestige. The whole labor force has been upgraded, but the relative position of various classes has evidently changed very little. There is, however, evidence that the share of all income going to the top 5 percent of all families declined considerably both during the Depression and during World War II. This suggests that these two upheavals may well have altered the occupational structure in significant ways, even though redistribution of workers among job categories was no more dramatic in these years than later. Although no good data are available on the overall income distribution before 1929, tax returns from the well-to-do suggest that their share of the pie changed very little between 1913 and

TABLE 2. *Share of All Income Going to Top 5 Percent and to Each Fifth of All American Families and Individuals, 1929–1962*

Year	Top 5 Percent	Net 15 Percent	Second Fifth	Third Fifth	Fourth Fifth	Bottom Fifth	Total
1929	30.0	24.4	19.3	13.8	12.5		100.0
1935–6	26.5	25.2	20.9	14.1	9.2	4.1	100.0
1941	24.0	24.8	22.3	15.3	9.5	4.1	100.0
1947	20.9	25.1	22.0	16.0	11.0	5.0	100.0
1957	20.2	25.3	22.4	16.3	11.1	4.7	100.0
1962	19.6	25.9	22.7	16.3	10.9	4.6	100.0

Source: Herman P. Miller, *Income Distribution in the United States*, Washington, U. S. Government Printing Office, 1966, p. 21. The data are from the series prepared by the Office of Business Economics. Miller also presents data from the Current Population Survey for years since 1947. Although the CPS data suggest that both the richest 5 percent and the poorest 20 percent are somewhat worse off than the above figures indicate, the differences are small and stability since 1947 is equally apparent. More recent data based on the CPS are shown in *Current Population Reports*, Series P-60, No. 51, January 12, 1967, Washington, U. S. Government Printing Office, 1967. These data suggest a slight decline in the proportion of income going to the top 5 percent between 1961 and 1965, but the overall pattern of postwar stability remains.

1929. This being the case, the safest working assumption is probably that there was little change in the overall distribution during those years.

Social Class and Social Mobility

What does this imply about social class in America? It seems clear that technological change and improvements in human skills have increased the productivity of the labor force and that the increase in productivity has led to rising living standards for virtually all Americans. Yet the distribution of goods and services has remained relatively constant despite the rise in absolute living standards. And it should be noted that, if both the rich and the poor increase their income at about the same rate over the years, the *absolute* gap between them will necessarily grow. Ten is to one as a hundred is to ten: but the absolute gap in the latter case is ten times greater than in the former. Between 1947 and 1962, for example, 80th-percentile income was always between 4.0 and 4.5 times as much as 20th-percentile income. But the absolute gap grew from $4,650 to $6,988 (in 1962 dollars).

So, if income distribution is taken as a crude index of the distribution of occupational skills, responsibilities, and prestige, it also seems fair to conclude that these latter have not been redistributed to any significant extent since 1945. In that case it also follows that the relative size of various social classes has remained essentially unchanged for the past twenty years. Nor is there much prospect of change in the near future.

The importance of this conclusion cannot be overemphasized. If, for example, the relative size of the various classes is taken as fixed, social mobility must be treated as a two-way street. Upward mobility will only be possible if vacancies occur in the higher strata. One reason for such vacancies is that the upper strata are less fertile than society as a whole and do not reproduce themselves. This used to be a major factor in American patterns of mobility, but fertility differentials between classes seem to have gradually narrowed over the years.[1]

If there is to be appreciable upward mobility, room at the top must be created by downward mobility among the sons and daughters of the elite. Since downward mobility is never pleasant to contemplate, this means that those who believe in equality of opportunity are under powerful ideological pressures to believe that the amount of room at the top is expanding, for otherwise their ideal will be hard to fulfill. It also means that the elite, while it may give lip-service to the idea of equalizing opportunity, is under powerful familial pressure to make sure that the opportunities available to its children are somewhat "more equal" than those available to the rest of the population.

Nonetheless, there has been a good deal of social mobility in America. Suppose, for example, that we imagine two alternative occupational systems. In one there is no mobility whatever: everyone inherits his parents' position. In the other there is perfect mobility: children from prosperous, well-placed families have no more chance of ending up in their parents' position than children born in the slums. Every country plainly falls somewhere between these two poles. America, like most industrial societies, falls closer to the equality model than to the hereditary model.[2] In interpreting this fact, it is important to bear in mind that the genes affecting both physical and mental competence are probably not randomly distributed across classes. Success in America has always depended to some extent on intelligence, and intelligence is to some extent hereditary. While clever parents tend to have children duller than themselves, and dull parents tend to have children cleverer than themselves, the clever parents' children are not typically so dull as the national average, nor are the dull parents' children typically as clever as the average. Thus, even a strictly meritocratic system for allocating class positions would probably put a slightly larger number of advantaged than disadvantaged children in the elite. Uneven distribuiton of talent cannot account for more than a fraction of all occupational

inheritance in America, but it probably does account for some of it.

Like the relative size of social classes, the rate of social mobility does not seem to be changing much, if at all. A man's chances of occupying the same place on the occupational totem pole as his father have not changed significantly in the past forty years, and there is no good reason to suppose they changed much in earlier times.[3]

Cultural Stratification

Up to this point we have been looking at class primarily in economic terms, defining men primarily as producers and consumers of goods and services. One can, however, take a less quantitative and more qualitative view, defining class as a broadly cultural rather than a narrowly economic phenomenon. Marx himself often looked at class this way, but in America this perspective owes more to cultural anthropology than to Marx and his followers.

When Lloyd Warner and his colleagues first began arguing this view in the 1930's, most readers' initial reactions were hostile. Warner's findings conflicted with the mythology of egalitarian pluralism even more sharply than studies of income distribution and occupational hierarchy. It was not that Americans denied the existence of diverse subcultures, but most people were inclined to assume that this diversity was only marginally related to differences in wealth and power.[4] In part, no doubt, public resistance to such arguments was a legacy of 19th-century America, in which subcultural differences really do seem to have been only loosely associated with wealth and power, at least west of the Appalachians. So long as most men's fathers had been farmers, High Culture remained at a definite discount and even formal education was often rejected in favor of "the school of hard knocks." By the 1930's, however, the situation had changed. It took the conventional wisdom a while to encompass the new reality, but this too has now been largely accomplished. Students, for example, are no longer surprised by Warner's view of small-town America as stratified. On the contrary, they have picked up his views and terms without even having read him, and now casually put their parents down by charging them with "middle-class" prejudices. Newspaper columnists hold forth in the same vein about the characteristics of "lower-class subcultures," and civil rights leaders rail against what they usually take to be an upper-class "power structure."

Nonetheless, cultural classes remain far less egregiously hierarchical than social classes. The time is largely past when the uneducated considered themselves superior to those with "book larnin,'" but the deference paid to expertise, sophistication, and Culture is still considerably less than in most countries. It is still very difficult, for example, to win political support for subsidies to symphonies, art, ballet, and other manifestations of upper-class taste. Nor does the *nouveau riche* seem as embarrassed by having unfashionable tastes and views as he would be in most European countries. Still, we would argue that American subcultures are more hierarchical than they used to be and that the "lower" cultural strata increasingly defer to the "higher." This means that even those who do not themselves have upper-middle class customs or share upper-middle class concerns nonetheless tend to accept their legitimacy and even their superiority. (The typical voter, for example, does not care for chamber music himself, but he may nonetheless be impressed by it and may have thought better

of President Kennedy because he had Casals play at the White House.) One result of this increase in the degree of consensus about the hierarchy of cultural values, assuming it is real, is that upward mobility is increasingly likely to mean cultural as well as socio-economic mobility.

This tendency toward congruence between social and cultural classes has led some sociologists to collapse the two into a single conglomerate conception. There are, however, dangers in this approach. For one thing, it is by no means self-evident that the relationship between social and cultural classes is fixed. What are today described as "middle class values," for example, may tomorrow be found waning among the middle classes but spreading among the working classes. Thus, the fact that the upper-middle class (in terms of income and occupation) is of relatively fixed size does not necessarily mean that what have traditionally beeen regarded as upper-middle class cultural values are confined to a fixed proportion of population. Many of the values traditionally associated with middle-class status could, for example, depend in large part on absolute living standards rather than relative status, and could be diffused to new groups in the same way that vacuum cleaners and football were. Under these circumstances it would seem useful to make a tentative distinction between social and cultural classes, and to treat their relationship as a problem for investigation rather than as a given.

Education as an Index

Such an investigation is not, however, a simple matter. There are, as we have indicated, serious difficulties in assessing the distribution of power between various job holders and consequent difficulties in discussing changes in the size of occupational classes. These difficulties are, however, trivial compared to those we encounter when we try to define cultural classes and to describe their relative size at different points in time. We cannot simply use behavioral indices (e.g., having a savings account or reading a news magazine), for the meaning of these acts varies over time. What were once primarily middle-class habits (e.g., small families and vacations) have in some cases now spread to the working class. The problem is even more serious if we take attitudes (regarding sex, for example) as an index of cultural class, for such attitudes vary from era to era as much as from stratum to stratum.

The impulse to quantify is, however, hard to resist. Just as we earlier took income as a crude measure of occupational power, so too we can take educational attainment as a crude index of cultural class. In doing this, we do not mean to imply a *causal* relationship between schooling and cultural level. While schooling may be an instrument for changing men's values, and more especially for disseminating the attitudes and skills which characterize the upper-middle class, evidence of this is by no means definitive. Instead, the relationship between schooling and cultural class may often work the other way. Young people's ultimate cultural class may be almost entirely determined by such factors as genetic ability, family structure, social connections, and so forth. Schools and colleges may simply be a sifting device for separating those whose talents and inclinations fit them for one cultural class from those whose talents and inclinations fit them for another. But whatever the cause-effect relationship, there does seem to be a strong *correlation* between educational attainment and cultural class.

TABLE 3. *Percent of All Individuals Born in Given Years Finishing High School and College, 1855–1944*

Years of Birth	Percent Finishing High School		Percent Finishing 4 Years College	
	Census	USOE	Census	USOE
1855–1859	—	—	—	1.1
1860–1864	11.5	2.5	2.3	—
1865–1869	13.1	—	2.6	1.3
1870–1874	14.2	3.5	2.9	—
1875–1879	16.4	—	3.3	1.7
1880–1884	17.1	6.4	3.4	—
1885–1889	18.5	—	3.8	2.0
1890–1894	20.7	8.8	4.1	—
1895–1899	24.6	—	5.0	2.7
1900–1904	28.5	16.8	6.1	—
1905–1909	34.9	—	7.3	5.8
1910–1914	40.6	29.0	7.4	—
1915–1919	43.4	—	8.1	8.1
1920–1924	54.7	50.8	9.5	—
1925–1929	55.8	—	10.9	—
1930–1934	60.5	59.0	11.0	14.1
1935–1939	63.6	61.1	—	18.2
1940–1944	—	65.1	—	20.0

Sources: The Census estimates for those born prior to 1890 are derived from the 1940 Census, as summarized in John Folger and Charles Nam's Census monograph, *The Education of the American Population*, Washington, U. S. Government Printing Office, 1967, Table A. 11. The estimates for those born subsequent to 1890 are derived from the *1960 Census*, I (1), Table 173. Those who report having completed four years of college include some who do not report having earned a degree. To obtain estimates of college degree holders, the figures for those born 1885–94 should be reduced by 20 percent, for those born 1895–1904 by 21 percent, for those born 1905–14 by 15 percent, for those born 1915–24 by 11 percent, and for those born 1925–34 by 10 percent. These discount rates are estimated from Mildred J. Schwartz, *The United States College Educated Population: 1960*, Chicago, National Opinion Research Center, 1965, Table 1.2, and *1960 Census*, I (1), Table 173. The U.S. Office of Education estimates are taken from the 1965 *Digest of Educational Statistics*, Tables 37, 53 and 74. They are based on institutional reports of degrees awarded divided by Census estimates of the total age group. We assumed that the median age of high school graduation was 17, since USOE makes this assumption, and that the median age at college graduation was 22, since the NORC survey of 1961 BA's showed this to be the case. (See James A. Davis, *Great Aspirations*, Chicago, Aldine, 1964. Table 1.1.)

On this basis, what can we say about the relative size of various cultural classes? To begin with, it must be said that data on the level and distribution of education before the 1930's are no more reliable than data on incomes before then. Table 3 gives two estimates of the proportion of various age groups completing high school and college, one based on the decennial Census, the other on the biennial institutional surveys by the U.S. Office of Education. It is apparent that, at least for those born before 1915, there is serious disagreement between these two sources. Individuals born before World War I reported receiving far more education than institutions reported giving in this period. Since then the discrepancy has narrowed. This means that institutional reports show a more rapid rate of growth in both high school and college graduation than do individual reports. The discrepancy in growth rates is particularly striking at the high school level, where Census data suggest that the proportion of the population graduating from high school rose by a factor of five between 1880 and 1940, while the USOE data suggest that it rose by a factor of twenty. On the whole we have more confidence in the Census statistics than in those supplied by USOE, but we cannot emphasize too strongly that neither series of statistics should be taken very seriously.

Tabular presentations of data on schooling may, however, conceal as much as they reveal. Table 3, for example, might give many readers an impression of an even, steady increase in both high school and college enrollment. The increase was, however, far from even. Despite growth in enrollment of higher levels, there was very little change in median attainment between the Civil War and World War I. The typical child got between 8 and 9 years of school. There was a sharp increase in median attainment during the 1920's and 1930's to about 12 years. Since World War II median attainment has risen relatively slowly.[5]

Despite the difficulty of estimating educational attainment for different groups and periods, one thing is clear: the level has risen. This raises the thorny question whether such general increases in attainment have affected the relative size of various cultural classes. If, for example, one were to define the cultural lower-middle class as anyone who had finished high school, and the cultural upper-middle class as anyone who had finished college, both classes would obviously be getting bigger. The lower cultural strata would be shrinking correspondingly. This procedure would clearly be justified if schooling were a primary cause of cultural characteristics. If we knew that the many observable differences between the college-educated and the high-school-educated were a direct consequence of attending college, we could feel fairly confident that the proportion of the population with traditional upper-middle class habits and values had risen in tandem with college enrollment. If, on the other hand, differences between the college-educated and the high-school-educated result largely from the more favored social background, greater intelligence, or more enterprising temperament of those who attend college, then increases in college enrollment may not contribute much to the diffusion of upper-middle class culture, but may simply place the collegiate imprimatur on hitherto marginal groups.

Our own view is that relatively few of the differences between the extensively educated and the briefly educated are caused directly by education per se. Most of the differences seem rather to result from selective withdrawal and ejection from the system. We would argue, in other words, that the differences between college graduates and high school dropouts are only occasionally caused by exposure to high school and college; mostly it is a matter of one sort of person finding high school and college tolerable, and so staying enrolled, while another finds them intolerable and withdraws.

The Distribution of Schooling

If this assumption is correct, what does it imply about the relationship between the absolute educational attainment of a given generation and the size of cultural classes in that generation? If the colleges' standards of selection were relatively stable over time, an increase in the proportion of young people earning degrees would clearly indicate an increase in the proportion of those who had the traditional upper-middle class virtues—verbal ability, perseverence, willingness to defer gratification, and so forth. This might have nothing to do with what is learned in colleges per se, but might be a result of urbanization, technological change, child rearing practices, the mass media, or other influences—yet it could still be measured by absolute levels of attainment. If, on the other hand, colleges have had no absolute standards, but have mostly graduated anyone willing to go through the motions of acquiring education, rising enrollment may not really indicate the growth of the more "sophisticated" cultural strata or a shrinkage of the more "benighted" strata.

Taken as a group, American educational institutions have not set many absolute requirements for entrance or graduation. The increase in high school graduation, for example, has been accomplished in good part by automatic promotion and by the creation of "general" or "basic" curricula which demand almost nothing of the student but persistence and docility. At the same time, however, the level of expectation in the academic curriculum has generally risen—as the spread of advanced placement courses indicates. Whether the net

result has been an increase or decrease in average competence we do not know; in either case, however, we suspect that the range of difference among high school graduates has grown. At the college level, there has been, at least until recently, less social and political pressure to accommodate everyone, and the maintenance of traditional upper-middle class norms has been more general and more successful. Indeed, the level of competence required for a B.A. has probably risen at the same time as the number earning it.

All this takes absolute levels of educational attainment as an index of cultural position. In order to give a more complete view, one must also look at an individual's standing relative to others of his generation. In 1900, for example, a man who completed high school was a member of his generation's educational elite. Most high school graduates of that era seem to have accepted most of the middle-class norms of their time. In 1967, on the other hand, about 75 percent of all young people were finishing high school. Secondary schools were willing to keep all but the most uncooperative students, even if they were not able to live up to middle-class expectations, and high teen-age unemployment made even rebellious youngsters stick around, simply because there were few attractive alternatives. As a result, the fact that a man survived twelve years in school no longer told much if anything about him. By 1967, colleges rather than high schools had become the instruments for separating out the prospective middle classes from the rest.

If we are interested in the changing size of cultural classes, then, we must look not just at absolute levels of schooling but at the distribution of schooling in different eras. We must ask how far it is from the bottom of the ladder to the top, and how the proportion of individuals on various rungs is changing. Table 4 estimates the distribution of schooling for three different generations.

At first glance this distribution looks much more equitable than the distribution of income shown in Table 2. This may, however, be an illusion. For one thing, Table 4 omits women. More important, a year of school does not have the same value under all conditions. The typical suburban school spends more than the typical rural one, and the typical college spends more than the typical elementary school. Our crude estimates suggest that the allocation of educational *resources* between various segments of the population is probably almost as inequitable as the income distribution. On the other hand, there is strong reason to doubt that there is anywhere nearly as much variation in what students learn as in the amounts spent on their education. A year of graduate school may cost ten times more than a year of elementary school, but an extra year of graduate school does not increase either a man's intellectual competence or his future income ten times as much as an extra year of elementary school. Thus, while Table 3 probably underestimates the inequalities in the distribution of schooling, a table showing the distribution of educational expenditures would overestimate these inequalities.

Whatever the absolute degree of inequality, it may be less important than the trend. Table 4 shows that if we imputed equal value to all years of schooling, regardless of what was spent on them, the trend was toward a more equal distribution. This would be even more true if we were to look at the distribution of days of schooling instead of years, for variations in lengths of school year and regularity of

TABLE 4. *Percentage Shares of Total Years of Schooling Obtained by Best- and Worst-Educated Twentieths and Thirds of U.S. Males, 1875–1934*

Year of Birth	Top 20th	Top Third	Middle Third	Bottom Third	Bottom 20th
1930–34	8	43	35	22	1
1910–14	9	46	34	20	1
1875–1885*	12	53	34	13	†

Source: John K. Folger and Charles B. Nam, *Education of the American Population*, Washington, D.C., U. S. Government Printing Office, 1967.
* Includes all those alive and over 75 in 1960.
† Less than 0.5 percent.

attendance have dropped sharply in recent times. It should also be borne in mind, however, that, just as with incomes, the rise in absolute attainment from one generation to another means that it takes a very considerable redistribution to prevent the absolute gap between the best and worst educated from growing. The absolute gap between the best and worst educated thirds, for example, widened from 5.8 to 7.0 years between the 1910–1914 generation and the 1930–1934 generation, even though the distribution of schooling had grown more equal.

Nor does the trend in the distribution of educational resources necessarily parallel the trend in the distribution of years of school. It is true that the expenditure differences among regions and jurisdictions are narrowing, so that eight years of elementary schooling or four years of high school have more nearly the same value for everyone. But a year of higher education is much more expensive than a year of either elementary or secondary education. As a result, a one year variation in the amount of college a man gets will affect the distribution of educational resources as much as a two or three year variation in the number of years of elementary or secondary school.[6] Our best guess is that the distribution of educational resources has changed relatively little in recent years.

Cultural and Social Stratification Compared

If the level of educational attainment is rising, while the distribution of educational resources remains relatively stable, what about intergenerational mobility? Are children from poorly educated families more or less likely to end up with a poor education today than in the past? If we judge cultural class by how long an individual has been in school, are upward and downward cultural mobility becoming more or less common?

The best available data suggest that a man's overall chances of improving on his father's position on the educational ladder has not changed significantly over the past forty years. But this fact is the gross result of two contrary trends. On the one hand, there seems to be somewhat more mobility in the middle of the educational distribution. On the other hand, there seems to be less at the top. If, for example, we rank men in quartiles according to the education of their fathers, we can make a crude estimate of educational mobility by looking at how many men born in the top quartile end up in the top quartile themselves. The greater the percentage of those who do so, the less room there is at the top. We find that among men born between 1927 and 1936, 49 percent of those who started in the top quartile remained there. Among men who had been born in the top quartile between 1897 and 1906, only 42 percent had remained there. This is not a dramatic change, but it certainly offers no support for the usual comfortable assumption that

educational opportunity is becoming more equal.

On the basis of the evidence on educational attainment just reviewed, it seems clear that cultural stratification follows many of the same patterns as social stratification:

1. The overall level of educational attainment seems to be rising, just as the overall income level is. The overall level of cultural sophistication is probably also rising, though not at anything like the same rate as the standard of living.

2. The distribution of years of schooling is more equal than the distribution of income, and unlike the income distribution is moving toward greater equality. The absolute attainment gap between the well educated and the poorly educated is growing, however, just as the absolute income gap between rich and poor is growing.

3. The distribution of educational resources, like the distribution of income, does not seem to be getting notably more or less egalitarian. What this implies for the distribution of intellectual competence is debatable, however, just as it is debatable whether a stable distribution of income indicates a stable distribution of occupational power and responsibility.

4. The rate of intergenerational mobility between cultural classes seems to resemble the rate of social mobility in that both are quite high and neither has changed significantly in the twentieth century.

Social and Cultural Classes Compared

Under these circumstances we must ask to what extent social and cultural classes are really identical. While there is considerable overlap, it is by no means complete. Those with "upper-middle" educations are by no means always "upper-middle" in occupation or income, and those with "lower" incomes and occupations are by no means always "lower" in educational attainment. In 1960, for example, 18 percent of the male labor force over 25 years old had completed at least one year of college. Only 45 percent of this educational elite were in the best paid fifth of the male work force; 25 percent were earning less than the national median. At the other end of the educational scale, 24 percent of the male labor force had not completed elementary school. Yet 21 percent of these semi-literates were earning more than the national median, and 5 percent were in the best paid fifth of the labor force.

Neither is the relationship between education and occupation as tight as many people suppose. It is true that in 1960 some 76 percent of all men over 25 in "professional, technical, and kindred" occupations reported a year or more of college, and about half held B.A.'s. But only 35 percent of all male "managers, officials, and proprietors" had ever been to college, and only 15 percent held B.A.'s. (Even if we exclude proprietors and include only salaried managers and officials, only 45 percent had finished a year of college.) Putting this the other way around: a man over 25 who had finished a year of college in 1960 had three chances in five of holding a professional or managerial job, but he also had one chance in six of holding a clerical or sales job and one chance in six of holding a blue-collar job.

While these relationships are all relatively loose, they are obviously not inconsequential. This becomes especially clear if, instead of looking at the relationship between only two of these hierarchies, we look at all three together. Taking men between 25 and 34 in 1960, for example, and then focusing on those in *both* the best paid fifth of the income distribution and the most prestigious fifth of the occupational distribution, we find that 68 percent are also in the best educated fifth of the male population. This suggests considerable overlap in America's economic, occupational, and cultural elites.

The most interesting point about all these relationships may not, however, be their absolute level but their trend. The overall relationship between education and occupational status has not changed much over the years, though earning a B.A. may be relatively more important while a high school diploma may be relatively less so. The relationship between education and income also seems to be fairly stable. The relationship between educational attainment and social mobility, while rather modest, also seems stable.

Loose as these relationships may be, their existence and persistence bring us back to the problem we raised earlier: namely, the character of the relationship between social and cultural class. Viewed from the top, the problem seems simple. There seem to be plenty of opportunities for those with appropriate skills, habits, and attitudes; the "problem" is the shortage of qualified men for available top-level jobs. The educational system is constantly criticized for not turning out enough men competent to fill these slots. Those at the top mostly assume that it is the difficulty of recruiting into their own cultural class which poses the crucial obstacle to both social progress and individual mobility. Hence their support for "more" and "better" education.

Viewed from the bottom, on the other hand, the situation looks very different. Employers seem to demand all sorts of irrelevant qualifications from applicants, and many fear that even if they meet these requirements they will not be allowed to climb very far. From the bottom, then, the main obstacle to upward mobility often appears to be the limited amount of room at the top, not the cultural characteristics of those at the bottom. To the extent that this is true, schooling and other invitations to character change depend for their success on convincing those involved that they are in fact headed for jobs and social milieus in which new habits and values will be both necessary and appropriate. This is often impossible. The excluded are constantly told they can be included if only they buy a new beauty cream, win at the races, do well in school, or whatever. They are rightly cynical, even though endlessly gullible. The changes required for success in school and for upward cultural mobility are painful, and skeptics are seldom willing to take the risks involved. Indeed, even the nonskeptic who takes the elite's claims at face value and believes he could get ahead by changing may be unwilling to do so, for he may feel that the material and psychic rewards are not worth the price of estrangement from family, friends, and childhood self.

The Function of Schooling

All this suggests a partial answer to another question we raised earlier: namely, how much of the difference between the uneducated and the educated should be attributed directly to school experiences and how much to external factors such as upbringing, intelligence, personality. A good portion of the apparent impact of schooling is, we would suggest, *anticipatory socialization*. Sending a child to school may be like telling him he has a rich maiden aunt and will eventually inherit a fortune. The aunt and her money have no direct effect on the child's life or growth. But the *idea* of the money—even if it is nonexistent—may have a considerable effect, for the child may feel he has special opportunities and responsibilities. So, too, with schooling. What actually happens from day to day in a school or college may have relatively little effect on the students—though it certainly has *some* effect. But a good student's knowledge that he can go to college, and that a college degree will be a passport to a good job and a comfortable standard of living, may have a significant effect on him. He is more likely to adopt the attitudes and acquire the skills he thinks he will need in the world he expects to enter. That he may not really be able to enter this world may be irrelevant at this stage, just as the actual terms of his aunt's will are.

This becomes critically important when we consider the possible impact on the overall social structure of equalizing educational opportunities and/or results. Suppose, to take an extreme example, that all students stayed in school precisely the same length of time. Employers interested in getting the most "suitable" students would then presumably rely on school grades to separate sheep from goats. Students would come to anticipate this, and would therefore be able to tell quite early what kinds of jobs and living standards were open to them. Most of those who knew they were going to have menial jobs and low incomes would sense that adults viewed them as failures and would probably begin to protect themselves psychologically from this eventuality by adopting something very like the current lower-class cultural style. Most of those who were going to have important jobs and live well would, on the other hand, sense that adults saw them as successes and would adapt themselves to the real or imagined requirements of this role. Such differentiation would occur even if all students attended the same schools for the same length of time, took the same courses with the same teachers, etc.

This fantasy suggests that the effects of schooling may depend as much on how well the student feels he is doing as on how long he stays enrolled. The apparent correlation between educational attainment and adult values is, in other words, at least partially due to the fact that high attainment is a surrogate for success (first in school itself and later in adult life). To the degree that this is so, neither expansion of schools and colleges, nor increases in the average length of schooling, nor even increases in the average academic competence of the population, will have much effect on the cultural characteristics of the adult population, for these measures will not affect people's sense of their own success or failure relative to others around them. These perceptions will be affected only by changes in the distribution of wealth and power among adults and, as we have seen, this distribution does not seem to be changing much at the present time.

Yet this is not quite the whole story. For one thing, while students tend to compare themselves to their contemporaries and adapt their personalities accordingly, they also compare themselves to their parents and respond to this comparison. If students feel they know more and are doing better than their parents did, this may give them self-confidence and a general sense of well-being even when their relative position vis-à-vis their agemates is identical to that of their parents among their contemporaries. In addition, it seems likely that schools and colleges do have some direct effect on the habits and values of those who pass through them, independent of the later fate of these youngsters. This is probably especially true in the younger grades.

Finally, it must be noted that there are a variety of other educational institutions, such as television and churches, working to change the customs and concerns of the American people.

All in all, it seems safe to conclude that the recent stability of the income distribution indicates a high degree of stability in the size of social classes and that this stability means considerable stability in the size of cultural classes. There may nonetheless be *some* changes in the latter. These changes are extremely difficult to describe in single summary measures comparable to income, but the evidence available from opinion surveys, consumer research, and the like suggests that there is a slow growth in the number of people having what have traditionally been called middle-class attitudes and tastes. Yet even here the most conspicuous fact is that the enormous rise in the standard of living over the past two decades has brought relatively few of the changes in basic values that the prophets of affluence perdicted.

Footnotes

[1] It should be noted that virtually all groups more than reproduce themselves in the narrow sense of averaging more than two children per family. But if, say, the upper-middle class included 15 out of every 100 people, and if they produced only 15 children while the remaining 85 people produced 105 children, then the top 15 percent of the next generation would have to include 18 people, at least 3 of whom would have to come from outside the elite of the previous generation.

[2] The skeptical reader interested in a statistical demonstration of this point is referred to Elton F. Jackson and Harry J. Crockett's "Occupational Mobility in the United States," *American Sociological Review*, February 1964.

[3] Peter Blau and Otis Dudley Duncan's difficult but enormously important study, *The American Occupational Structure,* shows that the simple correlation between father's and son's occupational status has been stable at 0.4 for sons born in the twentieth century.

[4] The issue is nicely embodied in the well-known Hemingway-Fitzgerald dialogue, in which Fitzgerald is said to have commented that "The rich are different from us," to which Hemingway replied, "Yes, they have more money." In the 1920's most Americans wanted to believe Hemingway's version; today Fitzgerald's view is more acceptable.

[5] Much of the increase in attainment in the 1920's and 1930's resulted from more regular progress through school rather than from more protracted schooling. The 1960 Census, I (1), Table 166, shows that between 1920 and 1960 the median school leaving age rose only two years, from 16 to 18. The relevant age groups show a four-year increase in attainment during this same period. This suggests that regular attendance and automatic promotion were crucial ingredients of the apparent change.

[6] If, for example, A gets four years of elementary education and B gets eight, B has gotten 100 percent more years of schooling than A and has absorbed about 100 percent more resources. If A's grandson gets 12 years of education while B's grandson gets 18 years, B's family advantage has been reduced from 100 percent to 50 percent and the distribution of years of school has grown more equitable. Yet if we assume that a year of high school costs 1.5 times as much as a year of elementary school, that a year of college costs three times as much, and that a year of graduate school costs ten times as much, B's grandson will consume 228 percent more resources than A's grandson. Thus while a change of this sort would make the distribution shown in Table 4 look more equal than before, it would make a distribution based on resource allocation look less equal.

9

The Invisible Poor

MICHAEL HARRINGTON

There is a familiar America. It is celebrated in speeches and advertised on television and in the magazines. It has the highest mass standard of living the world has ever known.

In the 1950's this America worried about itself, yet even its anxieties were products of abundance. The title of a brilliant book was widely misinterpreted, and the familiar America began to call itself "the affluent society." There was introspection about Madison Avenue and tail fins; there was discussion of the emotional suffering taking place in the suburbs. In all this, there was an implicit assumption that the basic grinding economic problems had been solved in the United States. In this theory the nation's problems were no longer a matter of basic human needs, of food, shelter, and clothing. Now they were seen as qualitative, a question of learning to live decently amid luxury.

While this discussion was carried on, there existed another America. In it dwelt somewhere between 40,000,000 and 50,000,000 citizens of this land. They were poor. They still are.

To be sure, the other America is not impoverished in the same sense as those poor nations where millions cling to hunger as a defense against starvation. This country has escaped such extremes. That does not change the fact that tens of millions of Americans are, at this very moment, maimed in body and spirit, existing at levels beneath those necessary for human decency. If these people are not starving, they are hungry, and sometimes fat with hunger, for that is what cheap foods do. They are without adequate housing and education and medical care.

The Government has documented what this means to the bodies of the poor, and the figures will be cited throughout this book. But even more basic, this poverty twists and deforms the spirit. The American poor are pessimistic and defeated, and they are victimized by mental suffering to a degree unknown in Suburbia.

This book is a description of the world in which these people live; it is about the other America. Here are the unskilled workers, the migrant farm workers, the aged, the minorities, and all the others who live in the economic underworld of American life. In all this, there will be statistics, and that offers the opportunity for disagreement among honest and sincere men. I would ask the reader to respond critically to every assertion, but not to allow statistical quibbling to obscure the huge, enormous, and intolerable fact of poverty in America. For, when all is said and done, that fact is unmistakable, whatever its exact dimensions, and the truly human reaction can only be outrage. As W. H. Auden wrote:

> Hunger allows no choice
> To the citizen or the police;
> We must love one another or die.

SOURCE: Reprinted from *The Other America* by Michael Harrington, by permission of The Macmillan Company and Penguin Books Ltd. Copyright © 1962 by Michael Harrington.

I

The millions who are poor in the United States tend to become increasingly invisible. Here is a great mass of people, yet it takes an effort of the intellect and will even to see them.

I discovered this personally in a curious way. After I wrote my first article on poverty in America, I had all the statistics down on paper. I had proved to my satisfaction that there were around 50,000,000 poor in this country. Yet, I realized I did not believe my own figures. The poor existed in the Government reports; they were percentages and numbers in long, close columns, but they were not part of my experience. I could prove that the other America existed, but I had never been there.

My response was not accidental. It was typical of what is happening to an entire society, and it reflects profound social changes in this nation. The other America, the America of poverty, is hidden today in a way that it never was before. Its millions are socially invisible to the rest of us. No wonder that so many misinterpreted Galbraith's title and assumed that "the affluent society" meant that everyone had a decent standard of life. The misinterpretation was true as far as the actual day-to-day lives of two-thirds of the nation were concerned. Thus, one must begin a description of the other America by understanding why we do not see it.

There are perennial reasons that make the other America an invisible land.

Poverty is often off the beaten track. It always has been. The ordinary tourist never left the main highway, and today he rides interstate turnpikes. He does not go into the valleys of Pennsylvania where the towns look like movie sets of Wales in the thirties. He does not see the company houses in rows, the rutted roads (the poor always have bad roads whether they live in the city, in towns, or on farms), and everything is black and dirty. And even if he were to pass through such a place by accident, the tourist would not meet the unemployed men in the bar or the women coming home from a runaway sweatshop.

Then, too, beauty and myths are perennial masks of poverty. The traveler comes to the Appalachians in the lovely season. He sees the hills, the streams, the foliage —but not the poor. Or perhaps he looks at a run-down mountain house and, remembering Rousseau rather than seeing with his eyes, decides that "those people" are truly fortunate to be living the way they are and that they are lucky to be exempt from the strains and tensions of the middle class. The only problem is that "those people," the quaint inhabitants of those hills, are undereducated, underprivileged, lack medical care, and are in the process of being forced from the land into a life in the cities, where they are misfits.

These are normal and obvious causes of the invisibility of the poor. They operated a generation ago; they will be functioning a generation hence. It is more important to understand that the very development of American society is creating a new kind of blindness about poverty. The poor are increasingly slipping out of the very experience and consciousness of the nation.

If the middle class never did like ugliness and poverty, it was at least aware of them. "Across the tracks" was not a very long way to go. There were forays into the slums at Christmas time; there were charitable organizations that brought contact with the poor. Occasionally, almost everyone passed through the Negro ghetto or the blocks of tenements, if only to get down town to work or to entertainment.

Now the American city has been transformed. The poor still inhabit the miserable housing in the central area, but they are increasingly isolated from contact with, or sight of, anybody else. Middle-class women coming in from Suburbia on a rare trip may catch the merest glimpse of the other America on the way to an evening at the theater, but their children are segregated in suburban schools. The business or professional man may drive along the fringes of slums in a car or bus, but it is not an important experience to him. The failures, the unskilled, the disabled, the aged, and the minorities are right there, across the tracks, where they have always been. But hardly anyone else is.

In short, the very development of the American city has removed poverty from the living, emotional experience of millions upon millions of middle-class Americans. Living out in the suburbs, it is easy to assume that ours is, indeed, an affluent society.

This new segregation of poverty is compounded by a well-meaning ignorance. A good many concerned and sympathetic Americans are aware that there is much discussion of urban renewal. Suddenly, driving through the city, they notice that a familiar slum has been torn down and that there are towering, modern buildings where once there had been tenements or hovels. There is a warm feeling of satisfaction, of pride in the way things are working out: the poor, it is obvious, are being taken care of.

The irony in this (as the chapter on housing will document) is that the truth is nearly the exact opposite to the impression. The total impact of the various housing programs in postwar America has been to squeeze more and more people into existing slums. More often than not, the modern apartment in a towering building rents at $40 a room or more. For, during the past decade and a half, there has been more subsidization of middle- and upper-income housing than there has been of housing for the poor.

Clothes make the poor invisible too: America has the best-dressed poverty the world has ever known. For a variety of reasons, the benefits of mass production have been spread much more evenly in this area than in many others. It is much easier in the United States to be decently dressed than it is to be decently housed, fed, or doctored. Even people with terribly depressed incomes can look prosperous.

This is an extremely important factor in defining our emotional and existential ignorance of poverty. In Detroit the existence of social classes became much more difficult to discern the day the companies put lockers in the plants. From that moment on, one did not see men in work clothes on the way to the factory, but citizens in slacks and white shirts. This process has been magnified with the poor throughout the country. There are tens of thousands of Americans in the big cities who are wearing shoes, perhaps even a stylishly cut suit or dress, and yet are hungry. It is not a matter of planning, though it almost seems as if the affluent society had given out costumes to the poor so that they would not offend the rest of society with the sight of rags.

Then, many of the poor are the wrong age to be seen. A good number of them (over 8,000,000) are sixty-five years of age or better; an even larger number are under eighteen. The aged members of the other America are often sick, and they cannot move. Another group of them live out their lives in loneliness and frustration: they sit in rented rooms, or else they stay close to a house in a neighborhood that has completely changed from the old days. Indeed, one of the worst aspects of poverty among the aged is that these people are out of sight and out of mind, and alone.

The young are somewhat more visible, yet they too stay close to their neighborhoods. Sometimes they advertise their poverty through a lurid tabloid story about a gang killing. But generally they do not disturb the quiet streets of the middle class.

And finally, the poor are politically invisible. It is one of the cruelest ironies of social life in advanced countries that the dispossessed at the bottom of society are unable to speak for themselves. The people of the other America do not, by far and large, belong to unions, to fraternal organizations, or to political parties. They are without lobbies of their own; they put forward no legislative program. As a group, they are atomized. They have no face; they have no voice.

Thus, there is not even a cynical political motive for caring about the poor, as in the old days. Because the slums are no longer centers of powerful political organizations, the politicians need not really care about their inhabitants. The slums are no longer visible to the middle class, so much of the idealistic urge to fight for those who need help is gone. Only the social agencies have a really direct involvement with the other America, and they are without any great political power.

To the extent that the poor have a spokesman in American life, that role is played by the labor movement. The unions have their own particular idealism, an ideology of concern. More than that, they realize that the existence of a reservoir

of cheap, unorganized labor is a menace to wages and working conditions throughout the entire economy. Thus, many union legislative proposals—to extend the coverage of minimum wage and social security, to organize migrant farm laborers—articulate the needs of the poor.

That the poor are invisible is one of the most important things about them. They are not simply neglected and forgotten as in the old rhetoric of reform; what is much worse, they are not seen.

One might take a remark from George Eliot's *Felix Holt* as a basic statement of what this book is about:

> . . . there is no private life which has not been determined by a wider public life, from the time when the primeval milkmaid had to wander with the wanderings of her clan, because the cow she milked was one of a herd which had made the pasture bare. Even in the conservatory existence where the fair Camellia is sighed for by the noble young Pineapple, neither of them needing to care about the frost or rain outside, there is a nether apparatus of hot-water pipes liable to cool down on a strike of the gardeners or a scarcity of coal.
>
> And the lives we are about to look back upon do not belong to those conservatory species; they are rooted in the common earth, having to endure all the ordinary chances of past and present weather.

Forty to 50,000,000 people are becoming increasingly invisible. That is a shocking fact. But there is a second basic irony of poverty that is equally important: if one is to make the mistake of being born poor, he should choose a time when the majority of the people are miserable too.

J. K. Galbraith develops this idea in *The Affluent Society,* and in doing so defines the "newness" of the kind of poverty in contemporary America. The old poverty, Galbraith notes, was general. It was the condition of life of an entire society, or at least of that huge majority who were without special skills or the luck of birth. When the entire economy advanced, a good many of these people gained higher standards of living. Unlike the poor today, the majority poor of a generation ago were an immediate (if cynical) concern of political leaders. The old slums of the immigrants had the votes; they provided the basis for labor organizations; their very numbers could be a powerful force in political conflict. At the same time the new technology required higher skills, more education, and stimulated an upward movement for millions.

Perhaps the most dramatic case of the power of the majority poor took place in the 1930's. The Congress of Industrial Organizations literally organized millions in a matter of years. A labor movement that had been declining and confined to a thin stratum of the highly skilled suddenly embraced masses of men and women in basic industry. At the same time this acted as a pressure upon the Government, and the New Deal codified some of the social gains in laws like the Wagner Act. The result was not a basic transformation of the American system, but it did transform the lives of an entire section of the population.

In the thirties one of the reasons for these advances was that misery was general. There was no need then to write books about unemployment and poverty. That was the decisive social experience of the entire society, and the apple sellers even invaded Wall Street. There was political sympathy from middle-class reformers; there were an élan and spirit that grew out of a deep crisis.

Some of those who advanced in the thirties did so because they had unique and individual personal talents. But for the great mass, it was a question of being at the right point in the economy at the right time in history, and utilizing that position for common struggle. Some of those who failed did so because they did not have the will to take advantage of new opportunities. But for the most part the poor who were left behind had been at the wrong place in the economy at the wrong moment in history.

These were the people in the unorganizable jobs, in the South, in the minority groups, in the fly-by-night factories that were low on capital and high on labor. When some of them did break into the economic mainstream—when, for instance, the CIO opened up the way for some Negroes to find good industrial jobs—they proved to be as resourceful as anyone else. As a group, the other Americans who stayed behind were not originally composed primarily of individual failures. Rather, they were victims of an impersonal process that selected some for progress and discriminated against others.

Out of the thirties came the welfare state. Its creation had been stimulated by mass impoverishment and misery, yet it helped the poor least of all. Laws like unemployment compensation, the Wagner Act, the various farm programs, all these were designed for the middle third in the cities, for the organized workers, and for the upper third in the country, for the big market farmers. If a man works in an extremely low-paying job, he may not even be covered by social security or other welfare programs. If he receives unemployment compensation, the payment is scaled down according to his low earnings.

One of the major laws that was designed to cover everyone, rich and poor, was social security. But even here the other Americans suffered discrimination. Over the years social security payments have not even provided a subsistence level of life. The middle third have been able to supplement the Federal pension through private plans negotiated by unions, through joining medical insurance schemes like Blue Cross, and so on. The poor have not been able to do so. They lead a bitter life, and then have to pay for that fact in old age.

Indeed, the paradox that the welfare state benefits those least who need help most is but a single instance of a persistent irony in the other America. Even when the money finally trickles down, even when a school is built in a poor neighborhood, for instance, the poor are still deprived. Their entire environment, their life, their values, do not prepare them to take advantage of the new opportunity. The parents are anxious for the children to go to work; the pupils are pent up, waiting for the moment when their education has complied with the law.

Today's poor, in short, missed the political and social gains of the thirties. They are, as Galbraith rightly points out, the first minority poor in history, the first poor not to be seen, the first poor whom the politicians could leave alone.

The first step toward the new poverty was taken when millions of people proved immune to progress. When that happened, the failure was not individual and personal, but a social product. But once the historic accident takes place, it begins to become a personal fate.

The new poor of the other America saw the rest of society move ahead. They went on living in depressed areas, and often they tended to become depressed human beings. In some of the West Virginia towns, for instance, an entire community will become shabby and defeated. The young and the adventurous go to the city, leaving behind those who cannot move and those who lack the will to do so. The entire area becomes permeated with failure, and that is one more reason the big corporations shy away.

Indeed, one of the most important things about the new poverty is that it cannot be defined in simple, statistical terms. Throughout this book a crucial term is used: aspiration. If a group has internal vitality, a will—if it has aspiration—it may live in dilapidated housing, it may eat an inadequate diet, and it may suffer poverty, but it is not impoverished. So it was in those ethnic slums of the immigrants that played such a dramatic role in the unfolding of the American dream. The people found themselves in slums, but they were not slum dwellers.

But the new poverty is constructed so as to destroy aspiration; it is a system designed to be impervious to hope. The other America does not contain the adventurous seeking a new life and land. It is populated by the failures, by those driven from the land and bewildered by the city, by old people suddenly confronted with the torments of loneliness and poverty, and by minorities facing a wall of prejudice.

In the past, when poverty was general in the unskilled and semiskilled work force, the poor were all mixed together. The bright and the dull, those who were going to escape into the great society and those who were to stay behind, all of them lived on the same street. When the middle third rose, this community was destroyed. And the entire invisible land of the other Americans became a ghetto, a modern poor farm for the rejects of society and of the economy.

It is a blow to reform and the political hopes of the poor that the middle class no longer understands that poverty exists. But, perhaps more important, the poor are losing their links with the great world. If statistics and sociology can measure a feeling as delicate as loneliness (and some of the attempts to do so will be cited later on), the other America is becoming increasingly populated by those who do not belong to anybody or anything. They are no longer participants in an ethnic culture from the old country; they are less and less religious; they do not belong to unions or clubs. They are not seen, and because of that they themselves cannot see. Their horizon has become more and more restricted; they see one another, and that means they see little reason to hope.

Galbraith was one of the first writers to begin to describe the newness of contemporary poverty, and that is to his credit. Yet because even he underestimates the problem, it is important to put his definition into perspective.

For Galbraith, there are two main components of the new poverty: case poverty and insular poverty. Case poverty is the plight of those who suffer from some physical or mental disability that is personal and individual and excludes them from the general advance. Insular poverty exists in areas like the Appalachians or the West Virginia coal fields, where an entire section of the country becomes economically obsolete.

Physical and mental disabilities are, to be sure, an important part of poverty in America. The poor are sick in body and in spirit. But this is not an isolated fact about them, an individual "case," a stroke of bad luck. Disease, alcoholism, low IQ's, these express a whole way of life. They are, in the main, the effects of an environment, not the biographies of unlucky individuals. Because of this, the new poverty is something that cannot be dealt with by first aid. If there is to be a lasting assault on the shame of the other America, it must seek to root out of this society an entire environment, and not just the relief of individuals.

But perhaps the idea of "insular" poverty is even more dangerous. To speak of "islands" of the poor (or, in the more popular term, of "pockets of poverty") is to imply that one is confronted by a serious, but relatively minor, problem. This is hardly a description of a misery that extends to 40,000,000 or 50,000,000 people in the United States. They have remained impoverished in spite of increasing productivity and the creation of a welfare state. That fact alone should suggest the dimensions of a serious and basic situation.

And yet, even given these disagreements with Galbraith, his achievement is considerable. He was one of the first to understand that there are enough poor people in the United States to constitute a subculture of misery, but not enough of them to challenge the conscience and the imagination of the nation.

Finally, one might summarize the newness of contemporary poverty by saying: These are the people who are immune to progress. But then the facts are even more cruel. The other Americans are the victims of the very inventions and machines that have provided a higher living standard for the rest of the society. They are upside-down in the economy, and for them greater productivity often means worse jobs; agricultural advance becomes hunger.

In the optimistic theory, technology is an undisguised blessing. A general increase in productivity, the argument goes, generates a higher standard of living for the whole people. And indeed, this has been true for the middle and upper thirds of American society, the people who made such striking gains in the last two decades. It tends to overstate the automatic character of the process, to omit the role of human struggle. (The CIO was organized by men in conflict, not by economic trends.) Yet it states a certain truth—for those who are lucky enough to participate in it.

But the poor, if they were given to theory, might argue the exact opposite. They might say: Progress is misery.

As the society became more technological, more skilled, those who learn to work the machines, who get the expanding education, move up. Those who miss out at the very start find themselves at a new disadvantage. A generation ago in American life, the majority of the working people did not have high-school educations. But at that time industry was organized on a lower level of skill and competence. And there was a sort of continuum in the shop: the youth who left school at sixteen could begin as a laborer, and gradually pick up skill as he went along.

Today the situation is quite different. The good jobs require much more academic preparation, much more skill from the very outset. Those who lack a high-school education tend to be condemned to the economic underworld—to low-paying service industries, to backward factories, to sweeping and janitorial duties. If the fathers and mothers of the contemporary poor were penalized a generation ago for their lack of schooling, their children will suffer all the more. The very rise in productivity that created more money and better working conditions for the rest of the society can be a menace to the poor.

But then this technological revolution might have an even more disastrous

consequence: it could increase the ranks of the poor as well as intensify the disabilities of poverty. At this point it is too early to make any final judgment, yet there are obvious danger signals. There are millions of Americans who live just the other side of poverty. When a recession comes, they are pushed onto the relief rolls. (Welfare payments in New York respond almost immediately to any economic decline.) If automation continues to inflict more and more penalties on the unskilled and the semiskilled, it could have the impact of permanently increasing the population of the other America.

Even more explosive is the possibility that people who participated in the gains of the thirties and the forties will be pulled back down into poverty. Today the mass-production industries where unionization made such a difference are contracting. Jobs are being destroyed. In the process, workers who had achieved a certain level of wages, who had won working conditions in the shop, are suddenly confronted with impoverishment. This is particularly true for anyone over forty years of age and for members of minority groups. Once their job is abolished, their chances of ever getting similar work are very slim.

It is too early to say whether or not this phenomenon is temporary, or whether it represents a massive retrogression that will swell the numbers of the poor. To a large extent, the answer to this question will be determined by the political response of the United States in the sixties. If serious and massive action is not undertaken, it may be necessary for statisticians to add some old-fashioned, pre-welfare-state poverty to the misery of the other America.

Poverty in the 1960's is invisible and it is new, and both these factors make it more tenacious. It is more isolated and politically powerless than ever before. It is laced with ironies, not the least of which is that many of the poor view progress upside-down, as a menace and a threat to their lives. And if the nation does not measure up to the challenge of automation, poverty in the 1960's might be on the increase.

II

There are mighty historical and economic forces that keep the poor down; and there are human beings who help out in this grim business, many of them unwittingly. There are sociological and political reasons why poverty is not seen; and there are misconceptions and prejudices that literally blind the eyes. The latter must be understood if anyone is to make the necessary act of intellect and will so that the poor can be noticed.

Here is the most familiar version of social blindness: "The poor are that way because they are afraid of work. And anyway they all have big cars. If they were like me (or my father or my grandfather), they could pay their own way. But they prefer to live on the dole and cheat the taxpayers."

This theory, usually thought of as a virtuous and moral statement, is one of the means of making it impossible for the poor ever to pay their way. There are, one must assume, citizens of the other America who choose impoverishment out of fear of work (though, writing it down, I really do not believe it). But the real explanation of why the poor are where they are is that they made the mistake of being born to the wrong parents, in the wrong section of the country, in the wrong industry, or in the wrong racial or ethnic group. Once that mistake has been made, they could have been paragons of will and morality,

but most of them would never even have had a chance to get out of the other America.

There are two important ways of saying this: The poor are caught in a vicious circle; or, The poor live in a culture of poverty.

In a sense, one might define the contemporary poor in the United States as those who, for reasons beyond their control, cannot help themselves. All the most decisive factors making for opportunity and advance are against them. They are born going downward, and most of them stay down. They are victims whose lives are endlessly blown round and round the other America.

Here is one of the most familiar forms of the vicious circle of poverty. The poor get sick more than anyone else in the society. That is because they live in slums, jammed together under unhygienic conditions; they have inadequate diets, and cannot get decent medical care. When they become sick, they are sick longer than any other group in the society. Because they are sick more often and longer than anyone else, they lose wages and work, and find it difficult to hold a steady job. And because of this, they cannot pay for good housing, for a nutritious diet, for doctors. At any given point in the circle, particularly when there is a major illness, their prospect is to move to an even lower level and to begin the cycle, round and round, toward even more suffering.

This is only one example of the vicious circle. Each group in the other America has its own particular version of the experience, and these will be detailed throughout this book. But the pattern, whatever its variations, is basic to the other America.

The individual cannot usually break out of this vicious circle. Neither can the group, for it lacks the social energy and political strength to turn its misery into a cause. Only the larger society, with its help and resources, can really make it possible for these people to help themselves. Yet those who could make the difference too often refuse to act because of their ignorant, smug moralisms. They view the effects of poverty—above all, the warping of the will and spirit that is a consequence of being poor—as choices. Understanding the vicious circle is an important step in breaking down this prejudice.

There is an even richer way of describing this same, general idea: Poverty in the United States is a culture, an institution, a way of life.

There is a famous anecdote about Ernest Hemingway and F. Scott Fitzgerald. Fitzgerald is reported to have remarked to Hemingway, "The rich are different." And Hemingway replied, "Yes, they have money." Fitzgerald had much the better of the exchange. He understood that being rich was not a simple fact, like a large bank account, but a way of looking at reality, a series of attitudes, a special type of life. If this is true of the rich, it is ten times truer of the poor. Everything about them, from the condition of their teeth to the way in which they love, is suffused and permeated by the fact of their poverty. And this is sometimes a hard idea for a Hemingway-like middle-class America to comprehend.

The family structure of the poor, for instance, is different from that of the rest of the society. There are more homes without a father, there is less marriage, more early pregnancy and, if Kinsey's statistical findings can be used, markedly different attitudes toward sex. As a result of this, to take but one consequence of the fact, hundreds of thousands, and perhaps millions, of children in the other America

never know stability and "normal" affection.

Or perhaps the policeman is an even better example. For the middle class, the police protect property, give directions, and help old ladies. For the urban poor, the police are those who arrest you. In almost any slum there is a vast conspiracy against the forces of law and order. If someone approaches asking for a person, no one there will have heard of him, even if he lives next door. The outsider is "cop," bill collector, investigator (and, in the Negro ghetto, most dramatically, he is "the Man").

While writing this book, I was arrested for participation in a civil-rights demonstration. A brief experience of a night in a cell made an abstraction personal and immediate: the city jail is one of the basic institutions of the other America. Almost everyone whom I encountered in the "tank" was poor: skid-row whites, Negroes, Puerto Ricans. Their poverty was an incitement to arrest in the first place. (A policeman will be much more careful with a well-dressed, obviously educated man who might have political connections than he will with someone who is poor.) They did not have money for bail or for lawyers. And, perhaps most important, they waited their arraignment with stolidity, in a mood of passive acceptance. They expected the worst, and they probably got it.

There is, in short, a language of the poor, a psychology of the poor, a world view of the poor. To be impoverished is to be an internal alien, to grow up in a culture that is radically different from the one that dominates the society. The poor can be described statistically; they can be analyzed as a group. But they need a novelist as well as a sociologist if we are to see them.

They need an American Dickens to record the smell and texture and quality of their lives. The cycles and trends, the massive forces, must be seen as affecting persons who talk and think differently.

I am not that novelist. Yet in this book I have attempted to describe the faces behind the statistics, to tell a little of the "thickness" of personal life in the other America. Of necessity, I have begun with large groups: the dispossessed workers, the minorities, the farm poor, and the aged. Then, there are three cases of less massive types of poverty, including the only single humorous component in the other America. And finally, there are the slums, and the psychology of the poor.

Throughout, I work on an assumption that cannot be proved by Government figures or even documented by impressions of the other America. It is an ethical proposition, and it can be simply stated: In a nation with a technology that could provide every citizen with a decent life,

it is an outrage and a scandal that there should be such social misery. Only if one begins with this assumption is it possible to pierce through the invisibility of 40,000,000 to 50,000,000 human beings and to see the other America. We must perceive passionately, if this blindness is to be lifted from us. A fact can be rationalized and explained away; an indignity cannot.

What shall we tell the American poor, once we have seen them? Shall we say to them that they are better off than the Indian poor, the Italian poor, the Russian poor? That is one answer, but it is heartless. I should put it another way. I want to tell every well-fed and optimistic American that it is intolerable that so many millions should be maimed in body and in spirit when it is not necessary that they should be. My standard of comparison is not how much worse things used to be. It is how much better they could be if only we were stirred.

10

The Merchants and the Low-Income Consumer

DAVID CAPLOVITZ

The visitor to East Harlem cannot fail to notice the sixty or so furniture and appliance stores that mark the area, mostly around Third Avenue and 125th Street. At first this may seem surprising. After all, this is obviously a low-income area. Many of the residents are on relief. Many are employed in seasonal work and in marginal industries, such as the garment industry, which are the first to feel the effects of a recession in the economy. On the face of it, residents of the area would seem unable to afford the merchandise offered for sale in these stores.

That merchants nevertheless find it profitable to locate in these areas attests to a commonly overlooked fact: low-income families, like those of higher income, are consumers of many major durables. The popular image of the American as striving for the material possessions which bestow upon him both comfort and prestige in the eyes of his fellows does not hold only for the ever-increasing middle class. The cultural pressures to buy major durables reach low- as well as middle-income families. In some ways, consumption may take on even more significance for low-income families than for those in higher classes. Since many have small prospect of greatly improving their low social standing through occupational mobility, they are apt to turn to consumption as at least one sphere in which they can make some progress toward the American dream of success. If the upper strata that were observed by Veblen engaged in conspicuous consumption to symbolize their social superiority, it might be said that the lower classes today are apt to engage in *compensatory consumption*. Appliances, automobiles, and the dream of a home of their own can become compensations for blocked social mobility.[1]

The dilemma of the low-income consumer lies in these facts. He is trained by society (and his position in it) to want the symbols and appurtenances of the "good life" at the same time that he lacks the means needed to fulfill these socially induced wants. People with small incomes lack not only the ready cash for consuming major durables but are also poorly qualified for that growing substitute for available cash —credit. Their low income, their negligible savings, their job insecurity all contribute to their being poor credit risks. Moreover, many low-income families in New York City are fairly recent migrants from the South or from Puerto Rico and so do not have other requisites of good credit, such as long-term residence at the same address and friends who meet the credit requirements and are willing to vouch for them.[2]

Not having enough cash and credit would seem to create a sufficient problem for low-income consumers. But they have other limitations as well. They tend to lack the information and training needed to be effective consumers in a bureaucratic society. Partly because of their limited education and partly because as migrants from more traditional societies they are

SOURCE: Reprinted from *The Poor Pay More* by David Caplovitz, by permission of the author and The Macmillan Company. Copyright © 1967 by The Free Press, a Division of The Macmillan Company.

unfamiliar with urban culture, they are not apt to follow the announcements of sales in the newspapers, to engage in comparative shopping, to know their way around the major department stores and bargain centers, to know how to evaluate the advice of salesmen—practices necessary for some degree of sophistication in the realm of consumption. The institution of credit introduces special complex requirements for intelligent consumption. Because of the diverse and frequently misleading ways in which charges for credit are stated, even the highly-educated consumer has difficulty knowing which set of terms is most economical.[3]

These characteristics of the low-income consumer—his socially supported want for major durables, his small funds, his poor credit position, his lack of shopping sophistication—constitute the conditions under which durables are marketed in low-income areas. To understand the paradox set by the many stores selling high-cost durables in these areas it is necessary to know how the merchants adapt to these conditions. Clearly the normal marketing arrangements, based on a model of the "adequate" consumer (the consumer with funds, credit, and shopping sophistication), cannot prevail if these merchants are to stay in business.

On the basis of interviews with fourteen of these merchants, the broad outlines of this marketing system can be described. This picture, in turn, provides a backdrop for the more detailed examination in later chapters of the marketing relationship from the viewpoint of the consumer.

Merchandising in a Low-Income Area

The key to the marketing system in low-income areas lies in special adaptations of the institution of credit. The many merchants who locate in these areas and find it profitable to do so are prepared to offer credit in spite of the high risks involved. Moreover, their credit is tailored to the particular needs of the low-income consumer. All kinds of durable goods can be obtained in this market at terms not too different from the slogan, "a dollar down, a dollar a week." The consumer can buy furniture, a TV set, a stereophonic phonograph, or, if he is so minded, a combination phonograph-TV set, if not for a dollar a week then for only a few dollars a week. In practically every one of these stores, the availability of "easy credit" is announced to the customer in both English and Spanish by large signs in the windows and sometimes by neon signs over the doorways. Of the fourteen merchants interviewed, twelve claimed that from 75 to 90 percent of their business consisted of credit and the other two said that credit made up half their business. That these merchants extend credit to their customers does not, of course, explain how they stay in business. They still face the problem of dealing with their risks.

The Markup and Quality of Goods

It might at first seem that the merchant would solve his problem by charging high rates of interest on the credit he extends. But the law in New York State now regulates the amount that can be charged for credit, and most of these merchants claim they use installment contracts which conform to the law. The fact is that they do not always use these contracts. Some merchants will give customers only a card on which payments are noted. In these transactions the cost of credit and the cash price are not specified as the law requires. The customer peddlers, whom we shall soon meet, seldom use installment contracts. In all these cases the consumer has no idea of how much he is paying for credit, for the cost of credit is not differentiated from the cost of the product.

Although credit charges are now regulated by law, no law regulates the merchant's markup on his goods. East Harlem is known to the merchants of furniture and appliances in New York City as the area in which pricing is done by "numbers." We first heard of the "number" system from a woman who had been employed as a bookkeeper in such a store. She illustrated a "one number" item by writing down a hypothetical wholesale price and then adding the same figure to it, a 100 percent markup. Her frequent references to "two number" and "three number" prices indicated that prices are never less than "one number," and are often more.

The system of pricing in the low-income market differs from that in the bureaucratic market of the downtown stores in another respect: in East Harlem there are hardly any "one price" stores. In keeping with a multi-price policy, price tags are conspicuously absent from the merchandise. The customer has to ask, "how much?," and the answer he gets will depend on several things. If the merchant considers him a poor risk, if he thinks the customer is naive, or if the customer was referred to him by another merchant or a peddler to whom he must pay a commission, the price will be higher. The fact that prices can be affected by "referrals" calls attention to another peculiarity of the low-income market, what the merchants call the "T.O." system.

Anyone closely familiar with sales practices in a large retailing establishment probably understands the meaning of "T.O." When a salesman is confronted with a customer who is not responding to the "sales pitch," he will call over another salesman, signal the nature of the situation by whispering, "this is a T.O.," and then introduce him to the customer as the "assistant manager." [4] In East Harlem, as the interviewers learned, T.O.'s extend beyond the store. When a merchant finds himself with a customer who seems to be a greater risk than he is prepared to accept, he does not send the customer away. Instead, he will tell the customer that he happens to be out of the item he wants, but that it can be obtained at the store of his "friend" or "cousin," just a few blocks away. The merchant will then take the customer to a storekeeper with a less conservative credit policy.[5] The second merchant fully understands that his colleague expects a commission and takes this into account in fixing the price.[6] As a result, the customer who happens to walk into the "wrong" store ends up paying more. In essence, he is being charged for the service of having his credit potential matched with the risk policy of a merchant.

As for the merchandise sold in these stores, the interviewers noticed that the furniture on display was of obviously poor quality. Most of all, they were struck by the absence of well-known brands of appliances in most of the stores. To find out about the sales of better-known brands, they initially asked about the volume of sales of "*high-price*" lines." But this question had little meaning for the merchants, because high prices were being charged for the low-quality goods in evidence. The question had to be rephrased in terms of "high *quality*" merchandise or, as the merchants themselves refer to such goods, "custom lines." To quote from the report of these interviews:

> It became apparent that the question raised a problem of communication. We were familiar with the prices generally charged for

high quality lines and began to notice that the same prices were charged for much lower quality merchandise. The markup was obviously quite different from that in other areas. The local merchants said that the sale of "custom" merchandise was limited by a slow turnover. In fact, a comparable markup on the higher quality lines would make the final price so prohibitively high that they could not be moved at all. A lower markup would be inconsistent with the risk and would result in such small profits that the business could not be continued.

The high markup on low-quality goods is thus a major device used by the merchants to protect themselves against the risks of their credit business. This policy represents a marked departure from the "normal" marketing situation. In the "normal" market, competition between merchants results in a pricing policy roughly commensurate with the quality of the goods. It is apparent, then, that these merchants do not see themselves competing with stores outside the neighborhood. This results in the irony that the people who can least afford the goods they buy are required to pay high prices relative to quality, thus receiving a comparatively low return for their consumer dollar.

In large part, these merchants have a "captive" market because their customers do not meet the economic requirements of consumers in the larger, bureaucratic marketplace. But also, they can sell inferior goods at high prices because, in their own words, the customers are not "price and quality conscious." Interviews found that the merchants perceive their customers as unsophisticated shoppers. One merchant rather cynically explained that the amount of goods sold a customer depends not on the customer but on the merchant's willingness to extend him credit. If the merchant is willing to accept great risk, he can sell the customer almost as much as he cares to. Another merchant, commenting on the buying habits of the customer, said, "People do not shop in this area. Each person who comes into the store wants to buy something and is a potential customer. It is just up to who catches him."

The notion of "who catches him" is rather important in this economy. Merchants compete not so much in price or quality, but in getting customers to the store on other grounds. (Some of these gathering techniques will shortly be described.)

Another merchant commented rather grudgingly that the Negroes were beginning to show signs of greater sophistication by "shopping around." Presumably this practice is not followed by the newer migrants to the area.

But although the merchants are ready to exploit the naivete of their traditionalistic customers, it is important to point out that they also cater to the customer's traditionalism. As a result of the heavy influx of Puerto Ricans into the area, many of these stores now employ Puerto Rican salesmen. The customers who enter these stores need not be concerned about possible embarrassment because of their broken English or their poor dress. On the contrary, these merchants are adept at making the customer feel at ease, as a personal experience will testify.

Visiting the area and stopping occasionally to read the ads in the windows, I happened to pause before an appliance store. A salesman promptly emerged and said, "I know, I bet you're looking for a nice TV set. Come inside. We've got lots of nice ones." Finding myself thrust into the role of customer, I followed him into the store and listened to his sales-pitch. Part way through his talk, he asked my name. I hesitated a moment and then provided him with a fictitious last name, at which point he said, "No, no—no last names. What's your first name? . . . Ah, Dave; I'm Irv. We only care about first names here." When I was ready to leave after making some excuse about having to think things over, he handed me his card. Like most business cards of employees, this one had the name and address of the enterprise in large type and in small type the name of the salesman. But instead of his full name, there appeared only the amiable, "Irv."

As this episode indicates, the merchants in this low-income area are ready to personalize their services. To consumers from a more traditional society, unaccustomed to the impersonality of the bureaucratic market, this may be no small matter.

So far, we have reviewed the elements of the system of exchange that comprise the low-income market. For the consumer, these are the availability of merchandise, the "easy" installments, and the reassurance of dealing with merchants who make them feel at home. In return, the merchant reserves for himself the right to sell low-quality merchandise at exorbitant prices.

But the high markup on goods does not insure that the business will be profitable. No matter what he charges, the merchant can remain in business only if customers actually pay. In this market, the customer's intention and ability to pay—the assumptions underlying any credit system—cannot be taken for granted. Techniques for insuring continuity of payments are a fundamental part of this distinctive economy.

Formal Controls

When the merchant uses an installment contract, he has recourse to legal controls over his customers. But as we shall see, legal controls are not sufficient to cope with the merchant's problem and they are seldom used.

Repossession.—The merchant who offers credit can always repossess his merchandise should the customer default on payments. But repossession, according to the merchants, is rare. They claim that the merchandise receives such heavy use as to become practically worthless in a short time. And no doubt the shoddy merchandise will not stand much use, heavy or light. One merchant said that he will occasionally repossess an item, not to regain his equity, but to punish a customer he feels is trying to cheat him.

Liens Against Property and Wages.— The merchant can, of course, sue the defaulting customer. By winning a court judgment, he can have the customer's property attached. Should this fail to satisfy the debt, he can take the further step of having the customer's salary garnisheed.[7] But these devices are not fully adequate for several reasons. Not all customers have property of value or regular jobs. Furthermore, their employers will not hesitate to fire them rather than submit to the nuisance of a garnishment. But since the customer knows he may lose his job if he is garnisheed, the mere threat of garnishment is sometimes enough to insure regularity of payments.[8] The main limitation with legal controls, however, is that the merchant who uses them repeatedly runs the risk of forfeiting good will in the neighborhood.

Discounting Paper.—The concern with good will places a limitation on the use of another legal practice open to merchants for minimizing their risk: the sale of their contracts to a credit agency at a discount. By selling his contracts to one of the licensed finance companies, the merchant can realize an immediate return on his investment. The problem with this technique is that the merchant loses control over his customer. As an impersonal, bureaucratic organization, the credit agency has recourse only to legal controls. Should the customer miss a payment, the credit agency will take the matter to court. But in the customer's mind, his contract exists with the merchant, not with the credit agency. Consequently, the legal actions taken against him reflect upon the merchant, and so good will is not preserved after all.

For this reason, the merchant is reluctant to "sell his paper," particularly if he has reason to believe that the customer will miss some payments. When he does sell some of his contracts at a discount, his motive is not to reduce risk, but rather to obtain working capital. Since so much of his capital is tied up in credit transactions, he frequently finds it necessary to make such sales. Oddly enough, he is apt to sell his better "paper," that is, the contracts of customers who pay regularly, for he wants to avoid incurring the ill will of customers. This practice also has its drawbacks for the merchant. Competitors can find out from the credit agencies which customers pay regularly and then try to lure them away from the original merchant. Some merchants reported that in order to retain control over their customers, they will buy back contracts from credit agencies they suspect are giving information to competitors.[9]

Credit Association Ratings.—All credit merchants report their bad debtors to the credit association to which they belong. The merchants interviewed said that they always consult the "skip lists" of their association before extending credit to a new customer.[10] In this way they can avoid at least the customers known to be bad risks. This form of control tends to be effective in the long run because the customers find that they are unable to obtain credit until they have made good on their past debts. During the interviews with them, some consumers mentioned this need to restore their credit rating as the reason why they were paying off debts in spite of their belief that they had been cheated.

But these various formal techniques of control are not sufficient to cope with the merchant's problem of risk. He also depends heavily on informal and personal techniques of control.

Informal Controls

The merchant starts from the premise that most of his customers are honest people who intend to pay but have difficulty managing their money. Missed payments are seen as more often due to poor management and to emergencies than to dishonesty. The merchants anticipate that their customers will miss some payments and they rely on informal controls to insure that payments are eventually made.

All the merchants described their credit business as operating on a "fifteen-month year." This means that they expect the customer to miss about one of every four payments and they compute the markup accordingly. Unlike the credit companies, which insist upon regular payments and add service charges for late payments, the neighborhood merchant is prepared to extend "flexible" credit. Should the customer miss an occasional payment or should he be short on another, the merchant considers this a normal part of his business.

To insure the close personal control necessary for this system of credit, the merchant frequently draws up a contract calling for weekly payments which the customer usually brings to the store. This serves several functions for the merchant. To begin with, the sum of money represented by a weekly payment is relatively small and so helps to create the illusion of "easy credit." Customers are apt to think more of the size of the payments than of the cost of the item or the length of the contract.

More importantly, the frequent contact of a weekly-payment system enables the merchant to get to know his customer. He learns when the customer receives his pay check, when his rent is due, who his friends are, when job layoffs, illnesses, and other emergencies occur—in short, all sorts of information which allow him to interpret the reason for a missed payment. Some merchants reported that when they know the customer has missed a payment for a legitimate reason such as illness or a job layoff, they will send a sympathetic note and offer the customer a gift (an inexpensive lamp or wall picture) when payments are resumed. This procedure, they say, frequently brings the customer back with his missed payments.

The short interval between payments also functions to give the merchant an early warning when something is amiss. His chances of locating the delinquent customer are that much greater. Furthermore, the merchant can keep tabs on a delinquent customer through his knowledge of the latter's friends, relatives, neighbors, and associates, who are also apt to be customers of his. In this way, still another informal device, the existing network of social relations, is utilized by the neighborhood merchant in conducting his business.[11]

The weekly-payment system also provides the merchant with the opportunity to sell other items to the customer. When the first purchase is almost paid for, the merchant will try to persuade the customer to make another. Having the customer in the store, where he can look at the merchandise, makes the next sale that much easier. This system of successive sales is, of course, an ideal arrangement—for the merchant. As a result, the customer remains continuously in debt to him. The pattern is somewhat reminiscent of the Southern sharecropper's relation to the company store. And since a number of customers grew up in more traditional environments with just such economies, they may find the arrangement acceptable. The practice of buying from peddlers, found to be common in these low-income areas, also involves the principle of continuous indebtedness. The urban low-income economy, then, is in some respects like the sharecropper system; it might almost be called an "urban share-cropper system."[12]

The Customer Peddlers

Characteristic of the comparatively tradi-tional and personal form of the low-income economy is the important role played in it by the door-to-door credit salesman, the customer peddler. The study of merchants found that these peddlers are not necessarily competitors of the store-owners. Almost all merchants make use of peddlers in the great competition for customers. The merchants tend to regard peddlers as necessary evils who add greatly to the final cost of purchases. But they need them because in their view, customers are too ignorant, frightened, or lazy to come to the stores themselves. Thus, the merchants' apparent contempt for peddlers does not bar them from employing outdoor salesmen (or "canvassers," as they describe the peddlers who work for one store or another). Even the merchants who are themselves reluctant to hire canvassers find they must do so in order to meet the competition. The peddler's main function for the merchant, then, is getting the customer to the store, and if he will not come, getting the store to the customer. But this is not his only function.

Much more than the storekeeper, the peddler operates on the basis of a personal relationship with the customer. By going to the customer's home, he gets to know the entire family; he sees the condition of the home and he comes to know the family's habits and wants. From this vantage point he is better able than the merchant to evaluate the customer as a credit risk. Since many of the merchant's potential customers lack the standard credentials of credit, such as having a permanent job, the merchant needs some other basis for discriminating between good and bad risks. If the peddler, who has come to know the family, is ready to vouch for the customer, the merchant will be ready to make the transaction. In short, the peddler acts as a fiduciary agent, a Dun and Bradstreet for the poor, telling the merchant which family is likely to meet its obligations and which is not.

Not all peddlers are employed by stores. Many are independent enterprisers (who may have started as canvassers for stores).[13] A number of the independent peddlers have accumulated enough capital to supply their customers with major durables. These are the elite peddlers, known as "dealers," who buy appliances and furniture from local merchants at a "wholesale" price, and then sell them on credit to their customers. In these transactions, the peddler either takes the customer to the store or sends the customer to the store with his card on which he has written some such message as "Please give

Mr. Jones a TV set."[14] The merchant then sells the customer the TV set at a price much higher than he would ordinarily charge. The "dealer" is generally given two months to pay the merchant the "wholesale" price, and meanwhile he takes over the responsibility of collecting from his customer. Some "dealers" are so successful that they employ canvassers in their own right.[15] And some merchants do so much business with "dealers" that they come to think of themselves as "wholesalers" even though they are fully prepared to do their own retail business.

Independent peddlers without much capital also have economic relations with local merchants. They act as brokers, directing their customers to neighborhood stores that will extend them credit. And for this service they of course receive a commission. In these transactions, it is the merchant who accepts the risks and assumes the responsibility for collecting payments. The peddler who acts as a broker performs the same function as the merchant in the T.O. system. He knows which merchants will accept great risk and which will not, and directs his customers accordingly.

There are, then, three kinds of customer peddlers operating in these low-income neighborhoods who cooperate with local merchants: the canvassers who are employed directly by the stores; the small entrepreneurs who act as brokers; and the more successful entrepreneurs who operate as "dealers." A fourth type of peddler consists of salesmen representing large companies not necessarily located in the neighborhood. These men are, for the most part, canvassers for firms specializing in a particular commodity, e.g., encyclopedias, vacuum cleaners, or pots and pans. They differ from the other peddlers by specializing in what they sell and by depending more on contracts and legal controls. They are also less interested in developing continuous relationships with their customers.

Peddlers thus aid the local merchants by finding customers, evaluating them as credit risks, and helping in the collection of payments. And as the merchants themselves point out, these services add greatly to the cost of the goods. One storekeeper said that peddlers are apt to charge five and six times the amount the store charges for relatively inexpensive purchases. Pointing to a religious picture which he sells for $5, he maintained that peddlers sell it for as much as $30. And he estimated that the peddler adds 30 to 50 percent to the final sales price of appliances and furniture.

Unethical and Illegal Practices

The interviewers uncovered some evidence that some local merchants engage in the illegal practice of selling reconditioned furniture and appliances as new. Of course, no merchant would admit that he did this himself, but five of them hinted that their competitors engaged in this practice.[16] As we shall see, several of the consumers we interviewed were quite certain that they had been victimized in this way.

One unethical, if not illegal, activity widely practiced by stores is "bait" advertising with its concomitant, the "switch sale." In the competition for customers, merchants depend heavily upon advertising displays in their windows which announce furniture or appliances at unusually low prices. The customer may enter the store assuming that the low offer in the window signifies a reasonably low price line. Under severe pressure, the storekeeper may even be prepared to sell the merchandise at the advertised price, for not to do so would be against the law. What most often happens, however, is that the unsuspecting customer is convinced by the salesman that he doesn't really want the goods advertised in the window and is then persuaded to buy a smaller amount of more expensive goods. Generally, not much persuasion is necessary. The most popular "bait ad" is the announcement of three rooms of furniture for "only $149" or "only $199." The customer who inquires about this bargain is shown a bedroom set consisting of two cheap and (sometimes deliberately) chipped bureaus and one bed frame. He learns that the spring and mattress are not included in the advertised price, but can be had for another $75 or $100. The living-room set in these "specials" consists of a fragile-looking sofa and one unmatching chair.[17]

The frequent success of this kind of exploitation, known in the trade as the "switch sale," is reflected in this comment by one merchant: "I don't know how they do it. They advertise three rooms of furniture for $149 and the customers swarm in. *They end up buying a $400 bedroom set for $600 and none of us can believe how easy it is to make these sales.*"

In sum, a fairly intricate system of sales-and-credit has evolved in response to the distinctive situation of the low-income consumer and the local merchant. It is a system heavily slanted in the direction of a traditional economy in which informal, personal ties play a major part in the transaction. At the same time it is connected to impersonal bureaucratic agencies through the instrument of the installment contract. Should the informal system break down, credit companies, courts of law, and agencies of law enforcement come to play a part.

The system is not only different from the larger, more formal economy; in some respects it is a *deviant* system in which practices that violate prevailing moral standards are commonplace. As Merton has pointed out in his analysis of the political machine, the persistence of deviant social structures can only be understood when their social functions (as well as dysfunctions) are taken into account. The basic function of the low-income marketing system is to provide consumer goods to people who fail to meet the requirements of the more legitimate, bureaucratic market, or who choose to exclude themselves from the larger market because they do not feel comfortable in it. As we have seen, the system is extraordinarily flexible. Almost no one—however great a risk—is turned away. Various mechanisms sift and sort customers according to their credit risk and match them with merchants ready to sell them the goods they want. Even the family on welfare is permitted to maintain its self-respect by consuming in much the same way as do its social peers who happen not to be on welfare.

Footnotes

[1] I am indebted to Robert K. Merton for suggesting the apt phrase, "compensatory consumption." The idea expressed by this term figures prominently in the writings of Robert S. Lynd. Observing the workers in Middletown, Lynd noted that their declining opportunities for occupational advancement and even the depression did not make them class-conscious. Instead, their aspirations shifted to the realm of consumption.

Fascinated by a rising standard of living offered them on every hand on the installment plan, they [the working class] do not readily segregate themselves from the rest of the city. They want what Middletown wants, so long as it gives them their great symbol of advancement—an automobile. Car ownership stands to them for a large share of the "American dream"; they cling to it as they cling to self respect, and it was not unusual to see a family drive up to the relief commissary in 1935 to stand in line for its four or five dollar weekly food dole. [The Lynds go on to quote a union official:] It's easy to see why our workers don't think much about joining unions. So long as they have a car and can borrow or steal a gallon of gas, they'll ride around and pay no attention to labor organization. . . . [Robert S. Lynd and Helen Merrill Lynd, *Middletown in Transition*, New York: Harcourt, Brace and Co., 1937, p. 26. See also pp. 447–448.]

It should be noted that the Lynds identify the installment plan as the mechanism through which workers are able to realize their consumption aspirations. Similar observations are to be found in *Knowledge for What?*, Princeton University Press: 1939, pp. 91, 198. Lynd's student, Eli Chinoy, also makes use of the idea of compensatory consumption in his study of automobile workers. He found that when confronted with the impossibility of rising to the ranks of management, workers shifted their aspirations from the occupational to the consumption sphere. "With their wants constantly stimulated by high powered advertising, they measure their success by what they are able to buy." Eli Chinoy, "Aspirations of Automobile Workers," *American Journal of Sociology*, 57, 1952, 453–459. For further discussion of the political implications of this process, see Daniel Bell, "Work and its Discontents" in *The End of Ideology*, New York: The Free Press of Glencoe, 1960, pp. 246 ff.

[2] A frequent practice in extending credit to poor risks is to have cosigners who will make good the debt should the original borrower default. The new arrivals are apt to be disadvantaged by their greater difficulty in finding cosigners.

[3] Professor Samuel S. Myers of Morgan State College has studied the credit terms of major department stores and appliance outlets in Baltimore. Visiting the ten most popular stores, he priced the same model of TV set and gathered information on down-payments and credit terms. He found that the cash price was practically the same in the various stores, but that there were wide variations in the credit terms leading to sizeable differences in the final cost to the consumer. (Based on personal communication with Professor Myers.)

In his statement to the Douglas Committee considering the "Truth in Interest" bill, George Katona presented findings from the consumer surveys carried out by the Survey Research Center of the University of Michigan. These studies show that people with high income and substantial education are no better informed about the costs of credit than people of low income and little education. See *Consumer Credit Labeling Bill, op. cit.,* p. 806.

[4] The initials stand for "turn over." The "assistant manager" is ready to make a small concession to the customer, who is usually so flattered by this gesture that he offers no further resistance to the sale. For further descriptions of the "T.O.," see Cecil L. French, "Correlates of Success in Retail Selling," *American Journal of Sociology,* 66, September, 1960, 128–134; and Erving Goffman, *Presentation of Self in Everyday Life,* New York: Doubleday, Anchor Books, 1959, pp. 178–180.

[5] The interviewers found that the stores closer to the main shopping area of 125th Street generally had more conservative credit policies than those somewhat farther away. This was indicated by the percentage of credit sales the merchants reported as defaults. The higher-rental stores near 125th Street reported default rates of 5 and 6 percent, those six or seven blocks away, as high as 20 percent.

[6] The referring merchant does not receive his commission right away. Whether he gets it at all depends upon the customer's payment record. He will keep a record of his referrals and check on them after several months. When the merchant who has made the sale has received a certain percentage of the payments, he will give the referring merchant his commission.

[7] It is of some interest that the low-income families we interviewed were all familiar with the word "garnishee." This may well be one word in the language that the poorly educated are more likely to know than the better educated.

[8] Welfare families cannot, of course, be garnisheed, and more than half the merchants reported that they sell to them. But the merchants can threaten to disclose the credit purchase to the welfare authorities. Since recipients of welfare funds are not supposed to buy on credit, this threat exerts powerful pressure on the family.

[9] Not all merchants are particularly concerned with good will. A few specialize in extending credit to the worst risks, customers turned away by most other merchants. These men will try to collect as much as they can on their accounts during the year and then will sell all their outstanding accounts to a finance company. As a result, the most inadequate consumers are apt to meet with the bureaucratic controls employed by the finance company. For a description of how bill collectors operate, see Hillel Black, *Buy Now, Pay Later,* New York: William Morrow and Co., 1961, chap. 4.

[10] See *Ibid.,* chap. 3, for a description of the world's largest credit association, the one serving most of the stores in the New York City area.

[11] The merchant's access to these networks of social relations is not entirely independent of economic considerations. Just as merchants who refer customers receive commissions, so customers who recommend others are often given commissions. Frequently, this is why a customer will urge his friends to deal with a particular merchant.

[12] The local merchants are not the only ones promoting continuous debt. The coupon books issued by banks and finance companies which underwrite installment contracts contain notices in the middle announcing that the consumer can, if he wishes, refinance the loan. The consumer is told, in effect, that he is a good risk because presumably he has regularly paid half the installments and that he need not wait until he has made the last payment before borrowing more money.

[13] A systematic study of local merchants and peddlers would probably find that a typical career pattern is to start as a canvasser, become a self-employed peddler, and finally a storekeeper.

[14] According to a former customer peddler, now in the furniture business, the peddlers' message will either read "Please *give* Mr. Jones . . ." or "Please let Mr. Jones *pick out* . . ." In the former case, the customer is given the merchandise right away; in the latter, it is set aside for him until the peddler says that it is all right to let the customer have it. The peddler uses the second form when his customer is already heavily in debt to him and he wants to be certain that the customer will agree to the higher weekly payments that will be necessary.

[15] One tiny store in the area, with little merchandise in evidence, is reported to employ over a hundred canvassers. The owner would not consent to an interview, but the student-observers did notice that this apparently small merchant kept some four or five bookkeepers at work in a back room. The owner is obviously a "dealer" whose store is his office. As a "dealer," he has no interest in maintaining stock and displays for street trade.

[16] Events are sometimes more telling than words. During an interview with a merchant, the interviewer volunteered to help several men who were carrying bed frames into the store. The owner excitedly told him not to help because he might get paint on his hands.

[17] In one store in which I inspected this special offer, I was told by the salesman that he would find a chair that was a "fairly close match."

PART FIVE Collective Behavior

Collective behavior is a general term used to refer to such phenomena as crowds, fads, mobs, riots, and social movements. The events that make up collective behavior occur in situations where the traditional modes of social control are no longer operating properly. That is, the traditional norms and values which govern and restrict behavior no longer function as realistic controls. Collective behavior may be spontaneous and brief or it may last for days, weeks, or even years. It may occur for quite frivolous reasons or it may result from the participants' desire to redress what they perceive as a serious social inequity.

In contemporary society collective behavior in the form of protests and riots has become one way in which various segments of the population attempt to create social change. The selections in this section describe three such occasions of collective behavior. The first piece is taken from the Walker Report—Rights in Conflict—*and describes citizen-police confrontation at the 1968 Democratic National Convention in Chicago, discussing in particular the bloody clash on the evening of August 28, 1968, in front of the Conrad Hilton Hotel. In Robert Blauner's essay on the Black ghetto three issues of protest-riots, cultural nationalism, and ghetto-control are analyzed as a collective response to colonial status. The final article, "Confrontation at Cornell" by William Friedland and Harry Edwards, analyzes campus conflict at Cornell University between students and authority.*

11
Action in Chicago

THE WALKER COMMISSION REPORT

.   .   .   .

Confrontation at the Conrad Hilton

The U.S. Attorney's report says about 2,000 persons, "mostly normally dressed," had already assembled at the Hilton. Many of these were demonstrators who had tired of waiting out the negotiations and had broken off from the marchers and made their way to the hotel. It appears that police already were having some difficulty keeping order at that location. Says the U.S. Attorney's report: "A large crowd had assembled behind the police line along the east wall of the Hilton. This crowd was heavily infiltrated with 'Yippie' types and was spitting and screaming obscene insults at the police."

A policeman on duty in front of the hotel later said that it seemed to him that the obscene abuses shouted by "women hippies" outnumbered those called out by male demonstrators "four to one." A common epithet shouted by the females, he said, was "Fuck you, pig." Others included references to policemen as "cock suckers" and "mother fuckers."

During this time, he said, the officers did and said nothing in retaliation. At one point, he recalled, a policeman made a retort to a "hippie" and "was immediately told to remain silent." All the while, he said, the policemen were "constantly being photographed by hippies with cameras."

According to his statement, "an Assistant U.S. Attorney and a policeman were sprayed in the face with oven cleaner. . . ." The police reporter mentioned earlier recalls that persons in the crowd were chanting, "Hump sucks" and "Daley sucks Hump."

A short time later the reporter noticed a lot of debris being hurled from one of the upper floors of the Hilton. He climbed into a police squad car parked in the area and with the aid of police binoculars saw that rolls of toilet paper were coming from the 15th floor, a location he pinpointed by counting down from the top of the building. He then went to the 15th floor and found that the section the paper was coming from was rented by Senator McCarthy campaigners. He was not admitted to the suite.

If Dellinger's marchers now moved to the Hilton area, an additional 5,000 demonstrators would be added to the number the police there would have to control.

.   .   .   .

The Crossing

At about 6 or 6:30 p.m., one of the march leaders announced by loudspeaker that the demonstrators would not be allowed to march to the Amphitheatre. He told the crowd to disperse and to re-group in front of the Conrad Hilton Hotel in Grant Park.

SOURCE: Reprinted from *Rights in Conflict*, a report submitted by Daniel Walker, Director of the Chicago Study Team, and Vice President of the Chicago Crime Commission, to the National Commission on the Causes and Prevention of Violence, November, 1968.

. . . .

Police in the area were in a far from cheerful mood. A neatly dressed sociology student from Minnesota says he stepped off the sidewalk onto the grass and two policemen pulled their billy clubs back as though ready to swing. One of them said, "You'd better get your fucking ass off that grass or I'll put a beautiful goddamm crease in your fucking queer head." The student overheard another policeman say to a "hippie-looking girl of 14 or 15, 'You better get your fucking dirty cunt out of here.'" Another witness recalls that while he was seeking an exit from the park, a young policeman "walked up to me and just looked at me and said, 'Fuck you, you son-of-a-bitch!'" The witness was getting scared and moved rapidly on. The growing feeling of entrapment was intensified and some witnesses noticed that police were letting people into the park but not out. The marshals referred to the situation as a "trap."

As the crowd moved north, an Assistant U.S. Attorney saw one demonstrator with long sideburns and hippie garb pause to break up a large piece of concrete, wrapping the pieces in a striped T-shirt.

Before the march formally disbanded, an early contingent of demonstrators, numbering about 30 to 50, arrived at the spot where Congress Plaza bridges the IC tracks at approximately the same time as a squad of 40 National Guardsmen. The Guard hurriedly spread out about three feet apart across Congress with rifles at the ready, gas masks on, bayonets fixed.

Now as the bulk of the disappointed marchers sought a way out of the park, the crowd began to build up in front of the Guard. Occasionally some managed to sneak through when Guard ranks parted

to let cars pass. Others jumped on the passing cars or hitched rides with "straights" and the noise of the crowd was joined by the klaxon sound of car horns. "I saw one woman driving a new red late-model car approach the bridge," a news correspondent says: "Two demonstrators, apparently badly gassed, jumped into the back seat and hoped to get through the Guard lines. Guardsmen refused to permit the car through, going so far as to threaten to bayonet her tires and the hood of her car if she did not turn around. One Guardsman fired tear gas point blank beside the car."

. . . .

The crowd's basic strategy, a medic recalls, was "to mass a sizable group at one end of the line," as if preparing to charge. Then, when Guardsmen shifted to protect that area, a comparatively small group of demonstrators would push through the weak end of the line. The physical violence included "grabbing the Guard's weapons, punching and kicking." Once the small group had penetrated the line, the medic says, members would "come up behind the Guardsmen and taunt them, as well as push and shove them from the rear." A Guard official said later that his men were attacked with oven cleaner and containers filled with excrement.

. . . .

As the crowd swelled, it surged periodically toward the Guard line, sometimes yelling, "Freedom, freedom." On one of these surges a Guardsman hurled two tear gas canisters.

. . . .

Some of the tear gas was fired directly into the faces of demonstrators. "We came across a guy really badly gassed," a college coed says. "We were choking, but we could still see. But this guy we saw was standing there helpless with mucous-type stuff on his face, obviously in pain. There was a medic near us with water and we washed this guy's eyes out and helped him along until he could see."

An Assistant U.S. Attorney says he saw "hundreds of people running, crying, coughing, vomiting, screaming." Some women ran blindly to Buckingham Fountain and leaped into the water to bathe their faces. The Guard medic quoted earlier says he was again assaulted by demonstrators when he went into the crowd to treat a man felled by "a particularly heavy dose of tear gas."

. . . . .

"In Grant Park, the gassed crowd was angered . . . more aggressive," says the history professor. Shortly after the gassing, says the Guard medic quoted earlier, "two forces of police arrived. . . . They immediately waded into the crowd with clubs swinging indiscriminately, driving them off the bridge and away from the area." Once more, the Guardsman said, he was assaulted by demonstrators—this time when he tried "to treat an individual who received a severe head injury from the police."

. . . . .

Surging north from Congress Plaza to a footbridge leading from the park, the crowd encountered more Guardsmen. More tear gas was dispensed. Surging north from the site of the gassings, the crowd found the Jackson Boulevard bridge unguarded. Word was quickly passed back by loud-speaker "Two blocks north, there's an open bridge; no gas." As dusk was settling, hundreds poured from the park into Michigan Avenue.

The Crowd on Michigan Avenue

At 7:14 p.m., as the first groups of demonstrators crossed the bridge toward Michigan Avenue, they noticed that the mule train of the Poor People's Campaign was just entering the intersection of Michigan and Jackson, headed south. The train consisted of three wagons, each drawn by two mules, and was accompanied by a number of SCLC blacks in fieldwork attire. The wagons were painted, "Jobs & Food for All." The train had a permit to parade within the Loop and south on Michigan Avenue.

The train was accompanied by 24 policemen on foot, five on three-wheelers, and four in two squadrols. A police official was in front with the caravan's leaders. The sight of the train seemed to galvanize the disorganized Grant Park crowd and those streaming over the bridge broke into cheers and shouts. "Peace now!" bellowed the demonstrators. "Dump the Hump!" This unexpected enthusiastic horde in turn stimulated the mule train marchers. Drivers of the wagons stood and waved to the crowd, shouting: "Join us! Join us!" To a young man watching from the 23rd floor of the Hilton Hotel, "the caravan seemed like a magnet to demonstrators leaving the park."

. . . . .

The Balbo-Michigan Crowd Builds Up

When the crowd's first rank reached the intersection of Balbo and Michigan, the northeast corner of the Hilton, it was close to the approximately 2,000 to 3,000 demonstrators and spectators. . . . The police were armed with riot helmets, batons, mace, an aerosol tear gas can and their service revolvers (which they always

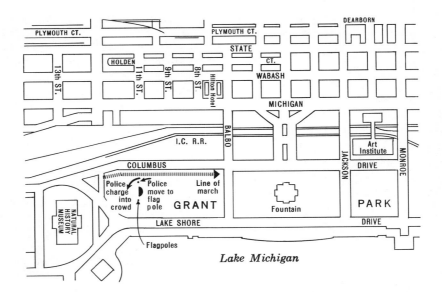

Lake Michigan

carry). Behind the police lines, parked in front of the Hilton, was a fire department high pressure pumper truck hooked up to a hydrant. Pairs of uniformed firemen were also in the vicinity. The growing crowds, according to the U.S. Attorney's report, were a blend of "young and old, hippies, Yippies, straights, newsmen and cameramen," even two mobile TV units.

.   .   .   .   .

From within the crowd were rising the usual shouts from some of the demonstrators: "Hell no, we won't go!" . . . "Fuck these Nazis!" . . . "Fuck you, L.B.J.!" . . . "No more war!" . . . "Pigs, pigs, pigs." . . . "The streets belong to the people!" . . . "Let's go to the Amphitheatre!" . . . "Move on, Move on!" . . . "You can't stop us." . . . "From the hotel," recalls a student, "people who sympathized were throwing confetti and pieces of paper out of the windows and they were blinking their room lights."

.   .   .   .   .

Isolated Incidents

Occasionally during the early evening, groups of demonstrators would flank the police lines or find a soft spot and punch through, heading off on their own for the Amphitheatre. On the periphery of the Hilton and on thoroughfares and side streets further southwest, a series of brief but sometimes violent encounters occurred.

For example, says the manager of a private club on Michigan Avenue, "a large band of long-haired demonstrators . . . tore down the American flag" overhanging the entrance to the club "and took it into Michigan Avenue attempting to tear it." . . . .

At about 7 p.m. from the window of a motel room in the 1100 block of South Michigan, a senator's driver noticed a group of demonstrators walking south, chanting: "Hell no, we won't go!" and "Fuck the draft." They were hurling insults at passing pedestrians and when one answered back, the witness says, "five demonstrators charged out of Michigan

Avenue onto the sidewalk, knocked the pedestrian down, formed a circle around his fallen body, locked their arms together and commenced kicking him in a vicious manner. When they had finished kicking their victim, they unlocked their arms and immediately melted back into the crowd. . . ."

. . . .

Back at the Conrad Hilton

Vice President Humphrey was now inside the Conrad Hilton Hotel and the police commanders were afraid that the crowd might either attempt to storm the hotel or march south on Michigan Avenue, ultimately to the Amphitheatre. The Secret Service had received an anonymous phone call that the Amphitheatre was to be blown up. A line of police was established at 8th and Michigan at the south end of the hotel and the squads of police stationed at the hotel doors began restricting access to those who could display room keys. Some hotel guests, including delegates and Senator McCarthy's wife, were turned away.

By 7:30 p.m., the SCLC people, too, were growing apprehensive. They were becoming concerned for the mule train because of the press of demonstrators and the crowd's escalating emotionalism. Also a rumor was passing around that the Blackstone Rangers and the East Side Disciples, two of Chicago's most troublesome street gangs, were on their way to the scene. (This was later proven to be untrue; neither of these South Side gangs was present in any numbers in either Lincoln Park or Grant Park.)

At this point, a Negro male was led through the police line by a police officer. He spoke to the police officer, a city official and a deputy superintendent of police. He

told them that he was in charge of the mule train and that his people wanted no part of this mob. He said he had 80 people with him, that they included old people and children, and he wanted to get them out of the mob. The police officer later stated the group wanted to go past the Hilton, circle it, and return to the front of the hotel where Reverend Ralph Abernathy could address the crowd.

. . . .

In a few minutes, Reverend Ralph Abernathy appeared and, according to the police officer's statement, "said he wanted to be taken out of the area as he feared for the safety of his group." The police officer directed that the train be moved south on Michigan to 11th Street and then, through a series of turns through the Loop, to the West Side.

. . . .

A policeman on Michigan later said that at about this time a "female hippie" came up to him, pulled up her skirt and said, "You haven't had a piece in a long time."

A policeman standing in front of the Hilton remembers seeing a blond female who was dressed in a short red minidress make lewd, sexual motions in front of a police line. Whenever this happened, he says, the policemen moved back to prevent any incident. The crowd, however, egged her on, the patrolman says. He thought that "she and the crowd wanted an arrest to create a riot." Earlier in the same general area a male youth had stripped bare and walked around carrying his clothes on a stick.

The intersection at Balbo and Michigan was in total chaos at this point. The street was filled with people. Darkness had fallen but the scene was lit by both police and television lights. As the mule train left, part of the group tried to follow the wagons through the police line and were stopped. According to the deputy superintendent of police, there was much pushing back and forth between the policemen and the demonstrators.

.　　.　　.　　.

Continual announcements were made at this time over a police amplifier for the crowd to "clear the street and go up on the sidewalk or into the park area for their demonstrations." The broadcast said "Please gather in the park on the east side of the street. You may have your peaceful demonstration and speechmaking there." The demonstrators were also advised that if they did not heed these orders they would face arrest. The response from many in the crowd, according to a police observer, was to scream and shout obscenities. A Chicago attorney who was watching the scene recalls that when the announcements were broadcast, "No one moved."

. . . The deputy superintendent then made another announcement: "Will any nondemonstrators, anyone who is not a part of this group, any newsmen, please leave the group." Despite the crowd noise, the loud-speaker announcements were "loud and plainly heard," according to this officer. Police state that the messages to clear the street were repeated—officers "walked to the front of the crowd and repeated these messages to individuals all along the line, all the while pointing over to the east side of the street where we wanted them to go."

.　　.　　.　　.

While this was happening on Michigan Avenue, a separate police line had begun to move east toward the crowd from the block of Balbo that lies between Michigan and Wabash along the north side of the Hilton.

.　　.　　.　　.

Just as the police in front of the Hilton were confronted with some sit-downs on the south side of the intersection of Balbo and Michigan, the police unit coming into the intersection on Balbo met the sitting demonstrators. What happened then is subject to dispute between the police and some other witnesses.

The Balbo police unit commander asserts that he informed the sit-downs and surrounding demonstrators that if they did not leave, they would be arrested. He repeated the order and was met with a chant of "Hell no, we won't go." Quickly a police van swung into the intersection immediately behind the police line, the officers opened the door at the rear of the wagon. The deputy chief "ordered the arrest process to start."

"Immediately upon giving this order," the deputy chief later informed his superiors, "we were pelted with rocks, bottles, cans filled with unknown liquids and other debris, which forced the officers to defend themselves from injury. . . . My communications officer was slugged from behind by one of these persons, receiving injuries to his right eye and cheekbone." That officer states: "All this debris came instantaneously, as if it was waiting for the signal of the first arrest."

.　　.　　.　　.

The many films and video tapes of this time period present a picture which does not correspond completely with the police view described above. First, the films do not show a mob moving west on Balbo; they show the street as rather clean of the demonstrators and bystanders, although the sidewalks themselves on both sides of the street are crowded. Second, they show the police walking east on Balbo, stopping in formation, awaiting the arrival of the van and starting to make arrests on order. A total of 25 seconds elapses between their coming to a halt and the first arrests.

Also, a St. Louis reporter who was watching from inside the Haymarket Lounge agrees that the police began making arrests "in formation," apparently as "the result of an order to clear the intersection." Then, the reporter adds, "from this apparently controlled beginning the police began beating people indiscriminately. They grabbed and beat anyone they could get hold of."

. . . . .

"The crowd tried to reverse gears," a reporter for a St. Louis paper says. "People began falling over each other. I was in the first rank between police and the crowd and was caught in the first surge. I went down as I tried to retreat. I covered my head, tried to protect my glasses which had fallen partially off, and hoped that I would not be clubbed. I tried to dig into the humanity that had fallen with me. You could hear shouting and screaming. As soon as I could, I scrambled to my feet and tried to move away from the police. I saw a youth running by me also trying to flee. A policeman clubbed him as he passed, but he kept running.

"The cops were saying, 'Move! I said, move, god dammit! Move, you bastards!'" A representative of the ACLU who was positioned among the demonstrators says the police "were cussing a lot" and were shouting, "Kill, kill, kill, kill, kill!" A reporter for the *Chicago Daily News* said after the melee that he, too, heard this

cry. A demonstrator remembers the police swinging their clubs and screaming, "Get the hell out of here." . . . "Get the fuck out of here." . . . "Move your fucking ass!"

. . . . .

The crowd frantically eddied in a half-moon shape in an effort to escape the officers coming in from the west. A UPI reporter who was on the southern edge of the crowd on Michigan Avenue, said that the advancing police "began pushing the crowd south." A cherry bomb burst overhead. The demonstrators strained against the deputy superintendent of police's line south of the Balbo-Michigan intersection. "When I reached that line," says the UPI reporter, "I heard a voice from behind it say, 'Push them back, move them back!' I was then prodded and shoved with nightsticks back in a northerly direction, toward the still advancing line of police."

"Police were marching this way and that," a correspondent from a St. Louis paper says. "They obviously had instructions to clear the street, but apparently contradicting one another in the directions the crowd was supposed to be sent."

. . . . .

The deputy superintendent of police recalls that he ordered his men to "hold your line there" . . . "stand fast" . . . "Lieutenant, hold your men steady there!" These orders, he said, were not obeyed by all.

"Two or three policemen broke formation and began swinging at everyone in sight," the McGovern worker says. The deputy superintendent states that police disregarded his order to return to the police lines—the beginning of what he says was the only instance in which he personally saw police discipline collapse. He estimates that ten to 15 officers moved off on individual forays against demonstrators.

.　.　.　.

The Clash

Thus, at 7:57 p.m., with two groups of club-wielding police converging simultaneously and independently, the battle was joined. The portions of the throng out of the immediate area of conflict largely stayed put and took up the chant, "The whole world is watching," but the intersection fragmented into a collage of violence.

Re-creating the precise chronology of the next few moments is impossible. But there is no question that a violent street battle ensued.

People ran for cover and were struck by police as they passed. Clubs were swung indiscriminately.

.　.　.　.

"I saw squadrols of policemen coming from everywhere," a secretary quoted earlier said. "The crowd around me suddenly began to run. Some of us, including myself, were pushed back onto the sidewalk and then all the way up against . . . the Blackstone Hotel along Michigan Avenue. I thought the crowd had panicked.

"Fearing that I would be crushed against the wall of the building . . . I somehow managed to work my way . . . to the edge of the street . . . and saw police everywhere.

"As I looked up I was hit for the first time on the head from behind by what must have been a billy club. I was then knocked down and while on my hands and knees, I was hit around the shoulders. I got up again, stumbling and was hit again. As I was falling, I heard words to

the effect of 'move, move' and the horrible sound of cracking billy clubs.

"After my second fall, I remember being kicked in the back, and I looked up and noticed that many policemen around me had no badges on. The police kept hitting me on the head."

Eventually she made her way to an alley behind the Blackstone and finally, "bleeding badly from my head wound," was driven by a friend to a hospital emergency room. Her treatment included the placing of 12 stitches.

.　.　.　.

A lawyer says that he was in a group of demonstrators in the park just south of Balbo when he heard a police officer shout, "Let's get 'em!" Three policemen ran up, "singled out one girl and as she was running away from them, beat her on the back of the head. As she fell to the ground, she was struck by the nightsticks of these officers." A male friend of hers then came up yelling at the police. The witness said, "He was arrested. The girl was left in the area lying on the ground."

.　.　.　.

A *Milwaukee Journal* reporter says in his statement, "when the police managed to break up groups of protesters they pursued individuals and beat them with clubs. Some police pursued individual demonstrators as far as a block . . . and beat them. . . . In many cases it appeared to me that when police had finished beating the protesters they were pursuing, they then attacked, indiscriminately, any civilian who happened to be standing nearby. Many of these were not involved in the demonstrations."

In balance, there is no doubt that police discipline broke during the melee. The deputy superintendent of police states that —although this was the only time he saw discipline collapse—when he ordered his men to stand fast, some did not respond and began to sally through the crowd, clubbing people they came upon. An inspector-observer from the Los Angeles Police Department, stated that during this week, "The restraint of the police both as individual members and as an organization, was beyond reason." However, he said that on this occasion:

There is no question but that many officers acted without restraint and exerted force beyond that necessary under the circumstances. The leadership at the point of conflict did little to prevent such conduct and the direct control of officers by first-line supervisors was virtually nonexistent.

The deputy superintendent of police has been described by several observers as being very upset by individual policemen who beat demonstrators. He pulled his men off the demonstrators, shouting "Stop, damn it, stop. For Christ's sake, stop it."

"It seemed to me," an observer says, "that only a saint could have swallowed the vile remarks to the officers. However, they went to extremes in clubbing the Yippies. I saw them move into the park, swatting away with clubs at girls and boys lying in the grass. More than once I witnessed two officers pulling at the arms of a Yippie until the arms almost left their sockets, then, as the officers put the Yippie in a police van, a third jabbed a riot stick into the groin of the youth being arrested. It was evident that the Yippie was not resisting arrest."

.   .   .   .

"In one incident, a young man, who apparently had been maced, staggered

across Michigan . . . helped by a companion. The man collapsed. . . . Medical people from the volunteer medical organization rushed out to help him. A police officer (a sergeant, I think) came rushing forward, followed by the two other nightstick-brandishing policemen and yelled, 'Get him out of here; this ain't a hospital.' The medical people fled, half dragging and half carrying the young man with them. . . .

"Another incident I vividly recall is two policemen dragging one protester by one leg, with his shoulders and possibly his head dragging on the pavement as they ran toward a paddy wagon. So much violence was going on at one time. . . ."

A university student who was watching the melee from a hotel window says she saw one young man attempting to flee the police. "Two or three grabbed him and beat him until he fell to the ground." Then, she says, "two or three more policemen were attracted to him and continued to beat him until he was dragged into a paddy wagon."

At another moment, the girl says, she saw another youth "felled by two or three policemen." A medic "dressed all in white and wearing a white helmet" came to aid him. When police saw him giving aid to the downed boy, "they came upon the medic and began to beat him."

.   .   .   .

. . . During the course of these arrests, one girl in this group lost her skirt. Although there have been unverified reports of police ripping the clothes from female demonstrators, this is the only incident on news film of any woman being disrobed in the course of arrest.

While violence was exploding in the street, the crowd wedged, behind the police sawhorses along the northeast edge of the Hilton, was experiencing a terror all its own. Early in the evening, this group had consisted in large part of curious bystanders. But following the police surges into the demonstrators clogging the intersection, protesters had crowded the ranks behind the horses in their flight from the police.

From force of numbers, this sidewalk crowd of 150 to 200 persons was pushing down toward the Hilton's front entrance. Policemen whose orders were to keep the entrance clear were pushing with sawhorses. Other police and fleeing demonstrators were pushing from the north in the effort to clear the intersection. Thus, the crowd was wedged against the hotel, with the hotel itself on the west, sawhorses on the southeast and police on the northeast.

Films show that one policeman elbowed his way to where he could rescue a girl of about ten years of age from the vise-like press of the crowd. He cradled her in his arms and carried her to a point of relative safety 20 feet away. The crowd itself "passed up" an elderly woman to a low ledge. But many who remained were subjected to what they and witnesses considered deliberate brutality by the police.

"I was crowded in with the group of screaming, frightened people," an onlooker states, "We jammed against each other, trying to press into the brick wall of the hotel. As we stood there breathing hard . . . a policeman calmly walked the length of the barricade with a can of chemical spray [evidently mace] in his hand. Unbelievably, he was spraying at us." Photos reveal several policemen using mace against the crowd.

.   .   .   .

"Some of the police then turned and attacked the crowd," a Chicago reporter says. The student says she could see police clubbing persons pinned at the edge of the crowd and that there was "a great deal of screaming and pushing within the group." A reporter for a Cleveland paper said, "The police indiscriminately beat those on the periphery of the crowd." An Assistant U.S. Attorney put it, "The group on the sidewalk was charged by police using nightsticks." A young cook caught in the crowd relates that:

The police began picking people off. They would pull individuals to the ground and begin beating them. A medic wearing a white coat and an armband with a red cross was grabbed, beaten and knocked to the ground. His whole face was covered with blood.

"The cops just waded into the crowd," says a law student. "There was a great deal of clubbing. People were screaming, 'Help.' "

As a result, a part of the crowd was trapped in front of the Conrad Hilton and pressed hard against a big plate glass window of the Haymarket Lounge. A reporter who was sitting inside said, "Frightened men and women banged . . . against the window. A captain of the fire department inside told us to get back from the window, that it might get knocked in. As I backed away a few feet I could see a smudge of blood on the glass outside."

With a sickening crack, the window shattered, and screaming men and women tumbled through, some cut badly by jagged glass. The police came after them.

.   .   .   .

In the heat of all this, probably few were aware of the Haymarket's advertising slogan: "A place where good guys take good girls to dine in the lusty, rollicking atmosphere of fabulous Old Chicago. . . ."

.   .   .   .

There is little doubt that during this whole period, beginning at 7:57 p.m. and lasting for nearly 20 minutes, the preponderance of violence came from the police. It was not entirely a one-way battle, however.

Firecrackers were thrown at police. Trash baskets were set on fire and rolled and thrown at them. In one case, a gun was taken from a policeman by a demonstrator.

"Some hippies," said a patrolman in his statement, "were hit by other hippies who were throwing rocks at the police." Films reveal that when police were chasing demonstrators into Grant Park, one young man upended a sawhorse and heaved it at advancing officers. At one point the deputy superintendent of police was knocked down by a thrown sawhorse. At least one police three-wheeler was tipped over. One of the demonstrators says that "people in the park were prying up cobblestones and breaking them. One person piled up cobblestones in his arms and headed toward the police." Witnesses reported that people were throwing "anything they could lay their hands on. From the windows of the Hilton and Blackstone hotels, toilet paper, wet towels, even ash trays came raining down." A police lieutenant stated that he saw policemen bombarded with "rocks, cherry bombs, jars of vaseline, jars of mayonnaise and pieces of wood torn from the yellow barricades falling in the street." He, too, noticed debris falling from the hotel windows.

.   .   .   .

A number of police officers were injured, either by flying missiles or in personal attacks. One, for example, was helping a fellow officer "pick up a hippie when another hippie gave [me] a heavy kick, aiming for my groin." The blow struck the officer partly on the leg and partly in the testicles. He went down, and the "hippie" who kicked him escaped.

.   .   .   .

In another instance, a Chicago police reporter said in his statement, "a police officer reached down and grabbed a person who dove forward and bit the officer on the leg. . . . Three or four fellow policemen came to his aid. They had to club the demonstrator to make him break his clamp on the officer's leg." In another case, the witness saw a demonstrator "with a big mop of hair hit a police officer with an old British Army type metal helmet." The reporter said he also heard "hissing sounds from the demonstrators as if they were spraying the police." Later he found empty lacquer spray and hair spray cans on the street. Also he heard policemen cry out, "They're kicking us with knives in their shoes." Later, he said, he found that demonstrators "had actually inserted razor blades in their shoes."

.   .   .   .

Wild in the Streets

By 8:15 p.m., the intersection was in police control. One group of police proceeded east on Balbo, clearing the street and splitting the crowd into two. Because National Guard lines still barred passage over the Balbo Street bridge, most of the demonstrators fled into Grant Park. A Guardsman estimates that 5,000 remained in the park across from the Hilton. Some clubbing by police occurred; a demonstrator says he saw a brick hurled at police; but few arrests were made.

Now, with police lines beginning to re-form, the deputy superintendent directed the police units to advance north on Michigan. He says announcements were again made to clear the area and warnings given that those refusing to do so would be arrested. To this, according to a patrol-man who was present, "The hippie group yelled 'fuck you' in unison."

. . . . .

Police units formed up. National Guard intelligence officers on the site called for Guard assistance. At 8:30 the Secret Service reported trucks full of Guard troops from Soldier Field moving north on Michigan Avenue to the Conrad Hilton and addi-tional units arrived about 20 minutes later. The troops included the same units that had seen action earlier in the day after the bandshell rally and had later been moved to 22nd Street.

By 8:55 p.m., the Guard had taken up positions in a U-shaped formation, block-ing Balbo at Michigan and paralleling the Hilton and Grant Park—a position that was kept until 4 a.m. Thursday. Although bayonets were affixed when the troops first hit the street, they were quickly removed. Explains a Guardsman who was there: "The bayonets had gotten in our way when we were on the Congress Street bridge.

"The crowd that remained behind in the park was very noisy and restless," he remembers. "People were milling around on the sidewalk. Police said that these people who were walking on the sidewalk could be subject to arrest. The parade marshals kept them away from the side-walk."

At one point, however, a demonstrator tried to "take the muzzle off" one of the

Guardsmen's rifle. "All the time the dem-onstrators were trying to talk to us. They said 'join us' or 'fuck the draft.' We were told not to talk to anyone in the crowd."

. . . . .

One Guard unit followed behind the police as a backup group.

With the police and Guard at its rear, the crowd fractured in several directions as it moved away from Balbo and Michigan.

. . . . .

Near Michigan and Monroe another casualty center had been set up in the head-quarters of the Church Federation of Greater Chicago. This, plus the melding of the crowds northbound on Michigan and eastbound on Monroe, brought about 1,000 persons to the west side of Michigan be-tween Adams and Monroe, facing the Art Institute. There were few demonstrators on the east side of Michigan.

At 9:25 p.m., the police commander ordered a sweep of Michigan Avenue south from Monroe. At about this same time the police still had lines on both the west and east sides of Michigan in front of the Hilton and additional National Guard troops had arrived at 8th Street.

At 9:57 p.m., the demonstrators still on Michigan Avenue, prodded along by the southward sweep of the police, began marching back to Grant Park, chanting "Back to the park." By 10:10 p.m., an estimated 800 to 1,000 demonstrators had gathered in front of the Hilton.

By then, two city street sweeping trucks had rumbled up and down the street in front of the hotel, cleaning up the residue of violence—shoes, bottles, rocks, tear gas, handkerchiefs. A police captain said the debris included: "Bases and pieces of broken bottles, a piece of board (1″ × 4″

× 14″), an 18-inch length of metal pipe, a 24-inch stick with a protruding sharpened nail, a 12-inch length of ½-inch diameter pipe, pieces of building bricks, an 18-inch stick with a razor blade protruding . . . several plastic balls somewhat smaller than tennis balls containing approximately 15 to 20 sharpened nails driven into the ball from various angles." When the delegates returned to the Hilton, they saw none of the litter of the battle.

As the crowd had dispersed from the Hilton, . . . the big war of Michigan and Balbo was, of course, over. But for those in the streets, as the rivulets of the crowd forked through the areas north of the hotel, there were still battles to be fought. Police violence and police baiting were some time in abating. Indeed, some of the most vicious incidents occurred in this "post-war" period.

．　　　．　　　．　　　．

The U.S. Attorney states that as the crowd moved north on Michigan Avenue, "they pelted the police with missiles of all sorts, rocks, bottles, firecrackers. When a policeman was struck, the crowd would cheer. The policemen in the line were dodging and jumping to avoid being hit." A police sergeant told the FBI that even a telephone was hurled from the crowd at the police.

．　　　．　　　．　　　．

In the first block north of the Hilton, recalls a man who was standing outside a Michigan Avenue restaurant, demonstrators "menaced limousines, calling the occupants 'scum,' telling them they didn't belong in Chicago and to go home."

As the police skirmish line moved north, the police lieutenant said he "saw people standing on the hoods and trunks of two marked police cars and one unmarked police car about 150 feet north of the skirmish line." He said he could hear windows being smashed and the crowd shouting its approval." (A college coed says a demonstrator first tried to kick in a squad car's back window and failing that, smashed it with a trash basket.) The lieutenant said he was approached by two young police officers, apparently refugees from one of the squad cars, who said they "were not supposed to be in that area and did not know what to do or where to go." They told the lieutenant they had been among the squads accompanying the mule train on its parade south on Michigan earlier, but had been cut off by the crowd. The lieutenant told them to report to their headquarters.

As the skirmish line drew nearer to the squad cars, the lieutenant said, he saw several persons shoving paper through the cars' broken windows—in his opinion, a prelude to setting the cars on fire. A theology student who was in the crowd states that "a demonstrator took a fire extinguisher and sprayed inside the car. Then he put paper on the ground under the gas tank. . . . People shouted at him to stop." To break up the crowd, the lieutenant said, he squirted tear gas from an aerosol container and forced the demonstrators back.

．　　　．　　　．　　　．

"Two or three policemen, one with a white shirt, advanced on the crowd," one witness said. "The white-shirted one squirted mace in arcs back and forth before him."

A cameraman for the *Chicago Daily News* photographed a woman cowering after she had been sprayed with mace. A *News* representative states that the officer administering the mace, whom the photographers identified as a police lieutenant, then turned and directed the spray at the cameraman. The cameraman shot a photograph of this as he ducked. The police lieutenant involved states that he does not remember this incident.

.   .   .   .

A priest who was in the crowd says he saw a "boy, about 14 or 15, white, standing on top of an automobile yelling something which was unidentifiable. Suddenly a policeman forced him down from the car and beat him to the ground by striking him three or four times with a nightstick. Other police joined in . . . and they eventually shoved him to a police van."

A well-dressed woman saw this incident and spoke angrily to a nearby police captain. As she spoke, another policeman came up from behind her and sprayed something in her face with an aerosol can. He then clubbed her to the ground. He and two other policemen then dragged her along the ground to the same paddy wagon and threw her in.

.   .   .   .

"At the corner of Congress Plaza and Michigan," states a doctor, "was gathered a group of people, number between 30 and 40. They were trapped against a railing . . . by several policemen on motorcycles. The police charged the people on motorcycles and struck about a dozen of them, knocking several of them down. About 20 standing there jumped over the railing. On the other side of the railing was a three-to-four-foot drop. None of the people who were struck by the motorcycles appeared to be seriously injured. However,

several of them were limping as if they had been run over on their feet."

A UPI reporter witnessed these attacks, too. He relates in his statement that one officer, "with a smile on his face and a fanatical look in his eyes, was standing on a three-wheel cycle, shouting, 'Wahoo, wahoo,' and trying to run down people on the sidewalk." The reporter says he was chased 30 feet by the cycle.

A few seconds later he "turned around and saw a policeman with a raised billy stick." As he swung around, the police stick grazed his head and struck his shoulders. As he was on his knees, he says someone stepped on his back.

A Negro policeman helped him to his feet, the reporter says. The policeman told him, "You know, man I didn't do this. One of the white cops did it." Then, the reporter quotes the officer as saying, "You know what? After this is all over, I'm quitting the force."

An instant later, the shouting officer on the motorcycle swung by again, and the reporter dove into a doorway for safety.

Near this same intersection, a Democratic delegate from Oklahoma was surrounded in front of his hotel by about ten persons, two of them with long hair and beards. He states that they encircled him for several minutes and subjected him to verbal abuse because they felt he "represented the establishment" and was "somewhat responsible for the alleged police brutality." The delegate stood mute and was eventually rescued by a policeman.

At Van Buren, a college girl states, "demonstrators were throwing things at passing police cars, and I saw one policeman hit in the face with a rock. A small paddy wagon drove up with only one policeman in it, and the crowd began rocking the wagon. The cop fell out and was surrounded by the crowd, but no effort was made to hurt him."

.   .   .   .

At Jackson, says the graduate student quoted earlier, "People got into the street on their knees and prayed, including several ministers who were dressed in clerical garb. These people, eight or ten of them, were arrested. This started a new wave of dissent among the demonstrators, who got angry. Many went forward to be arrested voluntarily; others were taken forcibly and some were beaten. . . . Objects were being thrown directly at police, including cans, bottles and paper."

"I was in the street," a witness who was near the intersection states, "when a fire in a trash basket appeared. . . . In a few minutes, two fire engines passed south through the crowd, turned west on Van Buren and stopped. They were followed by two police wagons which stopped in the middle of the block. As I walked north past the smaller of the two wagons, it began to rock." (The wagon also was being pelted by missiles, the U.S. Attorney states, and "PIGS" was painted on its sides.)

"I retreated onto the east sidewalk," the witness continued. "The two policemen jumped out of the smaller wagon and one was knocked down by a few demonstrators, while other demonstrators tried to get these demonstrators away. The two policemen got back to the wagon, the crowd having drawn well back around them." The U.S. Attorney's report states that one of the policemen was "stomped" by a small group of the mob.

A young woman who was there and who had attended the bandshell rally earlier in the afternoon states that the crowd rocked the wagon for some time, while its officers stayed inside. "Then," she says, "the driver came out wildly swinging his club and shouting. About ten people jumped on him. He was kicked pretty severely and was downed. When he got up he was missing his club and his hat."

A police commander says that at about this moment he received "an urgent radio message" from an officer inside the van. He radioed that "demonstrators were standing on the hood of his wagon . . . and were preparing to smash the windshield with a baseball bat," the commander recalled. The officer also told him that the demonstrators were attempting to overturn the squadrol and that the driver "was hanging on the door in a state of shock." The commander told the officer that assistance was on the way.

"I heard a '10–1' call on either my radio or one of the other hand sets being carried by other men with me," the U.S. Attorney states, "and then heard, 'Car 100-sweep!' [Car 100 was assigned to the police commander.] With a roar of motors, squads, vans and three-wheelers came from east, west and north into the block north of Jackson."

"Almost immediately a CTA bus filled with police came over the Jackson Drive bridge and the police formed a line in the middle of the street," says a witness. "I heard shouts that the police had rifles and that they had cocked and pumped them. Demonstrators began to run."

.   .   .   .

"I ran north of Jackson . . . just as police were clearing the intersection and forming a line across Michigan," says the witness quoted above. "The police who had formed a line facing east in the middle of Michigan charged, yelling and clubbing into the crowd, running at individuals and groups who did not run before them."

.   .   .   .

"As the fray intensified around the intersection of Michigan and Jackson, a big group ran west on Jackson, with a group of blue-shirted policemen in pursuit, beating at them with clubs," says the U.S. Attorney's report. "Some of the crowd would jump into doorways, and the police would rout them out. The action was very tough and, in my judgment, unnecessarily so. The police were hitting with a vengeance and quite obviously with relish because of what had happened to the men in the van. Some of the crowd ran up the alleys; some north on Wabash; and some west on Jackson to State with the police in pursuit."

.   .   .   .

An Assistant U.S. Attorney later reported that "the demonstrators were running as fast as they could but were unable to get out of the way because of the crowds in front of them. I observed the police striking numerous individuals, perhaps 20 or 30. I saw three fall down and then overrun by the police. I observed two demonstrators who had multiple cuts on their heads. We assisted one who was in shock into a passerby's car.

"A TV mobile truck appeared . . . and the police became noticeably more restrained, holding their clubs at waist level rather than in the air," a witness relates. "As the truck disappeared . . . the head-clubbing tactics were resumed."

.   .   .   .

One demonstrator states that he ran off Michigan Avenue onto Jackson. He says he and his wife ran down Jackson and

were admitted, hesitantly, into a restaurant. They seated themselves at a table by the window facing onto Jackson and, while sitting at the table, observed a group of people running down Jackson with policemen following them and striking generally at the crowd with their batons. At one instance, he saw a policeman strike a priest in the head with a baton. He said he saw the policeman strike the priest only once and then go on. The clergyman also moved on.

At the intersection of Jackson and Wabash, says the student whose wife was beaten in the race from Michigan, "the police came from all four directions and attacked the crowd. Demonstrators were beaten and run to the paddy wagons. I saw a black policeman go berserk. He charged blindly at the group of demonstrators and made two circles through the crowd, swinging wildly at anything."

An Assistant U.S. Attorney watching the action on various side streets reported, "I observed police officers clearing people westward . . . using their clubs to strike people on the back of the head and body on several occasions. Once a policeman ran alongside a young girl. He held her by the shoulder of her jacket and struck at her a few times as they were both running down the sidewalk.

.   .   .   .

A traffic policeman on duty on Michigan Avenue says that the demonstrators who had continued north often surrounded cars and buses attempting to move south along Michigan Avenue. Many males in the crowd, he says, exposed their penises to passers-by and other members of the crowd. At times, they would run up to cars clogged by the crowd and show their private parts to the passengers.

To men, the officer says, they shouted such questions as, "How would you like me to fuck your wife?" and "How would you like to fuck a man?" Many of the demonstrators also rocked the automobiles in an effort to tip them over.

. . . .

A policeman states that bags of feces and urine were dropped on the police from the building.

. . . .

As the crowd moved south again on Michigan, a traffic policeman, who was in the vicinity of Adams Street, recalls, "They first took control of the lions in front of the Art Institute. They climbed them and shouted things like, "Let's fuck" and "Fuck, fuck, fuck!"

. . . .

At this same intersection, an officer rescued two Loop secretaries from being molested by demonstrators. He asked them, "What are you doing here?" They replied, "We wanted to see what the hippies were like." His response: "How do you like what you saw?"

. . . .

Old Town: The Mixture as Before

While all that was going on in and around Grant Park, Lincoln Park on Wednesday was quiet and uncrowded; but there was sporadic violence in Old Town again that night. Two University of Minnesota students who wandered through the park in the morning say they heard small groups of demonstrators saying things like "Fuck the pigs," and "Kill them all," but by this time that was not unusual. They also heard a black

man addressing a group of demonstrators. He outlined plans for the afternoon, and discussed techniques for forming skirmish lines, disarming police officers, and self defense.

Also during the morning Abbie Hoffman was arrested at the Lincoln Hotel Coffee Shop, 1800 North Clark, and charged with resisting arrest and disorderly conduct. According to Hoffman's wife, Anita, she and her husband and a friend were eating breakfast when three policemen entered the coffee shop and told Hoffman they had received three complaints about an obscene word written on Hoffman's forehead. The word was "Fuck." Hoffman says he printed the word on his forehead to keep cameramen from taking his picture.

. . . .

Most of the violence against police, from all reports, was the work of gang-type youths called "greasers." They dismantled police barricades to lure squad cars down Stockton Drive, where one observer says "punks engaged in some of the most savage attacks on police that had been seen." Ministers and hippies in the area were directing traffic around the barricades and keeping people from wandering into the danger area. Two ministers in particular were trying to "keep the cool."

. . . .

Back at the Hilton

By 10:30 p.m., most of the action was centered once more in Grant Park across from the Hilton, where several hundred demonstrators and an estimated 1,500 spectators gathered to listen to what one observer describes as "unexciting speeches." There was the usual singing and shouting. Twice during the evening police and Hilton security officers went into the hotel and went to quarters occupied by McCarthy personnel—once to protest the ripping of sheets to bandage persons who had been injured and a second time to try to locate persons said to be lobbing ashtrays out of the windows. But compared to the earlier hours of the evening, the rest of the night was quiet.

In Grant Park, the sullen crowd sat facing the hotel. Someone with a transistor radio was listening to the roll call vote of states on the nomination and broadcasting the count to the rest of the throng over a bullhorn. There were loud cheers for Ted Kennedy, McCarthy, McGovern and Phillips. ("He's a black man," said the youth with the bullhorn.) Boos and cries of "Dump the Hump" arose whenever Humphrey received votes. "When Illinois was called," says the trained observer, "no one could hear totals because of booing and the chant, 'To Hell with Daley.' "

During this time the police line was subject to considerable verbal abuse from within the crowd and a witness says that both black and white agitators at the edge of the crowd tried to kick policemen with razor blades embedded in their shoes. Periodically several policemen would make forays into the crowd, punishing demonstrators they thought were involved.

At about "Louisiana," as the roll call vote moved with quickening pace toward the climax of Humphrey's nomination, the crowd grew restless, recalls a trained observer. About this same time, according to the Log, the police skirmish line began pushing the demonstrators farther east into the park. A report of an officer being struck by a nail ball was received by police. Film taken at about this time shows an officer being hit by a thrown missile, later identified as a chunk of concrete with a steel reinforcement rod in it. The blow knocked him down and, as he fell, the crowd cheered and yelled, "More!" The chant, "Kill the pigs," filled the air.

"At 'Oklahoma,' " recalls an observer, "the Yippie on the bullhorn said, 'Marshals ready. Don't move. Stay seated.'

"The front line rose [facing the police] and locked arms, and the others stayed seated. Humphrey was over the top with Pennsylvania, and someone in the Hilton rang a cow bell at the demonstrators. Boos went up, as did tension. A bus load of police arrived. Others standing in front of the Hilton crossed Michigan and lined up behind those in front of the demonstrators.

"The chant of 'Sit down, sit down' went out. An American flag was raised on a pole upside down. Wandering began among demonstrators and the chant continued."

Shortly before midnight, while Benjamin Ortiz was speaking, National Guard troops of the 2/129 Inf. came west on Balbo to Michigan to replace the police in front of the Hilton. "For the first time," says an observer, "machine guns mounted on trucks were pulled up directly in front of the demonstrators, just behind the police lines. The machine guns, and the Guard's mesh-covered jeeps with barbed wire fronts made the demonstrators angry and nervous. Bayonets were readied. In films of this period the word "pig" can be seen written on the street.

"Ortiz continued, 'Dig this man, just 'cause you see some different pigs coming here, don't get excited. We're going to sleep here, sing here, sex here, live here!' "

As the police moved off, one of the first Guard maneuvers was to clear demonstrators from Michigan's east sidewalk. This was done to allow pedestrian traffic. The crowd reacted somewhat hostilely to the maneuver, but by and large, the demonstrators seemed to view the Guard as helpless men who had been caught up in the events and did not treat them as badly as they had the police. Having secured the sidewalk, the guards shortly retired to the east curb of Michigan Avenue. A line of "marshals" sat down at the edge of the grass at the feet of the guards. Access to the hotel was restored and people began to move from the hotel to the park and vice versa. By now, there were an estimated 4,000 persons assembled across from the Hilton. Most of the crowd sat down in a mass and became more orderly, singing "America" and "God Bless America."

· · · · ·

McCarthy supporters jointed the crowd and were welcomed.

By 12:20 a.m., Thursday, the crowd had declined to 1,500 and was considered under control. By 12:33 a.m., the police department had retired from the streets entirely and the Guard took over the complete responsibility of holding Michigan from Balbo to 8th Street. At 12:47 a.m., another contingent of Guard troops arrived and was posted at the Hilton. At about this time delegates were returning and were being booed and jeered unless they could be identified as McCarthy or McGovern supporters. Those delegates were cheered and asked to join the group.

The crowd grew in number. By 1:07 a.m., the Secret Service estimated 2,000 persons in the park across from the hotel. Ten minutes later the crowd had grown by another 500. Those in the park were "listening to speeches—orderly" according to the log.

12

Internal Colonialism and Ghetto Revolt

ROBERT BLAUNER

It is becoming almost fashionable to analyze American racial conflict today in terms of the colonial analogy. I shall argue in this paper that the utility of this perspective depends upon a distinction between colonization as a process and colonialism as a social, economic, and political system. It is the experience of colonization that Afro-Americans share with many of the non-white people of the world. But this subjugation has taken place in a societal context that differs in important respects from the situation of "classical colonialism." In the body of this essay[1] I shall look at some major developments in Black protest—the urban riots, cultural nationalism, and the movement for ghetto control—as collective responses to colonized status. Viewing our domestic situation as a special form of colonization outside a context of a colonial system will help explain some of the dilemmas and ambiguities within these movements.

The present crisis in American life has brought about changes in social perspectives and the questioning of long accepted frameworks. Intellectuals and social scientists have been forced by the pressure of events to look at old definitions of the character of our society, the role of racism, and the workings of basic institutions. The depth and volatility of contemporary racial conflict challenge sociologists in particular to question the adequacy of theoretical models by which we have explained American race relations in the past.

For a long time the distinctiveness of the Negro situation among the ethnic minorities was placed in terms of color, and the systematic discrimination that follows from our deep-seated racial prejudices. This was sometimes called the caste theory, and while provocative, it missed essential and dynamic features of American race relations. In the past ten years there has been a tendency to view Afro-Americans as another ethnic group not basically different in experience from previous ethnics and whose "immigration" condition in the North would in time follow their upward course. The inadequacy of this model is now clear —even the Kerner Report devotes a chapter to criticizing this analogy. A more recent (though hardly new) approach views the essence of racial subordination in economic class terms: Black people as an underclass are to a degree specially exploited and to a degree economically dispensable in an automating society. Important as are economic factors, the power of race and racism in America cannot be sufficiently explained through class analysis. Into this theory vacuum steps the model of internal colonialism. Problematic and imprecise as it is, it gives hope of becoming a framework that can integrate the insights of caste and racism, ethnicity, culture, and economic exploitation into an overall conceptual scheme. At the same time, the danger of the colonial model is the imposition of an artificial analogy which might keep us from facing up to the fact (to quote Harold

SOURCE: Reprinted from *Social Problems*, Spring, 1969, 16:393–408, by permission of the author and The Society for the Study of Social Problems.

Cruse) that "the American black and white social phenomenon is a uniquely new world thing." [2]

During the late 1950's, identification with African nations and other colonial or formerly colonized peoples grew in importance among Black militants.[3] As a result the U.S. was increasingly seen as a colonial power and the concept of domestic colonialism was introduced into the political analysis and rhetoric of militant nationalists. During the same period Black social theorists began developing this frame of reference for explaining American realities. As early as 1962, Cruse characterized race relations in this country as "domestic colonialism." [4] Three years later in *Dark Ghetto*, Kenneth Clark demonstrated how the political, economic, and social structure of Harlem was essentially that of a colony.[5] Finally in 1967, a full-blown elaboration of "internal colonialism" provided the theoretical framework for Carmichael and Hamilton's widely read *Black Power*.[6] The following year the colonial analogy gained currency and new "respectability" when Senator McCarthy habitually referred to Black Americans as a colonized people during his campaign. While the rhetoric of internal colonialism was catching on, other social scientists began to raise questions about its appropriateness as a scheme of analysis.

The colonial analysis has been rejected as obscurantist and misleading by scholars who point to the significant differences in history and social-political conditions between our domestic patterns and what took place in Africa and India. Colonialism traditionally refers to the establishment of domination over a geographically external political unit, most often inhabited by people of a different race and culture, where this domination is political and economic, and the colony exists subordinated to and

dependent upon the mother country. Typically the colonizers exploit the land, the raw materials, the labor, and other resources of the colonized nation; in addition a formal recognition is given to the difference in power, autonomy, and political status, and various agencies are set up to maintain this subordination. Seemingly the analogy must be stretched beyond usefulness if the American version is to be forced into this model. For here we are talking about group relations within a society; the mother country—colony separation in geography is absent. Though whites certainly colonized the territory of the original Americans, internal colonization of Afro-Americans did not involve the settlement of whites in any land that was unequivocally Black. And unlike the colonial situation, there has been no formal recognition of differing power since slavery was abolished outside the South. Classic colonialism involved the control and exploitation of the majority of a nation by a minority of outsiders. Whereas in America the people who are oppressed were themselves originally outsiders and are a numerical minority.

This conventional critique of "internal colonialism" is useful in pointing to the differences between our domestic patterns and the overseas situation. But in its bold attack it tends to lose sight of common experiences that have been historically shared by the most subjugated racial minorities in America and non-white peoples in some other parts of the world. For understanding the most dramatic recent developments on the race scene, this common core element—which I shall call colonization—may be more important than the undeniable divergences between the two contexts.

The common features ultimately relate to the fact that the classical colonialism of the imperialist era and American racism developed out of the same historical situation and reflected a common world economic and power stratification. The slave trade for the most part preceded the imperialist partition and economic exploitation of Africa, and in fact may have been a necessary prerequisite for colonial conquest— since it helped deplete and pacify Africa, undermining the resistance to direct occupation. Slavery contributed one of the basic raw materials for the textile industry which provided much of the capital for the West's industrial development and need for economic expansionism. The essential condition for both American slavery and European colonialism was the power domination and the technological superiority of the Western world in its relation to peoples of non-Western and non-white origins. This objective supremacy in technology and military power buttressed the West's sense of cultural superiority, laying the basis for racist ideologies that were elaborated to justify control and exploitation of non-white people. Thus because classical colonialism and America's internal version developed out of a similar balance of technological, cultural, and power relations, a common *process* of social oppression characterized the racial patterns in the two contexts—despite the variation in political and social structure.

There appear to be four basic components of the colonization complex. The first refers to how the racial group enters into the dominant society (whether colonial power or not). Colonization begins with a forced, involuntary entry. Second, there is an impact on the culture and social organization of the colonized people which is more than just a result of such "natural" processes as contact and acculturation. The colonizing power carries out a policy which constrains, transforms, or destroys indige-

nous values, orientations, and ways of life. Third, colonization involves a relationship by which members of the colonized group tend to be administered by representatives of the dominant power. There is an experience of being managed and manipulated by outsiders in terms of ethnic status.

A final fundament of colonization is racism. Racism is a principle of social domination by which a group seen as inferior or different in terms of alleged biological characteristics is exploited, controlled, and oppressed socially and psychically by a superordinate group. Except for the marginal case of Japanese imperialism, the major examples of colonialism have involved the subjugation of non-white Asian, African, and Latin American peoples by white European powers. Thus racism has generally accompanied colonialism. Race prejudice can exist without colonization— the experience of Asian-American minorities is a case in point—but racism as a system of domination is part of the complex of colonization.

The concept of colonization stresses the enormous fatefulness of the historical factor, namely the manner in which a minority group becomes a part of the dominant society.[7] The crucial difference between the colonized Americans and the ethnic immigrant minorities is that the latter have always been able to operate fairly competitively within that relatively open section of the social and economic order because these groups came voluntarily in search of a better life, because their movements in society were not administratively controlled, and because they transformed their culture at their own pace—giving up ethnic values and institutions when it was seen as a desirable exchange for improvements in social position.

In present-day America, a major device

of Black colonization is the powerless ghetto. As Kenneth Clark describes the situation:

> Ghettoes are the consequence of the imposition of external power and the institutionalization of powerlessness. In this respect, they are in fact social, political, educational, and above all—economic colonies. Those confined within the ghetto walls are subject peoples. They are victims of the greed, cruelty, insensitivity, guilt and fear of their masters. . . .
>
> The community can best be described in terms of the analogy of a powerless colony. Its political leadership is divided, and all but one or two of its political leaders are shortsighted and dependent upon the larger political power structure. Its social agencies are financially precarious and dependent upon sources of support outside the community. Its churches are isolated or dependent. Its economy is dominated by small businesses which are largely owned by absentee owners, and its tenements and other real property are also owned by absentee landlords.
>
> Under a system of centralization, Harlem's schools are controlled by forces outside of the community. Programs and policies are supervised and determined by individuals who do not live in the community . . .[8]

Of course many ethnic groups in America have lived in ghettoes. What make the Black ghettoes an expression of colonized status are three special features. First, the ethnic ghettoes arose more from voluntary choice, both in the sense of the choice to immigrate to America and the decision to live among one's fellow ethnics. Second, the immigrant ghettoes tended to be a one and two generation phenomenon; they were actually way-stations in the process of acculturation and assimilation. When they continue to persist as in the case of San Francisco's Chinatown, it is because they are big business for the ethnics themselves and there is a new stream of immigrants. The Black ghetto on the other hand has been a more permanent phenomenon, although some individuals do escape it. But most relevant is the third point. European ethnic groups like the Poles, Italians, and Jews generally only experienced a brief period, often less than a generation, during which their residential buildings, commercial stores, and other enterprises were owned by outsiders. The Chinese and Japanese faced handicaps of color prejudice that were almost as strong as the Blacks faced, but very soon gained control of their internal communities, because their traditional ethnic culture and social organization had not been destroyed by slavery and internal colonization. But Afro-Americans are distinct in the extent to which their segregated communities have remained controlled economically, politically, and administratively from the outside. One indicator of this difference is the estimate that the "income of Chinese-Americans from Chinese-owned businesses is in proportion to their numbers 45 times as great as the income of Negroes from Negro owned businesses."[9] But what is true of business is also true for the other social institutions that operate within the ghetto. The educators, policemen, social workers, politicians, and others who administer the affairs of ghetto residents are typically whites who live outside the Black community. Thus the ghetto plays a strategic role as the focus for the administration by outsiders which is also essential to the structure of overseas colonialism.[10]

The colonial status of the Negro community goes beyond the issue of ownership and decision-making within Black neighborhoods. The Afro-American population in most cities has very little influence on the power structure and institutions of the larger metropolis, despite the fact that in numerical terms, Blacks tend to be the most sizable of the various interest groups. A recent analysis of policy-making in Chicago estimates that "Negroes really hold less than 1 percent of the effective power in the Chicago metropolitan area. [Negroes are 20 percent of Cook County's population.] Realistically the power structure of Chicago is hardly less white than that of Mississippi." [11]

Colonization outside of a traditional colonial structure has its own special conditions. The group culture and social structure of the colonized in America is less developed; it is also less autonomous. In addition, the colonized are a numerical minority, and furthermore they are ghettoized more totally and are more dispersed than people under classic colonialism. Though these realities affect the magnitude and direction of response, it is my basic thesis that the most important expressions of protest in the Black community during the recent years reflect the colonized status of Afro-America. Riots, programs of separation, politics of community control, the Black revolutionary movements, and cultural nationalism each represent a different strategy of attack on domestic colonialism in America. Let us now examine some of these movements.

Riot or Revolt?

The so-called riots are being increasingly recognized as a preliminary if primitive form of mass rebellion against a colonial status. There is still a tendency to absorb their meaning within the conventional scope of assimilation-integration politics: some commentators stress the material motives involved in looting as a sign that the rioters want to join America's middle-class affluence just like everyone else. That motives are mixed and often unconscious, that Black people want good furniture and television sets like whites is beside the point. The guiding impulse in most major outbreaks has not been integration with American society, but an attempt to stake out a sphere of control by moving against that society and destroying the symbols of its oppression.

In my critique of the McCone report I observed that the rioters were asserting a claim to territoriality, an unorganized and rather inchoate attempt to gain control over their community or "turf." [12] In succeeding disorders also the thrust of the action has been the attempt to clear out an alien presence, white men and officials, rather than a drive to kill whites as in a conventional race riot. The main attacks have been directed at the property of white business men and at the police who operate in the Black community "like an army of occupation" protecting the interests of outside exploiters and maintaining the domination over the ghetto by the central metropolitan power structure.[13] The Kerner report misleads when it attempts to explain riots in terms of integration: "What the rioters appear to be seeking was fuller participation in the social order and the material benefits enjoyed by the majority of American citizens. Rather than rejecting the American system, they were anxious to obtain a place for themselves in it." [14] More accurately, the revolts pointed to alienation from this system on the part of many poor and also not-so-poor Blacks. The sacredness of private property, that unconsciously accepted bulwark of our social arrangements, was rejected; people who looted apparently without guilt generally remarked that they were taking things that "really belonged" to them anyway.[15] Obviously the society's bases of legitimacy and authority have been attacked. Law and order has long been viewed as the white man's law and order by Afro-Americans; but now this perspective characteristic of a colonized people is out in the open. And the Kerner report's own data question how well ghetto rebels are buying the system: In Newark only 33 percent of self-reported rioters said they thought this country was worth fighting for in the event of a major war; in the Detroit sample the figure was 55 percent.[16]

One of the most significant consequences of the process of colonization is a weakening of the colonized's individual and collective will to resist his oppression. It has been easier to contain and control Black ghettoes because communal bonds and group solidarity have been weakened through divisions among leadership, failures of organization, and a general dispiritment that accompanies social oppression. The riots are a signal that the will to resist has broken the mold of accommodation. In some cities as in Watts they also represented nascent movements toward community identity. In several riot-torn ghettoes the outbursts have stimulated new organizations and movements. If it is true that the riot phenomenon of 1964–68 has passed its peak, its historical import may be more for the "internal" organizing momentum generated than for any profound "external" response of the larger society facing up to underlying causes.

Despite the appeal of Frantz Fanon to young Black revolutionaries, America is not Algeria. It is difficult to foresee how riots in our cities can play a role equivalent to rioting in the colonial situation as an integral phase in a movement for national liberation. In 1968 some militant groups (for example, the Black Panther Party in Oakland) had concluded that ghetto riots were self-defeating of the lives and interests of Black people in the present balance of organization and gunpower, though they had served a role to stimulate both Black consciousness and white awareness of the depths of racial crisis. Such militants have been influential in "cooling" their communities during periods of high riot potential. Theoretically oriented Black radicals see riots as spontaneous mass behavior which must be replaced by a revolutionary organization and consciousness. But despite the differences in objective conditions, the violence of the 1960's seems to serve the same psychic function, assertions of dignity and manhood for young Blacks in urban ghettoes, as it did for the colonized of North Africa described by Fanon and Memmi.[17]

Cultural Nationalism

Cultural conflict is generic to the colonial relation because colonization involves the domination of Western technological values over the more communal cultures of non-Western peoples. Colonialism played havoc with the national integrity of the peoples it brought under its sway. Of course, all traditional cultures are threatened by industrialism, the city, and modernization in communication, transportation, health, and education. What is special are the political and administrative decisions of colonizers in managing and controlling colonized peoples. The boundaries of African colonies, for example, were drawn to suit the political conveniences of the European nations without regard to the social organization and cultures of African tribes and kingdoms. Thus Nigeria as blocked out by the British included the Yorubas and the Ibos, whose civil war today is a residuum of the colonialist's disrespect for the integrity of indigenous cultures.

The most total destruction of culture in the colonization process took place not in traditional colonialism but in America. As Frazier stressed, the integral cultures of the diverse African peoples who furnished the slave trade were destroyed because slaves from different tribes, kingdoms, and linguistic groups were purposely separated to maximize domination and control. Thus language, religion, and national loyalties were lost in North America much more completely than in the Caribbean and Brazil where slavery developed somewhat differently. Thus on this key point America's internal colonization has been more total and extreme than situations of classic colonialism. For the British in India and the European powers in Africa were not able—as outnumbered minorities—to destroy the national and tribal cultures of the colonized. Recall that American slavery lasted 250 years and its racist aftermath another 100. Colonial dependency in the case of British Kenya and French Algeria lasted only 77 and 125 years respectively. In the wake of this more drastic uprooting and destruction of culture and social organization, much more powerful agencies of social, political, and psychological domination developed in the American case.

Colonial control of many peoples inhabiting the colonies was more a goal than a fact, and at Independence there were undoubtedly fairly large numbers of Africans who had never seen a colonial administrator. The gradual process of extension of control from the administrative center on the African coast contrasts sharply with the total uprooting involved in the slave trade and the totalitarian aspects of slavery in the United States. Whether or not Elkins is correct in treating slavery as a total

institution, it undoubtedly had a far more radical and pervasive impact on American slaves than did colonialism on the vast majority of Africans.[18]

Yet a similar cultural process unfolds in both contexts of colonialism. To the extent that they are involved in the larger society and economy, the colonized are caught up in a conflict between two cultures. Fanon has described how the assimilation-oriented schools of Martinique taught him to reject his own culture and Blackness in favor of Westernized, French, and white values.[19] Both the colonized elites under traditional colonialism and perhaps the majority of Afro-Americans today experience a parallel split in identity, cultural loyalty, and political orientation.[20]

The colonizers use their culture to socialize the colonized elites (intellectuals, politicians, and middle class) into an identification with the colonial system. Because Western culture has the prestige, the power, and the key to open the limited opportunity that a minority of the colonized may achieve, the first reaction seems to be an acceptance of the dominant values. Call it brainwashing as the Black Muslims put it; call it identifying with the aggressor if you prefer Freudian terminology; call it a natural response to the hope and belief that integration and democratization can really take place if you favor a more commonsense explanation, this initial acceptance in time crumbles on the realities of racism and colonialism. The colonized, seeing that his success within colonialism is at the expense of his group and his own inner identity, moves radically toward a rejection of the Western culture and develops a nationalist outlook that celebrates his people and their traditions. As Memmi describes it:

Assimilation being abandoned, the colonized's liberation must be carried out through a recovery of self and of autonomous dignity. Attempts at imitating the colonizer required self-denial; the colonizer's rejection is the indispensible prelude to self-discovery. That accusing and annihilating image must be shaken off; oppression must be attacked boldly since it is impossible to go around it. After having been rejected for so long by the colonizer, the day has come when it is the colonized who must refuse the colonizer.[21]

Memmi's book, *The Colonizer and the Colonized,* is based on his experience as a Tunisian Jew in a marginal position between the French and the colonized Arab majority. The uncanny parallels between the North African situation he describes and the course of Black-white relations in our society is the best impressionist argument I know for the thesis that we have a colonized group and a colonizing system in America. His discussion of why even the most radical French anti-colonialist cannot participate in the struggle of the colonized is directly applicable to the situation of the white liberal and radical vis-à-vis the Black movement. His portrait of the colonized is as good an analysis of the psychology behind Black Power and Black nationalism as anything that has been written in the U.S. Consider for example:

Considered *en bloc* as *them, they,* or *those,* different from every point of view, homogeneous in a radical heterogeneity, the colonized reacts by rejecting all the colonizers *en bloc.* The distinction between deed and intent has no great significance in the colonial situation. In the eyes of the colonized, all Europeans in the colonies are de facto colonizers, and whether they want to be or not, they are colonizers in some ways. By their privileged economic position, by belonging to the political system of oppression, or by partici-

pating in an effectively negative complex toward the colonized, they are colonizers. . . . They are supporters or at least unconscious accomplices of that great collective aggression of Europe.[22]

The same passion which made him admire and absorb Europe shall make him assert his differences; since those differences, after all, are within him and correctly constitute his true self.[23]

The important thing now is to rebuild his people, whatever be their authentic nature; to reforge their unity, communicate with it, and to feel that they belong.[24]

Cultural revitalization movements play a key role in anti-colonial movements. They follow an inner necessity and logic of their own that comes from the consequences of colonialism on groups and personal identities; they are also essential to provide the solidarity which the political or military phase of the anti-colonial revolution requires. In the U.S. an Afro-American culture has been developing since slavery out of the ingredients of African world-views, the experience of bondage, Southern values and customs, migration and the Northern lower-class ghettoes, and most importantly, the political history of the Black population in its struggle against racism.[25] That Afro-Americans are moving toward cultural nationalism in a period when ethnic loyalties tend to be weak (and perhaps on the decline) in this country is another confirmation of the unique colonized position of the Black group. (A similar nationalism seems to be growing among American Indians and Mexican-Americans.)

The Movement for Ghetto Control

The call for Black Power unites a number of varied movements and tendencies.[26]

Though no clear-cut program has yet emerged, the most important emphasis seems to be the movement for control of the ghetto. Black leaders and organizations are increasingly concerned with owning and controlling those institutions that exist within or impinge upon their community. The colonial model provides a key to the understanding of this movement, and indeed ghetto control advocates have increasingly invoked the language of colonialism in pressing for local home rule. The framework of anti-colonialism explains why the struggle for poor people's or community control of poverty programs has been more central in many cities than the content of these programs and why it has been crucial to exclude whites from leadership positions in Black organizations.

The key institutions that anti-colonialists want to take over or control are business, social services, schools, and the police. Though many spokesmen have advocated the exclusion of white landlords and small businessmen from the ghetto, this program has evidently not struck fire with the Black population and little concrete movement toward economic expropriation has yet developed. Welfare recipients have organized in many cities to protect their rights and gain a greater voice in the decisions that affect them, but whole communities have not yet been able to mount direct action against welfare colonialism. Thus schools and the police seem now to be the burning issues of ghetto control politics.

During the past few years there has been a dramatic shift from educational integration as the primary goal to that of community control of the schools. Afro-Americans are demanding their own school boards, with the power to hire and fire principals and teachers and to construct a curriculum which would be relevant to the special needs and culture style of ghetto youth. Especially active in high schools and colleges have been Black students, whose protests have centered on the incorporation of Black Power and Black culture into the educational system. Consider how similar is the spirit behind these developments to the attitude of the colonized North African toward European education:

He will prefer a long period of educational mistakes to the continuance of the colonizer's school organization. He will choose institutional disorder in order to destroy the institutions built by the colonizer as soon as possible. There we will see, indeed a reactive drive of profound protest. He will no longer owe anything to the colonizer and will have definitely broken with him.[27]

Protest and institutional disorder over the issue of school control came to a head in 1968 in New York City. The procrastination in the Albany State legislature, the several crippling strikes called by the teachers union, and the almost frenzied response of Jewish organizations make it clear that decolonization of education faces the resistance of powerful vested interests.[28] The situation is too dynamic at present to assess probable future results. However, it can be safely predicted that some form of school decentralization will be institutionalized in New York, and the movement for community control of education will spread to more cities.

This movement reflects some of the problems and ambiguities that stem from the situation of colonization outside an immediate colonial context. The Afro-American community is not parallel in structure to the communities of colonized nations under traditional colonialism. The significant difference here is the lack of fully developed indigenous institutions besides the church. Outside of some areas of the South there is really no Black economy, and most Afro-Americans are inevitably caught up in the larger society's structure of occupations, education, and mass communication. Thus the ethnic nationalist orientation which reflects the reality of colonization exists alongside an integrationist orientation which corresponds to the reality that the institutions of the larger society are much more developed than those of the incipient nation.[29] As would be expected the movement for school control reflects both tendencies. The militant leaders who spearhead such local movements may be primarily motivated by the desire to gain control over the community's institutions—they are anti-colonialists first and foremost. Many parents who support them may share this goal also, but the majority are probably more concerned about creating a new education that will enable their children to "make it" in the society and the economy as a whole—they know that the present school system fails ghetto children and does not prepare them for participation in American life.

There is a growing recognition that the police are the most crucial institution maintaining the colonized status of Black Americans. And of all establishment institutions, police departments probably include the highest proportion of individual racists. This is no accident since central to the workings of racism (an essential component of colonization) are attacks on the humanity and dignity of the subject group. Through their normal routines the police constrict Afro-Americans to Black neighborhoods by harassing and questioning them when found outside the ghetto; they break up groups of youth congregating on corners or in cars without any provocation;

and they continue to use offensive and racist language no matter how many intergroup understanding seminars have been built into the police academy. They also shoot to kill ghetto residents for alleged crimes such as car thefts and running from police officers.[30]

Police are key agents in the power equation as well as the drama of dehumanization. In the final analysis they do the dirty work for the larger system by restricting the striking back of Black rebels to skirmishes inside the ghetto, thus deflecting energies and attacks from the communities and institutions of the larger power structure. In a historical review, Gary Marx notes that since the French revolution, police and other authorities have killed large numbers of demonstrators and rioters; the rebellious "rabble" rarely destroys human life. The same pattern has been repeated in America's recent revolts.[31] Journalistic accounts appearing in the press recently suggest that police see themselves as defending the interests of white people against a tide of Black insurgence; furthermore the majority of whites appear to view "blue power" in this light. There is probably no other opinion on which the races are as far apart today as they are on the question of attitudes toward the police.

In many cases set off by a confrontation between a policeman and a Black citizen, the ghetto uprisings have dramatized the role of law enforcement and the issue of police brutality. In their aftermath, movements have arisen to contain police activity. One of the first was the Community Alert Patrol in Los Angeles, a method of policing the police in order to keep them honest and constrain their violations of personal dignity. This was the first tactic of the Black Panther Party which originated in Oakland, perhaps the most significant group to challenge the police role in maintaining the ghetto as a colony. The Panther's later policy of openly carrying guns (a legally protected right) and their intention of defending themselves against police aggression has brought on a series of confrontations with the Oakland police department. All indications are that the authorities intend to destroy the Panthers by shooting, framing up, or legally harassing their leadership—diverting the group's energies away from its primary purpose of self-defense and organization of the Black community to that of legal defense and gaining support in the white community.

There are three major approaches to "police colonialism" that correspond to reformist and revolutionary readings of the situation. The most elementary and also superficial sees colonialism in the fact that ghettoes are overwhelmingly patrolled by white rather than by Black officers. The proposal—supported today by many police departments—to increase the number of Blacks on local forces to something like their distribution in the city would then make it possible to reduce the use of white cops in the ghetto. This reform should be supported, for a variety of obvious reasons, but it does not get to the heart of the police role as agents of colonization.

The Kerner report documents the fact that in some cases Black policemen can be as brutal as their white counterparts. The report does not tell us who polices the ghetto, but they have compiled the proportion of Negroes on the forces of the major cities. In some cities the disparity is so striking that white police inevitably dominate ghetto patrols. (In Oakland 31 percent of the population and only 4 percent of the police are Black; in Detroit the figures are 39 percent and 5 percent; and in New Orleans 41 and 4.) In other cities,

however, the proportion of Black cops is approaching the distribution in the city: Philadelphia 29 percent and 20 percent; Chicago 27 percent and 17 percent.[32] These figures also suggest that both the extent and the pattern of colonization may vary from one city to another. It would be useful to study how Black communities differ in degree of control over internal institutions as well as in economic and political power in the metropolitan area.

A second demand which gets more to the issue is that police should live in the communities they patrol. The idea here is that Black cops who lived in the ghetto would have to be accountable to the community; if they came on like white cops then "the brothers would take care of business" and make their lives miserable. The third or maximalist position is based on the premise that the police play no positive role in the ghettoes. It calls for the withdrawal of metropolitan officers from Black communities and the substitution of an autonomous indigenous force that would maintain order without oppressing the population. The precise relationship between such an independent police, the city and county law enforcement agencies, a ghetto governing body that would supervise and finance it, and especially the law itself is yet unclear. It is unlikely that we will soon face these problems directly as they have arisen in the case of New York's schools. Of all the programs of decolonization, police autonomy will be most resisted. It gets to the heart of how the state functions to control and contain the Black community through delegating the legitimate use of violence to police authority.

The various "Black Power" programs that are aimed at gaining control of individual ghettoes—buying up property and businesses, running the schools through community boards, taking over anti-poverty programs and other social agencies, diminishing the arbitrary power of the police —can serve to revitalize the institutions of the ghetto and build up an economic, professional, and political power base. These programs seem limited; we do not know at present if they are enough in themselves to end colonized status.[33] But they are certainly a necessary first step.

The Role of Whites

What makes the Kerner report a less-than-radical document is its superficial treatment of racism and its reluctance to confront the colonized relationship between Black people and the larger society. The report emphasizes the attitudes and feelings that make up white racism, rather than the system of privilege and control which is the heart of the matter.[34] With all its discussion of the ghetto and its problems, it never faces the question of the stake that white Americans have in racism and ghettoization.

This is not a simple question, but this paper should not end with the impression that police are the major villains. All white Americans gain some privileges and advantage from the colonization of Black communities.[35] The majority of whites also lose something from this oppression and division in society. Serious research should be directed to the ways in which white individuals and institutions are tied into the ghetto. In closing let me suggest some possible parameters.

1. It is my guess that only a small minority of whites make a direct economic profit from ghetto colonization. This is hopeful in that the ouster of white businessmen may become politically feasible. Much more significant, however, are the private and corporate interests in the land and residential property of the Black community; their holdings and influence on urban decision-making must be exposed and combated.

2. A much larger minority have occupational and professional interests in the present arrangements. The Kerner Commission reports that 1.3 million non-white men would have to be upgraded occupationally in order to make the Black job distribution roughly similar to the white. They advocate this without mentioning that 1.3 million specially privileged white workers would lose in the bargain.[36] In addition there are those professionals who carry out what Lee Rainwater has called the "dirty work" of administering the lives of the ghetto poor: the social workers, the school teachers, the urban development people, and of course the police.[37] The social problems of the Black community will ultimately be solved only by people and organizations from that community; thus the emphasis within these professions must shift toward training such a cadre of minority personnel. Social scientists who teach and study problems of race and poverty likewise have an obligation to replace themselves by bringing into the graduate schools and college faculties men of color who will become the future experts in these areas. For cultural and intellectual imperialism is as real as welfare colonialism, though it is currently screened behind such unassailable shibboleths as universalism and the objectivity of scientific inquiry.

3. Without downgrading the vested interests of profit and profession, the real nitty-gritty elements of the white stake are political power and bureaucratic security. Whereas few whites have much under-

standing of the realities of race relations and ghetto life, I think most give tacit or at least subconscious support for the containment and control of the Black population. Whereas most whites have extremely distorted images of Black Power, many—if not most—would still be frightened by actual Black political power. Racial groups and identities are real in American life; white Americans sense they are on top, and they fear possible reprisals or disruptions were power to be more equalized. There seems to be a paranoid fear in the white psyche of Black dominance; the belief that Black autonomy would mean unbridled license is so ingrained that such reasonable outcomes as Black political majorities and independent Black police forces will be bitterly resisted.

On this level the major mass bulwark of colonization is the administrative need for bureaucratic security so that the middle classes can go about their life and business in peace and quiet. The Black militant movement is a threat to the orderly procedures by which bureaucracies and suburbs manage their existence, and I think today there are more people who feel a stake in conventional procedures than there are those who gain directly from racism. For in their fight for institutional control, the colonized will not play by the white rules of the game. These administrative rules have kept them down and out of the system; therefore they have no necessary intention of running institutions in the image of the white middle class.

The liberal, humanist value that violence is the worst sin cannot be defended today if one is committed squarely against racism and for self-determination. For some violence is almost inevitable in the decolonization process; unfortunately racism in America has been so effective that the

greatest power Afro-Americans (and perhaps also Mexican-Americans) wield today is the power to disrupt. If we are going to swing with these revolutionary times and at least respond positively to the anti-colonial movement, we will have to learn to live with conflict, confrontation, constant change, and what may be real or apparent chaos and disorder.

A positive response from the white majority needs to be in two major directions at the same time. First, community liberation movements should be supported in every way by pulling out white instruments of direct control and exploitation and substituting technical assistance to the community when this is asked for. But it is not enough to relate affirmatively to the nationalist movement for ghetto control without at the same time radically opening doors for full participation in the institutions of the mainstream. Otherwise the liberal and radical position is little different than the traditional segregationist. Freedom in the special conditions of American colonization means that the colonized must have the choice between participation in the larger society and in their own independent structures.

Footnotes

[1] This is a revised version of a paper delivered at the University of California Centennial Program, "Studies in Violence," Los Angeles, June 1, 1968. For criticisms and ideas that have improved an earlier draft, I am indebted to Robert Wood, Lincoln Bergman, and Gary Marx. As a good colonialist I have probably restated (read: stolen) more ideas from the writings of Kenneth Clark, Stokely Carmichael, Frantz Fanon, and especially such contributors to the Black Panther Party (Oakland) newspaper as Huey Newton, Bobby Seale, Eldridge Cleaver, and Kathleen Cleaver than I have appropriately credited or generated myself. In self-defense I should state that I began working somewhat independently on a colonial analysis of American race relations in the fall of 1965; see my

"Whitewash Over Watts: The Failure of the McCone Report," *Trans-action*, 3, March–April, 1966, pp. 3–9, 54.

[2] Harold Cruse, *Rebellion or Revolution*, New York: 1968, p. 214.

[3] Nationalism, including an orientation toward Africa, is no new development. It has been a constant tendency within Afro-American politics. See Cruse, *ibid.*, esp. chaps. 5–7.

[4] This was six years before the publication of *The Crisis of the Negro Intellectual*, New York: Morrow, 1968, which brought Cruse into prominence. Thus the 1962 article was not widely read until its reprinting in Cruse's essays, *Rebellion or Revolution, op. cit.*

[5] Kenneth Clark, *Dark Ghetto*, New York: Harper and Row, 1965. Clark's analysis first appeared a year earlier in *Youth in the Ghetto*, New York: Haryou Associates, 1964.

[6] Stokely Carmichael and Charles Hamilton, *Black Power*, New York: Random, 1967.

[7] As Eldridge Cleaver reminds us, "Black people are a stolen people held in a colonial status on stolen land, and any analysis which does not acknowledge the colonial status of black people cannot hope to deal with the real problem." "The Land Question," *Ramparts*, 6, May, 1968, p. 51.

[8] *Youth in the Ghetto, op. cit.*, pp. 10–11; 79–80.

[9] N. Glazer and D. P. Moynihan, *Beyond the Melting Pot*, Cambridge, Mass.: M.I.T., 1963, p. 37.

[10] "When we speak of Negro social disabilities under capitalism, . . . we refer to the fact that he does not own anything—*even what is ownable in his own community*. Thus to fight for black liberation *is to fight for his right to own*. The Negro is politically compromised today because he owns nothing. He has little voice in the affairs of state because he owns nothing. The fundamental reason why the Negro bourgeois-democratic revolution has been aborted is because American capitalism has prevented the development of a black class of capitalist owners of institutions and economic tools. To take one crucial example, Negro radicals today are severely hampered in their tasks of educating the black masses on political issues because Negroes do not own any of the necessary means of propaganda and communication. The Negro owns no printing presses, he has no stake in the networks of the means of communication. Inside his own communities he does not own the house he lives in, the property he lives on, nor the wholesale and retail sources from which he buys his commodities. He does not own the edifices in which he enjoys culture and entertainment or in which he socializes. In capitalist society, an individual or group that does not own anything is powerless." H. Cruse, "Behind the Black Power Slogan," in Cruse, *Rebellion or Revolution, op. cit.*, pp. 238–239.

[11] Harold M. Baron, "Black Powerlessness in Chicago," *Trans-action*, 6, Nov., 1968, pp. 27–33.

[12] R. Blauner, "Whitewash Over Watts," *op. cit.*

[13] "The police function to support and enforce the interests of the dominant political, social, and economic interests of the town" is a statement made by a former police scholar and official, according to A. Neiderhoffer, *Behind the Shield*, New York: Doubleday, 1967 as cited by Gary T. Marx, "Civil Disorder and the Agents of Control," *Journal of Social Issues*, forthcoming.

[14] Report of the National Advisory Commission on Civil Disorders, N.Y.: Bantam, March, 1968, p. 7.

[15] This kind of attitude has a long history among American Negroes. During slavery, Blacks used the same rationalization to justify stealing from their masters. Appropriating things from the master was viewed as "*taking* part of his property for the benefit of another part; whereas *stealing* referred to appropriating something from another slave, an offense that was not condoned." Kenneth Stampp, *The Peculiar Institution*, Vintage, 1956, p. 127.

[16] Report of the National Advisory Commission on Civil Disorders, *op. cit.*, p. 178.

[17] Frantz Fanon, *Wretched of the Earth*, New York: Grove, 1963; Albert Memmi, *The Colonizer and the Colonized*, Boston: Beacon, 1967.

[18] Robert Wood, "Colonialism in Africa and America: Some Conceptual Considerations," December, 1967, unpublished paper.

[19] F. Fanon, *Black Skins, White Masks*, New York: Grove, 1967.

[20] Harold Cruse has described how these two themes of integration with the larger society and identification with ethnic nationality have struggled within the political and cultural movements of Negro Americans. *The Crisis of the Negro Intellectual, op. cit.*

[21] Memmi, *op. cit.*, p. 128.

[22] *Ibid.*, p. 130.

[23] *Ibid.*, p. 132.

[24] *Ibid.*, p. 134.

[25] In another essay, I argue against the standard sociological position that denies the existence of an ethnic Afro-American culture and I expand on the above themes. The concept of "Soul" is astonishingly parallel in content to the mystique

of "Negritude" in Africa; the Pan-African culture movement has its parallel in the burgeoning Black culture mood in Afro-American communities. See "Black Culture: Myth or Reality" in Peter Rose, editor, *Americans From Africa,* Atherton, 1969.

[26] Scholars and social commentators, Black and white alike, disagree in interpreting the contemporary Black Power movement. The issues concern whether this is a new development in Black protest or an old tendency revised; whether the movement is radical, revolutionary, reformist, or conservative; and whether this orientation is unique to Afro-Americans or essentially a Black parallel to other ethnic group strategies for collective mobility. For an interesting discussion of Black Power as a modernized version of Booker T. Washington's separatism and economism, see Harold Cruse, *Rebellion or Revolution, op. cit.,* pp. 193–258.

[27] Memmi, *op. cit.,* pp. 137–138.

[28] For the New York school conflict see Jason Epstein, "The Politics of School Decentralization," *New York Review of Books,* June 6, 1968, pp. 26–32; and "The New York City School Revolt," *ibid.,* 11, no. 6, pp. 37–41.

[29] This dual split in the politics and psyche of the Black American was poetically described by Du Bois in his *Souls of Black Folk,* and more recently has been insightfully analyzed by Harold Cruse in *The Crisis of the Negro Intellectual, op. cit.* Cruse has also characterized the problem of the Black community as that of underdevelopment.

[30] A recent survey of police finds "that in the predominantly Negro areas of several large cities, many of the police perceive the residents as basically hostile, especially the youth and adolescents. A lack of public support—from citizens, from courts, and from laws—is the policeman's major complaint. But some of the public criticism can be traced to the activities in which he engages day by day, and perhaps to the tone in which he enforces the 'law' in the Negro neighborhoods. Most frequently he is 'called upon' to intervene in domestic quarrels and break up loitering groups. He stops and frisks two or three times as many people as are carrying dangerous weapons or are actual criminals, and almost half of these don't wish to cooperate with the policeman's efforts."

Peter Rossi *et al.,* "Between Black and White—The Faces of American Institutions and the Ghetto," in Supplemental Studies for The National Advisory Commission on Civil Disorders, July 1968, p. 114.

[31] "In the Gordon Riots of 1780 demonstrators destroyed property and freed prisoners, but did not seem to kill anyone, while authorities killed several hundred rioters and hung an additional 25. In the Rebellion Riots of the French Revolution, though several hundred rioters were killed, they killed no one. Up to the end of the Summer of 1967, this pattern had clearly been repeated, as police, not rioters, were responsible for most of the more than 100 deaths that have occurred. Similarly, in a related context, the more than 100 civil rights murders of recent years have been matched by almost no murders of racist whites." G. Marx, "Civil Disorders and the Agents of Social Control," *op. cit.*

[32] Report of The National Advisory Commission on Civil Disorders, *op. cit.,* p. 321. That Black officers nevertheless would make a difference is suggested by data from one of the supplemental studies to the Kerner report. They found Negro policemen working in the ghettoes considerably more sympathetic to the community and its social problems than their white counterparts. Peter Rossi *et al.,* "Between Black and White—The Faces of American Institutions in the Ghetto," *op. cit.,* chap. 6.

[33] Eldridge Cleaver has called this first stage of the anti-colonial movement *community* liberation in contrast to a more long-range goal of *national* liberation. E. Cleaver, "Community Imperialism," Black Panther Party newspaper, 2, May 18, 1968.

[34] For a discussion of this failure to deal with racism, see Gary T. Marx, "Report of the National Commission: The Analysis of Disorder or Disorderly Analysis," 1968, unpublished paper.

[35] Such a statement is easier to assert than to document but I am attempting the latter in a forthcoming book tentatively titled *White Racism, Black Culture,* to be published by Little Brown, 1970.

[36] Report of The National Advisory Commission on Civil Disorders, *op. cit.,* pp. 253–256.

[37] Lee Rainwater, "The Revolt of the Dirty-Workers," *Trans-action,* 5, Nov., 1967, pp. 2, 64.

13

Confrontation at Cornell

WILLIAM H. FRIEDLAND AND HARRY EDWARDS

Bandoliers across their shoulders, rifles and shotguns casually held ready, the black students of Cornell broke into American consciousness one morning last April like an advance patrol of that army of barbarians which is the special nightmare of the affluent and, for some, their dream of regeneration. In that moment, fear—which everyone on the campus, both black and white, had known for days—rippled out and touched everyone.

Cornell seems an unlikely, not to say preposterous setting for such an event. Tucked away in rural upstate New York, the college until recently was comfortably settled in an atmosphere of genteel "waspishness." There was also an Ivy League rah-rah spirit about the place which only partially obscured the substantial number of lower-class youths who came to Ithaca under State University auspices to study agriculture, education and home economics. True, there had been a riot in 1958 (memorialized in Richard Farina's novel *Been Down So Long It Looks Like Up to Me*) over the right of students to have mixed parties without chaperons. But *political* activism came late to Cornell.

The trigger was pulled at Berkeley in 1964. After that, Cornell students began to organize themselves, somewhat feebly, into a group called Students For Education. SFE, before being washed away by the Vietnam escalation of 1965, brought into being a good many study commissions and some small changes, among them the conversion of the campus bookstore into a bookstore rather than a purveyor of required texts, setting up an on-campus coffee house, and some very limited changes in the grading system.

But as the Vietnam war went on and was intensified, students at Cornell, like those elsewhere, stepped up their protests. One major confrontation took place during an ROTC review in the college's cavernous Barton Hall, which later figured so importantly in the events of the Spring. Throughout this period, most student activism revolved around the Students for a Democratic Society. Like SDS everywhere, the Cornell group was anti-organizational, anti-leadership, using consensus decision-making procedures, committed to spontaneity. Despite this (or because of it), SDS has been remarkably efficient in mobilizing on the part of the students and a few faculty members.

The Race Issue

Until recently, the number of blacks at Cornell has been negligible. Indeed, into the early 1960's, those from outside the United States were far more numerous than American blacks. Furthermore, as at most American universities, the atmosphere at Cornell was almost unashamedly racist. Many fraternities, for example, constitu-

SOURCE: Reprinted from *Trans-action*, June, 1969, 6:29–36, 76, by permission of the authors and the publisher. Copyright © June, 1969, by Trans-action, Inc., New Brunswick, New Jersey.

153

tionally denied membership to non-Caucasians. But as the civil rights movement gathered force in the country, Cornell's liberals began to put pressure on the restrictive practices of the fraternities and tried to eliminate discrimination in off-campus housing. And Cornell students were among those who participated in the Freedom Summer of 1964, working on voter registration in Fayette County, Tennessee.

White involvement in civil rights activities fell off in 1965, however. The development of racial consciousness among blacks led to the belief that blacks had to make their own way and shed themselves of their white supporters if their movement was to be their own. Then, too, the escalation of the Vietnam war increasingly provided a focus for liberal and radical whites. At the same time, more significant changes were taking place at Cornell as the number of American black students began to increase. A Committee on Special Educational Projects (COSEP) was set up to locate and recruit black students and provide them with financial and other support. COSEP's success, while small, was such that by September 1968 there were 240 blacks at Cornell in a total of some 13,200.

But even before then, the presence of black students was causing considerable strain in the university. The separatist issue broke into the open when a black girl, living in the girls' dorms, experienced difficulties with her dormmates. The girl was referred to Cornell's clinic for psychiatric assistance and apparently found little sympathy there. Ordered to leave Cornell, she refused. This precipitated a crisis out of which came demands for separate housing so that blacks could be free of the pressures of living in a hostile environment. Reluctantly, the college made arrangements to establish several black co-ops.

Later, academic freedom seemed to many to be called into question when black students and others became convinced that a visiting professor was teaching racism. After complaining to every relevant agency of the university and being put off time after time, the blacks confronted the professor with the demand that he read a statement in class. When he insisted on reading it in advance and the blacks rejected this, he dismissed the class. The blacks thereupon sat in at the professor's department offices, holding the department chairman in his office.

Confrontation 1969: The Immediate Background

On that same day occurred the assassination of Martin Luther King and the two events provided the university community with a rarely experienced shock. In addition, several fires were set and later, blacks used Cornell's memorial service to King as an opportunity to attack the university and America's whites.

If nothing else, these events during the year 1967–68 indicated that the blacks at Cornell had layed a strong base for their organization which soon everyone would know as the Afro-American Society.

In response to events of the 1968 spring term, the university moved to set up an Afro-American studies program. Throughout the summer and fall a committee made up of nine faculty and administration members and eight black students met to work out the program. But in the second week of December the black students revolted against what they saw as stalling tactics. They demanded total control of the program and refused to cooperate any further with the existing committee. The same week, six members of the Afro-American Society forced three whites to leave their offices in a university building on Waite Avenue—a building that the administration had promised to the Afro-American studies program, and during the same affair a photographer for the *Cornell Daily Sun* was roughed up when he refused to turn over a film.

At the same time, however, covert negotiations between the black students and the administration continued over the demands for an autonomous black studies program, but little progress was made and the blacks saw this as another expression of Cornell's unwillingness to take their demands seriously. Consequently, one week before the Christmas recess, black students at Cornell staged a number of demonstrations. Groups of them marched around the quadrangles playing bongo drums, while another contingent entered the President's office with water pistols. They also pushed white students away from several tables in the student union and claimed them for themselves as "black tables." Another time, they carried hundreds of books from the library shelves to the checkout counters, and dumped them there as "irrelevant." They also went to the clinic and demanded treatment by a black physician. Despite their sometimes playful aspects, these demonstrations had an ugly and threatening undercurrent that left most whites tense. Nevertheless, the administration did move toward implementing a black studies program. Not all black demands were met, but a black was chosen to be acting director and compromises were worked out that made the program a degree-granting one. Another

consequence was that the black students saw their demonstrations as part of a political program necessary to help them gain a meaningful education at Cornell.

Still, the faculty and administration response to the demonstrations had been hostile and the process of finding scapegoats upon whom retribution might be visited got underway. In January, six students were charged before the Student-Faculty Conduct Board. The decision with respect to these students was one of the important factors leading to the 1969 confrontation.

The disciplinary issues were complicated by what happened during a conference on apartheid sponsored by Cornell's Center for International Studies. The 25 speakers, of whom only three were black, were not greeted sympathetically by an audience composed for the most part of Afro-Americans, black Africans, and SDS supporters. The latter moved rapidly from verbal hostility to more openly disruptive interventions. At a meeting on the second evening of the conference, the blacks turned out en masse to challenge Cornell President James Perkins on university investments in South Africa. As Perkins was speaking, one black student grabbed him by the collar and pulled him from the podium. Perkins, badly shaken, left the room. The campus reaction to this incident was hardly in favor of the blacks, despite the fact that there was an increasing sentiment that Cornell's endowments should be free of the taint of apartheid.

Meanwhile, preliminary to the trial of the six members of the Afro-American Society before the Student-Faculty Conduct Board, the AAS was claiming that the demonstrations of December had been political acts for which the organization should be held responsible. Selection of a few members could only be regarded as victimization. Accordingly, the six refused to appear before the Conduct Board. Then followed a period in which the six students were verbally threatened with suspension if they failed to appear before the Board. When they didn't show up, letters were sent. In April, just before the events that brought Cornell into the head-lines, an obscure clause was discovered that permitted the Conduct Board to take action without the black students being present. On April 18, the Conduct Board reprimanded three of the blacks, dismissed charges against two others, while the charge against the last student was dropped because of his departure from the university.

Throughout this period, campus groups had been enunciating principles to support their positions on the issues involved. For the Conduct Board (and implicitly for the faculty and much of the student body) the issue raised was: Is the university a single community? If it is *a* community, must all "citizens" adhere to its rules? The blacks not only challenged the idea of *a* community but put forward the principle that no man should be judged except by a jury of his peers. The blacks also chal-lenged the legitimacy of the Board, con-tending it was not a voluntary product of the campus community but one imposed by the racist apparatus of American society. In partial justification of their statement, the Afro-Americans pointed out that there was no black representation on the Board. A second conflict of principle arose over the issue of how personal, in contrast to political, acts could be judged. Some university groups argued that individuals rather than organizations had to be held responsible for their acts; organizations could not be tried before the Conduct Board. The blacks asserted

the reverse was true: their actions were political, therefore their responsibility was collective. The blacks also argued that the university was not only the aggrieved party but the judge and jury as well, and prin-ciples of Anglo-Saxon justice declared that this should not be done. The Afro-American Society suggested that "arbi-tration" as in industrial-relations might be the appropriate model for a resolution of the problem.

In addition to the disciplinary issue, a number of other questions were deeply troubling to numbers of both students and faculty. During their seizure of the Waite Avenue building the blacks had insisted that their demands for an Afro-American studies program were "nonnegotiable." This was pure rhetoric, negotiations were going on through intermediaries, and most people knew it. Nevertheless, many faculty members interpreted the position of the blacks as needlessly intransigent. The black separatism issue had not gone down well with much of the university community either, especially those tables in the student union which had been claimed as black territory. Blacks moved around the campus in groups and were never found fraternizing with whites. This was upsetting to most faculty and students.

While attention centered on the blacks during the spring, a host of other issues affected large numbers of white students. SDS had made demands that the university provide housing not only for students but for the Ithaca community. Arguing that Cornell had thrown the burden of housing upon the community, SDS insisted that the university provide low-cost housing units for underprivileged groups in Ithaca. This issue generated considerable support in faculty and student circles: a network of housing organizations was created to bring pressures for a university commitment. A second issue burgeoned over the impending departure of several noted historians and humanities professors. Humanities has not been strong at Cornell; it is not an area to which the administration has paid any serious attention. So the issue was one that mobilized many Arts and Sciences students. Still other grievances were those of graduate assistants over financial support, and Cornell's South African investments. And, in mid-April, just before the confrontation, a popular sociology professor, one of the first winners of a teaching award, was, refused tenure because of his weak publication record.

These issues, and others, created an atmosphere of tension that threatened to come to a crisis on Wednesday, March 12, when the university faculty was scheduled to meet. But when the day came, the faculty adopted a resolution supporting the integrity of the adjudicatory machinery of the Conduct Board and the situation continued to bubble with neither confrontation nor resolution.

Confrontation 1969: The Seizure of the Student Union

At 3:00 a.m. on the morning of Friday, April 18, persons still unknown threw a burning cross on the porch of the black girls' co-operative. Responding to a call, the campus safety patrol reached the co-op where the fire was stamped out. What exactly the campus safety patrol did at the scene of the cross-burning is not clear, but apparently all seven officers covering the incident withdrew, ostensibly on other business, leaving no protection at the

co-op. Much later, a guard was established, but by that time the blacks had evidently lost any confidence they may have had in campus protection. This was to be exacerbated as campus officials, while strongly deploring the incident, referred to it as a "thoughtless prank." To the blacks, the symbolism of the event was as powerful as if someone had burned a *Mogen David* in front of a Jewish fraternity. Had such a thing occurred, the blacks reasoned, all the powers of the university would have been brought to bear and the cries of outrage would have been mighty indeed. As it was, the somewhat cavalier attitudes of the university seemed still another reflection of institutional racism, less open perhaps than the occasional group of white boys who had shouted "nigger" at black girls, but racism it was, nevertheless.

As word of the cross-burning spread among the blacks, they assembled at the co-op to decide what action was necessary to protect their women. The defense of their own kind, this was to become a central symbol of the events that followed. As for their choice of target—the student union at Willard Straight Hall, this was in part dictated by the dramatic possibilities implicit in the fact that Parents' Weekend had begun and the opportunity to demonstrate before thousands of parents was tactically so tempting that rumors had been circulating that some group would seize some building somewhere regardless of the issue. How significant a role the rumors played in the deliberations of the blacks is not known, but the tactical impact of the seizure was clear. But it is clear that in deciding to take over the student union, the blacks were intent only on giving an emphatic warning to the campus to "get off our backs," they were not concerned with specific demands. Indeed, the original intent was to seize the building for one day only and then surrender it peaceably.

At 6:00 a.m. on Saturday, April 19, the blacks marched into Willard Straight Hall, calmly ordered service personnel preparing for the day's activities to remove themselves, expelled from guest rooms in the loft a number of visiting parents, and locked up the building.

News of the seizure soon spread throughout the campus; by 8:00 a.m. everyone knew the university was on the brink of another confrontation. For many of the students, particularly those at either end of the political spectrum, having an audience of parents probably served as a stimulus to action. The conservative students tend to be concentrated in a small number of houses that remain "lily-white" and in the fraternities. One of these, Delta Upsilon, is known as the "jock house," because of its unusual number of athletes. It is also one of the most "waspish" houses and at present includes no Negro members. Around 9:00 in the morning, about 15 to 20 DU members attempted to break into Straight Hall, and some eight or nine succeeded in getting in before a group of SDS people prevented the rest from entering. While a good deal of pushing, shoving, and arguing was going on outside, inside there was a brief but violent battle between the blacks and the DU men. Three whites and one black were injured, no one seriously. The battle ended with the expulsion of the fraternity boys, but the blacks, even though badly shaken, announced that any other attack would be met by mounting escalation of force. SDS members, standing outside in sympathy with the blacks, rejected a proposal to seize another building and maintained

a picket around the entire building to show their support.

The DU attack can be, and was, interpreted in various ways. But from the viewpoint of the blacks, it represented a university attempt to oust them from the building. The campus patrol was supposed to have been guarding the building to prevent entry. Therefore, the fact that the DU people had gotten in was all too easily understood by the blacks as administrative complicity, rather than what it probably was—a spontaneous, self-organized attempt by frat boys. For their part, the DU men insisted that they had entered the building to engage in discussion with black athletes inside and that there was no intent to recapture the building. (There is no evidence, however, that there were ever any black athletes involved in the seizure of the student union.) The DU men claimed that they went in empty-handed; the blacks insisted that they came in with clubs.

Following this incident, the campus gave itself up to an orgy of rumors. Throughout the day, it was circulated about that armed vigilante groups were preparing to mount an attack on Straight Hall. Inside the Hall, the blacks received continuous telephone messages about these vigilantes. By Saturday afternoon, according to the testimony of the blacks and the administrators in telephone contact with them, the occupiers were in a state of terrible tension. It was then that they decided to bring in guns to protect themselves. In the end, they were to have 13 rifles, and two shotguns.

Saturday night passed quietly, but the tension throughout the campus was approaching a critical point. By Sunday morning, Cornell administrators had decided that it would be necessary to end the occupation of the Straight at almost any cost.

That the occupation of the Straight was a precipitous act, probably triggered by the cross-burning, is attested to, first, by the lengthy time it took the blacks to formulate demands; and, second, the relatively flimsy nature of the demands. By Saturday afternoon, three had emerged from Willard Straight, of which one was subsequently withdrawn. The first demand called for a nullification of the three reprimands handed down by the Conduct Committee after the demonstrations of December; the second called for a full investigation and report of the Afro-American Society of the cross-burning incident. That the blacks would take such very serious steps for such tired and modest demands indicates their state of fear and tension. But this was never communicated to the campus, except to those in the administration, Dean Robert Miller especially, who were in direct contact with them. With the latter, the blacks entered into a six-point agreement to end the Straight occupation. It included a commitment to call a full faculty meeting and recommend that the reprimands be declared null and void.

However, the occupiers of Straight Hall were still determined to demonstrate to Cornell whites that they were no longer sitting ducks. So it was that despite pressure from administrators for a decorous exit, the blacks proceeded to make a dramatic exit, brandishing their weapons. It soon became convenient for the shocked white majority of the university to look upon this as a new escalation in student activism; while campus after campus had experienced confrontation, it was argued that this was the first time that students had taken up guns. It was within this context that Cornell arrived at a new level of internal tension on Monday, April 21.

Confrontation 1969: Into the Crucible

The sight of armed students marching across their campus was too much for the overwhelming majority of the faculty. Unable to understand, or ignorant of, the black students' side of the story, their immediate reaction on Monday, April 21, was one of bitter hostility to any compromise or accommodation of black demands. Their antagonism focused on the six-point agreement reached between the administration and the blacks. Some forty members of the faculty, largely in the government and history departments, signed a statement declaring they would resign if the reprimands were nullified at the Monday faculty meeting.

Tension increased during the day as the opposition to nullification crystallized in the faculty. What the reaction of the blacks would be to a refusal to nullify was unclear, but there was an unspoken and widespread fear that Cornell might be headed toward some kind of shoot-out. In these circumstances, President Perkins called a convocation in Barton Hall just before the university faculty meeting. Some 10,000 students, faculty and staff assembled to hear an innocuous 20-minute statement by the President that left issues more undefined than before. There had been an expectation that presidential leadership was to be asserted.

Instead, in an atmosphere of diffuse fear and anger, in which the focused hostility of the government and history departments stood out, the faculty assembled at 4:00 p.m. in unprecedented numbers. The meeting began with a report by Dean of the Faculty, Robert Miller, who introduced a formal motion calling for nullification of the reprimands. The Dean's assessment was that the danger to human life at Cornell was real and had to be avoided even at the cost of failing to sustain the authority of the adjudicatory machinery, the Conduct Board. This approach was rejected by the faculty. Instead, they voted a substitute motion that upheld the legitimacy of the adjudicatory machinery and took no action on the nullification of the reprimands. Continuing for over four hours of intricate parliamentary maneuvers, the faculty meeting showed that the majority was adamantly opposed to nullification, but there was also an obdurate, vocal minority supporting the blacks or concerned with the consequences of refusal to nullify. President Perkins had little political capital at this meeting despite his earlier proclamation of limited emergency, a statement that anyone carrying guns on university property would be suspended summarily, or that disruptive demonstrations would lead to immediate suspensions. Nevertheless, he was able to achieve minimal consensus with a resolution calling for the initiation of discussions between the Faculty Council and the Afro-American Society and calling for another full faculty meeting.

Dean Miller now tendered his resignation, stating that by the refusal to vote on his motion, the faculty was repudiating his estimate of the situation. He was promptly given a standing ovation, which neatly illustrated the faculty's dilemma. They respected him and wanted peace, but they felt they had to refuse to make concessions under what they saw as the threat of armed coercion. As the meeting ended at 8:15 and the faculty departed for long-delayed dinners, there was the sense that no solution had been found and that the campus was entering a new and more dangerous situation.

On Monday evening, SDS called a meeting attended by 2,500, but it ended inconclusively. SDS was waiting for the blacks.

The Campus in Chaos

By Tuesday morning the campus was in chaos. Many classes did not meet, and in those that did the only topics were those raised by the confrontation. The university leadership, seeking desperately to remedy a deteriorating situation, consulted the deans of the colleges and proposed meetings of college faculties and the beginning of a broad-based discussion at all levels. The intent was to structure free-floating campus anxieties into organized meetings geared to a search for solutions. In the leadership vacuum created by the conflict between the administration's willingness to make concessions and an obdurate faculty, the administration sought only to keep a dialogue going. The fear of bloodshed was everywhere.

At noon, an ephemeral organization named "The Concerned Faculty," consisting largely of elements supporting the blacks, convened for several hours. Urged on by members of the Afro-American Society, "The Concerned Faculty" were unable to decide on anything more than gestures of solidarity. Twenty-six of those attending agreed to seize a building if necessary, while some 60-odd announced their willingness to strike.

Meanwhile, however, at meetings of the faculties of the various colleges, an apparent change in campus opinion began to be felt. The colleges of Arts and Sciences and Home Economics voted to recommend nullification of the Conduct Board's reprimands, and at its 7:00 p.m. meeting, the Faculty Council did the same, while calling for another meeting of the faculty for Wednesday noon. But several other faculties were still determined to maintain business as usual.

That same Tuesday, student opinion on campus began crystallizing around a call by SDS and the Inter-Fraternity Council for a teach-in at Barton Hall, the largest building on campus. By early evening, thousands of students had begun moving to the Hall. Like the faculty, they too seemed intent on avoiding violence between the blacks and other forces. Somewhere between 8,000 to 10,000 people gathered there and as the evening went on, a consensus emerged that it was vital for Cornell students to remain in the building and act as a pressure group on the Cornell faculty, which was scheduled to meet the next day, Wednesday, April 23. SDS speakers proposed that the students declare that they had seized the building, thereby defying President Perkins' new regulation prohibiting such actions. Only a handful objected, and later in the evening Perkins condoned the occupation of Barton Hall, though he persisted in defining it as a teach-in rather than as the seizure the students had declared it to be. This "legal" anomaly continued through the night. Thousands made preparations for the all-night meeting; a collection was taken and soon sandwiches and drinks were being passed out among the teeming mass of students.

As the evening of Tuesday, April 22 wore on, students organized according to their colleges to lobby faculty members for their vote on Wednesday. Around the edges of the Hall, there were dozens of meetings involving tens and hundreds of students. At 3:00 a.m. meetings were still

continuing; they included not only groups from different colleges, but various ad hoc committees on the press, particularly the *Sun,* the university's student operated newspaper. One large group of biology students was attempting to deal with the problem of a professor who refused to cancel a quiz scheduled for the next day. The mood in Barton Hall was tensely hopeful; that such an incredible outpouring of students could take place showed that student sentiment had shifted to the blacks, although it was less clear whether the shift had occurred for substantive reasons or because of the fear of violence.

On Wednesday, April 23, the students were wakened by a banjo ensemble and the speech-making began again in the Hall. Elsewhere on the campus, hundreds of meetings were taking place as faculty members were visited by student lobbyists.

Soon after the faculty meeting was gavelled into session by Provost Dale Corson, it became evident that a clear shift had occurred among the members. Despite hardline speeches by government and history faculty members, a motion to nullify was replaced by a second motion which not only called for nullification but also for restructuring the university. The substitute was introduced by Professor Clinton Rossiter who had signed, only two days before, the statement threatening resignation if the reprimands were nullified. Biology professor William Keaton explained how a large delegation of his students from Barton Hall had asked him to change his vote, not because of the threat of violence, but because they wanted him to have faith in them. But the probable major reason for the shift was expressed by Nobel physicist, Hans Bethe, who said that since the moderates were moving toward the SDS left, it was necessary for the faculty to reverse itself to occupy the middle ground and isolate radicals. The resolution calling for nullification and restructuring the university carried by a voice vote probably on the order of three or four to one. The faculty now accepted a resolution by philosopher Max Black informing the students, "We hear you. . . ."

A thousand faculty members then moved to Barton Hall where they received a standing ovation. The faculty action demonstrated to the students the latter's influence on the decision-making process; from this point, emphasis shifted to the second part of the Rossiter resolution on restructuring the university.

As the faculty arrived, Eric Evans, vice president of the Afro-American Society was talking. President Perkins came to the podium where, according to Evans, he put his arm around him, smiled in fatherly fashion, and said "Sit down, I want to talk." Evans refused to surrender the microphone. Nothing better demonstrated the students' new mood than the hilarious cheering that broke out when Evans informed them of this exchange. While Perkins fidgeted uncomfortably on the floor with the students and faculty, Evans continued a leisurely review of events leading up to the Willard Straight seizure. When he finished, Perkins spoke and was followed by a succession of others. Slowly the Barton Hall meeting achieved a catharsis from the tensions of the past five days. By 5:00 p.m. the teach-in had ended. Cornell now entered a new phase ostensibly dedicated to a restructuring of the university.

Foundations of the Next Confrontation

The period immediately following the Barton Hall catharsis was characterized by what can only be called organizational withdrawal symptoms. The most dramatic occurred within SDS which either could not or would not come to grips with its lack of organization and need for leadership. The faculty, too, lost the capacity to function coherently as a corporate body. The Afro-Americans managed to rename themselves the Black Liberation Front but otherwise they also retreated into themselves to try to decide how to relate to the college community under the new circumstances.

Administration officials and traditionally apathetic students also withdrew. The administration was in a state of shock; all that emerged from Day Hall, the administration building, were generalized statements reinforcing previous statements about guns and disruptive demonstrations. Beyond that, Day Hall demonstrated no capacity to provide any structure, guidance, or direction. As for the students, once catharsis had been achieved on Wednesday they lost the capacity to act.

Traditional Structure

In these circumstances, the tendency was to revert to the traditional, though weakened, institutional structure. Students and faculty turned to colleges and departments, that is, to more manageable social units. With this, the cooling-off process began. It was not that everyone's behavior was as in the past, but students once again came into direct face-to-face relations with teachers, to whom they had always exhibited deference. In a (crude) word, the "reniggerization" of the students had begun.

But the cooling-off took time. It was a week before student statements became more qualified and less concrete and hard-line. Faculty statements, too, became tougher as the teachers reverted to traditional issues of teaching vs. research, academic freedom, and the like.

What this means is that any action with respect to change in university structure, functioning, and priorities will be based on traditional university norms and values. Moreover, the summer will be used as a cooling-off period. Once again there will be the gradual accretion of "data," the rational consideration of infinitesimal details. This does not mean that the faculty will be unwilling to change at all; rather that change will be oriented toward maintaining basic structures. Cooptation of student dissidents will become the major mechanicism for attempting to alleviate pressure, for it is evident that the major emphasis is now on alleviating pressure, not solving problems. More fundamental commitment to change in the governance of the university or the educational process remains small.

In the weeks following the adjournment of Barton Hall, the administration, the students, and the faculty have been inadvertently laying the foundation for the next confrontation by reversion to old structures.

But first, it is perhaps worth a short digression to examine why so few black students at Cornell have been able to create such enormous pressures (and we limit ourselves to Cornell here, although some of this analysis is appropriate to black-student experience at other universities).

There is, first of all, a reservoir of readily exploitable guilt in liberal academic circles, but much more depends upon the social situation of a relatively small number of blacks resident in an overwhelmingly white university. All students experience adaptation and living problems in residential universities. Thrown together

for long periods of intensive community living and having to navigate a host of curricular and extracurricular problems and opportunities, most students have to find ways of making it all manageable.

As blacks increased at Cornell they experienced the usual problems that blacks undergo in a white environment. But the present generation of black collegians entered the university just as black-power ideology began to affect black intellectuals. This, and the antipathy they felt on the part of the whites, led black students into closer and more intensive relations with each other. The coalescence was further intensified by such incidents as that of whites yelling "nigger" at black girls. Each incident was stored away and became the subject of continual discussion. In these circumstances, black students began to act against their environment and their number was exactly right for the maximum cohesiveness needed to generate pressures. If larger number of blacks were present, this cohesiveness would be difficult, if not impossible.

But the main grounds on which we would predict further troubles for Cornell are the discrepancies between student hopes for change and the structural inabilities of universities to obtain significant change, especially in the educational process. This will create serious problems because the demand of students for restructuring the learning process remains unresolved. At the same time, the social conditions contributing to this demand also remain unresolved: poverty, discrimination, racism, the war in Vietnam, continue and are interpreted, probably correctly, as worsening. Most students are naive in that they think university reform will take place by itself, and many believe that something tangible will come out of Barton Hall. As students realize that little or nothing can emerge, they will find themselves increasingly frustrated.

The specific issue that will trigger the next action can come from a variety of sources: recruitment by employers (which most universities will not eliminate because a majority of students want it), pressures for open recruitment of blacks or other deprivileged groups, financial shortages as alumni react against campus actions, relations with the surrounding community, university investments, and so on. Thus, the institutional inabilities to change rapidly and drastically practically guarantee new confrontations in the next academic year at Cornell.

PART SIX Social Organization

The study of social organization may be approached from a number of levels. In its most broad sense, social organization may refer to the broad social institutions such as economics, family, government, and religion. In a narrower sense it may refer to formalized bureaucratic organizations set up to carry out limited functions. A third level of social organization refers to the informal structure which arises out of individuals interacting.

The first article in this section, "Work Behavior in a Service Industry" by Dean Harper and Frederick Emmert, discusses the formalized bureaucratic structure of the United States Postal System and the manner by which the formalized rules and regulations are partially subverted by the informal development of unofficial norms and standards. In light of the 1970 postal strike for higher wages, this article should prove interesting to many. The second article, written by Walter Gerson, describes the sorority as a social system, and discusses the mechanisms by which the system is perpetuated. The concluding selection, by Julian Roebuck and S. Lee Spray, illustrates the functions of a cocktail lounge and the informal organization of individuals which develops through continued interaction.

14

Work Behavior in a Service Industry

DEAN HARPER AND FREDERICK EMMERT

Industrial sociologists have described in detail the organization of work behavior of those in manufacturing and production industries. These studies have outlined the formal or official organization of activities on the assembly line or in the shop and have indicated how an informal or unofficial organization of work activities develops to supplement, modify, or oppose the formal organization.[1] However, little work has been done on workers in service industries which is comparable to that obtained from research on manufacturing and production workers.[2]

This paper will be concerned with the organization of work behavior in one large public service industry—the postal service.[3] It will focus on the recurring patterns of behavior of postal workers and on how these are determined by the official rules and regulations supplemented and modified by unofficial norms and standards. The purpose of this paper is (1) to contribute to the literature of industrial sociology a further illustration of the emergence of unofficial organization in an official context and (2) to make some theoretical observations on the factors underlying this behavior. By providing a further example of this phenomena the range of situations where such behavior is found will be extended. This, in turn, should contribute to a better understanding of such behavior.

The example which will be reported in this paper has been drawn from the authors' research on the postal service. Attention will be focused on the work behavior of those who occupy one particular position in the postal service; that is the letter carrier or as he is labeled by the general public—the mail man. Two aspects of the organization of behavior of the letter carrier will be described. These are the organization of behavior involved in sorting and delivering mail and the concomitant hierarchies of personnel.

The data for this paper were obtained by (1) participant observation, (2) interviews with postal employees, (3) discrete observation of letter carriers at work and (4) the examination of various written materials dealing with the Post Office Department or its workers. All of the various observations except those involving the written materials were made on letter carriers who worked out of one Post Office and its branch stations in a large eastern city. Strictly speaking, then, these observations hold only for the behavior of postal workers in this one city. However, interviews with those who had experience working in the Post Offices of other cities and areas of the country suggest that the descriptions presented here would apply for most letter carriers working in large urban residential areas throughout the country; at most, the specific details vary from place to place.

By the organization of behavior or social organization is meant that there are certain

SOURCE: Reprinted from *Social Forces*, December, 1963, 42:216–225, by permission of the authors and the University of North Carolina Press.

patterns of repetitive, recurring behavior. It is meant that in a group or in society there is a division of labor, that certain individuals perform certain activities which are different from those activities which others perform. This notion further denotes that individuals have certain relationships to each other which vary according to where the individuals are located in the group.

An alternative way of referring to the organization of behavior in the postal service is to say that the Post Office has a *social structure*. The elements in this structure are *positions* or *statuses*. The relationship between these elements is a behavioral one. It consists of the set of *role expectations* which define what is appropriate behavior for an individual who is occupying one status in the post office in his interactions with an individual who is occupying another status.

These patterns of repetitive, recurring behavior develop because of the existence of the role expectations. However, these role expectations are not all of the same type. One important distinction has to do with whether the expectations are *explicit* or *implict*. In a bureaucratic organization such as the Post Office there develop rules and regulations, job descriptions, organizational charts, policy pronouncements, and so on. These all represent codified or explicit role expectations. These are official definitions of appropriate behavior and carry the sanctions of the bureaucracy. These explicit expectations are supplemented and modified by a set of implicit expectations. Workers, in their mutual interactions and primary group affiliations, create a set of implicit role expectations. These expectations are not codified; they exist only in the minds of the interacting individuals. They are unofficial; they are sanctioned by small

primary groups of workers. Behavior is geared to these implicit expectations as much as it is to the explicit expectations. Hence, the actual patterns of behavior of group members is partly determined by the explicit expectations and partly by the implicit expectations.

The Sorting and Delivery of Mail

The official job of the letter carrier is to sort incoming mail for those on his route, to deliver it, to collect mail deposited in collection boxes along his route, and to perform various duties associated with these activities. Before describing the official rules which specify how this should be done and indicating how the letter carrier actually performs his duties, a brief description of the typical career of the letter carrier will be given.

The Career of the Letter Carrier

The carrier applicant who passes the Civil Service examination and accepts employment is first appointed as a substitute carrier. He is paid on an hourly basis and is assured a minimum of two hours of work a day. His main duties are to serve as a substitute carrier on the route of a regular carrier when the regular carrier has his day off, is sick, or on vacation; in this he will work a number of different routes, moving about the city from day to day.[4] In addition, the substitute carrier works two or three evenings a week collecting mail. He also can on occasion be pressed into work as a distribution clerk. As regular carriers retire or die, routes become available for reassignment. The substitute carrier with seniority is promoted to a salaried regular carrier position and temporarily assigned to the vacant route. Periodically all such vacant routes are bid for by regular carriers; each route goes to the carrier with seniority. There is considerable variability in the recruitment problems of different local Post Offices. In some areas of the country a substitute is able to obtain a regular route of his own after a few months; in other areas it may take him up to three years.

The next step in the career of the carrier, if he is motivated to seek promotion, is to a supervisory position. Those appointed to supervisory positions are selected by each local postmaster from the list of postal employees who have successfully passed Civil Service tests. A further aspect of the career of some letter carriers is a second job. Since the postal work day of most carriers ends at 3:30, a number of them work at second jobs.[5]

The Official Organization of Work Behavior

The activities of the letter carrier are circumscribed by various prescriptions and proscriptions. First, activities are determined by the order book for the carrier's route. This is a book which states pertinent information about the carrier, indicates the time he is to report to work, leave for his route, return from it, and to quit work. It further indicates the streets on his route, the order in which they are to be walked, how these streets are broken down for bundling mail, which bundles are to be put in which relay boxes and the time at which uncanceled mail is to be collected from the collection boxes along the route. It further lists all patrons who have moved in the last two years and their forwarding addresses; "special orders" such as withholding mail for certain patrons for brief periods of time are also indicated. Hence,

each letter carrier has his activities rigidly prescribed by a route order book.

Second, the behavior of the postal carrier is further determined by rules and regulations of the Postal Manual (which contains Postal Laws and rules prescribed by the Postmaster General by virtue of prerogatives granted him by Congress) and by directives and orders periodically promulgated by the Postmaster General or his assistants.

Some of the important general official rules which define the activities of the letter carrier can be paraphrased as follows:

1. The carrier will deliver mail in the sequence indicated in the order book and will follow the special orders.
2. Carriers are not to use private vehicles for carrying their mail unless they have a mounted route where such use is authorized.
3. Mail is to be placed only in the proper receptacle or given to a definitely known or identified recipient.
4. All mail is to be delivered on the day of reception by the carrier unless instructions to the contrary are received.
5. Mail must never be delayed by the carrier. No one is allowed to intercept it or handle it unless authorized.
6. Carriers are not to walk across grass nor any area except the standard sidewalks.

Supervision of the Letter Carrier

The carrier's work is supervised in several ways. First, of course, is the day-to-day supervision from his immediate superiors. In the larger post offices this includes the carrier superintendent and a greater or lesser number of personnel intermediate in the hierarchy. This supervision frequently tends to be nominal. It arises when the carrier is informed of rule changes, complaints of patrons, and so on.

The "annual count" provides a further means of supervising the carrier. Once each year the carrier's work is officially checked. He is observed in "casing the mail," i.e., sorting the mail for his patrons. He must do this accurately and at a given minimum rate. His delivery of the mail is also observed. He must deliver the mail in the time allotted, in the order specified in his order book and following departmental rules. The annual count not only serves as a check upon the carrier's performance, but it also serves as a basis for making modifications in the route—lengthening or shortening it.

In addition, the postal worker is "supervised" by postal inspectors. (One of the bureaus in the Post Office Department is that of Postal Inspection. Postal Inspectors oversee the activities of postal personnel, as well as the activities of users of the postal service, relative to fraudulent and illegal activities.) In large post offices there is a catwalk near the ceiling from which postal inspectors observe the handling of mail. Postal inspectors occasionally check on the carrier while he is on his route. They also "seed" the mails by depositing a letter in a collection box shortly before the stated collection time; this is done to determine if the carrier is collecting mail before the prescribed time.

Officially, the Department is equally adamant about all rules and regulations, although some regulations are more important than others as evidenced by the different sanctions applied or threatened. The major sanctions used by the Department are suspension from duty, loss of job, and fine or imprisonment. Those rules which are considered most inviolate, obviously, have to do with theft of mail and withholding delivery of mails. Violation of rules dealing with these matters calls for the strongest

sanctions, which at the very minimum is the loss of job. Periodically, a letter carrier may be suspended from duty for minor rule infractions such as taking too much time for lunch. Within the Department this is publicized so that other letter carriers will be reminded that deviations do not go unpunished. Although Department officials are aware of the violations of official rules and are aware of the unofficially prescribed patterns of behavior (to be described below), it is difficult for them to detect specific instances of deviance. Hence a large amount of rule violation is undetected and unpunished.

Unofficial Work Rules

Above were listed the more important official work rules. The behavior of most letter carriers deviates, to a greater or lesser degree, from all of these rules. In some instances this deviation results from the presence of conflicting unofficial work rules. Some of this deviant behavior is similar to the "restriction of output" observed in manufacturing enterprises.[6]

One of these unofficial work rules has to do with the way a route is worked. Recall that for each route the order book clearly and precisely states how the mail will be sorted, how it will be combined into bundles and the order in which it will be delivered. This "job description" is devised so that on the average it will take the carrier about eight hours to sort and deliver the mail. However, the unofficial norm develops which states that each carrier will reorganize his route so that it can be walked in the most convenient and fastest time possible. This means that even on the heaviest of mail days the carrier who reorganizes his route is likely to finish it before the allotted time. The question can be asked: how is this so? How can a route be timed inaccurately? If a carrier can work a route faster than it has been originally timed, then certainly this should be evident when the route is retimed.

This situation comes about because a carrier walks his route in one way when he is being timed and a different way when he is not being timed. Other studies have detailed how machinists, in dealing with time-and-motion study men in a factory, can have a piece of work timed for a longer period of time than it really takes to adequately do; the machinist does this by adding "embellishments" to the way he does the job when being timed which he does not use otherwise.[7] A letter carrier also embellishes his work performance when he is being timed. These embellishments consist of following the official work rules. The carrier conforms to the official work rules when he is being timed and violates them at other times. Recall that the official work rules state that the carrier should follow the order book in delivering mail, that he should use public transportation and not his own car in getting to and from his route and in carrying and delivering mail (unless he has a mounted route in which such is prescribed), that he should not walk across lawns and that he should deliver all mail on the day he receives it unless otherwise instructed by the appropriate postal authorities. Each of these four rules is frequently violated by most carriers in the regular course of working their routes.

In the first place the carrier violates the rule about following the order book; he alters the order in which he delivers the mail. The way he alters it depends upon the physical aspects of his route. He may find it more convenient to criss-cross the street when his order book states that he should deliver one side of the street and then the other. The order book prescribes certain loops in his delivery route in order to return to relay boxes to pick up mail; he may alter this looping arrangement. His route is usually organized so that each stop at a relay box results in a full satchel of mail. He may alter this so that he makes frequent stops at the relay box, each time picking up only as much mail as he can carry without a satchel; a carrier can walk his route much faster without 25 to 35 pounds of mail on his back. Thus, there are a number of ways in which the carrier alters the order of mail delivery on his route and consequently shortens the time it takes to walk the route.

Second, the carrier's automobile may be used for the route. Many carriers use them as transportation to and from the route. On the route it may be used as a "mobile relay box"—being moved from one part of the route to another as bundles of mail are removed from it. This saves time because the carrier does not have to walk back to relay boxes covering a block of houses he has already delivered. If a route contains empty fields, lots, factories, such that patrons are sparsely distributed over a large area, then the carrier has considerable walking to do. Here the use of an automobile saves time. However, even if the automobile is used only as transportation to and from the route, time is still saved.

Third, the carrier frequently violates the rule about walking on lawns. Wherever it will save time, most carriers walk from house to house by cutting across lawns rather than using sidewalks. Of course, some patrons request that the carriers not do this and most carriers abide by these requests.

Fourth, the carrier occasionally violates the rule about delivering all mail each day.

On a few heavy mail days the Superintendent of Mails at the local Post Office may indicate that certain third-class bulk mail (e.g., advertising circulars sent to every household in the city) can be held until the following day in order to "even out" the amount of mail delivered on different days. More frequently, as the carrier sorts his mail, he may decide that it is too heavy on that particular day and that some second or third class mail should be held until the following day. Further, when he is walking his route and a particular patron may have only one or two pieces of mail, the carrier may decide not to deliver to that patron but to withhold it until the following day. (This is referred to as "backslapping" the mail; the letter is put at the bottom of the stack of letters the carrier sorts through as he walks along. The phrase "taking it for a ride" is also used to refer to this practice.) By not having to deliver that patron and a number of such patrons, the carrier can save time. First class mail is seldom withheld; most of the time carriers are quite responsible in seeing that it is delivered on the day it is received. Most of the "back-slapped" mail is second and third class mail.

The question of what the carrier does with the saved time naturally arises. There are a variety of ways the carrier spends the hour or so which he may be able to save. If the carrier lives near his route, he goes home and then returns to the station near the officially prescribed time. He may spend the time shopping. He may join fellow carriers at a nearby restaurant or tavern. He may sit in his car and read. Further, the time saved may not all be used after the mail is delivered. A lunch period of thirty minutes is officially prescribed. The carrier frequently extends this to an hour or more.

Associated with the unofficial norm of walking a route in the most convenient and fastest manner is another norm about returning to the station. Even if a carrier has finished his route early, he should not return to the station too soon before the time prescribed in his order book (usually 2:30 p.m.); and if he returns early he should not do so too frequently. If he does return early too frequently, then this is interpreted by his supervisor that his route is too short and must be lengthened. Carriers try to adjust their time of return according to the amount of mail they have delivered. As one substitute stated:

> The amount of free time is generally maintained a constant by carriers. When the mail takes longer to deliver we return to the station later. If you return at the same time every day, whether it's a light day or a heavy day, they might think something is fishy.

When a regular substitute or summer substitute is assigned to work a route, this role expectation is strongly emphasized and reemphasized in such terms as "Don't kill the route." The substitute carrier should not be better than the regular carrier at working the regular carrier's route; rather it should take him longer. Therefore, the substitute should return somewhat later than the prescribed time.

Violation of this last unofficial rule by the substitute is readily observable to all. The major sanction used by letter carriers is that of making the job more difficult for the deviating carrier. This is done by either withholding information from him or by deliberately interfering with his work activity. When the substitute carrier who is known to be deviant ("fence-jumper" is the letter carrier's term for "rate-buster") is assigned to take over a particular route and he asks how the route is worked by the regular carrier, he is told that it is all in the order book. When he asks about patrons and patrons' dogs,[8] he meets with silence; this is referred to by the regular carriers as "feeding him to the dogs." If the substitute carrier still deviates from the unofficial work rules, then the regular carriers apply further pressures by subtly interfering with his work. The mail which is tied and sacked is trucked to relay boxes. Each mail sack has a label put on it indicating to the driver where it should be taken. When the substitute carrier finds that the labels on his mail sacks have been switched, he has to walk over his entire route searching for the mail sacks which have been placed in the wrong relay boxes. These tactics are usually sufficient to enforce conformity to the informal work rules.

It should not be concluded from this discussion that *all* carriers violate the rules in this way; nor should it be concluded that *all* carriers violate the rules to the same extent. However, the descriptions above characterize, to a greater or lesser extent, the behavior of many carriers.

There are a number of other similar patterns which can be described; one further pattern will be indicated. The mounted carrier is one who delivers mail from his car placing it in roadside mailboxes. He generally works in an expanding residential area. Because of this expansion, his route may require more than eight hours to complete on "heavy days." Whether a particular day is "heavy" or not is determined by supervisory personnel. Days which are classified as "heavy mail" days by the carrier's supervisor are days when the mounted carrier is certified for overtime pay and when a substitute carrier is assigned to assist him. Because of this the mounted carrier desires that a maximum of days be defined as "heavy mail" days.

This involves a struggle between the mounted carrier and his supervisor; it requires concerted action on the part of the mounted carriers. In one branch station which was examined, the mounted carriers had developed a norm of accepting no fewer than four "heavy mail" days in the six day work-week regardless of what the real volume of mail was during those six days. This struggle arose in the mounted carriers' collective efforts to obtain from their supervisors, definitions of the mail being heavy so that this goal of four heavy mail days a week was met. The strategy used by mounted carriers is *to act as if* the mail is heavy regardless of its real volume. Mail is dumped from sacks into a tub and then sorted from the tub. On those days which the carriers want defined as heavy, they will place the bulkier, heavier pieces of mail on the bottom of the tub and the thinner, smaller pieces on top. This gives an appearance of more pieces of mail than in reality. The mounted carriers will sort the mail at a slower pace than usual, will take a longer coffee break than usual and will attempt to prolong the sorting of mail. The mounted carriers will strictly follow the scheduled departure time, frequently being "forced" to leave behind some unsorted second and third class mail for the following day. In addition, the mounted carriers will typically be late in returning to the station in the afternoon with excuses such as having to instruct patrons in the proper placement of their roadside mailboxes, detours because of road construction, slippery roads in winter, and so on. What the late return means is that the afternoon dispatch of mail will not be sorted by the carrier until the next morning which increases the likelihood of a "heavy mail" day the next day. These various practices must be performed by each of the carriers. There is usually consensus among the carriers that a particular day "should" be a "heavy mail" day and they work together to obtain this designation from their supervisor. It can be further noted in this connection that some animosity develops between the mounted carriers and the unmounted carriers. The foot carriers feel that the mounted carrier, with his car allowance, overtime pay and assistance, has a "good deal" and by comparison with their own situation is being granted special privileges that are not really due him. As one foot carrier put it: "Never has so much been given to so few. The mounted carrier is the real nephew of Uncle Sam." [9]

Official and Unofficial Hierarchies

In the official organization of the Post Office there exist several hierarchies. Many statuses are related to each other in terms of an authority relationship; further, one individual may "stand higher" in the hierarchy than another, but yet not have any legitimate direct authority over the other. In addition, there is a reward hierarchy—the pay scale —which is closely correlated with the authority hierarchy.

In addition to the hierarchies which are stated or implied by the official rules and regulations there are also unofficial hierarchies which are supplementary to and grow out of the official hierarchies. These have to do with power, privilege and prestige.

Among the carriers three distinct work statuses will be compared. First, regular carriers can be distinguished from substitute carriers; second, as was indicated, among the regulars there are mounted carriers who deliver mail to roadside mailboxes from their cars and unmounted or foot carriers who deliver mail on foot.

The mounted carrier and the unmounted carrier are at an equal level in the official hierarchies. One does not have authority over the other and, apart from longevity, both receive the same base pay. The regular carrier does not have authority over the substitute except for those specific occasions when a particular substitute is assisting a particular regular carrier. However, since all carriers are promoted from substitute to regular carrier status the latter is higher in the official hierarchy.

First of all, it can be noted that the regular carrier is granted more prestige than the substitute carrier. This is due to the different official rewards which regular status brings, i.e., definite work hours rather than hourly wages, a five-day work week rather than a six-day week and the psychological security of a fixed work assignment. Secondly, prestige differences develop between the mounted carrier and the foot carrier. The mounted carrier receives a car allowance, overtime pay, and help from substitute carriers. Because he receives these things and the foot carrier does not, the mounted carrier is accorded more prestige; in general, a mounted route is valued more than a foot route and those who have them are esteemed. This is an addition to the hostility felt toward the mounted carrier by the foot carrier.

By virtue of the prestige differences, two other hierarchies emerge; these are the privilege hierarchy and the power hierarchy. The substitute carrier is frequently denied certain privileges. Unofficial norms prescribe that no substitute carrier shall leave the station to deliver his mail before all regular carriers have their mail sorted, that substitute carriers will help each other if they have difficulty in sorting mail, that substitute carriers will not have their morning coffee in the "swing room" (the employee's locker room found in most stations) on "heavy mail" days and that on "light" days substitute carriers will not spend as much time in the "swing room" as regular carriers.

The substitute is typically younger than the regular carrier, has been in the postal service a shorter time, and since he may move around from substation to substation in his work assignments, he frequently becomes peripheral to the *unique* informal organization of any substation. Because of these factors the regular carriers are able to exert influence on the substitute and they tend to enforce these privilege differences. As several subs were told by a regular carrier in the "swing room" on a heavy day: "What are you guys doing in here? Why the ink isn't even dry on your applications yet!" Comments such as these from a fairly cohesive regular carrier group are usually sufficient to enforce these privilege differences.

Thus, emerging out of the official authority and reward hierarchies is a prestige hierarchy. Associated with the prestige hierarchy is a privilege hierarchy reinforced by a power hierarchy. These unofficial hierarchies are supplementary to the official hierarchies.

Other studies in industrial sociology have described the emergence of some of these unofficial hierarchies. Cottrell describes a prestige hierarchy among the various railroad work statuses where prestige is correlated with skill required for the job, pay and conditions of work.[10] Roethlisberger and Dickson indicated that in the bank wiring room the wiremen were superior to the soldermen and those who wired connectors were more esteemed than those who wired selectors; these prestige differences were associated with skill required for the job and pay differences.[11]

Whyte has pointed out that distinctions are made among the various jobs in the kitchens of restaurants which partially depend upon the prestige value of the materials used and the position of the job in the flow of work.[12]

Discussion

Two patterns of behavior of letter carriers have been described. Each is determined by official expectations supplemented or modified by unofficial expectations. In one case—that having to do with the sorting and delivery of mail—the actual patterns of behavior represent deviation in some respects from the official expectations. In the second case—that of the hierarchical relations—the official expectations are not countermanded by unofficial expectations; the actual pattern of behavior does not constitute deviation from the official expectations. The actual pattern is not completely prescribed by the official expectations but it is consistent with them.

How can these patterns of behavior be explained? To give an explanation requires the answering of two questions: (1) How did the patterns come to be? (2) How do the patterns persist? An answer to the first question requires a history of work behavior in the Post Office; the second question is more easily answered. One answer to the second question is that these patterns persist because individuals are motivated to behave in these patterned ways. Then the question becomes: what motivates individuals to behave in these patterned ways? These patterns can be understood if we assume that most men, within the circumstances of their lives, attempt to maximize the rewards they receive. In the following discussion it will be argued that these patterns of behavior do provide such rewards.

Let us consider the sorting and delivering of mail first. Since the Post Office produces nothing it may be misleading to make comparisons in the work behavior of the letter carrier with that of the man on the assembly line or the worker in the factory. However, some general comparisons can be made. What has been described above can be thought of as a form of *restriction of output* but it is restriction in a *service industry* rather than in a *manufacturing industry*.

Productivity can be defined in terms of the number of pieces of mail handled and the number of patrons on a route. The management of the Post Office obviously wants this to be a maximum for each carrier within the limitations of what can be done by the average man working at the average pace. By the nature of the work no wage incentive plan can readily be devised to motivate the carrier to increase his productivity. His productivity is initially determined and is re-examined annually.

The goal of the letter carrier is to limit this official standard of productivity so that it can be achieved in less than eight hours. Hence, the letter carrier does engage in restriction of output. An unofficial expectation prescribes this behavior. Once this goal has been achieved then other unofficial role expectations prescribe that nothing be done to jeopardize it.

Other studies have indicated that work restriction has been perceived by workers as behavior which satisfies their best economic interests. The worker feels that if he attempts to maximize his pay under a wage incentive play then eventually the job will be retimed, rates will be cut, and he will be earning no more while working harder; further, with this increased productivity some workers may be laid off. This same kind of thinking can be applied

by the letter carrier to his job. If he "allows" his route to be expanded, it does not mean greater pay. He will work harder for the same pay. It further means that there will be fewer routes and hence fewer letter carriers will be needed. Hence, it can be argued that such behavior is motivated by a desire to keep from working harder for the same pay and by the desire to maximize the number of routes so that there will be a need for more carriers.[13]

A further motivation for the letter carrier to make his job as easy as possible can be postulated. If he can finish his work in less than eight hours, then it is easier for him to spend the remaining time on his own activities than it is for the worker who is confined to the shop. The factory worker may keep working just to have something to do and to escape the pressures of supervision. The letter carrier is free from direct observation and direct supervision; he is not confined to the work place. He can go home or do whatever he wants; hence, there is a strong motivation to finish his work so that he has extra time to spend on his own activities.

The same explanation can be postulated for the second behavior pattern—the unofficial hierarchies. Prestige, privilege, and power are three further rewards or gratifications which most individuals seek. In some instances, these rewards can only be measured comparatively. Individuals feel satisfied with the prestige, privilege, or power they receive if they perceive them to be greater than those received by others with whom they interact. That is, an individual has maximized privilege or prestige when these are greater for him than for many of those in his reference group. Further, it is only just that unofficial rewards be commensurate with official rewards.[14]

This brief analysis would seem to apply to the letter carrier. Where differences in reward are officially prescribed, then carriers will attempt to do those things which earn them the greater rewards. Hence, the substitute will attempt to become a regular carrier and, other things being equal, the regular will attempt to obtain a mounted route. Carriers will attempt to maximize their power over others and their relative privileges. If official prescriptions and rewards will be helpful in this, then they will be used. Thus, the regular carrier uses his regular carrier position and its associated obligations and rewards as a basis for earning unofficial power and privileges.

Footnotes

[1] For a good review of some of this work see William Foote Whyte, *Money and Motivation,* New York: Harpers, 1955, Part 1, "The Worker and His Work Group." More recently, research on the activities of the executive in the manufacturing concern have been reported. For example, see Melville Dalton, *Men Who Manage,* New York: Wiley, 1959.

[2] There has been some research on the organization of work behavior of public employees but this research has typically been motivated out of a concern with problems of bureaucratic change. For example, see Peter M. Blau, *The Dynamics of Bureaucracy,* Chicago: University of Chicago Press, 1955.

[3] The study of work behavior in the public service is of considerable significance for industrial sociology. This is evident, if for no other reason, from the fact that in 1961 over 13 percent of the labor force in the United States worked for national, state, or local governments. See U.S. Department of Commerce, *Survey of Current Business,* Vol. 42, August 1962, pp. S11–S12. This proportion has increased over the years and will undoubtedly continue to grow. Of the 9.2 million people in public employment, about 2.4 million work for the federal government with about a quarter of these in the Post Office Department. See U.S. Senate, Committee on Government Operations, *Organization of Federal Executive Departments and Agencies,* Report No. 22, 87th Congress, 2nd Session, March 28, 1962, Washington: Government Printing Office, 1962. Of the executive departments only the Department of Defense has more employees than the Post Office Department. The Post Office Department has nearly as many employees as the largest private industrial concern—General Motors. In 1959 General Motors reported 577,218 employees. See *Fortune,* Vol. 66, July 1962, p. 173.

[4] Thus, the substitute can and usually does serve as an important link in the informal communications within the Post Office.

[5] According to a survey made by the National Association of Letter Carriers, the letter carriers union, 39 percent of all letter carriers have second jobs. See U.S. Senate, Committee on the Post Office and Civil Service, *Federal Employee Compensation Study of 1960,* Hearings before the Committee, 86th Congress, 2nd Session, Washington: Government Printing Office, 1960, pp. 174–175. According to a Bureau of the Census Survey, in December 1959, 12.6 percent of all postal employees worked at a second job. This was a larger proportion than that for any other occupational category. See Gertrude Bancroft, "Multiple Job Holders in December 1959," *U.S. Monthly Labor Review,* Vol. 83, October 1960, p. 1047.

[6] For example, see Donald Roy, "Quota Restriction and Goldbricking in a Machine Shop," *American Journal of Sociology,* Vol. 57, March 1952, pp. 427–442.

[7] Donald Roy, "Efficiency and the Fix: Informal Intergroup Relations in a Piecework Machine Shop," *American Journal of Sociology,* Vol. 60, November 1954, p. 257.

[8] One might think that the situation of a dog biting a carrier is a joke perpetuated by cartoonists and seldom happens. However, this is a real occupational hazard for many postmen. In one six-month period the Buffalo Post Office recorded 63 dog bites which resulted in 123 lost work days costing $1,715 in lost time and $1,003 in medical expenses. This prompted the Buffalo Post Office to instigate a training program on how to deal with patrons' dogs. See *Postal Service News,* January 1960, p. 13.

[9] The reader should not conclude from this discussion that the Post Office is an inefficient, badly managed bureaucracy nor that postal patrons receive poor service. The authors of this paper are skeptical of the accuracy of either of these propositions. "The general patterns described here are similar to those found in any large organization—whether it be public or private. What is described here is a struggle between the carrier and the Post Office and not between the carrier and the public. We feel that most carriers are quite concerned about the kind of service they give and that they desire to give the postal patron the best

service they can. They are cognizant of how their relations with the public affect their relations with Congress. If the Post Office was a private corporation this attitude toward the public might be somewhat different.

[10] See W. Fred Cottrell, *The Railroader,* Palo Alto, California: Stanford University Press, 1940, pp. 12–41.

[11] F. J. Roethlisberger and William J. Dickson, *Management and the Worker,* Cambridge, Massachusetts: Harvard University Press, 1950, pp. 495–496.

[12] William Foote Whyte, *Human Relations in the Restaurant Industry,* New York: McGraw-Hill Book Company, 1948, pp. 33–46.

[13] The National Association of Letter Carriers has as one of its goals the restoration of two-a-day deliveries in residential areas. See NALC, AFL-CIO, *Official Proceedings of the 42nd Biennial Convention,* April 21 to April 26, 1960, pp. 34, 44. Whatever else this means, it means more work and, therefore, a need for more letter carriers. It also means, of course, a larger, stronger union.

[14] George Caspar Homans, *Social Behavior: Its Elementary Forms,* New York: Harcourt, Brace and World, 1961.

15

The College Sorority as a Social System

WALTER M. GERSON

Subcultures constitute a prevalent phenomenon in American society, for in a complex society people tend to form subsystems through which they can "belong." Because of the complexity and number of different groups in our society, individuals can isolate themselves from their more obvious, all-inclusive and common American culture by joining certain organizations and associating with persons with whom they share similar interests and values. These subsystems can subsequently become highly structured subcultures with specific patterns of behavior and activity beyond the more loosely integrated and extensive American system. One such subculture is the social sorority for college women. Sororities as fraternal social systems were formed as special organizations for elite young women in the latter half of the nineteenth century.[1]

The sorority is a stable, durable subculture in that recurrent patterns can be observed in it during a long period of time, for there is a regularity of expected behavior in the relationship and interactions of the members. A continuity in these patterns among the girls produces circumstances which are predictable, making for a well-ordered and structured system. It must be stressed, however, that the component parts of the sorority subculture, or those of any other culture for that matter, are both cultural and social. Not only do the individual members bring into the group their learned

behavior in terms of American culture, as it has been handed down through the generations and inculcated in them by agents of socialization, but also they learn to share a new set of cultural ideals, patterns, values, symbols, and norms which will thereby manifest themselves in the social action that ensues. The everyday person-to-person interactions give a sense of group identity to the sorority girls, because transcending the interactions is a regulatory cultural structure by which the group maintains itself through careful sanctioning of norms of conduct. Because of the high degree of interaction and the stress on obligations in social relations, the members of the society see their living situation as a very solid, unified structure. In sharing interests, values, and behavioral patterns, they create a social organization which they feel is unique from others.

In this article, sororities are analytically treated as social systems. As on-going social systems, sororities have developed mechanisms to deal with the functional problem of survival. This article constitutes a descriptive analysis of some of the mechanisms of maintenance of one empirical type sorority —which we shall call Gamma Sigma.[2] Gamma Sigma represents a composite picture of Greek-letter social sororities at a large Western or Midwestern state university. Data for this report were gathered from: (1) approximately 100 written analyses of sorority houses by sorority girls

---

SOURCE: Reprinted from *Sociology and Social Research,* An International Journal, University of Southern California, Los Angeles, April, 1969, 53:385–394, by permission of the author and the publisher.

who were students of the author; (2) extensive conversations with a large number of sorority members over the past few years; and (3) extended observations by the author of various aspects of sorority life.

Membership Recruiting: Pattern Maintenance

In Gamma Sigma, there are restrictions on the acceptance of potential members, for they will later have to carry on the traditions of the sorority to new members in order to maintain continuity in the subculture. Two important aspects in the selection of members are: (1) the criteria by which someone is judged a tentatively satisfactory Gamma Sigma, and (2) the whole mechanical and emotional process of rushing. The criteria of membership are, in general, consistent with those of the middle class in America. A girl must have made fairly good grades in high school so that there is an assurance that she will be scholastically eligible for the sorority's initiation. Recommendations from alumnae of the "house," [3] personal character, and "personality" are usually carefully considered.[4] Often, lists of potential pledges are organized during the summer before the freshman girls are ever seen during fall rush week.[5]

The most important mechanism for perpetuating the social system is "rushing," a process centered around effective and close social interaction on the part of the "actives," who are already members, and the "rushees," who are prospective potential members. "Rush week" is a highly organized phenomenon which is planned and expedited by Panhellenic Council. Panhellenic Council is composed of representatives from all of the individual sororities on the campus.[6] All of the various sororities cooperate with one another, then, in producing rush week, although during the process of rushing, each house actively competes with the other houses in the courting of prospective members. During rush week, rushees are ushered around, in relatively small groups, to the various sorority houses. Each group spends a certain allotted amount of time at a sorority; at the end of that time, the group is ushered on to the next house. At each stop, the rushees meet a large number of members of that given house. The process continues for most of a week, during which the anxieties and emotions of many rushees approach the straining point. Near the end of the week, sororities "bid" for the loyalties of various rushees.

Gamma Sigma has institutionalized certain techniques which the actives use in attracting desirable rushees. During rush week, the actives give the outward appearance of glowing with sisterly love. They smile continuously, so that the nervous rushee who is attempting to make a good impression feels more comfortable with a Gamma Sigma girl. However, the member is only practicing a method that the rush chairman repeatedly stressed to her—that of "eye-contact." This technique is especially effective during the last day of rush when sentimental sorority songs are sung. Upon hearing and singing these songs, the active is supposed to become so emotional that her eyes water. When the watery-eyed active stares into a rushee's eyes, the rushee may become so emotionally involved she will wish to join the house. In addition, the Gamma Sigma member is trained never to sit above the rushee during rush week. Since height is often symbolic of superiority, her being above a rushee might not make a good impression or may make the rushee feel uncomfortable. Hence, the active sits at the same level with or below the rushee, if possible. The eventual success of these techniques for attracting new participants into the social system are determined by the overall quality of the girls who "pledge" Gamma Sigma. The formal ceremony of pledging occurs at the very end of rush week when a certain number of girls, determined by a quota system set up by Panhellenic Council and by the preferences of the individual sorority, join Gamma Sigma.[7] These pledges are then ready to take the steps toward becoming full members of the sorority. If they have been carefully selected—and they usually are—the outcome of rush week for Gamma Sigma is that of pattern maintenance.

Ceremony and Ritual: Symbolic Boundary Maintenance

Not all of the secrets of the subculture are revealed in the short ritual of the pledging ceremony, for the real sacredness of Gamma Sigma is exposed only later in the initiation ceremony.[8] The pledging rite of passage is part of the anticipatory socialization process which is built into the social system. Each pledge in the ceremony is assigned a mystagogue, an older active who will guide and educate her like a sister. The manifest function of this "big sister" is to ensure the socialization of the pledge into the subculture. The big sister's latent function is to teach the pledge how to pass the culture effectively on to others when the pledge eventually becomes a big sister. Each specific sister-relationship, then, results in continuity for three separate generations of members: the present big sister, the little sister who will later become a big sister, and the little sister of the following generation.

The period between the initial pledging ritual and the ceremony at which the girls are initiated as full members of the sorority is called the pledge training period. This period of socialization usually is about four months in duration.[9] It is a period of cultural transmission during which the pledge learns the norms, values, and beliefs of the subculture.[10] A pledge trainer—an active who has been elected to this position—directs the socialization of the pledges. The pledges study a pledge book which contains the important norms, values, information, and history of the sorority. Before initiation, every girl will have to pass a comprehensive test on the content of the pledge book. Some of the symbols of the organization, such as the significant crest, are learned, but some of the symbolic content of the subculture is not revealed until the initiation ceremony. The new girls are taught traditional sentimental sorority songs which inspire a feeling of solidarity in the group. During the socialization process, the pledges learn the proper manners of a lady, so that one always butters one bite of bread at a time and never passes a dish without changing hands. The girls learn the normative standards of the sorority concerning smoking and the drinking of alcoholic beverages.

The pledge training period functions as a mechanism for the accomplishment of pattern maintenance, which is necessary for the perpetuation of the social system. During the entire period, there is constant reinforcement of the anticipation of gaining full membership in the sorority.[11] Initiation into active membership is the goal for the pledge; if she performs satisfactorily during the trial period—pledge-training—she will be invited to become an active. Pledges are excluded from initiation rites if they cannot pass the pledge tests or if they have not achieved a certain minimum grade average after a term of school work.

In many cultures, rites of passage are important features in introducing adolescents to a serious adult world and to the sacred ritual of their culture. The rites of initiation in the Gamma Sigma sorority subculture are also sacred, and the secrets learned are never to be revealed to anyone outside of the social system.[12] The initiation rite is an effective mechanism for maintaining the social system as a distinct subculture because it is structured so as to be binding and meaningful for the participants. The ceremony itself begins after a solemn dinner whereby those select novices dress completely in white as the actives prepare a ceremonial room. In this sorority the costumes include a large, white net veil worn over the face and a white robe with a colored sash and white stockings, with the effect that the costume symbolizes that of a virgin bride. During the rite the secrets such as the special grip, the special knock, and the meanings of symbolic Greek words are revealed. Several active members portray important Greek goddesses who are the patrons of Gamma Sigma; they deliver speeches on the ideal of the sorority. The ceremony institutionalizes the initiate's new status, that of active member of the sorority system. As the novices become active members of the sorority at the end of the ritual and receive their pins, they are symbolically wed to Gamma Sigma. They then lift the veils from their faces to see the true light after being children of darkness. Finally, after all of the solemnity, there is a party for the new members.

Initiation and the subsequent seeing of the truth constitutes a very important part of Gamma Sigma ceremony and ritual,

but the weekly chapter meetings embody symbolic ceremony which is also characteristic of the subculture's traditions. "Chapter" (the subcultural terminology for a weekly meeting for the members of the system) is significant in that its secrets are revealed only during the initiation rites, and only actives participate in chapter meetings. Lowly pledges must remain in separate pledge meetings held at the same time. A typical chapter meeting, which always follows the same order of ceremony, includes much symbolic activity —in the order of entrance into the chapter room, the songs sung, and the special words used in answering the roll call. In role call, each girl replies with a word formulated from the syllables of the name of the house, Gamma Sigma, such as "Gam-Sig-Ma." Symbolic names and gestures are used, and one refers to the president of Gamma Sigma, who is leading chapter meetings, as "Prettiness," and one stands, salutes her, and uses this title of address in order to speak at the meeting. Singing is always included in Gamma Sigma ceremony and ritual, whether the specific occasion is the pledging or the initiation ceremony or chapter meeting. A special rite signifies the end of Chapter so that the bonds of friendship are strengthened and there is a reaffirmation of the subcultural values.

The In-Group: Social Insulation and Integration

Gamma Sigma is not a total or twenty-four hour institution. Not all of the members live in the sorority house; several live at home or in dormitories or rooming houses. Especially for these girls who do not live "in," there is not complete social control over their social interactions and dating behavior. If Gamma Sigma does function as a partially total institution for any of its members, these participants will most likely be those who live in the house. The social system is apt to be more of a twenty-four hour phenomenon for them, even though a good portion of the waking hours of each day are actually spent outside the physical confines of the building. Their social world and role behaviors do not necessarily have to be as segmented as those of the "townies" who do not live in the house. The townie may, by necessity, have to perform several roles which often cannot be easily related to that part of her life which occurs within the Gamma Sigma social system. She participates in many role networks which are outside the symbolic boundary of the Gamma Sigma social system: the automobile traffic network as she drives or rides to school, the network of family relationships which cannot be avoided if she lives at home, the network of social interactions with non-Gamma Sigma girls if she lives in a rooming house or in a dormitory, and the greater possibility of dating nonfraternity boys due to not living at the sorority house.

Still, the social interaction patterns of Gamma Sigma girls are, for the most part, in-group oriented. Most of the primary group relationships of the members are with other members of the sorority or at least with other "Greeks" (members of social sororities or fraternities). Most of the girl's significant others, then, are part of the "Greek" system. The sorority girl is insulated from nonparticipants. She often does not have enough time, even if she desired, to maintain extensive contacts with non-Greeks. There is, then, an indirect (and occasionally direct) control on the selection of dating partners. Overall, there is relatively little opportunity for close

friendships with "independents" (those who are not part of the Greek system) and only limited chances for extensive inter-actions with non-Gamma Sigma girls. Social insulation operates as a boundary-maintaining mechanism for the Gamma Sigma social system.

A number of sanctions operate to produce conformity within the social system. Those who deviate from the norms of the subculture are negatively sanctioned. They may have to pay fines either with money or with their service and time (clean-up work) or they may be "campused" for a weekend or more. To be campused means that the girl may not "go out" or have any dates during the specified time period; she is supposed to stay home and study. Probably the most serious negative sanction is the disapproval of one's sorority sisters. Since most of a girl's friends are likely to be from the ranks of her sorority sisters, the disapproval of these significant others function as a strong incentive toward future conformity to the norms of the subculture.

However, not all sanctions are punish-ments. Active participation in the Gamma Sigma social system (hence, continued conformity to the norms) has many rewards for the participants. The Gamma Sigma girl is trained to feel more fortunate or superior than nonsorority girls. The social system offers status, a feeling of belonging, group support, and ready-made opportunities for primary relationships— which can be very important to a student in the mass society of a large university. There is structured group recognition for achievements of any member; the sorority periodically announces members' achieve-ments at dinner so that all participants are made aware of the achievements.

In addition, participation in the social

system opens up vistas and behavioral opportunities which would not likely be possible without sorority membership. For example, during a four-year time span, quite a large proportion of the members will be selected as Gamma Sigma's candidate in one queen contest or another. During an average school year, from eight to ten fraternity houses will select queens (such as the Sweetheart of Sigma Chi), and other annual queens may include the Homecoming Queen, May Day Queen, Miss University, Miss Forestry, Miss Neighborhood, Miss Winter Carnival, Miss Ski Queen, and Miss Bermuda Shorts. Gamma Sigma will probably be asked to select one of its members as a candidate in each one of the separate queen contests.

Although some girls appear to make careers of queen contests, there is a definite attempt in the Gamma Sigma sorority to pass the honor around and to allow many different girls to have the opportunity to be queen candidates. Hence, participation-in-full in the social system "pays off" for many of the members.

Conclusion

Little actual social change occurs in the social system of the sorority. Every year seniors graduate and freshmen or sophomores pledge. Thus, there is a succession of new individuals arriving each autumn who are new to the subculture and to the adjustments it requires. However, the social system is perpetuated through the various mechanisms that are inherent in the fraternal system of social organization. These mechanisms ensure that, even with some deviant behavior, the reverence of what is traditional, authoritative, and socially acceptable, will continue to maintain a cultural and social system.

Footnotes

[1] Although a very large number of fraternal-type organizations exist in American society, there has been surprisingly little systematic research of them. About thirty years ago, Gist gathered data on 70 American fraternal groups. In an excellent paper, he said, "In the character of organizational structure, in the methods of selection, and control of members, in the ideological framework, in the general character of origin myths, and in the content and character of fraternal symbols the fraternities have tended to develop according to a rather uniform basic design." Noel P. Gist, "Culture Patterning in Secret Society Ceremonials," *Social Forces,* 14, May, 1936, 497–505 (quotation from p. 505).

[2] The term "empirical type" is used rather than "ideal type" (in the Weber sense). Gamma Sigma is an empirical type insofar as it is a composite sorority. It is not an "ideal type" because I am generalizing from empirical information and I do not imply that the system is "closed." An ideal type often conceptualizes a closed logical system; this composite sorority does not represent a closed logical system. The empirical type is an analytical device; it is unlikely that any actual sorority will have all of the exact characteristics of Gamma Sigma.

[3] "House" appears to have a double meaning to sorority and fraternity members—one limited and the other broader. (1) Frequently the term is used to refer to the specific building in which the specific sorority social system is centered. For example, a girl may say, "I must go back to the house." (2) On the other hand, "house" also appears to be synonymous with the sorority itself in its use. Girls often refer to members or alumnae of the house, whether or not those persons ever actually resided in the sorority building. House, then, refers to the social system of the sorority.

[4] It is likely that much anticipatory socialization for sorority living occurs during high school or perhaps, even junior high school periods. Sorority membership is already a goal for some girls when they are preteenagers. Very early, then, they begin developing and improving the social traits felt to be desirable for sorority membership.

A recent study by Levine and Sussman of fraternity pledging at a technical school in the East is relative to our discussion. Levine and Sussman found that the more dating and socializing a boy did in high school, the higher his family's income, and the less time he spent on studying on homework in high school, the more likely he will go through rush week. However, we feel that their findings of fraternity pledging can be extended to sorority pledging only with extreme caution.

See Norman Levine and Leila A. Sussman, "Social Class and Sociability in Fraternity Pledging," *American Journal of Sociology,* 65, January, 1960, 391–399.

[5] Some universities have a rule which states that students cannot pledge sororities or fraternities until their sophomore year. At those schools, sororities frequently informally "court" outstanding potential pledges during their freshman year. The courting behavior takes the form of anticipatory socialization, with the effect that the freshman looks forward to the benefits to be derived from her pledging the sorority when she becomes a sophomore.

[6] There is a formal bifurcation of social control for the Gamma Sigma social system. The Gamma Sigs are controlled, in part, by authorities who are outside the immediate social system. Two outside sources of authority with considerable control are Panhellenic Council and university officials such as the dean of students.

Certain controls are exerted on Gamma Sigma and the behavior of its members. The sorority must conform to these restrictions whether or not the rules are preferred by or functional to Gamma Sigma. As part of the broader university system, it is subject to outside sanctions. This situation is of considerable importance, since it may generate tensions within the organization.

[7] The demographic or generational problem of Gamma Sigma is not primarily a problem of numbers. The problem of members is, to some degree, a controllable one: they can aspire for a fixed number of pledges, and can cut off the number at any point. Their problem lies in making sure that they have a sufficient number of *satisfactory* applicants and recruits.

[8] A classic work on the process of admission to secret societies and other aspects of secret societies is Georg Simmel, "The Sociology of Secrecy and Secret Societies," *American Journal of Sociology,* 11, January, 1906, 441–98.

[9] If the pledges are freshmen, the first several weeks of college are likely to constitute a time of rapid and pervasive changes in value-orientations and attitudes. Empirical support for the generalization is offered by Walter L. Wallace, "Institutional and Life-Cycle Socialization of College Freshmen," *American Journal of Sociology,* 70, November, 1964, 303–18. It is likely that while many of these changes are related to or are part of the sorority socialization, some changes experienced by the pledges are independent of the sorority social system, i.e. they would have taken place whether or not the girl had pledged a sorority.

[10] Numerous authors have reported on the socialization of new members of a wide variety of other social systems. One of the most interesting, for comparative purposes, is by Sanford M. Dornbusch, "The Military Academy as an Assimilating Institution," *Social Forces,* 33, May, 1955, 3–16–21.

[11] Not all sorority pledges reside in the sorority house. At some universities, all or most sorority pledges reside in dormitories, at home, or in some other non-sorority housing. Frequently, they cannot actually reside at the sorority house until they have been formally initiated as full-time active members of the social system. In such cases, the right to live at the house is a privilege, a reward for behaving properly and becoming properly socialized as a pledge.

[12] The phenomenon of secrecy is not unique to sororities. Gist has stated that "institutionalized secrecy constitutes an important feature of American civilization." Noel P. Gist, "Structure and Process in Secret Societies," *Social Forces,* 16, March, 1938, 349–57 (quotation from p. 357).

16

The Cocktail Lounge: A Study of Heterosexual Relations in a Public Organization

JULIAN ROEBUCK AND S. LEE SPRAY

An important setting for social contact among urban residents from the upper-middle and upper classes is the cocktail lounge. Despite this obvious fact, little, if any, research has been done on such establishments. The reasons for the surprising paucity of data on this social setting seem to stem from (1) the assumption that the cocktail lounge caters to an individualized, transient population and (2) the assumption that any organized group behavior found in such a setting is for instrumental purposes. As a result, the literature includes materials on the neighborhood bar and on taverns and restaurants where musicians, entertainers, prostitutes, criminals, and others gather for a variety of purposes. There are virtually no data available on the social organization of the plush cocktail lounge.[1]

Who frequents these quiet, well-furnished establishments where the employees are well dressed, where the bartenders often have college degrees, where the patrons are well dressed and well behaved, where formal entertainment is limited to soft music, and where one never sees a uniformed policeman? The existing popular literature suggests that attendance at a cocktail lounge is a pattern of the affluent but lonely transients without their spouses, alcoholics, call girls, young people out for kicks, men and women looking for spouses, etc. Undoubtedly all these types do frequent cocktail lounges. But is this the only support base for such an establishment, or does it, like the working-class bar, also draw support from persons whose attendance is sufficiently frequent as to classify them as regulars? If so, who are they, and what are their reasons for going to the lounge? The purpose of this paper is to provide tentative answers to these questions by presenting data gathered in the course of a two-year study of an upper- and upper-middle-class cocktail lounge in a middle-sized West Coast city (250,000 population).

Methods

Our interests led to the adoption of the following methods of investigation. First, a variety of persons who were knowledgeable about the city were interviewed regarding the presence of "high-class" cocktail lounges in the city. Those contacted included cab drivers, bartenders, bar owners, employees of the local Chamber of Commerce, businessmen, psychiatrists, college professors, ministers, and restaurateurs. Consensus was reached on two cocktail lounges in the central area as meeting the criteria outlined above. The attributes most often mentioned in identifying these lounges as "high class" were: (1) the quality of service was polite and attentive; (2) the clientele included suc-

SOURCE: Reprinted from *American Journal of Sociology*, January, 1967, 72:388–395, by permission of the authors and the University of Chicago Press. Copyright © 1967 by the University of Chicago.

cessful business and professional men who frequented these bars at the cocktail hour (and later); and (3) young, attractive, sociable females were generally present. One of the two cocktail lounges was located in what was generally considered the finest hotel in the city, and it was under the general supervision of the manager of the hotel, who agreed to cooperate in the study. With the help of the manager, the cooperation of all the employees of the lounge —four bartenders (three of them college graduates), two cocktail waitresses, and a female pianist—was secured.[2] After sufficient rapport was established, the purpose of the project was explained to each employee individually, and the anonymity of their responses was guaranteed. At the same time, the necessity of keeping the data collection procedures and all information absolutely confidential was stressed. The employees initially served as informants and were told to work alone and to reveal their information to no one but the researcher.

The first step was to secure information on the characteristics of the lounge patrons. To this end, each of the employees was given four cards and instructed to list the regular male patrons on one card and the regular female patrons on another card. A "regular" was defined as a person who visited the lounge at least once a week. On the remaining two cards, the employees were instructed to list the irregular male and female patrons; an "irregular" was defined as a man or woman who visited the lounge at least once every three weeks. The employees were instructed to withhold their lists from each other so the ratings would be independent. When all the lists had been completed, they were pooled and discussed by all of the employees, the manager, and the

researcher. Unanimous agreement was reached on the four lists of names composed of twenty female regulars, twenty male regulars, ten female irregulars, and ten male irregulars. Those listed were well known to all members of the group. The list of patrons was used to construct a set of cards, each containing the code number of the patron and a list of variables (22 for the men and 24 for the women) considered important to the research objectives. A set of cards was given to each employee, and the variables were defined and explained to them. The instructions were for each employee to keep the cards behind the bar and to record information acquired by listening to conversations or by occasionally asking direct questions. Information coming directly from the patrons was to be checked with information coming from other patrons about their peers in the lounge. The employees were also instructed to use any information about patrons gained from sources outside the lounge (e.g., from acquaintances of the patrons, from reading about them in the newspapers, or by driving by a patron's home and rating his house by type and neighborhood). Both direct and indirect information were recorded immediately after the period of observation. At the end of two years, the cards were examined and edited by the researcher and the hotel manager. Few inconsistencies were found in the data on each card. Since the manager was well acquainted with the study sample, he was able to resolve the few inconsistencies found.

The second method of data gathering was that of participant observation. By "participant observation" we mean that the fieldworker observed and participated in the group in the sense that he had durable social relations with members of the study group.[3] The researcher was present a minimum of five hours a week in the lounge for the two-year duration of the study. A minimum of two visits per week was maintained during this period, with all hours of the day from 4:00 p.m. to 2:00 a.m. and all days of the week being covered systematically. In addition, each of the sixty members of the study sample were informally interviewed on three separate occasions over the two-year observation period, with each interview lasting approximately one hour.[4]

For the purpose of analysis, the data on regulars and irregulars of each sex were combined, since the data collected by the lounge employees and those obtained by the researcher in the interviews revealed no differences between them.

Findings

In analyzing the data, it was apparent that the patrons studied spent a sufficiently large amount of time in the lounge to warrant classifying their behavior as habitual. (The men averaged ten visits per week and the women six visits per week.) The fact that the initial sample of sixty persons remained available, without attrition, for the entire two-year period of observation indicates that the voluntary relationships in the lounge were highly stable. Clearly, the lounge was an important center of activity for these people.

In attempting to assess the importance of engaging in the activities of the cocktail lounge, two broad alternative interpretations were available. The first alternative, which is consistent with the deviant-behavior approach to the study of activities in settings of this type, would start with two assumptions: (1) the activities in the lounge would be related

to the disruption of other social ties (e.g., family, occupation, community, etc.), and (2) the importance of the lounge to the patrons would be related to the extent to which the individual has failed to achieve primary goals in other settings and has turned to the lounge as a second-best alternative setting. The second alternative, and the one considered most consistent with the findings, was to consider the importance of participating in the activities of the lounge to be related to obtaining gratifications in this setting that were not possible in other settings.

An examination of these two alternatives led to a focus on three questions: (1) What kinds of social ties characterize the regular patrons of the lounge? (2) What kinds of goals were the individuals pursuing in this particular social setting? (3) How did the social organization of the lounge contribute to the attainment of personal goals at a level sufficient to retain the participation of these persons over an extended period of time?

We will first consider some of the major social characteristics of these people. In addition to the findings presented in Table 1, it should be added that two-thirds of the men had an annual income over $10,000 (the top being $75,000) with the remainder earning between $8,500 and $10,000. (None of the employed women earned as much as $9,000 annually.) With regard to religion, two-thirds of the men were Catholics and the remainder were Protestants, while 60 percent of the women were Catholics and the remainder were Protestants. All the respondents expressed a belief in God, and all attended church.[5] Finally, we had the employees of the lounge rate the women patrons as to their relative attractiveness. The following distribution resulted: "Very Sharp" = 30

TABLE 1. *Social Characteristics of Respondents*

Variable	Men (N=30)	Women* (N=30)
Marital status:		
Single..................	13%	60%
Married.................	70	0
Divorced or separated......	17	40
Age (median: men = 39; women = 24):		
20 and under............	0	13
21–25...................	0	37
26–30...................	7	37
31–35...................	27	13
36–40...................	27	0
41–45...................	23	0
46 and over..............	16	0
Occupation of father:		
Professional..............	37	30
Manager, official, proprietor.................	33	10
Clerical and sales.........	10	27
Craftsman...............	7	13
Farm manager and owner...	13	20
Education of respondent:		
College graduate.........	53	20
Attended college.........	20	40
High school graduate.....	27	33
Less than high school graduate...............	0	7
Home ownership of respondent:		
Owned own home:		
Upper class (dwelling and neighborhood, $60,000 homes)........	23	0
Upper-middle class (dwelling and neighborhood, $40,000–$59,000 homes)........	17	0
Middle class (dwelling and neighborhood, $30,000–$39,000 homes)..............	37	3
Rented apartment.........	23	83
Lived with parents........	0	13
Occupation of respondent:		
Professional..............	40	10
Manager, official, or proprietor.................	53	....
Farm owner and manager...	7	....
Secretary...................	....	33
Clerk.....................	....	17
Cocktail waitress..........	....	17
Service worker............	....	3
College student...........	....	20

* The percentages do not always total to 100 because of rounding error.

percent; "Sharp" = 50 percent; "Average" = 20 percent.[6]

Table 1 clearly indicates a general difference between the men and women in terms of social status, although none of the patrons was lower class in origin or current position. Specifically, the men who frequent the cocktail lounge tend to be older, married men of high-class position while the women are young, attractive, unattached and of somewhat lower-class position. What influence does this status differential have on the development of social relationships in the lounge? Does it provide support for a distinct sex-role differentiation in the cocktail lounge that the patrons believe is absent in their relationships outside the lounge? Or is it simply irrelevant because the regular patrons frequent the lounge to engage in "retreatist," "criminalistic," or "escapist" sexual deviation and drinking behavior? To answer the last question first, the interviews revealed that none of these men and women considered themselves, or were considered by their peers, to have a drinking problem. This was further supported by the employees of the lounge who believed that only four of the men and four of the women could be considered to be relatively heavy drinkers. Similarly, while both men and women admitted to occasional sexual relations with other regular patrons, none of the women were considered, either by themselves or by the employees and other patrons, to be prostitutes or call girls. None of the patrons had a delinquent or criminal history. None of the male patrons had illegitimate children, and only one female had an illegitimate child. Finally, with regard to personal aberration, we had the employees classify the patrons according to their personality stability. The results shown in

Table 2 indicate that the vast majority of both the men and women were considered to be reliable, predictable persons.

TABLE 2. *Personality Characteristics of Regular Patrons*

Type of Personality*	Men (N = 30)	Women† (N = 30)
Stable...............	80%	80%
Unstable...........	20	20

* While the terms "stable" and "unstable" may not be satisfactory from a clinical point of view, they were the terms used by the employees of the lounge and seemed to be very meaningful to them. Using these terms, the employees were able to achieve complete agreement in classifying the patrons of the lounge.
† Two of the women were referred to as "Very Unstable," while none of the men was referred to in this manner.

The evidence indicates, then, that the regular patrons of the cocktail lounge were not anomic, personally disorganized or disturbed individuals driven to frequent the lounge for deviant purposes. Rather, these people seemed to visit the lounge because it was a preferred recreational pattern. Furthermore, this particular preference did not seem to set them apart from other persons of similar social status. Finally, the other activities they mentioned as preferred recreational activities were quite standard. For example, when the women were asked to list their preferred recreational patterns, they most often mentioned dancing, going to parties, and listening to jazz music, while the men mentioned playing golf, fishing, and hunting. Given these findings, the important question becomes one of determining what it is about the cocktail lounge that makes it such a desirable setting for these individuals.

In the interviews, each respondent was asked to list his reasons for frequenting the cocktail lounge. Table 3 presents the answers given by the men and women. In examining these findings, it is apparent

TABLE 3. *Reasons for Frequenting the Cocktail Lounge*

Reasons Stated by Respondents	Percentage*
Male (N = 30):†	
To meet attractive women......	73
To relax......................	23
To meet male friends..........	20
To meet business acquaintances..	14
Female (N = 30):‡	
To meet men with money who could take her out..........	48
To meet men who would keep quiet about sexual and drinking behavior...............	19
To meet men who did not want to get involved.............	15
To enjoy the company of older men........................	10
To meet eligible men for marriage.....................	7

* The percentage figures do not total 100 because multiple reasons for frequenting the lounge could be given by each respondent.
† Total number of reasons = 51. Total number of sex-linked reasons = 48.
‡ Total number of reasons = 52. Total number of sex-linked reasons = 52.

that they are direct extensions of the various dimensions of feminine and masculine roles. That is, the emphasis the women placed on financial dependence and the maintenance of a "good reputation" combined with the emphasis the men placed on having earned the rewards of relaxation with attractive young women portrays sex-role differentiation in a heightened form. The fact that a great emphasis was placed on conducting these heterosexual activities between married men and unattached women according to a specific code of "proper" behavior clearly indicates that the behavior was institutionalized. Basically, what these men and women had done was to accept the definition of appropriate behavior for one age level (youth) and certain settings (marital) and apply them to new age categories (those represented in the lounge) and new social settings (the lounge and hotel). The popularity of the cocktail lounge, then, stems from the fact that it is a setting in which casual sexual affairs between unattached women and higher-class men can be conducted in a context of respectability. From the standpoint of the patrons, these activities tend to be viewed more in terms of reaffirming social identities than rejecting social norms.

The above argument implies that participating in the activities of the cocktail lounge may not necessarily disrupt marital and other social ties. To gain evidence on this point, we asked the respondents to evaluate their behavior in and related to the lounge. The men explained their behavior in the following terms:

1. They accepted part of their behavior as wrong in a technical-legal sense but not in a social sense.

2. They insisted that certain extenuating circumstances (e.g., busy wives, family pressures, business pressures, "cold" wives, etc.) created a need for extracurricular activities in the cocktail lounge.

3. They deserved romantic interludes with attractive, decent women because earlier in life they did not have the time for such interludes, and such women were not available to them.

4. They did not permit themselves or the young women with whom they consorted to become emotionally involved.

5. They maintained friendly relationships with the young women which were devoid of exploitation.

6. The women were not *virgins*.

7. They were discreet and protective of the women and themselves in securing safe places of assignation and in preventing pregnancy.

8. They believed in the double standard.

9. They remained good husbands and fathers at home where they were loved and loved in return.

10. They did not feel guilty but would feel shame if caught.

The female respondents' rationale for consorting with older married men, as reported during the interviews, closely parallels the reasons they gave for frequenting the cocktail lounge. In sum, with men who were older, married, sophisticated, protective, and friendly, they could enjoy sex and companionship in pleasant and discreet circumstances without having to play a competitive, exploitive courtship game. They all insisted that they were not interested in breaking up any man's home. Moreover, they did not feel that their behavior in the lounge in any way precluded or endangered their social and occupational roles in the larger community.[7] As in the case of the male respondents, the women expressed no guilt feelings about their behavior but did express the fear of shame if exposed.

Given these findings we have to conclude that participation in the activities of the cocktail lounge does not lead to a disruption of family ties. Further, it seems clear that the married men were not driven to participate in the activities of the lounge by disintegrating marriage and family relations. Finally, if the cocktail lounge does provide a setting in which gratifications can be obtained, which cannot be achieved in other settings, it becomes important to ask what type of social organization makes this possible. To throw some light on this question, we will turn to a consideration of the structural properties of the cocktail lounge.

In investigating the social organization of the cocktail lounge, it was expected that the strongest normative regulation of behavior would be found in areas having the greatest consequence to the group, such as the motives that brought the people together and the activities affecting the maintenance of the group. As we have indicated, most of the norms surrounded heterosexual interaction. These included the following patterns, which were rarely violated by the regular patrons. First, women usually came in alone and did not sit at the bar unless a previous date had been arranged with a man already at the bar. The men came in alone or in pairs and took a position at the bar. Women who did not have dates sat at a table, and men who were well acquainted with them might ask if they could join them at a table. The usual pattern was for one couple to occupy a table, but occasionally two couples would share a table. When this happened, however, the interaction still took place primarily on a couple basis and not as a group. Men who were not acquainted with the women sitting at tables would watch them and look for social cues defining their status. Women who were waiting for a date pointedly looked at their watches, asked the waitresses and the bartenders if the awaited party had been in yet, and in other ways signaled their unavailability. The unattached males at the bar who were interested were expected to wait out a woman through one drink, during which time they made inquiries to the bartenders and/or cocktail waitresses about them and their attachments. If they found the woman unattached, they would ask that she be served a drink of her choice. By accepting the drink and nodding her thanks, the woman indicated her willingness to engage in conversation. It was only at that time that the man could go over to the woman's table. At times the invitee would ask the cocktail waitress for a

run-down on the inviter before accepting the drink.

In short, the bartenders and cocktail waitresses played an important mediating role in the proper introduction; they knew the male and female patrons well, and they accepted the responsibility of facilitating contact between people who would be compatible. They knew the social, emotional, and physical attributes that appealed to the various patrons. Occasionally the bartender or waitress would parry an introduction by politely remarking something as follows: "Lorraine, I tried to check Joe's play. I told him you were not his type. I know you can't stand bald-headed fat men, but he insisted. It's up to you now. Do you want to drink with him or not?" The regular patrons who were well acquainted were very informal in their polite salutations. However, they invariably made their "play" through the hired help. The exceptions to this rule occurred among the patrons who were first-timers or who came in very infrequently. The aggressive male or female who bypassed the hired help in a direct approach to an unknown person was referred to as a "burglar." He was not appreciated by his fellows, the hired help, or the unknown person contacted. At times such a person would be "called down" by any one or all three of these categories of persons; the expression used by the employees would be something like: "Charlie, slow down and use a little class. If she is available and interested, everything will work out. You know what is right. Of course, you do what you want." The women, of course, by declining or accepting a drink, exerted some control over the choice; but they did not enjoy unlimited freedom. Should an unattached woman (alone or in twos or threes) decline more than two invitations, she took the chance of losing the aid of the employees. The bartenders and waitresses could and did discourage other males from making further invitations. As one bartender put it, "If they come to play, O.K., we'll help, but if they get too choosy or just come to build their egos and look pretty, let them hustle their drinks elsewhere." In essence, the expectations were that polite behavior was to be used at all times, and the power of initiating interaction always resided in the men but was supposed to be channeled through the employees of the lounge.

Conclusion

Popular myth has it that the cocktail lounge is a place where strangers pick up sexual partners. The major role of the high-class cocktail lounge studied was to facilitate casual sexual affairs in the context of respectability but not among strangers. In fact, the regular patrons of the lounge constituted a highly stable group of persons who considered the lounge to be an important center of activity. The implication is that the cocktail lounge (*a*) provides gratifications that may not be available in other spheres of life for these people and (*b*) serves to drain off energies which might otherwise be invested in change by the individuals of other aspects of their life situations. For the unattached women this means that the availability of the "consort status" at the lounge may operate as a substitute for, or enable them to postpone, the ordinary heterosexual concern of women their age—the location of a suitable marriage partner.[8] For the married men, the relationships established in the cocktail lounge may actually serve to maintain marital ties that would otherwise be dissolved. In general, then, the cocktail lounge seems to perform many of the functions

frequently attributed to the "mistress complex" in society and may, in fact, be related to the practical disappearance of this pattern in American society. This suggests, if true, that other public organizations (e.g., ski lodges, resorts, night clubs, etc.) may perform similar functions and that one key to understanding the sexual norms in upper-middle- and upper-class society lies in the study of such settings.

Footnotes

[1] Most of the literature dealing with establishments of this type focuses either on the extent to which the tavern or bar contributes to various "social problems" or on the deviant behavior of the patrons, rather than on the organization of the establishment. For a notable exception to this statement, see David Gottlieb, "The Neighborhood Tavern and Cocktail Lounge: A Study of Class Differences," *American Journal of Sociology,* 62, May, 1957, 559–62.

[2] Several factors contributed to the excellent cooperation of the employees of the lounge. First, the hotel manager was a long-time friend of one of the researchers and, hence, accepted the promise of confidentiality without question. Second, the manager had had a great deal of experience managing large, exclusive hotels throughout California and elsewhere and did not feel threatened in any way by the researchers' desire to gather data on a lounge that even the manager felt was rather typical of establishments of its kind. Third, two of the bartenders were part-time graduate students in sociology who used their experiences in the lounge to develop Masters' theses which were later written under the supervision of one of the researchers. A third bartender was a college graduate who had taken courses in sociology, understood the research objectives, and was interested in participating in the research project. These three employees were invaluable aids in assuring the other employees that the research was important and that the researchers could be trusted. Finally, it quickly became known to the patrons that the observer was a college professor (though they never knew that he was doing research in the lounge). While this fact made him somewhat "different" from the other patrons, it also carried a certain amount of prestige and gave him a "license" to ask questions which were not normally asked by other patrons.

[3] For a discussion of this particular definition of "participant observation," see Morris Zelditch, Jr., "Some Methodological Problems of Field Studies," *American Journal of Sociology*, 67, March, 1962, 566–76.

[4] These informal interviews seemed to have no adverse effect on the on-going observations that were being made. For an interesting discussion of interviewing during a period of field observation, see Howard Becker, "Interviewing Medical Students," *American Journal of Sociology*, 62, September, 1956, 199–201.

[5] All of the respondents were Caucasian, and none were members of ethnic minority groups. With regard to nativity, twenty-six of the males and twenty-seven of the females were born in urban areas outside of California, while the remaining three females were born in rural areas outside of California.

[6] The terms used to classify the women as to their attractiveness were those given by the employees of the lounge. While these are very general categories, they were commonly defined by the employees of the lounge inasmuch as they were able to reach complete consensus on which of the three categories each of the women should be placed in.

[7] A follow-up study, conducted two years after the completion of the original study, indicated that the women's views were correct. By this time, slightly more than one-half of the women were married and no longer frequented the cocktail lounge. By all available evidence, the women had made "good" marriages with high-status men. However, none of the women had married regular patrons of the cocktail lounge. The follow-up study also revealed that the women who left the cocktail lounge were replaced by other young, unattached women with similar characteristics. Much less attrition had occurred among the men, involving at most five of the regular patrons. The reason given by the employees for the disappearance of these men was that they had either become too old for the activities in the cocktail lounge or they had moved out of the area. Among the married men, none was known to have been divorced since the study ended. Finally, observation (averaging three times per week over a three-month period) during the follow-up study revealed that the same pattern of behavior among the patrons still persisted even though the personnel had changed somewhat.

[8] This idea was suggested by Jeanne Watson Eisenstadt in a personal communication.

PART SEVEN Social Change

Frequently, social systems are discussed by sociologists in a way that leaves one with the impression that the systems are static and unchanging. Actually, all social systems, to one degree or another, are in a constant state of change. In some societies, particularly those that are pre-industrial, change may be minimal and may occur at a relatively slow rate. In modern industrial societies, however, the vast technological advances, which seem to compound each other, create very rapid social change.

In a modern industrial state such as the United States, the rate of social change tends to create various types of stress. As new technology and knowledge are developed, they tend to be accompanied by changes in values and norms. As a result, a "generation gap" appears to be nearly inevitable in modern societies. The twenty years or so between generations means that parents and children are socialized into at least partially different values and beliefs. These differences, particularly those concerned with traditionally accepted morality, tend to create conflict and misunderstanding.

The first article in this section, written by Robert Rosenstone, examines social change from the viewpoint of youth and their music. The second article, "Changing Sexual Standards" by Ira L. Reiss, examines an area in which considerable change has occurred in recent years. Reiss relates and contrasts the changing sexual behavior standards with observations of actual behavior. In the final selection, Daniel Bell attempts to predict aspects of the future United States society from the viewpoint of technological change.

17

"The Times They Are A-Changin' ": The Music of Protest

ROBERT A. ROSENSTONE

At the beginning of the 1960's, nobody took popular music very seriously. Adults only knew that rock n' roll, which had flooded the airwaves in the 1950's, had a strong beat and was terribly loud; it was generally believed that teen-agers alone had thick enough eardrums, or insensitive enough souls, to enjoy it. Certainly, no critics thought of a popular star like the writhing Elvis Presley as being in any way a serious artist. Such a teen-age idol was simply considered a manifestation of a subculture that the young happily and inevitably outgrew—and, any parent would have added, the sooner the better.

Today, the view of popular music has drastically changed. Some parents may still wonder about the "noise" that their children listen to, but important segments of American society have come to recognize popular musicians as real artists saying serious things.[1] An indication of this change can be seen in magazine attitudes. In 1964, the *Saturday Evening Post* derided the Beatles—recognized giants of modern popular music—as "corny," and *Reporter* claimed: "They have debased Rock 'n Roll to its ultimate absurdity." Three years later the *Saturday Review* solemnly discussed a new Beatles record as a "highly ironic declaration of disaffection" with modern society, while in 1968 *Life* devoted a whole, laudatory section to "The New Rock," calling it music "that challenges the joys and ills of the . . . world." [2] Even in the

intellectual community, popular music has found warm friends. Such sober journals as *The Listener, Columbia University Forum, New American Review,* and *Commentary* have sympathetically surveyed aspects of the "pop" scene, while in *The New York Review of Books*—a kind of house organ for American academia—composer Ned Rorem has declared that, at their best, the Beatles "compare with those composers from great eras of song: Monteverdi, Schumann, Poulenc." [3]

The reasons for such changes in attitude are not difficult to find: there is no doubt that popular music has become more complex, and at the same time more serious, than it ever was before. Musically, it has broken down some of the old forms in which it was for a long time straight-jacketed. With a wide-ranging eclecticism, popular music has adapted to itself a bewildering variety of musical traditions and instruments, from the classic Indian sitar to the most recent electronic synthesizers favored by composers of "serious" concert music.

As the music has been revolutionized, so has the subject matter of the songs. In preceding decades, popular music was almost exclusively about love, and, in the words of poet Thomas Gunn, "a very limited kind [of love], constituting a sort of fag-end of the Petrarchan tradition." [4] The stories told in song were largely about lovers yearning for one another in some

SOURCE: Reprinted from *The Annals*, March, 1969, 382:132–144, by permission of the author and The American Academy of Political and Social Science.

vaguely unreal world where nobody ever seemed to work or get married. All this changed in the 1960's. Suddenly, popular music began to deal with civil rights demonstrations and drug experiences, with interracial dating and war and explicit sexual encounters, with, in short, the real world in which people live. For perhaps the first time, popular songs became relevant to the lives of the teenage audience that largely constitutes the record-buying public. The success of some of these works prompted others to be written, and the second half of the decade saw a full efflorescence of such topical songs, written by young people for their peers. It is these works which should be grouped under the label of "protest" songs of the 1960's, for, taken together, they provide a wide-ranging critique of American life. Listening to them, one can get a full-blown picture of the antipathy that the young song writers have toward many American institutions.

Serious concerns entered popular music early in the 1960's, when a great revival of folk singing spread out from college campuses, engulfed the mass media, and created a wave of new "pop" stars, the best known of whom was Joan Baez. Yet, though the concerns of these folk songs were often serious, they were hardly contemporary. Popular were numbers about organizing unions, which might date from the 1930's or the late nineteenth century, or about the trials of escaping Negro slaves, or celebrating the cause of the defeated Republicans in the Spanish Civil War. Occasionally, there was something like "Talking A-Bomb Blues," but this was the rare exception rather than the rule.[5]

A change of focus came when performers began to write their own songs, rather than relying on the traditional folk repertoire. Chief among them, and destined to become the best known, was Bob Dylan. Consciously modeling himself on that wandering minstrel of the 1930's, Woody Guthrie, Dylan began by writing songs that often had little to do with the contemporary environment. Rather, his early ballads like "Masters of War" echoed the leftist concerns and rhetoric of an earlier era. Yet, simultaneously, Dylan was beginning to write songs like "Blowin' In the Wind," "A Hard Rain's A-Gonna Fall," and "The Times They Are A-Changin'," which dealt with civil rights, nuclear war, and the changing world of youth that parents and educators were not prepared to understand. Acclaimed as the best of protest song writers, Dylan in mid-decade shifted gears, and in the song "My Back Pages," he denounced his former moral fervor. In an ironic chorus claiming that he was much younger than he had been, Dylan specifically made social problems the worry of sober, serious, older men; presumably, youths had more important things than injustice to think about. After that, any social comment by Dylan came encapsulated in a series of surrealistic images; for the most part, he escaped into worlds of aestheticism, psychedelic drugs, and personal love relationships. Apparently attempting to come to grips in art with his own personality, Dylan was content to forget about the problems of other men.[6]

The development of Dylan is important not only because he is the leading song writer, but also because it parallels the concerns of popular music in the 1960's. Starting out with traditional liberal positions on war, discrimination, segregation, and exploitation, song writers of the decade turned increasingly to descriptions of the private worlds of drugs, sexual experience, and personal freedom. Though social concerns have never entirely faded, the private realm has been increasingly seen as the only one in which people can lead meaningful lives. Now, at the end of the decade, the realms of social protest and private indulgence exist side by side in the popular music, with the latter perceived as the only viable alternative to the world described in the former songs.[7]

The Negro in Song

In turning to the protest songs of the 1960's, one finds many of the traditional characters and concerns of such music missing. Gone are exploited, impoverished people, labor leaders, "finks," and company spies. This seems natural in the affluent 1960's, with youths from middle-class backgrounds writing songs. Of course, there has been one increasingly visible victim of exploitation in this decade, the Negro; and the songsters have not been blind to his plight. But, egalitarian as they are, the white musicians have not been able to describe the reality of the black man's situation.[8] Rather, they have chronicled Northern liberal attitudes towards the problem. Thus, composer-performer Phil Ochs penned works criticizing Southern attitudes towards Negroes, and containing stock portraits of corrupt politicians, law officials, and churchmen trembling before the Ku Klux Klan, while Paul Simon wrote a lament for a freedom rider killed by an angry Southern mob.[9] Similarly white-oriented was Janis Ian's very popular "Society's Child," concerned with the problem of interracial dating. Here a white girl capitulates to society's bigotry and breaks off a relationship with a Negro boy with the vague hope, "When we're older things may change/ But for now this is the way they must remain." [10]

Increasingly central to white-Negro relationships have been the ghetto and urban riots, and a taste of this entered the popular music. Phil Ochs, always on top of current events, produced "In the Heat of the Summer" shortly after the first major riot in Harlem in 1964. Partially sympathetic to the ghetto-dwellers' actions, he still misjudged their attitudes by ascribing to them feelings of shame—rather than satisfaction—in the aftermath of the destruction.[11] A later attempt, by Country Joe and the Fish, to describe Harlem ironically as a colorful vacation spot, verged on patronizing blacks, even while it poked fun at white stereotypes. Only the closing lines, "But if you can't go to Harlem . . ./Maybe you'll be lucky and Harlem will come to you," followed by sounds of explosion, thrust home what indifference to the ghetto is doing to America.[12] The most successful song depicting the situation of the Negro was "Trouble Coming Everyday," written by Frank Zappa during the Watts uprising in 1965. Though the song does not go so far as to approve of rioting, it paints a brutal picture of exploitation by merchants, bad schooling, miserable housing, and police brutality—all of which affect ghetto-dwellers. Its most significant lines are Zappa's cry, "You know something people, I ain't black, but there's a whole lots of times I wish I could say I'm not white." No song writer showed more empathy with the black struggle for liberation than that.[13]

Politicians

While the downtrodden are heroes of many traditional protest songs, the villains are often politicians. Yet, politics rarely enters the songs of the 1960's. Ochs, an unreconstructed voice from the 1930's, depicts vacillating politicians in some works, and

Dylan mentions corrupt ones early in the decade. But the typical attitude is to ignore politics, or, perhaps, to describe it in passing as "A yardstick for lunatics, one point of view." [14] It is true that the death of President Kennedy inspired more than one song, but these were tributes to a martyr, not a politician.[15] If Kennedy in death could inspire music, Lyndon Johnson in life has seemed incapable of inspiring anything, except perhaps contempt. In a portrait of him, Country Joe and the Fish pictured the, then, President as flying through the sky like Superman ("It's a bird, it's a plane, it's a man insane/It's my President L. B. J."). Then they fantasized a Western setting:

Come out Lyndon with your hands held high
Drop your guns, baby, and reach for the sky
I've got you surrounded and you ain't got a
    chance
Send you back to Texas, make you work on
    your ranch.[16]

One traditional area, antiwar protest, does figure significantly in the music of the 1960's. With America's involvement in Vietnam and mounting draft-calls, this seems natural enough. Unlike many songs of this genre, however, the current ones rarely assess the causes of war, but dwell almost exclusively with the effect which war has on the individual. Thus, both Love and the Byrds sing about what nuclear war does to children, while the Peanut Butter Conspiracy pictures the effect of nuclear testing on everyone: "Firecracker sky filled with roots of fusion . . ./We're so far ahead we're losing." [17] Most popular of the antiwar songs was P. F. Sloan's "Eve of Destruction," which, for a time in 1965, was the best-selling record in the country (and which was banned by some patriotic radio station directors). The title obviously gives the author's view of the world situation; the content deals mostly with its

relationship to young men like himself: "You don't believe in war, but what's that gun you're totin'?" [18] There are alternatives to carrying a gun, and defiance of the draft enters some songs, subtly in Buffy St. Marie's "Universal Soldier" and stridently in Ochs' "I Ain't Marching Any More." [19] Perhaps more realistic in its reflection of youthful moods is the Byrds' "Draft Morning," a haunting portrait of a young man reluctantly leaving a warm bed to take up arms and kill "unknown faces." It ends with the poignant and unanswerable question, "Why should it happen?" [20]

If many songs criticize war in general, some have referred to Vietnam in particular. The Fugs give gory details of death and destruction being wreaked on the North by American bombers, which unleash napalm "rotisseries" upon the world.[21] In a similar song, Country Joe and the Fish describe children crying helplessly beneath the bombs, and then comment ironically, "Super heroes fill the skies, tally sheets in hand/Yes, keeping score in times of war takes a superman." [22] No doubt, it is difficult to make music out of the horrors of war, and a kind of black humor is a common response. In a rollicking number, the Fugs, with irony, worry that people may come to "love the Russians" and scream out a method often advocated for avoiding this: "Kill, kill, kill for peace." [23] And one of Country Joe's most popular numbers contains the following:

Well come on generals let's move fast
Your big chance has come at last
We gotta go out and get those reds
The only good Commie is one that's dead
And you know that peace can only be won
When we blow 'em all to kingdom come.[24]

The injustice and absurdity of America's Asian ventures, perceived by the song writers, does not surprise them, for they feel that life at home is much the same. The songs of the 1960's show the United States as a repressive society, where people who deviate from the norm are forced into conformity—sometimes at gunpoint; where those who do fit in lead empty, frustrated lives; and where meaningful human experience is ignored in a search for artificial pleasures. Such a picture is hardly attractive, and one might argue that it is not fair. But it is so pervasive in popular music that it must be examined at some length. Indeed, it is the most important part of the protest music of the decade. Here are criticisms, not of exploitation, but of the quality of life in an affluent society: not only of physical oppression, but also of the far more subtle mental oppression that a mass society can produce.

Youth as Victim

Throughout the decade, young people have often been at odds with established authority, and, repeatedly, songs picture youth in the role of victim. Sometimes the victimization is mental, as when the Mothers of Invention complain of outworn thought patterns and say "All your children are poor/Unfortunate victims of lies/You believe." [25] On a much simpler level, Sonny Bono voices his annoyance that older people laugh at the clothes he wears, and he wonders why they enjoy "makin' fun" of him.[26] Now, Bono could musically shrug off the laughs as the price of freedom, but other songs document occasions when Establishment disapproval turned into physical oppression. Thus, Canned Heat tells of being arrested in Denver because the police did not want any "long hairs around." [27] The Buffalo Springfield, in a hit record, describe gun-bearing police rounding up teen-agers on the Sunset Strip,

and draw the moral, "Step out of line the men come and take you away." [28] On the same theme, Dylan ironically shows that adults arbitrarily oppose just about all activities of youths, saying that they should "look out" no matter what they are doing.[29] More bitter is the Mothers' description of police killing large number of hippies, which is then justified on the grounds "They looked too weird . . . it served them right." [30] Though the incident is fictional, the Mothers clearly believe Americans capable of shooting down those who engage in deviant behavior.

Though the songs echo the oppression that youngsters have felt, they do not ignore the problems that all humans face in a mass society. Writer Tom Paxton knows that it is not easy to keep one's life from being forced into a predetermined mold. In "Mr. Blue" he has a Big-Brother-like narrator telling the title character, a kind of Everyman, that he is always under surveillance, and that he will never be able to indulge himself in his precious dreams of freedom from society. This is because society needs him to fill a slot, no matter what his personal desires. Of that slot, the narrator says, "You'll learn to love it/Or we'll break you." And then comes the chilling chorus:

> What will it take to whip you into line
> A broken heart?
> A broken head?
> It can be arranged.[31]

Though no other writer made the message so explicit, a similar fear of being forced into an unwelcome slot underlies many songs of the period.

The society of slotted people is an empty one, partly described as "TV dinner by the pool,/I'm so glad I finished school." [32] It is one in which people have been robbed of their humanity, receiving in return the "transient treasures" of wealth and the useless gadgets of a technological age. One of these is television, referred to simply as "that rotten box," or, in a more sinister image, as an "electronic shrine." This image of men worshipping gadgets recurs. In the nightmare vision of a McLuhanesque world —where the medium is the message— Simon and Garfunkle sing of men so busy bowing and praying to a "neon god" that they cannot understand or touch one another. Indeed, here electronics seem to hinder the process of communication rather than facilitate it. People talk and hear but never understand, as the "sounds of silence" fill the world.[33] Such lack of communication contributes to the indifference with which men can view the life and death of a neighbor, as in Simon's "A Most Peculiar Man." [34] It also creates the climate of fear which causes people to kill a stranger for no reason other than his unknown origins in Strawberry Alarm Clock's "They Saw the Fat One Coming." [35]

Alienated from his fellows, fearful and alone, modern man has also despoiled the natural world in which he lives. With anguish in his voice, Jim Morrison of the Doors asks:

What have they done to the earth?
What have they done to our fair sister?
Ravished and plundered and ripped her and bit her
Stuck her with knives in the side of the dawn
And tied her with fences and dragged her down.[36]

In a lighter tone but with no less serious an intent, the Lewis and Clark Expedition describe the way man has cut himself off from nature.

There's a chain around the flowers
There's a fence around the trees

This is freedom's country
Do anything you please.

With a final thrust they add, "You don't need to touch the flowers/They're plastic anyway." [37]

This brings up a fear that haunts a number of recent songs, the worry that the technological age has created so many artificial things that nothing natural remains. Concerned with authenticity, the songsters are afraid that man himself is becoming an artifact, or, in their favorite word, "plastic." Thus, the Jefferson Airplane sing about a "Plastic Fantastic Lover," while the Iron Butterfly warn a girl to stay away from people "made of plastic." [38] The image recurs most frequently in the works of the Mothers of Invention. In one song, they depict the country as being run by a plastic Congress and President.[39] Then, in "Plastic People," they start with complaints about a girlfriend who uses "plastic goo" on her face, go on to a picture of teen-agers on the Sunset Strip—who are probably their fans—as being "plastic," too, and finally turn on their listeners and say "Go home and check yourself/You think we're talking about someone else." [40] Such a vision is frightening, for if the audience is plastic, perhaps the Mothers, themselves, are made of the same phony material. And if the whole world is plastic, who can be sure of his own authenticity?

Love Relationships

Toward the end of "Plastic People," the Mothers say, "I know true love can never be/A product of plasticity." [41] This brings up the greatest horror, that in a "plastic" society like the United States, love relationships are impossible. For the young song writers, American love is viewed as warped and twisted. Nothing about Establishment society frightens them more than its attitudes towards sex. Tim Buckley is typical in singing that older Americans are "Afraid to trust in their bodies," and in describing them as "Faking love on a bed made of knives." [42] Others give graphic portraits of deviant behavior. The Fugs tell of a "Dirty Old Man" hanging around high school playgrounds; the Velvet Underground portray a masochist; and the Mothers depict a middle-aged man lusting after his own thirteen-year-old daughter.[43] The fullest indictment of modern love is made by the United States of America, who devote almost an entire album to the subject. Here, in a twisted portrait of "pleasure and pain," is a world of loveless marriages, homosexual relationships in men's rooms, venomous attractions, and overt sadism—all masked by a middle-class, suburban world in which people consider "morality" important. To show that natural relationships are possible elsewhere, the group sings one tender love lyric; interestingly, it is the lament of a Cuban girl for the dead Ché Guevara.[44]

The fact that bourgeois America has warped attitudes towards sex and love is bad enough; the songsters are more worried that such attitudes will infect their own generation. Thus, the Collectors decry the fact that man-woman relationships are too often seen as some kind of contest, with a victor and vanquished, and in which violence is more acceptable than tenderness.[45] Perhaps because most of the singers are men, criticisms of female sexual attitudes abound. The Mothers say disgustedly to the American woman, "You lie in bed and grit your teeth," while the Sopwith Camel object to the traditional kind of purity by singing, "I don't want no woman wrapped up in cellophane." [46] This is because such

a woman "will do you in/Bending your mind with her talking about sin." [47] All the musicians would prefer the girl about whom Moby Grape sings who is "super-powered, deflowered," and over eighteen.[48]

Living in a "plastic" world where honest human relationships are impossible, the song writers might be expected to wrap themselves in a mood of musical despair. But they are young—and often making plenty of money—and such an attitude is foreign to them. Musically, they are hopeful because, as the title of the Dylan song indicates, "The Times They Are A-Changin'." Without describing the changes, Dylan clearly threatens the older generation, as he tells critics, parents, and presumably anyone over thirty, to start swimming or they will drown in the rising floodwaters of social change.[49]

In another work, Dylan exploits the same theme. Here is a portrait of a presumably normal, educated man, faced with a series of bizarre situations, who is made to feel like a freak because he does not understand what is going on. The chorus is the young generation's comment to all adults, as it mocks "Mr. Jones" for not understanding what is happening all around him.[50]

The changes going on are, not surprisingly, associated with the carefree, joyful experiences of youth. As Jefferson Airplane sings, "It's a wild time/I see people all around me changing faces/It's a wild time/ I'm doing things that haven't got a name yet." [51] The most full-blown description of the changing world is Tim Buckley's "Goodbye and Hello," a lengthy and explicit portrait of what the youth hope is happening. Throughout the song the author contrasts two kinds of people and their environments. On the one hand are the "antique people"—godless and sexless—

of an industrial civilization, living in dark dungeons, working hard, worshipping technology and money, sacrificing their sons to placate "vaudeville" generals, and blinding themselves to the fact that their "masquerade towers" are "riddled by widening cracks." Opposed to them are the "new children," interested in flowers, streams, and the beauty of the sky, who wish to take off their clothes to dance and sing and love one another. What's more, the "antique people are fading away"; in fact, they are already wearing "death masks." As the song says, "The new children will live because their elders have died." [52]

Buckley's vision of the new world that is coming is obviously that of a kind of idyllic Eden before the fall, a world in which men will be free to romp and play and indulge their natural desires for love. It is a pagan world, the antithesis of the Christian ideal that would postpone fulfillment to some afterlife. Elsewhere, Buckley explicitly condemns Christianity, saying "I can't hesitate and I can't wait for pleasant street." [53] Similarly, the Doors' Jim Morrison states, "Cancel my subscription to the resurrection," and in the same song literally shrieks, "We want the world and want it now." [54] Here is the impatient demand of youth that all problems be swept aside and the world be made into paradise without delay.

How to Live

Though the times may be changing, the songsters are well aware that—despite their brave words and demands—there is plenty of strength left in the old social order. Obviously, they can see the war continuing, Negro demands not being met, and the continuing hostility of society toward their long hair, music, sexual behavior, and experimentation with drugs. Faced with these facts, the musicians must deal with the problem of how to live decently within the framework of the old society. Here they tend toward the world of private experience mentioned earlier in this article in connection with Dylan. Many of their songs are almost programs for youth's behavior in a world perceived as being unlivable.

The first element is to forget about the repressive society out there. As Sopwith Camel says, "Stamp out reality . . ./Before reality stamps out you." [55] Then it is imperative to forget about trying to understand the outside world rationally. In a typical anti-intellectual stance, the Byrds describe such attempts as "scientific delirium madness." [56] Others combine a similar attitude with a strong measure of *carpe diem*. Spirit deride people who are "always asking" for "the reason" when they should be enjoying life, while H. P. Lovecraft admits that the bird is on the wing and states, "You need not know why." [57] What is important is that the moment be seized and life lived to the fullest. As Simon and Garfunkel say, one has to make the "moment last," and this is done best by those who open themselves fully to the pleasures of the world. [58]

The most frequent theme of the song writers is the call to freedom, the total freedom of the individual to "do his own thing." Peanut Butter Conspiracy carry this so far as to hope for a life that can be lived "free of time." [59] Circus Maximus and the Byrds—despite the fact that they are young men—long to recapture some lost freedom that they knew as children. [60] Such freedom can be almost solipsistic; Jimi Hendrix claim[ed] that even if the sun did not rise and the mountains fell into the sea, he would not care because ha[d] his "own world to live through." [61] But for others, it can lead to brotherhood. As H. P. Lovecraft says, "C'mon people now, let's get together/ Smile on your brother,/Try and love one another right now." [62]

A desire for freedom is certainly nothing new. What is different in the songs of the 1960's is the conviction that this freedom should be used by the individual in an extensive exploration of his own internal world. Central to the vision of the song writers is the idea that the mind must be opened and expanded if the truths of life are to be perceived. Thus, the importance of external reality is subordinated to that of a psychological, even a metaphysical, realm. The most extensive treatment of this subject is by the Amboy Dukes, who devote half of a long-playing record to it. Their theme is stated quite simply: "How happy life would be/If all mankind/Would take the time to journey to the center of the mind." [63] Like any mystical trip, what happens when one reaches the center of the mind is not easy to describe. Perhaps the best attempt is by the Iron Butterfly, who claim that an unconscious power will be released, flooding the individual with sensations and fusing him with a freedom of thought that will allow him to "see every thing." At this point, man will be blessed with the almost supernatural power of knowing "all." [64]

Such a journey is, of course, difficult to make. But youth has discovered a short cut to the mind's center, through the use of hallucinogenic drugs. Indeed, such journeys are almost inconceivable without hallucinogens, and the so-called "head songs" about drug experiences are the most prevalent of works that can be classified as "protest." [65] In this area, the songs carefully distinguish between "mind-expanding," nonaddictive marijuana and LSD, and hard, addictive drugs which destroy the body. Thus, the Velvet Underground and Love both tell of the dangers of heroin, while Canned Heat warn of methedrine use and the Fugs describe the problems of cocaine. [66] But none of the groups hesitate to recommend "grass" and "acid" trips as a prime way of opening oneself to the pleasures and beauties of the universe. As the Byrds claim in a typical "head song," drugs can free the individual from the narrow boundaries of the mundane world, allowing him to open his heart to the quiet joy and eternal love which pervade the whole universe. [67] Others find the reality of the drug experience more real than the day-to-day world, and some even hope for the possibility of staying "high" permanently. More frequent is the claim that "trips" are of lasting benefit because they improve the quality of life of an individual even after he "comes down." [68] The Peanut Butter Conspiracy, claiming that "everyone has a bomb" in his mind, even dream of some day turning the whole world on with drugs, thus solving mankind's plaguing problems by making the earth a loving place. [69] An extreme desire, perhaps, but one that would find much support among other musicians.

A Repressive Society

This, then is the portrait of America that emerges in the popular songs of the 1960's which can be labelled as "protest." It is, in the eyes of the song writers, a society which makes war on peoples abroad and acts repressively toward helpless minorities like Negroes, youth, and hippies at home. It is a land of people whose lives are devoid of feeling, love, and sexual pleasure. It is a country whose institutions are crumbling away, one which can presumably only be saved by a sort of cultural and spiritual revolution which the young themselves will lead.

Whether one agrees wholly, partly, or

not at all with such a picture of the United States, the major elements of such a critical portrait are familiar enough. It is only in realizing that all this is being said in popular music, on records that sometimes sell a million copies to teenagers, in songs that youngsters often dance to, that one comes to feel that something strange is happening today. Indeed, if parents fully understand what the youth are saying musically to one another, they must long for the simpler days of Elvis Presley and his blue suede shoes.

If the lyrics of the songs would disturb older people, the musical sound would do so even more. In fact, a good case could be made that the music itself expresses as much protest against the status quo as do the words. Performed in concert with electronic amplification on all instruments—or listened to at home at top volume—the music drowns the individual in waves of sound; sometimes it seems to be pulsating inside the listener. When coupled with a typical light show, where colors flash and swirl on huge screens, the music helps to provide an assault on the senses, creating an overwhelming personal experience of the kind that the songs advise people to seek. This sort of total experience is certainly a protest against the tepid, partial pleasures which other songs describe as the lot of bourgeois America.

Another aspect of the music which might be considered a kind of protest is the attempt of many groups to capture in sound the quality of a drug "trip," to try through melody, rhythm, and volume to—in the vernacular—"blow the mind" of the audience. Of course, youngsters often listen to such music while under the influence of hallucinogens. In such a state, the perceptive experience supposedly can have the quality of putting one in touch with regions of the mind and manifestations of the universe that can be felt in no other way. Such mysticism, such transcendental attitudes, are certainly a protest against a society in which reality is always pragmatic and truth instrumental.

To try to explain why the jingles and vapid love lyrics of popular music in the 1950's evolved into the social criticism and mystical vision of the 1960's is certainly not easy. Part of it is the fact that performers, who have always been young, started writing their own songs, out of their own life experiences, rather than accepting the commercial output of the older members of tin pan alley. But this does not explain the popularity of the new songs. Here one must look to the youthful audience, which decided it preferred buying works of the newer kind. For it was the commercial success of some of the new groups which opened the doors of the record companies to the many that flourish today.

The Function of Music

Though one cannot make definitive judgments about this record-buying audience, some things seem clear. Certainly, it is true that with increasingly rapid social change, parents—and adults in general—have less and less that they can tell their children about the ways of the world, for adult life experiences are not very relevant to current social conditions. Similarly, institutions like the school and the press suffer from a kind of cultural lag that makes their viewpoints valueless for youth. Into the place of these traditional sources of information have stepped the youth themselves, and through such things as the "underground" press and popular music they are telling each other exactly what is happening. In this way, the music has achieved popularity—at least in part—because it telegraphs important messages to young people and helps to define and codify the mores and standards of their own subculture. A youngster may personally feel that there is no difference between his parents' drinking and his use of marijuana. Certainly, it is comforting to him when his friends feel the same way, and when popular songs selling millions of copies deliver the same message, there are even stronger sanctions for his "turning on." Thus, the lyrics of the music serve a functional role in the world of youth.

It is interesting to note that the popular music also puts youth in touch with serious, intellectual critiques of American life. Perhaps it starts only as a gut reaction in the song writers, but they have put into music the ideas of many American social critics. Without reading Paul Goodman, David Riesman, C. Wright Mills, or Mary McCarthy, youngsters will know that life is a "rat race," that Americans are a "lonely crowd," that "white-collar" lives contain much frustration, and that the war in Vietnam is far from just. And they will have learned this from popular music, as well as from their own observation.

The other side of the coin from criticism of contemporary life is the search for personal experience, primarily of the "mind-expanding" sort. As is obvious by now, such expansion has nothing to do with the intellect, but is a spiritual phenomenon. Here a final critique is definitely implicit. Throughout the music —as in youth culture—there is the search for a kind of mystical unity, an ability to feel a oneness with the universe. This is what drugs are used for; this is what the total environment of the light and music shows is about; and this is what is sought in the sexual experience—often explicitly evident in the orgasmic grunts and moans of performers. Through the search for this unity, the music is implicitly condemning the fragmentation of the individual's life which is endemic in the modern world. The songsters are saying that it is wrong to compartmentalize work and play, wrong to cut men off from the natural rhythms of nature, wrong to stifle sex and love and play in favor of greater productivity, wrong to say man's spiritual needs can be filled by providing him with more material possessions.

This is obviously a criticism that can only be made by an affluent people, but these youth do represent the most affluent of all countries. And rather than wallow in their affluence, they have sensed and expressed much of the malaise that plagues our technological society. The charge may be made against them that they are really utopians, but the feeling increases today that we are in need of more utopian thinking and feeling. And while one might not wish to follow their prescriptions for the good life, they have caught something of the desire for freedom that all men feel. What could be more utopian and yet more inviting in its freedom than the hopeful picture which the Mothers of Invention paint of the future:

There will come a time when everybody
Who is lonely will be free . . .
TO SING AND DANCE AND LOVE
There will come a time when every evil
That we know will be an evil
WE CAN RISE ABOVE
Who cares if hair is long or short
Or sprayed or partly grayed . . .
WE KNOW THAT HAIR
AINT WHERE IT'S AT
(There will come a time when you
won't even be ashamed if you are fat!)

Who cares if you're so poor
You can't afford to buy a pair
Of mod a-go go stretch elastic pants
THERE WILL COME A TIME
WHEN YOU CAN EVEN
TAKE YOUR CLOTHES OFF WHEN
YOU DANCE [70]

Footnotes

[1] The definition of "popular music" being used in this article is a broad one. It encompasses a multitude of styles, including folk, folk-rock, acid-rock, hard-rock, and blues, to give just a few names being used in the musical world today. It does so because the old musical classifications have been totally smashed and the forms now overlap in a way that makes meaningful distinction between them impossible. Though not every group or song referred to will have been popular in the sense of selling a million records, all of them are part of a broad, variegated scene termed "pop." Some of the groups, like Buffalo Springfield, Strawberry Alarm Clock, or the Byrds, have sold millions of records. Others, like the Fugs or Mothers of Invention, have never had a real hit, though they are played on radio stations allied to the "underground." Still, such groups do sell respectable numbers of records and do perform regularly at teen-age concerts, and thus must be considered part of the "pop" scene.

[2] *Saturday Evening Post,* Vol. 237, March 21, 1964, p. 30; *Reporter,* Vol. 30, Feb. 27, 1964, p. 18; *Saturday Review,* Vol. 50, August 19, 1967, p. 18; *Life,* Vol. 64, June 28, 1968, p. 51.

[3] "The Music of the Beatles," *New York Review of Books,* Jan. 15, 1968, pp. 23–27. See also "The New Music," *The Listener,* Vol. 78, August 3, 1967, pp. 129–130; *Columbia University Forum,* Fall 1967, pp. 16–22; *New American Review,* Vol. 1, April 1968, pp. 118–139; Ellen Willis, "The Sound of Bob Dylan," *Commentary,* Vol. 44, November 1967, pp. 71–80. Many of these articles deal with English as well as American popular groups, and, in fact, the music of the two countries cannot, in any meaningful sense, be separated. This article will only survey American musical groups, though a look at English music would reveal the prevalence of most of the themes explored here.

[4] "The New Music," *loc. cit.,* p. 129.

[5] *Time,* Vol. 80, Nov. 23, 1962, pp. 54–60, gives a brief survey of the folk revival.

[6] Wills, *op. cit.,* gives a good analysis of his work.

[7] It must be pointed out that, in spite of the large amount of social criticism, most songs today are still about love, even those by groups such as Country Joe and the Fish, best known for their social satire.

[8] This article is concerned almost exclusively with music written and performed by white musicians. While popular music by Negroes does contain social criticism, the current forms—loosely termed "soul music"—make comments about oppression similar to those which Negroes have always made. The real change in content has come largely in white music in the 1960's.

[9] Phil Ochs, "Talking Birmingham Jam" and "Here's to the State of Mississippi," *I Ain't Marching Any More* (Elektra, 7237); Simon and Garfunkel, "He Was My Brother," *Wednesday Morning 3 A.M.* (Columbia, CS 9049). (Songs from records will be noted by performer, song title in quotation marks, and album title in italics, followed by record company and number in parentheses.)

[10] Copyright 1966 by Dialogue Music, Inc. Used by permission.

[11] Ochs, *I Ain't Marching Any More.*

[12] "The Harlem Song," *Together* (Vanguard, VSD 79277). Copyright by Joyful Wisdom Music, Inc.

[13] Mothers of Invention, *Freak Out* (Verve, 65005). Copyright 1968 by Frank Zappa Music, Inc. All rights reserved.

[14] Strawberry Alarm Clock, "Incense and Peppermints," written by John Carter and Tim Gilbert, *Strawberry Alarm Clock* (Uni., 73014). Copyright by Claridge Music, Inc.

[15] Phil Ochs, "That Was the President," *"I Ain't Marching Any More;* the Byrds, "He Was A Friend of Mine," *Turn! Turn!* (Columbia, CS 9254).

[16] "Superbird," *Electric Music for the Mind and Body* (Vanguard, 79244). Copyright by Tradition Music Company.

[17] Love, "Mushroom Clouds," *Love* (Elektra, EKL 4001); the Byrds, "I Come and Stand at Every Door," *Fifth Dimension* (Columbia, CS 9349); Peanut Butter Conspiracy, "Wonderment," written by John Merrill, *Great Conspiracy* (Columbia, CS 9590). Copyright by 4-Star Music Company, Inc.

[18] Copyright 1965 by Trousdale Music Publishers, Inc.

[19] Buffy St. Marie, "Universal Soldier," Southern Publishing, ASCAP; Ochs, *I Ain't Marching Any More.*

[20] *The Notorious Byrd Brothers* (Columbia, CS 9575).

[21] "War Song," *Tenderness Junction* (Reprise, S 6280).

[22] "An Untitled Protest," *Together.* Copyright by Joyful Wisdom Music.

[23] "Kill for Peace," *The Fugs* (Esp. 1028).

[24] "I Feel Like I'm Fixin' to Die," *I Feel Like I'm Fixin' to Die* (Vanguard, 9266). Copyright by Tradition Music Company.

[25] *We're Only in It for the Money* (Verve, 65045). Copyright by Frank Zappa Music, Inc. All rights reserved.

[26] "Laugh at Me," *Five West Cotillion,* BMI.

[27] "My Crime," *Boogie* (Liberty, 7541).

[28] "For What It's Worth." Copyright 1966 by Cotillion Music, Inc.—Ten East Music—Springaloo Toones. Reprinted by permission.

[29] "Subterranean Homesick Blues," *Bob Dylan's Greatest Hits* (Columbia, KCS 9463).

[30] *We're Only in It for the Money.* Copyright 1968 by Frank Zappa Music, Inc. All rights reserved.

[31] "Mr. Blue," written by Tom Paxton, *Clear Light* (Elektra, 74011). Copyright 1966 by Deep Fork Music, Inc. All rights reserved. Used with permission.

[32] Mothers of Invention, "Brown Shoes Don't Make It," *Absolutely Free* (Verve, 65013). Copyright 1968 by Frank Zappa Music, Inc. All rights reserved.

[33] "Sounds of Silence," *Sounds of Silence* (Columbia, CS 9269).

[34] *Sounds of Silence.*

[35] *Wake Up . . . It's Tomorrow* (Uni., 73025).

[36] "When the Music's Over," *Strange Days* (Elektra, 74014). Copyright 1967 by Nipper Music, Inc. All rights reserved.

[37] "Chain Around the Flowers," *The Lewis and Clark Expedition* (Colgems, COS 105). Words and music by John Vandiver. Copyright 1967 by Screen Gems—Columbia Music, Inc. Used by Permission. Reproduction prohibited.

[38] *Surrealistic Pillow* (Victor, LSP 3766); "Stamped Ideas," *Heavy* (Atco, S 33-227).

[39] Uncle Bernie's Farm," *Absolutely Free.*

[40] "Plastic People," *Absolutely Free.* Copyright 1968 by Frank Zappa Music, Inc. All rights reserved.

[41] *Ibid.*

[42] "Goodbye and Hello," written by Tim Buckley, *Goodbye and Hello* (Elektra, 7318). Copyright 1968 by Third Story Music, Inc. All rights reserved.

[43] *The Fugs;* "Venus in Furs," *The Velvet Underground and Nico* (Verve, V6-5008); "Brown Shoes Don't Make It," *Absolutely Free.*

[44] *The United States of America* (Columbia, CS 9614).

[45] "What Love," *The Collectors* (Warner Bros.- Seven Arts, WS 1746).

[46] *We're Only in It for the Money;* "Cellophane Woman," *The Sopwith Camel* (Kama Sutra, KLPS 8060). Copyright by Great Honesty Music, Inc.

[47] "Cellophane Woman." Copyright by Great Honesty Music, Inc.

[48] "Motorcycle Irene," *Wow* (Columbia, CS 9613).

[49] *Bob Dylan's Greatest Hits.*

[50] "Ballad of a Thin Man/Mr. Jones," *Highway 61 Revisited* (Columbia, CS 9189). Though this song has obvious homosexual overtones, it also stands as youth's criticism of the older generation.

[51] "Wild Tyme (H)," *After Bathing at Baxter's* (Victor, LSO-1511). Copyright by Ice Bag Corporation.

[52] "Goodbye and Hello," written by Tim Buckley, *Goodbye and Hello.* Copyright 1968 by Third Story Music, Inc. All rights reserved.

[53] "Pleasant Street," written by Tim Buckley. Copyright 1969 by Third Story Music, Inc. All rights reserved.

[54] "When the Music's Over," *Strange Days.* Copyright 1967 by Nipper Music Company, Inc. All rights reserved.

[55] "Saga of the Low Down Let Down," *The Sopwith Camel.* Copyright by Great Honesty Music, Inc.

[56] "Fifth Dimension," *Fifth Dimension.*

[57] "Topanga Window," *Spirit* (Ode, 212 44004); "Let's Get Together," *H. P. Lovecraft* (Phillips, 600-252).

[58] "Feeling Groovy," *Sounds of Silence.*

[59] "Time Is After You," *West Coast Love-In* (Vault, LP 113).

[60] "Lost Sea Shanty," *Circus Maximus* (Vanguard, 79260); "Going Back," *The Notorious Byrd Brothers.*

[61] "If 6 Was 9," *Axis* (Reprise, S 6281).

[62] H. P. Lovecraft, "Let's Get Together," written by Chester Powers, *H. P. Lovecraft.* Copyright by Irving Music, Inc.

[63] "Journey to the Center of the Mind," *Journey to the Center of the Mind* (Mainstream, S 6112). Copyright 1968 by Brent Music Coropration.

[64] "Unconscious Power," *Heavy*.

[65] There are so many "head songs" that listing them would be an impossibly long task, Some of the most popular protest songs of the decade have been such works. They include Jefferson Airplane, "White Rabbit," *Surrealistic Pillow;* the Doors, "Light My Fire," *The Doors* (Elektra EKS 74007); Strawberry Alarm Clock, "Incense and Peppermints," *Incense and Peppermints;* and the Byrds, "Eight Miles High," *Fifth Dimension*.

[66] "Heroin," *Velvet Underground;* "Signed D. C.," *Love* (Elektra, 74001); "Amphetamine Annie," *Boogie;* "Coming Down," *The Fugs*.

[67] "Fifth Dimension," *Fifth Dimension*.

[68] See Country Joe and the Fish, "Bass Strings," *Electric Music for the Mind and Body;* or United States of America, "Coming Down," *United States of America*.

[69] "Living, Loving Life," *Great Conspiracy*.

[70] "Take Your Clothes Off When You Dance," *We're Only in It for the Money*. Copyright 1968 by Frank Zappa Music, Inc. All rights reserved.

18

Changing Sexual Standards

IRA L. REISS

Available Evidence

Scientific research into the sexual standards of different countries is extremely new. It has been in the last thirty years only that good researches into this area have been carried out. Indeed, even today the evidence is uneven and sparse. The majority of extensive research into sexual standards and behavior has been carried out in America. To be sure, there is evidence on other countries; for example, Anna-Lisa Kalveston has reported on sexual research in Sweden, and in England, Eustace Chesser has conducted some elaborate research. Mention should also be made here of the extensive anthropological evidence on nonliterate cultures (cultures that have not as yet achieved a written language, such as aboriginal African and South Pacific cultures).

Perhaps the greatest drawback of present-day research is the accent on sexual behavior rather than on the sexual standards that underlie that sexual behavior. The author has recently published a comprehensive study that tries to summarize all the evidence on sexual standards that can be deduced from the major American studies on sexual behavior by Kinsey,[1] Burgess and Wallin,[2] Terman,[3] Ehrmann,[4] Locke,[5] and others. Elaboration of many of the points in this article can be found there. Another drawback of much of the available research is the fact that, especially in

America, it applies mostly to the upper segments of the white-urban population and not to all classes.

Despite these weaknesses, the evidence today is sufficient to make some key observations about sexual standards and their trends in America and in some other parts of the world. Science is a continuing process and one cannot give up the search because it does not give full information immediately. We must be content that what we have is surely better than any blind hunches.

Premarital Sexual Standards

The area of behavior involving kissing, petting, and coitus before marriage is the one about which most is known. In most cases, the standards that underlie these behaviors must be inferred from the behavior itself. For example, Kinsey found that 90 percent of the females in his sample who had had premarital intercourse had no serious regrets about it. This is taken as evidence that many of these women did not have a belief in abstinence that they were violating but that, in part at least, they must have accepted another standard that was more permissive and did not make them feel guilty about their behavior.

In this area of premarital sexual behavior, there are, in America, four major standards that young people accept and that find support in the research evidence.

SOURCE: Reprinted from "Standards of Sexual Behavior," by Ira L. Reiss, *The Encyclopedia of Sexual Behavior*, ed. Ellis and Abarbanel, New York: Hawthorn Books Inc., 1961, pp. 996–1004, by permission of the author and the publisher.

Standard of Abstinence

First, there is the formal standard of abstinence, which forbids coitus before marriage for both men and women. This standard has several subtypes, some of which allow petting, others of which allow only kissing. Petting is used here to refer to sexual stimulation short of full coitus, involving those parts of the body that are ordinarily clothed, such as the breast or genital area.

Double Standard

The second major premarital standard in America is the ancient double standard, which basically states that premarital intercourse is forbidden to women but not to men. Females who indulge are therefore considered immoral, but males who indulge are not. Under this standard, petting and kissing are not so severely restricted as coitus but here, too, the male is given much freer rights than the female.

Permissiveness without Affection

The third major standard in America, less widespread than preceeding ones, may be called permissiveness without affection, which holds that if two people are attracted physically to each other and both desire to have coitus, they may do so. Petting and kissing are, of course, also allowed on the same basis under this standard.

Permissiveness with Affection

The fourth and final premarital sexual standard is called permissiveness with affection. This standard is also less prevalent than the first two. It allows coitus for both men and women, but it requires that a strong, stable, and affectionate relationship be present.

Although these four standards have been best demonstrated to exist in America, I believe they are common to Western society and are applicable to most all the South American and European countries. However, there is a difference in the popularity of each standard; for example, the permissive standards are probably not as widespread in South America, where abstinence and the double standard seem to be overwhelmingly present. The opposite type of situation seems to prevail in the Scandinavian countries, in particular in Sweden, where permissiveness with affection seems to be more prevalent than the other standards; in fact, many of the young people are taught that if they are in love it is permissible to engage in coitus. England appears to be the country whose sexual standards most closely approximate our own in terms of the relative strength of each of the four standards.

There is only scanty evidence on the Oriental countries, but it is known that the double standard is quite widespread there. This is particularly true of China. Of course, industrialization in China and also in India is probably having a slow but sharp effect on the Oriental way of life and we may soon see a noticeable weakening of the double standard because of this.

The Polynesian cultures of the South Pacific are distinguished by their strong emphasis on the two permissive standards. This is also true for many African societies. In several of these areas the virginal and sexually apathetic woman is scorned and thought to be abnormal. This situation is also true for several of our Indian tribes in the American Southwest. The studies of Murdock[6] and Ford[7] indicate that the majority of these nonliterate cultures take a permissive attitude toward premarital petting and coitus. These researchers have made use of the Yale University Human Relations Area Files, which contain information on almost 300 nonliterate cultures—probably the best source for such information today.

Thus, there is a good deal of individuality among different cultures as to their sexual standards, even though there may be some general similarities; and each culture must be carefully studied in order to fully understand the relative power of each subtype of sexual standard. Nevertheless, it seems safe to say that most of the Western world *formally* favors a standard of abstinence and *informally* favors a double standard, although there are strong trends working in a more permissive direction.

Standards on Adultery, Homosexuality, and Masturbation

In addition to standards concerning premarital sexual relations, there are standards concerning adultery, homosexuality, masturbation, and other forms of sexual behavior. The formal norms in America forbid adultery, homosexuality, and masturbation. However, there is a sort of informal double standard for adultery and to a lesser extent for masturbation that frowns upon these behaviors in women much more so than in men. Homosexuality is largely rejected by all major sexual codes in America.

It should be noted that since much of the past sociological research focused on premarital sexual relations, we do not know as much about other standards, such as those regarding adultery, homosexuality, and masturbation. However, we do have evidence from Kinsey that all three of these types of behavior are quite common in American society; for example, Kinsey

reports that in his sample of married people of 40 years or over, about one-fourth of the wives and one-half of the husbands had committed adultery. In most cases some sort of disturbance in the marital relationship was involved and adultery was the outcome, but in other cases adultery as such was accepted. Many double-standard husbands took such liberties without feeling they were harming their marriages and without being willing to grant equal rights to their wives.

Homosexual behavior was also found to be quite common by Kinsey. He found that 37 percent of the males and 13 percent of the females had engaged in such behavior to orgasm at least once. But here too we know too little about how these people felt about their behavior. One could assume that, since all major American standards reject such behavior, most of these people suffered guilt reactions.

Attitudes toward masturbation, although still negative, seem to have become liberalized in America. Thus, many more people who masturbate today probably do so without as strong a guilt reaction. However, here too we lack sufficient information. We do know that in Kinsey's sample of several thousand men and women, by age 20 about one-third of the females and about nine of every ten men had masturbated.

Standards in other Western cultures regarding these three areas should be somewhat similar but one cannot be sure of the full picture until more research is carried out. For information on nonliterate cultures, we turn again to the work of Ford and Beach and of Murdock. Their findings indicate that casual adultery is commonly forbidden, as it too often leads to complications that disrupt the social organization. When it is allowed, it is usually strictly regulated so that it can occur only between certain people such as a husband and his sister-in-law. However, these restrictions are not required in several societies, such as the Eskimo, where during the winter months young married couples play a game called "putting out the lamps." In this game the oil lamps are extinguished and all the individuals scramble for a partner other than their mate, spending the night with the one they find.

Ford and Beach give evidence on masturbation and homosexuality in nonliterate societies. Masturbation seems to be very common but is most frequent among nonadults; homosexuality is much less common but many societies permit it under certain conditions for both men and women. As can be seen, our own attitudes on almost all sexual practices in the Western world are much more restrictive than those of nonliterate cultures.

Trends in Premarital Sexual Standards

Since exact sociological evidence on sexual behavior goes back less than thirty years, there is much in the area of trends that must be qualified and investigated more thoroughly. However, the evidence we have on America is consistent and points strongly in one direction. Starting in the 1920's, the Victorian "sexual dams" were breached and increases occurred in almost all forms of sexual behavior.

It should be clear that much of the permissive behavior that began in the 1920's occurred more on impulse or for excitement than for purposes of abiding by any standard, whether old or new. In time, standards did develop and in premarital relations the two older standards were liberalized and the two newer permissive standards were greatly enlarged.

Abstinence formerly placed a strong emphasis on the "untouched" quality of virginity. This has been sharply altered and today we find many women who believe in abstinence yet feel it is quite proper to pet to orgasm or masturbate their date. Thus, the standard of abstinence has been liberalized, adapting itself to the more sexually permissive changes that have been going on.

During this same time period the double standard also seems to have been severely weakened. There are probably fewer people today who can fully accept an unequal standard of behavior for men and women. Many people who formerly believed in the double standard have begun to feel that if they accept coitus for men they must also accept it for women. Frequently, however, these people cannot bring themselves to give full equality to the female so they have merely liberalized the double standard and have said that men can have coitus whenever they want but women can have coitus only when they are in love and/or engaged. Here, as in the case of abstinence, we find a liberalization occurring in order to make the standard adjust to a more permissive society.

Those who have found the liberalization of the standard of abstinence and of the double standard to be too conservative have joined the ranks of those who accept the standards of permissiveness without affection and of permissiveness with affection. Social changes occur gradually, so most of the shift seems to have gone to the less radical of these two standards, namely, permissiveness with affection, which requires a stable, affectionate relationship as a prerequisite for sexual intercourse.

Research Evidence on Changing Trends

Some of the research evidence on trends in standards will be seen in the following tables. Table 1 shows the increase in inci-

TABLE 1. *Accumulative Incidence of Petting to Orgasm among Females*

Age	Born before 1900	Born 1900– 1909	Born 1910– 1919	Born 1920– 1929
		Percentage*		
14	1	1	1	1
16	3	5	6	6
18	6	10	13	18
20	10	17	22	28
25	15	30	34	43
30	24	39	45	
35	26	44	53	

Source: Kinsey, *Sexual Behavior in the Human Female*, p. 275. Present-day rates for males are quite similar but the increase over previous generations is much smaller and such petting makes up a smaller percentage of the total male sex outlet.
* Accumulative incidence is a rate figured by taking all those eligible for an experience and seeing what percentage actually have the experience. For a full explanation, see Kinsey (1948), pp. 114–119.

dence of petting to orgasm in females of various generations, starting with the generation born between 1900 and 1910, which reached maturity in the 1920's. One can also see how such behavior increases as they became older.

TABLE 2. *Premarital Coitus of Women by Decade of Birth*

Age	Born before 1900	Born 1900– 1909	Born 1910– 1919	Born 1920– 1929
None	73.4	48.7	43.9	48.8
Spouse only	10.4	24.4	23.3	27.3
Others only	5.5	5.4	7.0	6.5
Spouse and others	10.4	21.0	25.6	17.4

Source: These data are based on Kinsey (1953), but were especially prepared for this paper through the kindness of Drs. Gebhard and Martin, of the Institute for Sex Research. These were based on 2,479 women who either were or had been married by the time of interview.

The decrease in the number of women who were virginal before marriage is clearly indicated in Tables 2 and 3, which are

TABLE 3. *Premarital Coitus of Women by Decade of Birth*

	Born before 1890	Born 1890– 1899	Born 1900– 1909
		Percentage	
None	86.5	74.0	51.2
Spouse only	8.7	17.7	32.7
Others only	1.9	2.5	2.1
Spouse and others	2.9	5.8	14.0

Source: Terman, p. 321. Rates for the 1910–1920 generation are not included here as they were based on few cases. Such rates can be found in the Kinsey studies.

from the studies of Kinsey and Terman, respectively. The weakening of the orthodox double standard is also supported by the data in Table 4, where the number

TABLE 4. *Premarital Coitus of Men by Decade of Birth*

	Born before 1890	Born 1890– 1899	Born 1900– 1909
		Percentage	
None	50.6	41.9	32.6
Spouse only	4.6	7.6	17.2
Others only	35.6	27.5	16.5
Spouse and others	9.2	23.0	33.7

Source: Terman, p. 321. The high rates of male virginity evidenced above are due to the high proportion of college men in this group. Kinsey found much lower percentages of virginity among those of lower education (by age 25, 90 percent of males whose education stopped in the eighth grade had premarital intercourse). The college-educated males exceed in petting to orgasm, where about 60 percent of them are involved by age 30, as compared to only about 15 percent of the low-education groups (Kinsey, 1948, pp. 536, 550).

of men who engage in coitus *only* with others besides their fiancées has been drastically reduced. This indicates that many more such men are now having coitus with their fiancées because they now accept such behavior as moral for engaged women. Finally, the increases in the "Spouse only" and the "Spouse and others" categories in Tables 2, 3, and 4 are also evidence that many more people accept permissiveness with affection, i.e., premarital coitus when love or engagement is present. Some of this increase may also be a further indication of the growth of a new subtype of the double standard, which allows coitus for women if they are in love and/or engaged. Thus Tables 1 through 4 tend to support my contentions regarding changes in premarital sexual standards. The majority of the men and women in the Kinsey study and the Burgess-Wallin study said they had no serious qualms about their behavior, thus further indicating acceptance of more liberal standards.

England is one of the few other countries for which we have comparable premarital trend data based on extensive studies. A glance at Table 5 indicates that, for the

TABLE 5. *Premarital Coitus for English Women by Decade of Birth*

	Born before 1904	Born 1904– 1913	Born 1914– 1923	Born 1924– 1933
	Percentage			
Coitus	19	36	39	43
Petting	7	22	29	25

Source: Chesser, p. 311.

sample Chesser used,[8] premarital coitus has also greatly increased in England among people born after 1900 who came to their maturity in the 1920's and later.

Reports regarding trends from other European countries are more difficult to obtain but basically they indicate that a more permissive sex code is in the making. Trend reports on nonliterate cultures are almost completely lacking since these cultures are usually studied only at one point in time.

Trends in Adultery, Homosexuality, and Masturbation Standards

Again, for data on America, the Kinsey studies can be taken as adequate, especially for the better-educated urban, white classes of our culture.

TABLE 6. *Accumulative Incidence of Extramarital Coitus for Females*

Age	Born before 1900	Born 1900– 1909	Born 1910– 1919	Born 1920– 1929
	Percentage			
18			10	9
19		4	7	10
20	2	3	5	9
25	4	8	10	12
30	10	16	19	
35	18	26	25	
40	22	30		
45	21	40		

Source: Kinsey, *Sexual Behavior in the Human Female*, p. 442. Men also increased in this area, except for the college-educated group. Data on men were not broken down as accurately by birth decades so these charts are for women only, with only summary statements for males given in the text.

Table 6 indicates that there has been an increase in extramarital coitus. However, here it is more difficult to determine standards since these data are not broken down into different types. The preponderance of men who commit adultery (by age 40, one-half of the men had committed adultery while only one-fourth of the women had done so) indicates that here too our culture is probably more liberal regarding men and that a sort of double standard exists in this area. However, it is unlikely that the increase in adultery is due to an increase in such double standard beliefs since there is strong evidence that the double standard is weakening. It is more likely that this increase is related to our present 1-in-4 divorce rate. Adultery may accompany the breakup of a marriage and with more divorces there may thus be more adultery. Of course, other reasons apply also; these are only a few possibly important factors.

Although Kinsey's figures for masturbation among males are only slightly higher in recent generations, the figures for women show a somewhat higher rate of increase. Table 7 indicates about 11 percent

TABLE 7. *Accumulative Incidence of Masturbation to Orgasm for Females*

Age	Born before 1900	Born 1900–1909	Born 1910–1919	Born 1920–1929
	Percentage			
5	3	3	2	1
10	12	12	10	6
15	25	25	24	17
20	33	34	36	30
25	38	43	46	47
30	44	51	53	
35	49	57	63	
40	52	63		

Source: Kinsey, *Sexual Behavior in the Human Female*, p. 180. For males there is only a slight increase in lower-education levels.

increase at age 40 for women born after 1900. Our standards seem to be more tolerant of masturbation today and this seems to be the trend despite the lack of any great increase in behavior. Most of the change in masturbation rates refers to women since the percentage of men who masturbate has been over 90 for several generations.

Homosexuality is even more evenly distributed over the various birth decades and there is practically no increase. Females, as seen in Table 8, by age 45 average

TABLE 8. *Accumulative Incidence of Homosexual Contacts to Orgasm for Females*

Age	Born before 1900	Born 1900–1910	Born 1910–1920	Born 1920–1930
	Percentage			
12				1
15	2	2	2	3
20	5	6	4	3
25	8	9	7	6
30	9	10	10	
35	11	11	13	
40	11	12		
45	12	17		

Source: Kinsey, *Sexual Behavior in the Human Female*, p. 495. The rate for men was 37 percent and also showed no increase.

about 13 percent homosexual experience to orgasm. The comparable rate for males is 37 percent. Again, I caution the reader that Kinsey qualified his findings and fully realized that they are not representative of all segments of American society. There is little evidence of an exact nature on trends in standards concerning homosexual behavior, but I believe that just as the rates have remained stable so have the attitudes toward such behavior. By and large, there is a strong feeling against homosexual contact, despite its apparent frequency. As our premarital sex codes become more liberalized, perhaps this attitude too will change, but as of today there is no firm evidence of such a change.

There is little evidence on trends in the above three areas (adultery, masturbation, and homosexuality) from other Western societies. As far as non-Western cultures are concerned, our evidence concerning trends is even more scanty. We do have some good information concerning standards at the time researchers visited the culture, but very few cultures have been investigated as to their past behavior, and thus trend information is sorely lacking on most cultures of the world. There is little question, however, that many countries such as India and China are undergoing changes in their sexual standards due to the effects of industrialization. But until more complete sociological researches are carried out in those areas, we can only put forth the speculation that as they industrialize their sexual codes will become more like those of other industrialized cultures.

Reasons for Recent Trends

What happened before 1920, particularly in America, to cause the sexual "explosion" of that decade?

The American and Western sexual standards of today have deep roots. They can be traced to the Hebrew, Greek, Roman, and early Christian cultures. Deuteronomy in the Old Testament gives us ample evidence of the source of our own male-dominant type of double standard. The Greeks had the hetaerae, an organization of highly cultured prostitutes, and they also had homosexuality; but both of these were for men only. The Romans followed the Greek example with their own, somewhat cruder, versions of male favoritism in the area of sexual permissiveness. Thus, the double standard had strong supports in Western society, so strong that the full force of Christianity and its demand for a single standard of abstinence failed to conquer it. The double standard is, of course, not "just natural"; witness the many cultures today that do not hold to the double standard. The double standard probably originally began due to man's physical superiority over woman, and it is difficult to change, for men are often unwilling to give up an "advantage" they have enjoyed for many centuries.

The nineteenth century dealt the double

standard its mortal blow. The urban industrial revolution had occurred by that time and the face of America, together with that of most of the Western world, was changing. For the first time, women were able to earn a living without entering prostitution. This new economic power meant that women could act, in general, more independently of men.

Particularly in America, young people began to choose their own mates on the basis of love, and the feminist movement continued in its drive to grant women the vote and general equality before the law. This trend toward permissiveness and equality was strongly reinforced by the improved economic position of women and the general urban-industrial type of society that was developing. Within a century women had carved an empire of wealth and status surpassing all previous achievements. Choice of mate by the young people themselves and consequent dating became widespread; contraceptive measures were developed that removed some of the fear of venereal disease and pregnancy; young people were allowed to go out alone; and Henry Ford gave them a "moving parlor" with his "invention."

Given this over-all picture, it is no wonder that by the 1920's there were great numbers of American men and women who no longer accepted the highly restrictive sexual codes of the nineteenth century. These people could afford to be independent, for all the new social forces were in their favor. Americans have come to accept a more permissive sexual attitude in a way that would shock our Victorian ancestors and with a nonchalance that would surprise even the iconoclasts of the 1920's. Since the 1920's, instead of increasing the frequency of sexual behaviors, the changes made have been consolidated. This, naturally, does not mean that Americans have fully thrown over the past. The older standards (abstinence and the double standard) are still very much present. But Americans have moved further away from orthodox forms of both these standards than ever before. Many similar forces have effected changes in European countries, England most likely being the closest in this respect to America. It is possible that as India, China, and other countries industrialize, such changes in their sex codes will also occur.

The Future of Premarital Sexual Standards

The area of premarital sexual standards in America is the one most studied, and although full evidence is lacking, much of what is said about America applies to many other Western cultures.

The evidence points clearly to increased permissiveness. This permissiveness will probably take three directions. First, there will be an increase in abstinent-believers who accept heavy petting. This seems to be the case in past generations (see Table 1) and should become increasingly true. The evidence indicates that very often petting standards are only temporary standards that girls drop when they fall in love and/or become engaged. At such times these people come to accept permissiveness with affection. The freedom granted young people, the intimacy they have in their "steady" and "pinned" relationships, makes this permissive trend quite likely. People do not like to feel guilty about their behavior, so it is likely that when they violate old standards they will come to accept more permissive ones in their place.

The second major direction our sexual standards will take will be toward continued modification of the double standard so as to permit coitus for women when in love but still allowing men coitus at any time. Equalitarian pressures strongly push in this direction. However, this trend is also probably only a transitory solution for it still contains too much inequality and female restrictiveness for our type of society.

The third direction in which our sexual standards will likely head is also in line with past trends: toward permissiveness with affection. The more conservative interpretation of this standard, which only allows coitus when love and/or engagement is involved, will become increasingly accepted. This standard is much more in accord with the strong equalitarian and permissive pressures that have developed with our urban-industrial type of society and, as Tables 2, 3, and 4 indicate, its acceptance has already greatly increased. Of course, there are elements that conflict with this standard, such as our religious institutions, but by and large it seems to have become integrated into our society. This does not mean that it is the most moral standard; many immoral customs fit very nicely into a society.

The standard of abstinence and the double standard will probably continue for many centuries more, but possibly within a hundred years or so they will no longer be the dominant standards in America, permissiveness with affection taking precedence. The college-educated group has most clearly demonstrated its tendencies in this direction and will probably lead the move in this direction.

As far as the fourth standard is concerned, permissiveness without affection is too radical to obtain a large following at the present time. If such a standard ever takes root in America it will probably be many centuries from today. Our extended permissiveness has been largely in the direction of affectionate, "person-centered coitus" rather than "body-centered coitus" and it is likely to remain that way for some time to come due to our strong association of deep affection with sexual behavior.

The Future of Other Sexual Standards

The evidence previously cited shows that, in America at least, there has been an increase in adultery. Unlike the trend toward increased premarital relations, however, this trend will probably slow down. Although our urban-industrial society is conducive to increased permissiveness, most of this permissiveness in the future will probably grow in the area of premarital relations. My own research in this area indicates that the same young people who strongly favor being allowed to engage in premarital coitus will argue quite firmly against extramarital coitus. For example, permissiveness with affection is a standard that has increased in importance in recent decades and this standard is one that stresses a monagamous type of love affair. Even on this premarital basis it emphasizes that one must be faithful to one's premarital partner. Thus, although there has been an increase in adultery, the association of love and sexual monogamy has shown no sign of weakening.

In regard to masturbation and homosexuality in America attitudes toward masturbation seem to have been liberalized, and this should continue since it agrees with the over-all courtship permissiveness. It is difficult to speak of changes in behavior in this area for, with increased liberalism in petting and coitus, masturbation, although more accepted, may ac-

tually decrease. Homosexual attitudes seem the least likely to alter and a strong general opposition appears to remain toward such behavior.

Conclusions

There is one important distinctive characteristic of the premarital trends discussed above. For the first time in Western society's written history our young people are devising a sexual code of their own making. Abstinence and double standard codes were parentally devised codes, codes that were integrated into a male-dominant, parentally run, extended-family type of system. In this sort of society parents chose the mates and women were valued for their economic assets and their ability to bear children. With the advent of a new kind of society, an urban-industrial society, the pressures for this older sort of courtship system have sharply decreased.

A new sexual code was needed to fit into this new type of society. It has been in process of development since the nineteenth century and its significance is that this time the young people themselves, in their new social relationships, are unconsciously evolving it. It is this newer sexual code that has modified and in some cases replaced the older, parentally devised sexual codes. The clash between the old and new codes is felt internally by many people in Western society, who are partly attached to both.

American society, together with most of the Western world, has had a severely restrictive sexual code. As time moves on this is becoming much less the case but there still is a strong general sexual taboo that is quite rare in non-Western societies. American and other Western cultures seem to be involved at present in a change in that over-all sexual taboo, and there will likely be much conflict involved. We are in a state of transition and those who cling to the past get hurt by the customs of the present and those who rush to the future are damaged by the traditions of the past.

Footnotes

[1] See: Alfred C. Kinsey, *et al.*, *Sexual Behavior in the Human Male*, Phila.: W. B. Saunders Co., 1948; Alfred C. Kinsey, *et al.*, *Sexual Behavior in the Human Female*, Phila.: W. B. Saunders Co., 1953.

[2] Ernest W. Burgess and Paul Wallin, *Engagement and Marriage*, Phila.: J. B. Lippincott Co., 1953.

[3] Lewis M. Terman, *Psychological Factors in Marital Happiness*, New York: McGraw-Hill Book Co., 1938.

[4] Winston Ehrmann, "Some Knowns and Unknowns in Research into Human Sex Behavior," *Marriage & Family Living*, 17, 1955, pp. 16–22.

[5] Harvey J. Locke, *Predicting Adjustment in Marriage*, New York: Henry Holt, 1951.

[6] George P. Murdock, *Social Structure*, New York: The Macmillan Co., 1949.

[7] Clellan S. Ford and Frank A. Beach, *Patterns of Sexual Behavior*, New York: Harper and Brothers, 1951.

[8] Eustace Chesser, *The Sexual, Marital and Family Relationships of the English Woman*, New York: Roy Publishers, 1957.

19

The Study of the Future

DANIEL BELL

I

This is an era in which society has become "future-oriented" in its thinking. The French Commissariat du Plan last year [1964] set up a 1985 Committee to explore different choices in the use of the expected increases in French national income. The American Academy of Arts and Sciences is creating a Commission on the Year 2000 (which, after all, is less than thirty-five years away), to anticipate social problems and to design new institutions to cope with them. The Ford Foundation has underwritten such varied projects as Resources for the Future, Inc., which has assembled statistical estimates, based on requirements and availabilities, of American physical resources (heat and power, metals, water, food, outdoor recreation, and the like), and the European-based project, Futuribles, directed by Bertrand de Jouvenel, which has sponsored almost a hundred speculative essays under the rubric "The Future of . . . Pakistan, Greece, India, etc.," as well as detailed studies of methods of planning and prediction, and of expected changes in the major institutions of society.

In the last few years, in fact, at least half a dozen nongovernmental organizations have begun in some serious way to anticipate or even "invent" the future, and there have been published, by cursory count, at least two dozen books that soberly attempt some broad or technical projection about the shape of society ahead and its problems— e.g., *The Future* (by Theodore Gordon), *The Foreseeable Future* (by Sir George Thomson), *The Future of Man* (by P. B. Medewar), *Man and His Future* (edited by Gordon Wolstenholme), *Inventing the Future* (by Dennis Gabor), *Profiles of the Future* (by Arthur C. Clarke), *Resources in America's Future* (by Landsberg, Fischman and Fisher), *The World in 1984* (edited by Nigel Calder), *The Next Generation* (by Donald Michael), *The Race to the Year 2000* (by Fritz Baade), *The Next Hundred Years* (by Brown, Bonner and Weir), *Life in the Twenty-First Century* (edited by Vassiliev and Gouschev), and on and on.

All of this is startling, and in some ways novel. Only seven years ago, Raymond Aron could remark (in his Auguste Comte lectures on *War and Industrial Society*) that "we are too much obsessed by the 20th century to spend time in speculating about the twenty-first. Long-range historical predictions have gone out of fashion." Aron, it is true, was talking about the apocalyptic modes of thought that dominated the 19th century: the contending forces of rationalistic optimism, nourished by utopian visions of earthly abundance, and the irrationalist pessimism derived from the aristocratic, Catholic and Nietzschean critiques of mass society, two modes that were caricatured and cruelly distorted by the Soviet effort to transform a lumbering society root and branch, had by the Nazi glorification of race and blood. While many

SOURCE: Reprinted from *The Public Interest*, Fall, 1965, 1:119–130, by permission of the author and the publisher. Copyright © 1965 by National Affairs, Inc.

ideologies of the *tiers monde* retain an apocalyptic air—precisely because of the discrepancy between the vaulting fantasies about a new role in world history and the recalcitrant reality of economic backwardness—that style of thought has largely disappeared among the Western intelligentsia, at least among those who have lived through several decades of wars, concentration camps and terror.

What has remained from the utopian tradition, however, and this is the underlying element in our renewed interest in the future, is its eudaemonism—the proposition that each person is entitled to happiness and that it is one of the functions of government to try and assure him at least the preconditions of happiness. Now, some persons may cavil that happiness is a subjective state that cannot be defined, let alone measured, and its pursuit is a personal matter to be defined by the individual in his own way. Whatever force this argument may have as a metaphysical statement, or as a statement about ultimate definitions, the simple sociological fact is that in a complex, interconnected society, the *conditions* of happiness for the mass of the people—social and economic security, education, equal opportunity, decent housing, medical care, and the like—involve a high degree of collective action through the agency of government, national or local. The creation of a welfare state which all this implies is thus linked with a concern about the future.

What has been added to the recurrent eudaemonism (one cannot call it eternal, since the proposition that to provide happiness is the function of government goes back principally to Saint-Just and the French Revolution) is a *technocratic* orientation about the achievement of happiness. The older utopian tradition assumed that all social problems would be solved simply by "abundance." Even such a hard-headed revolutionist as Lenin assumed (in *State and Revolution*) that most functions of state administration had "become so simplified and . . . reduced to such simple operations of registration, filing, and checking" that they would be within the "reach of every literate person." What is clear today is that planning is a highly technical skill and involves a host of equally specialized skills. Planning itself, whether city or economic, has become a profession, complete with its own arcane language and hieratic knowledge. And many of the planners "foresee" themselves as the forerunners of a new class—*les dirigeants,* the future governors of the future society.

How does one explain this resurgence of interest in "the future"? And why has it become so technocratically oriented? One can identify a number of elements that have conjoined to produce this new future-orientation:

1. The fading of the horrors of the past—the recession of Nazism and Stalinism—and the rise of a new generation (as well as new states) have created new demands upon society, and a new optimism about fulfillment. To this has been added the "romance of space." What science fiction (the genre is less than eighty years old, and mass-produced science fiction is only about thirty years old) had foretold as a fantasy became a possibility with the launching of the first Sputnik in 1957. Within less than a decade, more than a dozen men have orbited the earth, space shots have reached the moon and have probed Mars, and a communications satellite that provides instant television and telephone linkage among almost all parts

of the world has become a permanent fixture in the skies. Thus man's technological powers have been given a new dimension and a new dramatic demonstration. The jump-off into space is also a jump-off into future time.

2. The rapid expansion of transportation and communication (five-hour jets from coast to coast; a hundred million persons, on 93 percent of all television sets in the United States, simultaneously watching the Kennedy funeral) has bound this country together in a new way and, perhaps for the first time, created a genuine national society. At the same time, the interdependence and the competition of people and enterprises have increased. Corporations have to anticipate technological trends, new products, changes in markets, capital needs, new plant locations, and must make more careful estimates of costs and output; today almost every company makes regular five-year budgets, many make ten- and twenty-year planning projections. Looking toward the future and planning for its consequence have increasingly become standard activities of the business firm.

3. The commitment to "economic growth" is an institutionalized feature of every modern society. Our ability to measure growth (dating back only twenty years or so, when the idea of Gross National Product was adopted as a measure of national achievement), our recognition of the role of government policy in stimulating or retarding growth, have made us all aware of the nature of social change and the role of government in directing social change.

4. The commitment to economic growth has meant, in many societies, an auxiliary commitment to "planning." Planning, as the Russians found out, need not mean a completely centralized, overadministered command economy. The French have developed indicative planning, which combines pooled market information—so that all firms are aware of each other's intentions and can adjust their targets accordingly—and government-induced investment in socially defined areas. The British are tinkering with an economic-development plan that combines a national incomes policy (primarily one of wage restraint) with a directed investment policy. Even the United States, while not formally committed to planning, has a set of national goals and purposes, proposed by the Commission that was set up by President Eisenhower. These goals—sixteen areas for the expansion of needs and services—have recently been "costed out" by the National Planning Association, which found that if all the projected expenditures were made by 1975, their expense would exceed the economy's capabilities by $150 billion. In all these ways, attention to planning and goals necessarily focuses attention on "the future," and how one can anticipate social and economic developments.

5. The development of a new intellectual technology—game theory, decision theory, linear programming, simulation, information theory, cybernetics, systems analysis—all of it tooled by the computer, allows us now to construct models of the future and assess possible consequences. The "input-output" models of Wassily Leontieff provide an interindustry matrix of 81 sectors, so that we can chart throughout the economy the "flows" of different economic combinations. Professor Richard Stone, of Cambridge, has created a simulation of the British economy that can demonstrate exactly which areas of investment or consumption have to be favored in order to

achieve designated growth rates or desirable allocations of resources. The Brookings Institution, and, independently—Robert Solow and James Tobin—have created "econometric forecasting" models, mathematical models of the American economy that will give us quarter-by-quarter forecasts of economic activities. The development of intellectual tools for planning thus provides the instruments for prediction, as well.

6. Finally, the heightened prestige of science and the crucial role of research have brought with them a new, optimistic temper about the future. Science, by its nature, is open, self-corrective, and often cumulative. Its very promise is one of new knowledge. We have recently been informed, principally by Derek Price, that knowledge has been growing at an "exponential rate"—i.e., the number of scientific articles, the holdings of major research libraries, the number of scientific periodicals have been "doubling" at a faster rate than ever before. Whatever caveats one may have about the genuine accretions of knowledge that might be reflected simply in the doubling of publications, the idea of the information explosion has reinforced the sense many people have —although it cannot be measured—that technology is increasing at an accelerating rate, and that new inventions, new modes of communication, new knowledge will demand new social forms necessary to cope with these changes.

In sum, there now exists the sense that social change, inevitably linked in its effects, must be guided in some conscious direction. Though this may not create the changes themselves, it will at least anticipate their direction and effects, and plan accordingly. In other words, we have become oriented toward the future.

The growing preoccupation with the future inevitably leads to the question of forecasting: how well can the future be predicted? Is such prediction possible when human affairs are so tangled or liable to irrational or capricious decisions, and when the elements that make up aggregate behavior are so multiple? The answer is not whether one can or cannot predict, but what kinds of things one can predict, and with what state of confidence.

Clearly the prediction of *single events* or the *singular decisions* men in power will make is very difficult, and is a function largely of intelligent information. (When one Kremlinologist was taxed with his failure to predict Khrushchev's downfall, his reply, quite correctly, was: Khrushchev didn't see what was coming, how did you expect me to see it?) Having reliable sources close to the decision-makers can, of course, facilitate prediction. But when a decision has to be *inferred,* then one is subject to many qualifying and even contradictory elements. For example, the question has been raised as to why, even though American Intelligence had broken the Japanese cipher codes and knew the imminence of war, the United States was unprepared at Pearl Harbor. The answer, as Roberta Wohlstetter points out (in her fascinating book *Pearl Harbor: Warning and Decision*), is that while we knew of the Japanese intention to attack Hawaii, we also knew a dozen other possibilities. We had no way of knowing which, among the dozen, was the most likely. The universal expectation among Americans, and others, was that when the Japanese attacked, they would move directly southward toward the Netherland East Indies, and the Philippines, as indeed they did. All that was expected at Pearl Harbor was sabotage against which precautions had been taken. "A warning signal," as Mrs. Wohlstetter observes, "is not likely to be heard if its occurrence is regarded as so improbable that no one is listening."

In similar fashion one can ask why the Hungarian revolt of 1956 which Paul Kecskemeti, in his study, has called *The Unexpected Revolution,* was not foreseen. The events of October, 1956, came as a total surprise to everyone in the West including people who were professionally concerned with what was going on in Hungary. A retrospective analysis by Donald D. Ranstead, which examined all the published material in English during the crucial period between July, 1953, and October 1, 1956, sheds some light on the matter. "Much of it was written under the spell of an academic concept of 'totalitarianism' that had come to be the standard basis of analyzing communist politics. Hannah Arendt's *Origins of Totalitarianism,* published in 1952, set the pattern. Kracauer and Berkman's *Satellite Mentality* which appeared, unfortunately, in the year of the upheavals only seemed to give empirical confirmation to the standard concept."

The concept of totalitarianism posited the idea that all social life within the totalitarian society had become atomized and subject to terror, and that internal revolt was highly unlikely, if not impossible. The different developments in Hungary, for example, which began with Nagy's launching of the "New Course" in July, 1953, were regarded only as a "seeming change," or simply as a factional struggle for power at the top with no consequences for the rest of the society. Thus, despite the open evidence of change, the failure was one of interpretation.

The prediction of political changes or of single decisions runs the hazard, thus, of

inadequate information, of too much "noise" (in the language of communication theory), or of dogmatic conceptualization which in itself sifts out inadequately the kind of signal the experts should be alert to. But there are different kinds of changes that do lend themselves to more accurate "plotting" of the future. One class of such changes is the crescive one—which, because of a time lag, is evident long before it comes to the fore. Demography, or population changes, represents the best example of such crescive changes, and most market research and planning are based exactly on such calculations.

Population forecasting does have its hazards. In the 1930's, for example, the National Resources Planning Board assumed that the American population would reach a peak of about 165 million between 1960 and 1965, and then decline to about 130 million or so by the year 2000. The error was based on a straight-line extrapolation of depression trends, and failed to take into account the decisions families made in conditions of postwar prosperity. (Today, all demographic projections are usually made on high-low-and-middle estimates, in which the assumptions for each level are carefully stipulated.)

How *many* persons will be born may be subject to a margin of error, but once individuals are born, we know that they will be available for work in about twenty years at some reasonable ratio; in this respect, labor-force data are the most solid of all facts available. In this and the next decade, for example, we face a tremendous influx of youngsters into the labor force simply because of the coming of age of the postwar babies. Compared to the 1950's, the increase is of a magnitude of 100 percent. We used to have two million youngsters reaching age eighteen in the early 1950's; we now have over four million a year. This data leads us to plan for increased needs not only in schools and jobs, but in other areas as well: in family formation, housing, automobiles, recreation, and the like. A study like the Unilever Corporation's *1984* is a fairly straightforward market projection of 25-year trends, using data beginning with 1959. Peter Hall's *London 2000* is, along the same lines, a meticulous examination of the probable growth of the London metropolis, and a suggestion about the balancing of residential, office, industrial, and recreational areas. Thus a great deal of prediction does go on, using this kind of material.

On the other side of the coin to crescive changes are the predictions based on *limits,* physical and institutional, which act as constraints to growth. Thus, as early as 1955, analysts of the Soviet scene predicted that the Russian government would have to make huge investments in agriculture and divert resources from other areas. The analysis was made simply by plotting the land available for *extensive agriculture* (most of Russia lies above the 55° parallel) and the yields per acre that were possible with existing methods. Though it was predicted that such a change was inevitable, no one could predict when such diversion would begin. In fact, it took ten years for the prediction to come true. Khrushchev sought to postpone the decision by opening up new "virgin lands"—forest tracts which many experts had deemed to be unsuitable for that purpose. When the virgin-lands policy failed, Khrushchev's successors finally took the long-delayed step and announced, in May, 1965, that in the next five years the Soviet Union would invest 71 billion rubles in intensive development of agriculture, a sum equal to all their agricultural investment in the previous twenty years.

Ultimately, all useful prediction is a function of tested theory. Much prediction —most prediction, so far—is derived from experience, which is a rough way of sifting out what is relevant from what is not in making an estimate of the future. But the function of theory is to "reduce" experience, and to identify the relevant variables that allow us to explain behavior. The most satisfactory theory, and the fullest prediction, are possible usually in a "closed system" whose boundaries are defined, and whose equilibriums can be established. In the human world there are few such closed systems. To a considerable extent, however, the development of modern economics has allowed us to identify the relevant variables that explain the operation of the economic system, and to establish some mathematical equations for the interaction of these variables. And this has led, in the last few years, to the development of econometric models that will attempt to forecast economic behavior. But in most other affairs our methods of forecasting are still primitive and essentially speculative, and it is only recently that some attention has been paid to the establishment of the "controls" of prediction, and a means of testing them—to some extent. For this reason, the first study that will be reported on in this department is a pioneer effort both to do some specific long-range forecasting and to study the methods whereby such forecasts can be refined. This study was done at the Rand Corporation by Olaf Helmer and Theodore Gordon, using what the authors have dubbed the Delphi Technique.

II

In planning our daily lives, we are accustomed to making daily, weekly and even yearly forecasts hopefully, with some reasonable degree of certainty, for if we are to function at all with some degree of rationality, a stable order is the primary need of individuals, as it is of governments.

Most planning, by individuals or by corporations or by governments, is based on extrapolation from the recent past, some knowledge of alternative possibilities, and some contingency planning (the most usual being insurance) against unforeseen hazards. For the more distant future—ten, twenty and fifty years ahead—one necessarily relies on more intuitive judgments about the future. The intention of the Delphi Technique is simply to obtain such intuitive judgments as systematically as possible from persons who are designated as experts in the area to be predicted.

The Rand study sought predictions in the following six areas:

(1) Scientific breakthroughs
(2) Population control
(3) Automation
(4) Space progress
(5) War prevention
(6) Weapon systems

Eighty-two experts participated. Professionally, there were twenty engineers, seventeen physical scientists, fourteen logicians and mathematicians, twelve economists, nine social scientists, five writers, four operations analysts, and one military officer; forty-two of the participants were Rand staff members or consultants; of the remaining forty participants, eight were from other countries.

In the first panel, on scientific breakthroughs, the experts produced a list of 49 possibilities. The list was submitted to the group and each person was asked to predict the probable time of each breakthrough. From the results, the median year and the quartile range for each item were established (e.g., the median year for a specific prediction might be the year 2000, the quartile range from 1980 to 2033.) On the second round, the study found a considerable consensus for ten breakthroughs. Of the remaining thirty-nine, seventeen were arbitrarily selected for further study. The experts were then asked, in the third round, to consider the probable time of the 17 remaining breakthroughs and, if the opinion fell outside the range of opinions shared by the middle 50 percent of the previous responses, the expert was asked to justify his answer. A fourth and final questionnaire refined the items and stated the majority and minority opinions.

Laborious as this procedure may be, this panel technique was adopted for a double reason: it eliminated or lessened the problems that arise out of fact-to-face discussion (e.g., the bandwagon effects of majority opinion, embarrassment in refusing to abandon a publicly expressed opinion, etc.), and it allowed the feedback through successive rounds, which gave a respondent the time to reconsider an opinion and to reassert or establish new probabilities for his choices.

All of the final answers were presented within time distributions. Thus it was predicted that economically useful desalination of sea water (the first on the list) would come between 1965 and 1980, though the median year was 1970. It was predicted that controlled thermonuclear power would be available in 1985, though the time range was put between 1978 to 2000. In presenting here the major findings of the study, however, these qualifications, because they are burdensome in exposition, are eliminated. Readers should note, therefore, that all dates given are the median year.

What, then, have the experts predicted?

The World of 1984

If we abstract the most significant items from the forecasts of all six panels, the following picture emerges of the state of the world in 1984:

The population of the world, because of the declining death rate in the *tiers monde,* will have increased by about 40 percent from its present size to 4.3 billion—that is, provided no third world war will have taken place before then. (There is, say the experts, a 15 to 25 precent probability that such a war may erupt, though this risk can be reduced to 5 percent by appropriate policy measures.)

To provide the increased quantities of food needed by this larger population, agriculture will be aided by automation and by the availability of desalinated sea water. Effective fertility control will be practiced, with the result that the birth rate will continue to drop.

In the field of medicine, transplantation of natural organs and implantation of artificial (plastic and electronic) organs will be common practice. The use of personality-control drugs will be widespread and widely accepted.

Sophisticated teaching machines will be in general use. Automated libraries, which look up and reproduce relevant material, will greatly aid research. Worldwide communication will be enhanced by a universal satellite relay system and by automatic translating machines. Automation will span the gamut from many service operations to some types of decision-making at the management level.

In space, a permanent lunar base will have been established. Manned Mars and Venus flybys will have been accomplished. Deep-space laboratories will be in operation.

Propulsion by solid-core nuclear-reactor and ionic engines will become available.

In the military arena, ground warfare will be modified by rapid mobility and a highly automated tactical capability, aided by the availability of a large spectrum of weapons, ranging from non-lethal biological devices and lightweight rocket-type personnel armament to small tactical nuclear bombs and directed-energy weapons of various kinds. Ground-launched anti-ICBM missiles will have become quite effective. Anti-submarine warfare techniques will have advanced greatly, but improved, deep-diving, hard-to-detect submarines will present new problems.

The World of 2000

When we continue our projection to the year 2000, the following major additional features emerge as descriptive of the world at that time:

The population size will be up to about 5.1 billion (65 percent more than 1963.) New food sources will have been opened up through large-scale ocean farming and the fabrication of synthetic protein. Controlled thermonuclear power will be a source of new energy. New mineral raw materials will be derived from the oceans. Regional weather control will be past the experimental stage.

General immunization against bacterial and viral diseases will be available. Primitive forms of artificial life will have been generated in the laboratory. The correction of hereditary defects through molecular engineering will be possible.

Automation will have advanced further, from many mental robot services to sophisticated, high-IQ machines. A universal language will have evolved through automated communication.

On the moon, the mining and manufacture of propellent materials will be in progress. Men will have landed on Mars, and permanent unmanned research stations will have been established there, and on earth commercial global ballistic transport will have been instituted.

Weather manipulations for military purposes will be possible. Effective anti-ICBM defenses in the form of air-launched missiles and directed-energy beams will have been developed.

The World in the Year 2100

When they tried to look as far ahead as the year 2100, there was no pretense regarding the existence of any consensus among the respondents. The following developments, for which there was a median forecast of no later than 2100, are reported not as a prediction of the state of the world at that time but as an indication of what a number of thoughtful people regard as conceivable during the next few generations that lie ahead of us:

By the year 2100, the world population may be on the order of 8 billion. Chemical control of the aging process may have been achieved, raising a person's life expectancy to over 100 years. The growth of new limbs and organs through biochemical stimulation may be possible. Man-machine symbiosis, enabling a person to raise his intelligence through direct electromechanical tie-in of his brain with a computing machine, is a distinct possibility. Automation, of course, will have taken further enormous strides, evidenced in all probability by such things as household robots, remote facsimile reproduction of newspapers and magazines in the home, completely automated highway transportation, and the like.

The problem of adequately providing the necessities of life for all people of the earth will presumably have been solved by international agreements based on the abundance of new sources of energy and raw materials opened up in the twenty-first century. As for materials, it is even possible that elaborate differential mining processes will have been abandoned in favor of commercially efficient transmutation of elements.

Conceivably, revolutionary developments will have become feasible as a result of the control of gravity through some form of modification of the gravitational field. A permanent lunar colony may well have been established, with regularly scheduled commercial traffic between the earth and the moon A permanent base on Mars, landings on Jupiter's moons, and manned flybys past Pluto are likely accomplishments. Possibly even a multi-generation mission to other solar systems may be on its way, aided perhaps by artificially induced long-duration coma.

If one turns from the "composite" picture of the worlds as envisaged at these detailed times to the specific areas of forecasts, the picture looks somewhat like this:

Scientific Breakthroughs. Most experts think that by 1990 thermonuclear power will be controlled; that there will be "economically useful exploitation of the ocean bottom through mining (other than just off-shore oil drillings)"; that "economic feasibility of commercial generation of synthetic protein for food" will be developed; that there will be an "increase by an order of magnitude in the relative number of psychotic cases amenable to physical or chemical therapy"; and that "biochemical general immunization against bacterial and viral diseases" may be possible.

Population. Population forecasts are more conservative than most estimates based on extrapolation from present and recent growth. Straightforward extrapolation puts the world population at 13 billion in 2050. The median estimate of the experts is slightly over 7 billion.

At the same time, however, the experts predicted that advances in medicine and in the production and distribution of food would further lower the death rate. In view of this lowered death rate, it would appear that the experts may have been unduly optimistic about population figures. A minority of experts thought that famine would lower the figure for 2050, but the majority disagreed. Most put their faith in the widespread acceptance of birth-control devices.

Automation. Forecasts about future developments in automation include within the next decade an "increase by a factor of 10 in capital investment in computers used for automated process control," air traffic control, teaching machines and automation of office work leading to the displacement of 25 percent of the current work force.

"Electronic prosthesis," "automated interpretation of medical symptoms," and "construction on a production line of computers with motivation by education" all await us before 2000. Also, there will be "widespread use of robot services for refuse collection, as household slaves, as sewer inspectors, etc.," as well as "widespread use of computers in tax collection, with access to all business records for automatic single tax deductions," and "availability of a machine which comprehends standard IQ tests and achieves scores above 150."

After 2000, the experts look for "evolution of a universal language from automated communication," "automated voting, in the sense of legislating through automated plebiscite," "automated highways and adaptive automobile auto-pilots," "remote facsimile newspapers and magazines, printed in the home," "man-machine symbiosis, enabling man to extend his intelligence by direct electro-mechanical interaction between his brain and a computing machine," and "international agreements which guarantee certain economic minima to the world's population as a result of high production from automation."

Space Progress. In forecasting progress in space, the experts agree remarkably on developments within the near future— the logical extension of current work. Thus, before 1980, we will witness, among other things, orbital rendezvous, "unmanned inspection and capability for destruction of satellites," "a manned lunar landing and return," and a "temporary lunar base (2 men, 1 month)."

By 2000, the experts tend to agree, there will be a "permanent base established on Moon (10 men, indefinite stay)," "manned landing on Mars and return," and "establishment of permanent research stations on near planets."

The twenty-first century can bring "commercial global ballistic transport," "manned landing on Jupiter's moons," "manned multigeneration missions to other solar systems," " regularly scheduled commercial traffic to a lunar colony," and "communication with extraterrestrials."

War Prevention. The mean estimates of the experts on this panel were a 10 percent probability of large-scale war within the next 10 years and a 20 percent probability within the next 25 years. If war comes, they see it as a result of (1) "escalation of a political crisis" (45 percent); (2) "escalation in the level of violence in an ongoing minor war" (37 percent); (3) "inadvertence" (11 percent); (4) "surprise attack at a time when there is no ostensible acute crisis" (7 percent).

The experts believe that the most realistic and effective measures that might reduce the chances of war include "buildup of Western-bloc conventional forces," "increased security of command-and-control and retaliatory capability," and "development on both sides of invulnerable delayed-response weapons that are incapable of surprise attack." Less effective, probable, or desirable measures, but still worthy of attention, include "greater political and economic unity among free advanced democracies," "establishment of a standing worldwide U.N. police force, not subject to veto," bilateral U.S.-S.U. arms control agreements," and "holding the status quo against even minor aggressions."

Least effective and least probable measures include "support and promotion of a United States of Africa, Latin America, Europe, Asia," a "clear U.S. statement as to which national interests are to be protected by nuclear deterrents, and orientation of our policies to that end," an "organized encouragement of conscientious objection on the part of scientists to cooperation in the improvement of weapon systems," and a "U.S.-initiated unilateral step toward disarmament."

The experts mitigated their Cassandra-like predictions by optimistically believing the chances of war would be reduced 75 percent within 10 years and 70 preent within 25 years if the suggested preventive measures were "vigorously pursued."

Weapon Systems. Panel predictions on weapon systems were doubtless affected by military secrecy, which would tend to restrain respondents having access to classified information.

Of the 32 developments in weapon systems eventually considered, the experts predicted on two levels: (1) when the weapons would be developed under "normal" conditions, and (2) when the weapons would be developed under "crash" conditions. They also weighed the effectiveness as well as the feasibility of each development.

Before 1980 the experts see "extensive use of devices which persuade without killing (water cannons, tear gas, etc.)" and "incapacitating biological agents." Before 2000 they expect "perishable counter-insurgent arms," "accurate intelligence correlation through the use of computers," "biological agents destroying the will to resist," and "massive civilian defense and postwar recovery plans." Experts disagree widely about the time when "effective terminal defense by air-launched anti-missiles" and "large orbiting satellite weapons for blackmail" will be operational, but they definitely feel such weapons will be developed.

Unlikely to be developed are such "weapons" as "mass-hypnotic recruitment of forces from enemy populations" and "mind-reading," although a few experts do not rule out their possibility.

What is one to make of these forecasts? Mr. Helmer and his colleagues express their surprise at some of the forecasts that have been propounded, and they list the ones that they had failed to anticipate:

The implication that the water-covered portions of the earth may become important enough to warrant national territorial claims.

The possibility that continued developments in automation will result in serious social upheavals; the almost complete acceptance of the necessity of regulative legislation.

The probability, in the relatively near future, of very widespread use of personality-control drugs.

The notion of an actual symbiosis of man and machine.

The fact that control of gravity was not rejected outright.

The relative confidence that the population curve would begin to level off during the next generation.

The strong likelihood of the emergence of weapons of a non-killing, nonproperty-destroying nature, covert perhaps, attacking on the psychological or biological level.

The general disagreement with the concept of deep-space military applications, such as heliocentric strategic fleets.

The anticipated relatively high probability of another major war. The absence, on the one hand, of significantly new ideas for the prevention of war, and the confidence, on the other, that the application of what may almost be called traditional proposals to this effect holds great promise for reducing the probability of war.

Helmer and his colleagues sought to point up certain warnings, not to prophesy doom but to indicate the areas in which a major effort would have to be concentrated in order to avoid future disaster. They were subsumed under four headings:

War prevention. While the odds against another war within the next generation are considered to be 80 percent (within 25 years), a 20 percent chance is intolerable. The main danger appears to be in mutually undesired escalation and downright inadvertence; hence a major effort to seek improved ways of forestalling such disaster becomes necessary.

Equitable distribution of resources. While there is a consensus that eventually there will be an abundance of resources in energy, food, and raw materials, there is no foregone conclusion that such resources will be available in time for the increasing world population, or that effective means of an equitable world distribution will have been found and agreed upon. To solve such problems would clearly be a great contribution toward the prevention of big or small wars.

Social reorganization. The anticipated growth in the amount of automation is likely to reshape the industrialized nations. While improved and highly automated methods of education will make the acquisition of technical skills available to a larger fraction of the population, only the very ablest people are likely to be needed to manage the new, automated economy. Since robots are apt to take over many of the services, especially the more menial ones, large segments of the population may find themselves without suitable employment within an economy of potential abundance. Farsighted and profoundly revolutionary measures may have to be taken to cope with this situation.

Eugenics. Finally, a problem, though not yet upon us, which will require much forethought and wisdom. There is the possibility —within a generation or two—of selectively extending an individual's life span through biochemical methods and of selective eugenic control through molecular genetic engineering.

These, then, are the forecasts that have resulted from a sophisticated use of expert talent to look at the future. With what "state of confidence" can we accept these previsions? The major difficulty, perhaps, lies not in any one item, but in the technique itself. Each prediction is made as a single instance isolated from the others, though all the participants probably recognized that the realization of any one prediction is not only dependent upon the others but, even more, is dependent on the state of the society itself. The implicit premise underlying all these predictions is that the *context* of the United States and the world will remain as it now stands. But the social systems and the relationships between them are bound to change, and these changes, more than the technical feasibility of any of the breakthroughs, will determine the possibility of these breakthroughs being realized. In short, if forecasting is to advance, it has to be within a *system context* which specifies the major social, political and economic relationships that will obtain at any given time. This is in no way to depreciate the Helmer study and its forecasts. What we are given is a set of *possibilities,* but the way in which these possibilities are combined depends upon the system in which they are received. And the art—or science—of forecasting can be extended only when we are able to advance in the creation of models of the social system itself.

PART EIGHT Minorities

When sociologists discuss minorities, they are not referring to population size, but to group dominance in terms of power. In a social system where the dominant power group distinguishes and discriminates against other groups of people, the group discriminated against may be referred to as a minority. Frequently, the interaction between the dominants and the minority are restricted by various norms and values. Common features are occupational restrictions and varying degrees of pro-hibitions against intermarriage. Typically, there are vast numbers of prescriptions which govern interaction between the groups.

In man's history, most minorities have been defined in terms of race, ethnic background, or religion. The prejudice and negative stereotypes assigned to minorities in present times is largely based on the alleged cultural and biological inferiorities of the oppressed groups. The Nazi persecution of the Jews offers a horrendous example of the possible results of prejudice and discrimination. Among contemporary societies, one can still hear arguments in many countries, including the United States, that the Black is inherently inferior. Needless to say, the consensus of opinion, based upon available data and research, is that the various groupings of the human race are more similar than different and no competent case can be made for the superiority of any particular group.

Another group which has only recently been seriously regarded as a minority is the female. Any rational appraisal of the evidence by we male chauvinists must lead us to the conclusion that women have indeed been discriminated against. This society, along with most others, has severely limited the types of roles and situations in which women can participate. There is, of course, much disagreement on the degree to which we should obliter-ate differences in sex roles. However, many of the traditional roles and tasks of women are obsolete, and society must come to task with such obvious discrimination as various types of non-physical occupational restrictions on career-minded females. The first article in this section, written by Jessie Bernard, seeks to assess the problems and position of women in modern society. The other two selections, Merwyn Gar-barino's "Seminole Girl" and Peter Weiss' "Nightmare in Mississippi," discuss the more traditional, and currently more press-ing, problems of the American Indian and American Negro.

20

The Status of Women in Modern Patterns of Culture

JESSIE BERNARD

I just happened to be in Kabul at the time when women began to appear in public with uncovered faces. The first ones were the airline stewardesses. They had been to Tashkent and New Delhi and seemed to feel no embarrassment, self-consciousness, or malaise in the exercise of their new freedom.

I was in Papeete a few years after its harbor was opened to tourist ships and the first air strips laid down. Already the young women performing in native dress for the tourists had begun to see themselves self-consciously, through tourist eyes, and knew how they looked to those people from beyond the seas. And the proud young women in Western dress bicycling to their jobs in shop and office had already acquired the tense expression resulting from schedules to keep and time to account for.

I was the recipient of the confidences of a wealthy young Arab flying back from the Middle East to school on the West Coast, anxious to see the American girl he hoped to marry. Yes, he would expect her to accept many of his ways; yes, he would expect to permit her many of her ways. No, he would not let her have a job for pay, certainly not one that involved contact with men. But what would he expect a university-trained girl to do all day? She could do volunteer work in a hospital. But he had said that she was interested in anthropology. Could she not, perhaps, do research? work in a

museum? Not if it meant dealing with men.

Last year's Christmas greetings from an old friend visiting in India included the announcement that his daughter, married to a Hindu, was getting a divorce and would return with her children to the United States; no ill will on anyone's part. It had just not worked out.

I listened last year to a debate between two teams of African women at Howard University on the topic: "Resolved that polygamy should be officially sanctioned in Africa." The male judges, admitting that they had started with a prejudice on the positive side, awarded victory to the negative side.

I was the chairman of the doctoral committee of a young Pakistani who, like most graduate students, skated constantly at the brink of insolvency. Still, when his widowed mother wrote from Pakistan that he must go to Beirut and find a husband for his sister who was studying at a university there, he did—protesting, resentful, hostile, vowing that his was the last generation that would bow to the past, but obedient.

I have, puzzled, watched the ongoing efforts of sociologists and anthropologists to understand the relations between the sexes among the Caribbean peoples: are they to be interpreted in class or in cultural terms? It makes a difference if one is interested in change.

SOURCE: Reprinted from *The Annals*, January, 1968, 375:4–14, by permission of the author and The American Academy of Political and Social Sciences.

Revolution has become commonplace, daily fare, almost—incongruously—part of the status quo everywhere.

The "Status of Women": A Changing Medley

The term "status of women" refuses to sit still for its portrait; it is one of those evocative expressions which have no precise referent but which nearly everyone understands. It can refer to almost anything having to do with women. On December 14, 1961, President Kennedy charged that "we have by no means done enough to . . . encourage women to make their full contribution as citizens." He thought it appropriate, therefore, for us "to set forth before the world the story of women's progress in a free, democratic society, to review recent accomplishments," but at the same time "to acknowledge frankly the further steps that must be taken." And this he rightly considered "a task for the entire nation." Accordingly, the President's Commission on the Status of Women was established by Executive Order 10980. Its reports covered the status water front, from restrictions on jury service to the degrading image of women projected by the mass media, from property rights to paid maternal leave.

Like the story of all reform movements, that of "woman's rights" has had to do with both enacted rules (legislation and administrative rulings) and so-called crescive rules (mores, custom, tradition, and convention). Until well into the twentieth century, the first predominated. The term "status of women" referred primarily to the political and legal rights of women, that is, to the kinds of rights that legislators or administrators could do something about. Most of those rights have now been

achieved, including, in the 1964 Civil Rights Act, the right to equal opportunity in employment. That battle is now a clean-up operation, bringing backward areas into the main stream. The term now has to do with such rights as the right to privacy and to contraception. The frontier battles have shifted from rights denied by enacted norms to rights denied by crescive norms.

Along with the movement for legal and political rights, there had been, even in the nineteenth century, a movement for "sexual emancipation." Sober demands by the more conservative leaders for the suffrage and for legal protection of women had been paralleled by demands of some, of the more radical, for "free love." Some Marxists—but not Karl Marx himself—had promised women this boon under socialism;[1] once women had achieved economic independence, they could also achieve sexual independence.

The two kinds of reform—political and sexual—were related, but by no means in a simple one-way manner. When lower-class women were at the mercy of exploitative men of all classes, the sexual revolution needed to protect them was one which gave them, as well as upper-class women, the prerogative of "respectability." Steven Marcus has shown how Victorian puritanism had an elevating effect on the status of women.

Among the urban lower classes until well into the ninteenth century . . . life was degraded and often bestial; drink, violence, early and promiscuous sexuality, and disease were the counterparts of poverty, endless labor, and a life whose vision of futurity was at best cheerless. In such a context, the typical Victorian values, and indeed Victorianism itself, take on new meaning. It is not usual nowadays to regard such values as chastity, propriety, modesty, even rigid prudery, as positive moral values, but it is difficult to doubt that in the situation of the urban lower social classes they operated with positive force. The discipline and self-restraint which the exercise of such virtues required could not but be a giant step toward the humanization of a class of persons who had been traditionally regarded as almost of another species. Indeed, the whole question of "respectability" stands revealed in a new light when we consider it from this point of view. One of the chief components of respectability is self-respect, and when we see this young girl [in *My Secret Life*] resisting all that money, class, privilege, and power, we understand how vital an importance the moral idea of respectability could have for persons in her circumstances.[2]

But the wall of mores which protected some women was seen by others as a wall which cut them off from male prerogatives. They aimed their attack on the subtler rights denied them not by law or administrative rules, but by mores, custom, tradition, and convention. Why should men have more freedom than women? Why should women have to use the family entrance? Why could they not smoke and drink as men did? Why one standard of behavior for men and another for women? Why should women not be permitted as much sexual satisfaction as men? This relative emphasis on rights in the area of crescive norms, especially the mores, as compared with enacted norms, characterizes the status issues at the present time.

In discussing changes over time, it is important to remind ourselves of the enormous stability of social forms. The modal or typical segments of a population show great inertia; they change slowly. The modal or typical college girl today is not astonishingly different from her counterpart of the 1940's—or even the 1930's or 1920's.

What does change, and rapidly, is the form which the nontypical takes. It is the nontypical which *characterizes* a given time: that is, the *typical* which tends to be stable, has to be distinguished from the *characteristic* or characterizing, which tends to be fluctuating. When we speak of "the silent generation" or "the beat generation" or the "anti-establishment generation" we are not referring to the typical member of any generation but to those who are not typical. To say, therefore, that the characteristic issues for young women of the 1960's are rights to privacy, to contraception, or to greater sexual freedom is not the same as saying that the typical young woman actively espouses these issues.

Technological Culture and the Status of Women

The term "culture" as popularly used has, like "status of women," only an imprecise referent which most people feel they understand until they try to define it. Actually, the norms which define the status of women constitute a considerable segment of any culture. They *are* major components of the culture—nonmaterial aspects, to be sure, but no less real for that. They act upon the material, especially the technological, aspects, as well as being themselves acted upon by them. If the mores had forbidden women to follow their work into the mills and factories, the technologies which depended on their work would have been retarded. But if the technology had not created the wage-paying jobs for them, the status of women would have continued to be one of universal dependence. It is a nice theoretical point to determine, in any one case, which way the influence operates. The emphasis for the most part has tended to be on the effect of material culture on the status of women rather than the other way around. And the effect, it has been found, has been great.

A generation ago, a team of cultural anthropologists surveyed the literature on the material culture of "the simpler peoples" to see how it related to their institutions. So far as the position of women was concerned, they concluded that it was "not favorable as judged by modern standards." [3] It was a little worse among pastoral peoples than among hunting or agricultural peoples and worse in some areas of the world than in others, but "the preponderance of the negative type holds throughout." [4]

Not so among industrialized cultures. Among them, the status of women goes up along with that of the other formerly disadvantaged. With industrialization and urbanization, families everywhere tend to converge on the so-called conjugal system, a system which favors women:

Everywhere the ideology of the conjugal family is spreading, even though a majority does not accept it. It appeals to the disadvantaged, to the young, to women, and to the educated. It promises freedom and new alternatives as against the rigidities and controls of traditional systems. It is as effective as the appeal of freedom or land redistribution or an attack on the existing stratification system. It is radical, and is arousing support [even] in many areas where the rate of industrialization is very slight. [5]

The "material culture" which we call industrialism is the first, Goode reminds us, which permits women to hold independent jobs, to control the money they earn—a fact which greatly improves their bargaining position within the family—

and to assert their rights and wishes within that group. In addition, the new system gives women allies in the outside world, third-party support for their demands within as well as outside the family.

Although there is nothing in the material culture of industrialized societies which precludes full equality for women, the actual prospects for full equality are not bright:

. . . we do not believe that any . . . system now in operation, or likely to emerge in the next generation, will grant full equality to women, although throughout the world the general position of women will improve greatly. The revolutionary philosophies which have accompanied the shifts in power in Communist countries or in the Israel *kibbutzim* have asserted equality, and a significant stream of philosophic thought in the West has asserted the right to equality, but no society has yet granted it. Nor does the movement in Western countries, including the Communist countries, suggest that the future will be greatly different. We believe that it is possible to develop a society in which this would happen, but not without a radical reorganization of the social structure. [6]

Two Roadblocks to Equality

Two roadblocks, Goode finds, stand in the way of this radical reorganization of the social structure, essential for full equality:

(1) The family base upon which all societies rest at present requires that much of the daily work of the house and children be handed over to women. Doubtless, men can do this nearly as well, but they have shown no eagerness to assume these tasks, and (2) families continue to rear their daughters to take only a modest degree of

interest in full-time careers in which they would have equal responsibilities with men.[7]

With respect to the care of the home, modern technology has reduced the time and effort required to a very moderate level.[8] And whether or not men show any eagerness to assume household tasks, they do show at least willingness to assume them, as studies of the marriages of working women show.[9] In any event, no radical reorganization of the social structure would be called for if care of the house were the only roadblock in the path of equality.

The care of children is a more difficult one to deal with. The President's Commission on the Status of Women recognized the need for services to help mothers carry their responsibilities. They recommended a wide array of such services, including child-care services, health services, and services related to the home, as well as services related to employment.[10] And they placed the responsibility for providing these services on the local community, on voluntary organizations, on professional associations, and on federal and state governments.[11] These are among the new rights women ask for in the drive for equality.

Even without them, the care of children, though difficult, is manageable when we are dealing with, let us say, two children, whose intensive care takes only about ten years of a woman's life. But it becomes formidable when we are dealing with four, five, or six children, whose care covers a span long enough to preclude other life options.

Motherhood and the Status of Women

Although the existence of abortion and infanticide in many past societies shows that motherhood *per se* is no guarantee of high status for women, still in many societies, both Oriental and Western, there has been a strong tendency to honor and encourage motherhood. "Facts about the desirability of offspring should [therefore] always be noted in a study of the status of mother and wife." [12] Actually, there has always been a reverse relationship between the birth rate and status as measured by such indexes as income, education, and occupation. This inverse relationship was, in fact, often invoked in the nineteenth century as an argument against the emancipation of women. Legal independence would create instability in marriage; economic independence would detract from motherhood or, worse still, lead to "race-suicide." [13] Such logic underlies the *Kirche, Küche, und Kinder* policy with respect to the status of women. Still, despite the jeremiads, the birth rate did go down and the status of women as measured in terms of political, legal, and economic rights did go up until well into the twentieth century.

Strange Interlude: The Motherhood Mania, 1946–1957

In addition to the expectable trend fluctuations, there occurred at mid-century— between 1940 and 1957—an enormous upsurge in the fertility rate in the United States. The first phase can be fairly well "explained" in terms of expectable post-depression and postwar babies. But, on the basis of past experience, the trend should thereafter have resumed the long-time downward slope characteristic of the twentieth century or at least should have leveled off. But it did not. When, instead, it continued to increase at an almost unprecedented rate into the 1950's, demographers ran out of precedents for explaining it. For the first time since records had been kept, there was actually an upward secular trend (as contrasted with fluctuations with the business cycle and with war) in the birth rate.

One explanation offered for this strange interlude is the capture of the minds of women by the so-called feminine mystique, a psychoanalytically-spawned doctrine that one could be a woman only by having children, that women who sought self-fulfillment outside of the home were a lost sex.[14] A whole generation of women returned to weaving, baking, and food-preservation—along with extravagant motherhood—to validate their femininity. Another explanation was that the retreat into maternity was a revulsion against the anomie and impersonality of modern life. Prosperity was another stand-by explanation.

The sheer satisfaction of parenthood, a kind of "child-hunger," has recently also been invoked. Judith Blake, on the basis of worldwide demographic data, concludes that having children is more satisfying to many people as a way of life than are the alternatives; they are therefore willing to make economic sacrifices to achieve it.[15]

And women in the United States were willing to sacrifice more—education and careers and status-equality—for that way of life. For, whatever the causes of the mania for maternity may have been, the concomitants and consequences were adverse for the status of women. It was accompanied by a decline in graduate study[16] (see Figure), in career aspirations,[17] and, in general, in participation in the world.[18]

During the great baby boom, women expected to be envied by women and approved of by men when they had a fourth, fifth, or even sixth child. At the very least, they could expect to be excused from other responsibilities. The ability to afford many babies was, in effect, a "status symbol." But mounting costs for schools, health

Inverse Relationship between Fertility Rate and Proportion of All Advanced Degrees Earned by Women*

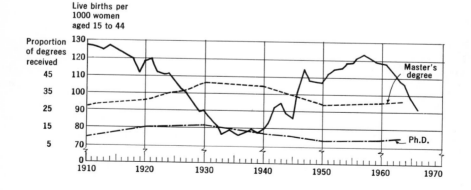

* Sources: Fertility data: Population Reference Bureau, *Population Profile*, March 1967; degree data: U.S., Department of Labor, Women's Bureau, *Trends in Educational Attainment of Women*, June 1966, Chart C.

facilities, and other community provisions for the onrushing generation began gradually to puncture the euphoric mood—as did, also, the frightening threat of uncontrolled population growth.

We have now come full circle. Judith Blake tells us that we are going to have to find acceptable nonfamilial substitute roles for women, to supply the satisfactions that they find in motherhood. In a world that, faced with a population crisis, cannot permit women to indulge their "child-hunger," jobs are needed that can supply companionship, recreation, and creative activity as alternatives to motherhood. Participation in the labor force, she notes, is the most relevant variable associated with family size in the Western world. If women can be deflected from familial roles, they may be satisfied with smaller families. "Until nonfamilial roles begin to offer significant competition to familial ones as avenues for adult satisfaction," [19] we can expect Spencer's "genesis" to win over female "individuation."

Only a Modest Degree of Interest in Equal Responsibilities

Goode's second major roadblock to equality—lack of interest on the part of women in assuming equal responsibilities—can be documented by a respectable research literature[20] which suggests that most women would reject any radical reorganization of the social structure required for the achievement of full equality. Under the impact of the pressures of sympathetic men and activist women, much-publicized campaigns are inaugurated to find women for top positions in the federal government; administrators are hounded by the White House to upgrade women staff members; honors are bestowed on top-level women;

a President's Commission is appointed and labors long and industriously to improve the status of women—all with less than spectacular success.

Thoughtful leaders look with a jaundiced eye on the refusal or unwillingness of women to take full advantage of their opportunities.[21] They have little patience with the regression of women into maternity. Hear Margaret Mead:

We may well ask, in these days of great fredom, when education is as open to women as men, when the great professions of medicine and law, teaching and scientific research are open to women, how do we stand?

The answer is very simple; we stand very badly indeed. . . . And we may well ask why. Why have we returned, for all our great advances in technology, to the Stone Age arrangement in which women's main ambition is to acquire and hold a mate, to produce or adopt children who are to be the exclusive delight and concern of a single married pair, and in which work outside the home . . . holds no attraction in itself, unless it is subservient to the demands of an individual household. . . . Woman has returned, each to her separate cave . . . almost totally unaware of any life outside her door.[22]

Pearl Buck observes that men have changed but women have not:

The door of the house is wide open for women to walk through and into the world, but the stupendous scene beyond terrifies her. She slams the door shut and pulls down the shades. She is so terrified that she sometimes even rails against the exceptional woman, the daring individual who accepts the invitation of the open door and enters into wider opportunity and assumes the new responsibility. . . . Old prejudices are fading, intelligent men are eagerly seeking intelligence wherever it can be found and they are impatient when intelligent women continue to live in narrow ways, apart from the world's problems and dangers. . . . The question which faces every woman is no longer, "Do I want to?" or "How can I?" The answer is simple. "You must!" [23]

And Agnes E. Meyer says sternly: "I feel very strongly that the educated women of America are not taking their responsibility to the nation's strength and welfare seriously enough." [24] Ethel J. Alpenfels documents the recession of women from the professional world, noting the decline of women in the professions from one half in 1930 to about one third in the 1960's.[25] "The status of women deteriorates," she notes, "even while the administrative heads of their universities and colleges ponder the ways and means of salvaging lost talent." [26]

Even when women are themselves held responsible for their inferior status, men are often blamed for making women what they are. Thus, Marya Mannes: "Women are not by nature denied the ability to think creatively and abstractly. It is rather that this ability is unpopular with women because it is unpopular with men." [27] Or culture in the form of a "climate of opinion" is blamed. "It is not the individual young girl, or young wife or older woman who is to blame; it is the climate of opinion that has developed in this country." [28] The most vitriolic attack on the refusal of women to take advantage of their opportunities, by what might be called the men-by-way-of-women approach, was that of Betty Friedan, whose excoriation of the feminine mystique, or what Margaret Mead had called a "retreat into fecundity," [29] precipitated one of the most heated controversies of the decade. Miss Friedan pointed an accusing finger at everyone responsible for glorifying the exaggerated

maternity of the postwar period—psychoanalysts, educators, advertisers, industry—and at women for succumbing.[30] Though she blamed men, she put millions of women on the defensive. Their lives *did* begin to look trivial under her unsympathetic eye; they *were* able-bodied; they *did* have little to do around the house; the children *did* resent too much meddling in their lives.

As frequently happens, the trends here attacked had already begun to moderate by the time they had been widely recognized and bemoaned. Five years before Betty Friedan's book appeared, women were already beginning to delay marriage,[31] return to college,[32] go on for graduate study,[33] as well as reduce the number of babies they bore.[34] Whether they would also now be willing to undertake full-time careers and assume equal responsibilities with men was still a question. It is too early as yet to discern trends. But the indications are that neither a full-time career nor unbridled motherhood will be the characteristic option. For even during the period that was dominated by the feminine mystique, there was almost a stampede of mothers back into the labor force; the feminine mystique did not keep millions of mothers from wanting jobs[35] —not, however, at the higher, more responsible levels. A job, not a career, was the trade-off in their dilemma. And even this compromise was far from achieving universal acceptance. Despite the urgent efforts of educators, counselors, and leaders, girls—and boys—are still unaware of the pattern of women's lives in this day and age. They "hold traditional attitudes about the place of women in modern society," and, as a result, "most of the girls will finish their education either unprepared or poorly prepared to take a place in society in which they will feel satisfied and fulfilled." [36] Goode's second roadblock stands firm.

Sexuality and the Status of Women

It was a standard argument against woman's rights in the nineteenth century that suffrage and political activity would "unsex" women. The converse was not usually articulated, namely, that emphasizing female sexuality would detract from serious participation in the outside world. But Agnes Meyer was making precisely this charge in the 1960's:

> It seems tragic that just when the challenge to women and their opportunities for service are greatest, the younger ones are so profoundly influenced by the overemphasis on sex now so prevalent in our whole culture that they are reverting to female rather than to womanly ideals. [37]

And Marya Mannes and Margaret Culkin Banning concurred. Miss Mannes noted that it was the *Playboy* Bunny and the whole *Playboy* psychology that degraded women; [38] and Mrs. Banning, that the emphasis on glamour tended to demote women. [39]

The men did not agree. They defended the idea of "an impossibly attractive, charming . . . woman" as an ideal. [40] And even from the Soviet Union came word that feminine beauty was a worthy goal.

Soviet women were advised to pay more attention to their looks and charm. Men were told to look upon them as something more than a comrade worker. "We need an art which educates young boys to admire the miracle of beauty in women and young girls to aspire to imitate the examples of such beauty," said *Literaturnaya Gazeta* (Literary Gazette).

"Along with the full equality of women we need a cult of women's charm." The publication complained that Soviet women often are negligent about their appearance. There has been a tendency under communism to regard attention to clothes, cosmetics, and hairdo as a waste of time. But "the esthetics of woman's beauty is needed by the whole population, both men and women," the article contended. It was written by 68-year-old Ilya Selvinsky, a poet. A common theme, repeated by Selvinsky, is that legal equality does not mean that the sexes should behave and be treated exactly alike. The article urged not only that women become more feminine, but that they be idealized. "For a barbarian a woman is simply a person of the opposite sex," Selvinsky said. "But art teaches men to idealize women. This distinguishes civilized people from primitive ones." [41]

To be sure, Agnes Meyer, Marya Mannes, and Mrs. Banning are not talking to the same issue as is the Soviet poet, Selvinsky. But in his plea for feminine glamour there are reverberations of the nineteenth-century lady-on-a-pedestal, adored at a distance, and not permitted to demean herself by entrance into the male world. And, as the women sense, "to be looked up to" is not a substitute for equality.

Changing Issues

The issues that engage young women today have little to do with the traditional rights-for-women issues of the past. It is revealing of the changes in issues to note that on the same day (March 31, 1967), the press reported that, although only "a little over four years ago, Afghan women rarely set foot inside a mosque because, as many men said, 'their presence would interfere with sober prayer,' . . . today . . . that is all changed"; [42] that in Korea today "instead of offering their daughters dowries and inheritances in cash and goods, farmers sell their land in order to send their daughters to college";[43] and that in the United States it was the right to the contraceptive pill that was being debated: "Any woman student over the age of 21 should be able to obtain contraceptive devices or prescriptions through the health service physician just as she could from the private physician." [44]

American women had never had to contend with religious exclusion; they have long since enjoyed the right to a college education; they are now asking for the right to get contraceptive help outside of marriage. There is little talk nowadays, as there was in the past, about "free love" but a considerable amount of discussion on the right to privacy, which may take the form of freedom from conventional controls. College students, for example, when interviewed about their position on the matter are often quoted as saying: "I don't care to indulge myself but I don't object if others do. They have a right to it if they want to." The rights which the current generation of women seek are personal, private, and often sexual. And the confronting parties on these issues are not women versus men but one generation versus another. Young people of both sexes affirm their right to privacy, which amounts in many cases to a right to unregulated—though not promiscuous— sexual relations.

Equality and Differences

How to equate differences in any area is a perennial and all-pervasive problem. As very young children, we are taught that we cannot add apples and puppies

and get fruits. A great deal of thought goes into ways to reduce different kinds of things to common units in order to deal with them logically, if not mathematically. In the area of sex differences, for example, we automatically adjust intelligence quotient (IQ) tests so that the average IQ of both sexes comes out 100.

Interesting in this connection is the trend among some young people in the mid-1960's toward a monosex or unisex, toward a convergence in dress and coiffure, toward a minimization of the usual, conventional sex distinctions. They emphasize their common status as human beings rather than their different statuses as males and females. Their stand could be interpreted as another aspect of the effort to remove all norms which make a distinction between the sexes in privileges, prerogatives, or responsibilities. But it seems to have little if any affinity with the traditional "woman's rights" movement which had the same goal. It is, however, as logical an outcome as the Equal Employment Opportunity Act of 1964.

A Zero-Sum Game?

There are even profounder aspects to the relationship between sexuality and the status of women. For women, the relevant problems have to do with the implications of sexuality for equality; for men, with the implications of equality for sexuality.

Some of the rights which women demanded in their movement for emancipation did not have the effect of seriously depriving men of their rights. Giving women the vote did not deprive men of theirs.[45] But granting other rights to women did deprive men. In such cases, it was a zero-sum situation. Laws, for example, which gave property rights took rights away from men. And laws which forbade discrimination in employment deprived men of an advantage in certain kinds of jobs. In a sense, any attempt to equalize unequal statuses can raise one only by lowering the other. In this sense, sexual equality is paid for by men.

In the past, when the drive toward equality of the sexes dealt with a single standard, it was the feminine standard that was sought; in recent years, the male standard. A cultural pattern inherited from Victorian times prescribing a passive, recipient, nondemanding role for women in the sexual encounter was transmuted into one which, at least in some circles, called for active, even aggressive, sexual behavior on their part. There was to be no double standard so far as sexual satisfaction was concerned. Orgasm became almost a civil right. Women had sexual rights as well as men (whether they wanted them or not).

We have been so amazed at these phenomena, so concentrated on the changes in female sexuality, that until now we have not noticed the effect they were having on men. Recently, however, the psychological costs to men have received attention. It now appears that granting women the privilege of sexual initiative, not to mention aggressiveness, can have a sexually depressing effect on men. A growing literature alerts us to the "masculinity crisis" of modern men.[46] It raises the question: How much equality can the sexes stand? Women who prize male sexuality may be willing to pay a price to protect it; they will guard Goode's second roadblock; they will settle for less than complete equality. But others will want to know: Why should we?

There are certainly no easy answers.

Footnotes

[1] For example, August Bebel, *Die Frau und der Sozialismus*, Zurich, 1883. Translated by M. L. Stern in 1910 as *The Soul of Woman under Socialism.*

[2] Steven Marcus, *The Other Victorians*, New York: Basic Books, 1966, p. 146.

[3] L. T. Hobhouse, G. C. Wheeler, and M. Ginsberg, *The Material Culture and Social Institutions of the Simpler Peoples*, London: Chapman and Hall, 1915, p. 173.

[4] *Ibid.*, p. 174.

[5] W. J. Goode, *World Revolution and Family Patterns*, New York: Free Press, 1963, p. 369.

[6] *Ibid.*, p. 373.

[7] *Ibid.*, p. 373.

[8] Robert W. Smuts, *Women and Work in America*, New York: Columbia University Press, 1959, p. 26; W. F. Ogburn and M. F. Nimkoff, *Technology and the Changing Family*, New York: Houghton Mifflin, 1955, *passim.*

[9] The research literature is summarized in F. Ivan Nye and Lois W. Hoffman (eds.), *The Employed Mother in America*, Chicago: Rand McNally, 1963, chap. xv.

[10] U.S., President (Kennedy), Commission on the Status of Women, *Report of the Committee on Home and Community*, October 1963, *passim.*

[11] No mention was made by the Commission of the responsibility of employers to supply help except in respect to paid maternity leave. For a discussion of employers' attitudes, see Nye and Hoffman (eds.), *loc. cit.*, chap. xxvi. Yet the question may well be raised with respect to motherhood: why should women have to pay the entire cost? When mechanization and automation began to deprive workers of their jobs, the same question was raised: why should one set of workers have to pay, with their unemployment, the entire cost of technological progress? Severance pay, retraining, and other devices were introduced to spread the costs. Perhaps the "right" of women to part-time jobs and to other concessions by industry to their peculiar career needs may be just around the corner. They may, in fact, constitute the radical reorganization of the social structure to which Goode referred.

[12] Elsie Clews Parsons, *The Family*, New York: G. P. Putnam's Sons, 1906, p. 229. Mary Wollstonecraft argued for the emancipation of women on the grounds of impaired maternity.

[13] *Ibid.*, p. 357.

[14] Betty Friedan, in *The Feminine Mystique*, New

York: W. W. Norton, 1963, summarized the literature on this curious phenomenon.

[15] Judith Blake, *Demographic Science and the Redirection of Population Policy,* Berkeley and Los Angeles: University of California Press, 1966.

[16] U.S., Department of Labor, Women's Bureau, *Trends in Educational Attainment of Women,* June 1966.

[17] Ethel J. Alpenfels, "Women in the Professional World," in Beverly Benner Cassara (ed.), *American Women: The Changing Image,* Boston: Beacon Press, 1962, pp. 73–89.

[18] *Ibid., passim.*

[19] Judith Blake, quoted in *The Public Interest,* Spring 1966, p. 128.

[20] Dael Wolfle, *America's Resources of Specialized Talent,* New York: Harper, 1954, pp. 234–236; Jessie Bernard, *Academic Women,* University Park: Pennsylvania State University Press, 1964, chap. xii.

[21] Margaret Mead, Introduction to Cassara (ed.), *loc. cit.,* pp. xi–xii.

[22] *Ibid.*

[23] Pearl Buck, "Changing Relationships between Men and Women," Cassara (ed.), *loc. cit.,* pp. 8–9.

[24] Agnes E. Meyer, "Leadership Responsibilities of American Women," Cassara (ed.), *loc. cit.,* p. 11.

[25] Ethel J. Alpenfels, "Women in the Professional World," in Cassara (ed.), *loc. cit.,* pp. 78–79.

[26] *Ibid.,* p. 79.

[27] Marya Mannes, "Female Intelligence—Who Wants It?," *New York Times Magazine,* January 3, 1960 (Cassara [ed.], *loc. cit.,* pp. 78–79).

[28] Mead, Introduction, Cassara (ed.), *loc. cit.,* p. xiii.

[29] *Ibid.,* p. xii.

[30] Friedan, *op. cit., passim.*

[31] The age at first marriage: 1940 (21.5); 1947 (20.5); 1955 (20.2); 1960 (20.3); 1963 (20.5); 1965 (20.6); 1966 (20.5).

[32] Percentage of high school graduates who were first-time college enrollees: 1950 (31.3); 1954

(36.9); 1958 (40.0); 1962 (44.4); 1964 (45.0).

[33] Proportion of all Master's and other second-level degrees granted to women: 1940 (38.2); 1950 (29.2); 1960 (31.6); 1964 (31.8). Proportion of doctorate and equivalent degrees granted to women: 1940 (13.0); 1950 (9.6); 1960 (10.5); 1964 (10.6).

[34] The rate of third births declined from 33 per 1,000 in 1957 to 24.4 per 1,000 in 1965; of fourth births, from 21 per 1,000 in 1961 to 15.7 in 1965; of fifth babies, from 12 per 1,000 in 1959–1962 to 9.3 in 1965. See "Baby Boom Ends," *Statistical Bulletin* of the Metropolitan Life Insurance Company, Vol. 47, October 1966, p. 1.

[35] Nye and Hoffman (eds.), *loc. cit.*

[36] Kenneth K. Kern, "High School Freshmen and Seniors View the Role of Women in Modern Society," *The Bulletin on Family Development* (of the Family Study Center, University of Missouri, Kansas City, Mo.), 5, Winter 1965, pp. 11, 12.

[37] Agnes Meyer, in Cassara (ed.), *loc. cit.,* p. 11.

[38] "Portrayal of Women by the Mass Media," *Report of the President's Commission on the Status of Women,* p. 22.

[39] *Ibid.*

[40] *Ibid.*

[41] "Charm Comes to Comrade Olga: Will She Ogle Back?," *Washington Post,* April 13, 1967.

[42] *Washington Post,* March 31, 1967.

[43] *Ibid.*

[44] *Ibid.* In the off-campus world, the issue of rights with respect to contraception took the form of the rights of relief recipients to such services. By the mid-1960's, this issue seemed to be settled; every woman had such a right, even young, unmarried women.

[45] Alan P. Grimes, *The Puritan Ethic and Woman Suffrage,* New York: Oxford University Press, 1967.

[46] See, for example, Myron Brenton, *The American Male: A Penetrating Look at the Masculinity Crisis,* New York: Coward-McCann, 1966; Hendrik M. Ruitenbeek, *The Male Myth,* New York: Dell, 1967.

21

Seminole Girl

MERWYN S. GARBARINO

One hundred and thirty miles of circuitous
road and 250 years of history separate the
city of Miami from the four federal
reservations that lock the Seminole Indians
into the Florida swamplands known as
Big Cypress Swamp. A new road is under
construction that will trim in half the
traveling distance between the city and
the reservations scattered along the present
winding U.S. Highway 41 or Tamiami
Trail as it is called by the Indians. But
the new road will only draw the two
communities closer on the speedometer;
it will not alter the vastly different lifeways
it links; it may only make more apparent
the historical inequities that brought the
two areas into existence.

The Seminoles are harsh examples of
what happened to American Indians caught
in the expansion process that saw the
United States swell from a federation of
13 colonies to a nation blanketing more
than half a continent. The peoples who
came to be known as "Seminole," which
means "wild" or "undomesticated," were
Indians who fled south from the guns and
plows of the whites. Some were Yamassee
who were driven from the Carolinas in
1715. Others were Hitchiti-speaking Oconee
who moved down the Apalachicola River
to settle in Spanish-held Florida. These two
groups were joined by others escaping
soldiers or settlers or other Indians demanding their lands.

The loose confederation of Seminoles
was tripled by a large influx of Creeks after
the Creek War of 1813–14. Although the
Creeks were linguistically related to the
Hitchiti, the primary factor uniting the
diverse groups was the hatred and fear
they felt toward their common foe, the
young United States. But this common
bond was enough to regroup the broken
political units into a single body that
absorbed not only Indians, but renegade
whites and Negroes escaping slavery.

In 1817–18, the United States sent
Andrew Jackson to Florida, ostensibly to
recover runaway slaves. This resulted in
the First Seminole War, one of the three
Seminole Wars that were among the
bloodiest ever fought by American forces
against Indians. The war also led to the
annexation of Florida by the U.S. in 1821
because Spain was in no position to
fight for it.

At the time of annexation, the Indians
held extensive farm and pasture lands that
the Spaniards had not wanted for themselves. American settlers, however, wanted
them very much. Insatiable, they forced
the Seminoles ever southward, until finally
they demanded that the Indians relocate
to the area of the Louisiana Purchase
which is now Oklahoma. Some Indians
went westward, but a number under the
leadership of Osceola fought bitterly.
When Osceola was captured under a flag
of truce, some of his warriors fled into the
Everglades where they could not be

SOURCE: Reprinted from *Trans-action*, February, 1970, 7:40–46, by permission of the author and the
publisher. Copyright © February, 1970, by Trans-action, Inc., New Brunswick, New Jersey.

*flushed out. To this day they haven't
recognized the treaty that drove their
fellow tribesmen to the West.*

*In 1911, Florida reservation land was set
aside by an executive order. The Seminoles,
however, were not pressured at that time
into moving on to the federal territory.
South Florida was a real wilderness; Miami
was little more than a town, and lavish
coastal resorts were unforeseen. Literally
no one but the alligators, snakes, birds and
the Indians wanted the land they lived on.
The climate is one of wet summers and
dry winters, and the area is often struck
by hurricanes from the Caribbean. Annual
rainfall is in excess of 60 inches and
without drainage, the prairie is almost
always under water. Brush fires in the dry
season destroy valuable hardwood trees on
the hummocks which are the low-lying
hills undulating through the swampland.
Fire also destroys the highly flammable
drained peat and for the same reason,
there is an absence of pines in many areas
suitable for their growth. Elsewhere however, there are moderately to heavily
wooded places, and sometimes great flocks
of white egrets alight in the branches of
the trees, looking like puffs of white
blossoms. Except for the hummocks, the
horizon is flat, a vista of sky and water,
broken only by the occasional wooded
clumps.*

*Most inhabitants of this waste and water
live on elevated platforms under thatched
roofs held in place by poles. Unemployment
is an ever-present problem helped
somewhat by seasonal agricultural work
or by crafts such as the gaily colored
garments, dolls, basketry and carvings
made for the tourists who are now visiting
their homeland on a year 'round basis.
Lands are leased to commercial vegetable
farmers and deer can still be hunted. So*

*subsistence living is still possible for the
"wild" Seminoles.*

*Somewhere along the Tamiami Trail,
Nellie Greene—a pseudonym of course—
was born a Seminole, raised in a chickee,
and learned the ways of her people. Her
father was a frog hunter and could neither
read nor write; her mother was a good
Seminole mother who later had troubles
with tuberculosis and drinking. No one
Nellie knew had much more education
than her father and mother. Yet, despite
the ignorance and illiteracy on the reservation, Nellie Greene wanted and was
encouraged to get a good education. As it
does for most Indians in the United States,
this meant leaving her "backward" people,
mixing with whites who at best patron-
ized her.*

*I first met Nellie Greene when she had
graduated from college and was living in
an apartment in Miami where she worked
as a bank clerk. I knew her background
from having spent three summers in the
middle sixties, thanks to the National
Science Foundation, on the Seminole reservations of Florida. In September of
1966 Nellie wrote me that she had been
offered a job as manager in the grocery
store back on the reservation. If she didn't
take it, a white person would, for she was
the only native with the necessary knowledge of bookkeeping. She had accepted the
job, she said, but since she had once told
me (in Miami) that she could never give
up the kind of life she had grown accustomed to there, I was curious to find out
why she had returned to the reservation.*

*She herself said that she took the job
to help her people, but she added that it
had not been an easy decision; in fact it
had been quite a struggle. I could have
guessed that this was so; many Indian*

tribes that offer educational grants to their younger members do so only with the stipulation that the recipients later return to the reservation. The stipulation is a measure of the difficulty in getting their educated members to come back to the tribe. In any event, I wanted to hear Nellie Greene tell her own story. I went to see her, and this is what she told me.

Nellie Greene's Story

I was born in a Miami hospital on February 6, 1943. At that time my parents were living on the [Tamiami] Trail, and my daddy was making his living frog hunting. He owned an air boat and everything that goes along with frog hunting. It was during the war, and at that time I guess it was hard to get gas. When it was time for me to be born, my father had to borrow gas from a farmer to get to Miami. But the tail light was broken, so my father took a flashlight and put a red cloth over it and tied it on to the truck and went to the hospital. My daddy often told me about that.

I had an older sister and an older brother. We lived in a chickee until 1961 when my daddy bought a CBS [a cement block structure, "hurricane proof" according to state standards] at Big Cypress, and we moved into it. When I was little, my daddy had to be out in the Everglades a lot, so he would take all of us out to a hummock, and we would make camp there and stay there while he went off to hunt for frogs. When he got back, he'd take the frog legs into the hotels and sell them. Then he would bring back something for each of us. When he would ask us what we wanted, I always asked for chocolate candy.

About all I remember of the Everglades is that it was a custom when you got up to take a bath or go swimming early in the morning. My mother says they always had to chase me because I didn't like to get wet in winter when it was cold. We were there four or five years, and then we moved near the Agency at Dania [renamed Hollywood in 1966]. I had never been to school until then. We were taught at home, the traditional things: to share with each other and with children of other families, to eat after the others—father and grandfather first, then mothers and kids. But lots of times us kids would climb up on our fathers' knees while they were eating. They didn't say anything, and they'd give us something. It just wasn't the custom for families to eat the way we do today, everybody sitting together around the table.

Folktales, too, we learned; they were like education for us, you know. The stories told about someone doing something bad, and then something bad happened to him. That was the way of teaching right and wrong.

When we were growing up we broke away from some family customs. My parents spanked us, for instance, not my mother's brother, who would have been the right person to punish his sister's children—one of the old ways. But they were not close to my mother's family because my daddy was a frog hunter, and we wandered around with him. My parents were chosen for each other by their families. I guess they learned to love each other in some ways, but I have heard my mother say that it is not the same kind of love she would have had if she had chosen her own husband. It was respect, and that was the custom of the Indians.

Most parents here show so little affection. Even if they love their kids, maybe they don't think they should show love. I know a lot of parents who really care, but they don't tell their kids how they feel. We always knew how our parents felt about us. They showed us affection. Sometimes I hear kids say, "My mother doesn't care whether I go to school or not." These kids have seen how others get care from their parents, like the white children at school. And that kind of concern doesn't show up here. A lot of parents don't even think of telling their children that they want them to succeed. They don't communicate with their children. You never see an Indian mother here kiss and hug children going to school. But white parents do that, and when Indian children see this in town or on TV, it makes them think that Indian parents just don't care. Kids are just left to go to school or not as they wish. Often the mothers have already left to work in the fields before the school bus comes. So no one sees whether children even go to school.

I felt loved. My parents never neglected us. We have never gone without food or clothes or a home. I have always adored my mother. She has made her mistakes, but I still feel the same about her as when I was a child.

We moved to Big Cypress around 1951 or 1952. I had been in first grade at Dania. I remember I didn't understand English at all when I started first grade. I learned it then. We moved around between Big Cypress and Dania, visiting, or because my father was doing odd jobs here and there.

Both my parents wanted me to go to school because they had wanted to go to school when they were kids. I can remember my mother telling me that she and her sister wanted to go to school. But the clan elders—their uncles—wouldn't let them. The uncles said they would whip the two girls if they went.

One of my father's greatest desires was to go to school when he was a boy. He said that he used to sneak papers and pencils into the camp so that he could write the things he saw on the cardboard boxes that the groceries came in, and figures and words on canned goods. He thought he would learn to read and write by copying these things. My daddy adds columns of figures from left to right, and he subtracts the same way. His answers will be correct, but I don't know how. Almost everything he knows he learned on his own. He can understand English, but he stutters when he talks. He has a difficult time finding the right word when he speaks English, but he understands it.

When my parents said no, they meant no. That was important to me. They could be counted on. The other thing that was important in my childhood schooling was that my daddy always looked at my report card when I brought it home from school. He didn't really know what it meant, and he couldn't read, but he always looked at my report card and made me feel that he cared how I did in school. Other parents didn't do this. In fact, most of the kids never showed their parents their report cards. But my daddy made me feel that it was important to him. I told him what the marks stood for. It was rewarding for me because he took the time.

"Nothing for Me to Do"

Public school was hard compared to what I'd had before, day school on the reservation and a year at Sequoyah Government School. I almost flunked eighth grade at the public school, and it was a miracle that I passed. I just didn't know a lot of things, mathematics and stuff. I survived it somehow. I don't know how, but I did. The man who was head of the department of education at the Agency was the only person outside of my family who helped me and encouraged me to get an education. He understood and really helped me with many things I didn't know about. For a long time the white public school for the Big Cypress area would not let Indian children attend. A boy and I were the first Big Cypress Indians to graduate from that school. He is now in the armed forces.

After I graduated from high school I went to business college, because in high school I didn't take courses that would prepare me for the university. I realized that there was nothing for me to do. I had no training. All I could do was go back to the reservation. I thought maybe I'd go to Haskell Institute, but my mother was in a TB hospital, and I didn't want to go too far away. I did want to go on to school and find some job and work. So the director of education said maybe he could work something out for me so I could go to school down here. I thought bookkeeping would be good because I had had that in high school and loved it. So I enrolled in the business college, but my English was so bad that I had an awful time. I had to take three extra months of English courses. But that helped me. I never did understand why my English was so bad— whether it was my fault or the English I had in high school. I thought I got by in high school; they never told me that my English was so inferior, but it was not good enough for college. It was *terrible* having to attend special classes.

"I Learned How to Dress"

At college the hardest thing was not loneliness but schoolwork itself. I had a roommate from Brighton (one of the three reservations), so I had someone to talk to. The landlady was awfully suspicious at first. We were Indians, you know. She would go through our apartment, and if we hadn't done the dishes, she washed them. We didn't like that. But then she learned to trust us.

College was so fast for me. Everyone knew so much more. It was as though I had never been to school before. As soon as I got home, I started studying. I read assignments both before and after the lectures. I read them before so I could understand what the professor was saying, and I read them again afterwards because he talked so fast. I was never sure I understood.

In college they dressed differently from high school, and I didn't know anything about that. I learned how to dress. For the first six weeks, though, I never went anywhere. I stayed home and studied. It was hard—real hard. (I can imagine what a real university would be like.) And it was so different. If you didn't turn in your work, that was just your tough luck. No one kept at me the way they did in high school. They didn't say, "OK, I'll give you another week."

Gradually I started making friends. I guess some of them thought I was different. One boy asked me what part of India I was from. He didn't even know there were Indians in Florida. I said, "I'm an American." Things like that are kind of hard. I couldn't see my family often, but in a way that was helpful because I had to learn to adjust to my new environment. Nobody could help me but myself.

Well, I graduated and went down to the bank. The president of the bank had called the Agency and said he would like to employ a qualified Indian girl. So I went down there and they gave me a test, and I was interviewed. And then they told me to come in the following Monday. That's how I went to work. I finished college May 29, and I went to work June 1. I worked there for three years.

In the fall of 1966, my father and the president of the Tribal Board asked me to come back to Big Cypress to manage a new economic enterprise there. It seemed like a dream come true, because I could not go back to live at Big Cypress without a job there. But it was not an easy decision. I liked my bank work. You might say I had fallen in love with banking. But all my life I had wanted to do something to help my people, and I could do that only by leaving my bank job in Miami. Being the person I am, I had to go back. I would have felt guilty if I had a chance to help and I didn't. But I told my daddy that I couldn't give him an answer right away, and I knew he was upset because he had expected me to jump at the chance to come back. He did understand though, that I had to think about it. He knew when I went to live off the reservation that I had had a pretty hard time, getting used to a job, getting used to people. He knew I had accomplished a lot, and it wasn't easy for me to give it up. But that's how I felt. I had to think. At one time it seemed to me that I could never go back to reservation life.

But then really, through it all, I always wished there was something, even the smallest thing, that I could do for my people. Maybe I'm helping now. But I can see that I may get tired of it in a year, or even less. But right now I'm glad to

help build up the store. If it didn't work out, if the store failed, and I thought I hadn't even tried, I would really feel bad. The basic thing about my feeling is that my brothers and sisters and nieces and nephews can build later on in the future only through the foundation their parents and I build. Maybe Indian parents don't always show their affection, but they have taught us that, even though we have a problem, we are still supposed to help one another. And that is what I am trying to do. Even when we were kids, if we had something and other kids didn't, we must share what we had with the others. Kids grow up the way their parents train them.

By the age of nine, girls were expected to take complete care of younger children. I too had to take care of my little brother and sister. I grew up fast. That's just what parents expected. Now teen-agers don't want to do that, so they get angry and take off. Headstart and nurseries help the working mothers because older children don't tend the little ones any more. The old ways are changing, and I hope to help some of the people, particularly girls about my age, change to something good.

There are people on the reservation who don't seem to like me. Maybe they are jealous, but I don't know why. I know they resent me somehow. When I used to come in from school or from work back to the reservation, I could tell some people felt like this. I don't think that I have ever, ever, even in the smallest way, tried to prove myself better or more knowing than other people. I have two close friends here, so I don't feel too lonely; but other people my age do not make friends with me. I miss my sister, and I miss my roommate from Miami. My two friends here are good friends. I can tell them anything I want. I can talk to them. That's important, that

I can talk to them. That's what I look for in a friend, not their education, but for enjoyment of the same things, and understanding. But there are only two of them. I have not been able to find other friends.

The old people think I know everything because I've been to school. They think it is a good thing for us to go to school. But the old people don't have the kind of experience which allows them to understand our problems. They think that it is easy somehow to come back here. They think there is nothing else. They do not understand that there are things I miss on the outside. They do not understand enough to be friends. They are kind, and they are glad that I am educated, but they do not understand my problems. They do not understand loneliness.

It was hard for me to get used again to the way people talk. They have nothing interesting to talk about. They are satisfied to have a TV or radio, but they don't know anything about good books or good movies or the news. There is almost no one I have to talk to about things like that. Here people don't know what discussion is. That's something I found really hard. They gossip: they talk about people, not ideas.

And it was hard getting used to what people think about time. You know, when you live in the city and work, everything is according to time. You race yourself to death, really. But I got used to that and put myself on a schedule. But here, when you want something done, people take their time. They don't come to work when they should, and I just don't want to push them. I would expect it of the older people, but the younger generation should realize how important time is. When you go to school, you just eat and study and go to school, and not worry too much about time; but

on a job, you must keep pace. You are being paid for a certain performance. If you do not do what you are supposed to, you do not get paid. But how do I get that across to my people?

"I Don't Know Why . . ."

I was lonely when I first came back here. I was ready to pack up and go back to Miami. People hardly talked to me— just a few words. I don't know why. I've known these people all my life. I don't know why they didn't know me after just three years. I couldn't carry on a conversation with anyone except my own family. I was working all day at the store, and then I had nothing to do but clean the house, or go fishing alone, or with someone from my family.

Coming back to the reservation to live did not seem to be physically hard. At first I lived in a house with a girl friend because I did not want to stay with my family. I wanted to be sure of my independence. I think this hurt my father. But later, when more of my friend's family moved back to the reservation, I decided it was too crowded with her and went back to live in my old home with my father and family. My father's CBS is clean and comfortable. It is as nice as an apartment in Miami.

My idea was that, being raised on the reservation and knowing the problems here, I could hope that the Indian girls would come to me and ask about what they could do after they finished high school: what they could do on the reservation, what jobs they could get off the reservation. I hoped they would discuss their problems with me, what their goals should be. I'd be more than happy to talk with them. But I can't go to them and tell them what to do. Just because I've worked outside for three years doesn't give me the right to plan for other people. But I thought I had something to offer the girls here, if only they would come for advice.

"They Say I'm Mean . . ."

I would like to see the financial records at the store so well kept that an accountant could come in at any time and check the books, and they would be in perfect order. It is difficult because only Louise and I can run the store, and if either of us gets sick, the other one has to be at the store from 7 A.M. to 9 P.M., or else close the store. At first I had to be very patient with Louise and explain everything to her. She had no training at all. Sometimes I started to get mad when I explained and explained, but then I'd remember that she can't help it. People do not know some of the things I know, and I must not get irritated. But if things go wrong, I am responsible, and it is a big responsibility. The younger people are not exactly lazy; they just don't know how to work. I want them to work and be on time. If they need time off, they should tell me, not just go away or not appear on some days.

So some of them start calling me bossy. But that is my responsibility. I tried to talk to them and tell them why I wanted them to come to work on time, but still they didn't. I want them to realize that they have to work to earn their money. It is not a gift. They were supposed to do something in return for their wages. They are interested in boys at their age, and that's why they aren't good workers. But still, the National Youth Corps, operating in Big Cypress, gives kids some idea of how it is to work, to have a job. If I don't make them do the job, they're

really not earning their money. That is one thing I had to face. I know that they are going to say I'm mean and bossy. I expect that. But if I'm in charge, they're going to do what they're supposed to do. That's the way I look at it. Everybody talks here. I know that, but I've been away, and I can take it.

I think people my own age are jealous. It is not shyness. Before I left, they were all friendly to me. I came back, and they all look at me, but when I go to talk to them, they just turn around, and it is so hard for me. They answer me, but they don't answer like they used to, and talk to me. That has been my main problem. It is hard for someone to come back, but if he is strong enough, you know, he can go ahead and take that. Maybe some day people will understand. There is no reason to come back if you really think you are better than the people. They are wrong if that is what they believe about me. There is not enough money here, and if I didn't really care about the people, then I would have no reason to return.

I am worried about my mother, and I want to stay where I can help her (my parents are now divorced). It is best to come back and act like the other people, dress like they dress, try to be a part of them again. So even if a person didn't have kinfolk here, if he wanted to help, he could. But he must not show off or try to appear better.

If I didn't have a family here, it would be almost like going to live with strangers. I have to work now. It has become a part of my life. People here just don't understand that. I can't just sit around or visit and do nothing. If there were no work here, I could not live here. It would be so hard for me to live the way the women here do, sewing all the time or working in the fields, but if I had to take care of my family and there was nothing else to do, I guess I would stay here for that. My aunt has taught me to do the traditional sewing, and how to make the dolls, so I could earn money doing that; but I wouldn't do it unless I had to stay here to take care of my family.

I think the reason almost all the educated Indians are girls is because a woman's life here on the reservation is harder than the man's. The women have to take all the responsibility for everything. To go to school and get a job is really easier for a woman than staying on the reservation. The men on the reservation can just lay around all day and go hunting. They can work for a little while on the plantations if they need a little money. But the women have to worry about the children. If the women go away and get jobs, then the men have to take responsibility.

A woman and a man should have about the same amount of education when they marry. That means there is no one at Big Cypress I can marry. The boys my age here do not have anything in common with me. If a girl marries an outsider, she has to move away, because the Tribal Council has voted that no white man can live on the reservation. A woman probably would miss the closeness of her family on the reservation. I would want to come back and visit, but I think I could marry out and make it successful. I would expect to meet and know his family. I would like to live near our families, if possible. I will always feel close to my family.

"I Think About the City . . ."

Sometimes I think about the city and all the things to do there. Then I remember my mother and how she is weak and needs someone who will watch over her and help her. You know my mother drinks a lot. She is sick, and the doctors want her to stop; but she herself cannot control her drinking. Well, I guess us kids have shut our eyes, hoping things will get better by themselves. I know you have not heard this before, and I wish I was not the one to tell you this sad story, but my move back to the reservation was partly brought on because of this. She has been to a sanitarium where they help people like her. It has helped her already to know that I want to see her get help and be a better person. I am having a chickee built for her, and I must stay here until she is well enough to manage alone.

Economic opportunity has been severely limited on the reservation until recently. Employment for field hands or driving farm machinery has been available on ranches in the area, but the income is seasonal. Both men and women work at crafts. The products are sold either privately or through the Arts and Crafts Store at the tribal agency on the coast but the income is inadequate by itself. Some of the men and one or two Indian women own cattle, but none of these sources of income would appeal to a person with higher education. Until the opening of the grocery store, there was no job on the reservation which really required literacy, let alone a diploma.

Examining these possibilities and the words of Nellie Greene, what would entice an educated Indian to come back to work and live on the reservation? A good paying job; a high status as an educated or skilled person; to be back in a familiar, friendly community; a desire to be with his family and to help them. Perhaps for the rare individual, an earnest wish to try to help

*his own people. But income from a job
on the reservation must allow a standard
of living not too much lower than that
previously enjoyed as a member of outer
society. Nellie never gave any consideration
to returning to the reservation until there
was the possibility of a job that challenged
her skills and promised a comparable
income. The salary she receives from
managing the store is close to what she
had made at the bank in Miami. In Miami,
however, she worked 40 hours a week,
while on the reservation she works nearly
60 hours a week for approximately the
same pay, because there are no trained
personnel to share the responsibility. Given
the isolation of Big Cypress, there is not
enough time, after she has put in her hours
at the store, to go anywhere off the reservation. It is not merely a question of total
pay; it is a problem of access to a way of
life unattainable on the reservation. Economic opportunity alone is not sufficient.*

*It is quite apparent from Nellie's inter-
views and from observation of the interaction between Nellie and other Indians,
both in the store and elsewhere on the
reservation, that her status is very low.
Her position appears to vary: from some
slight recognition that her training places
her in a category by herself, to distinct
jealousy, to apparent puzzlement on the
part of some of the old folks as to just what
her place in the society is. Through the
whole gamut of reaction to Nellie, only
her proud family considers her status a
high one.*

*The primary reason Nellie gave for
returning to the reservation was to help
her people, but the reservation inhabitants
did not indicate that they viewed her
activities or presence as beneficial to them.
Older Indians, both male and female, stated*

*that it was "right" that she returned because
Indians should stay together, not because
she might help her people or set an example
to inspire young Indians who might otherwise be tempted to drop out of school.
Younger people regard her as bossy and
trying to act "white." She does not even
have the status of a marriageable female.
There is no Indian man on the reservation
with the sort of background that would
make him a desirable marriage partner,
from her standpoint; in their traditional
view of an ideal wife, she does not display
the qualities preferred by the men. At the
same time, there is a council ordinance
which prohibits white men from living
on the reservation, and therefore marriage
to a white man would mean that she would
have to leave the reservation to live. There
is no recognized status of "career woman,"
educated Indian, or marriageable girl, or
any traditional status for her.*

*Obviously, with an inferior status, it is
unlikely that a person would perceive the
community as a friendly, familiar environment. From the point of view of the
reservation people, who have had contacts
with her, she is no longer truly "Indian,"
but rather someone who has taken over so
much of the Anglo-American ways as to
have lost her identity as an Indian woman.
Nearly all of Nellie's close acquaintances
are living off the reservation. The only two
girls she considers friends on the reservation
are, like herself, young women with more
than average contact with outside society,
although with less formal education.*

*Nellie may have rationalized her decision
to return by stressing her determination to
help the people, but her personal concern
for her mother probably influenced her
decision to return more than she herself
realized. Nellie was the only person in the
family who had the ability, knowledge and*

willingness to see that her mother received the proper supervision and help.

The Bureau of Indian Affairs is attempting to increase the economic opportunities on the reservations, but I believe their efforts at holding back the "brain drain" of educated Indians will not be effective. Retraining the reservation people who do not have an education is certainly desirable. But, as the story of Nellie Greene points out, it takes more than good pay and rewarding work to keep the educated Indians down on the reservations. If the educated Indian expects to find status with his people, he is going to be disappointed. White people outside are apt to pay more attention to an educated Seminole than his own Indian society will. If the Indian returns from college and expects to find warm personal relationships with persons of his own or opposite sex, he is going to find little empathy, some distrust and jealousy because of his training and experiences outside the reservation. For Nellie Greene there was a personal goal, helping her sick mother. She was lucky to find a job that required her skills as an educated person, and which paid her as well as the bank at Miami. Her other goal, to help her own people, was thwarted rather than helped by her college education.

22

Nightmare in Mississippi

PETER WEISS

In Mississippi this summer [1964], against the background of the jack-booted terror of official and unofficial reprisals, one could not avoid being startled by the success of the Summer Project, an educational and voter registration program sponsored by the Council of Federated Organizations (COFO), and by the enthusiasm and concentration of the young civil rights volunteers working on it. It has split Mississippi wide open and revealed to the nation a social order so rotten and corrupt that it defies comprehension. The student volunteers who came here from middle-class Northern homes early in the summer are already veterans, as hardened to their battle as any soldiers can be, and the likelihood of frightening them away has all but disappeared from the mind of white Mississippi.

The war on racism is a serious one, and these student volunteers have moved constantly in the shadow of violence and death. But the words *"freedom now"* burn in their stomachs, and they have learned to live with their fear and perpetual concern about safety. In doing so, they have implicated all of us and revealed that had we thought of the Negroes as people we would have been implicated long ago.

Such courage born of purpose is still hard for us to believe. In Jackson, I met a tall, soft spoken, tow-headed Stanford University student who had just been bombed out of the Freedom House in McComb and was

recuperating from his injuries. His ear drums had been split, and he had a mild concussion and cuts from glass. He was frightened and at first spoke little (the night before he had awakened screaming in a thunderstorm).

He told me that he was on his way back to McComb to help with repairs and to continue canvassing for voters. He explained that McComb was a new project (in the dangerous southwest hill country where the Klan has been very active) and that in time the community would become more tolerant. "When they see that we mean to stay, then they will slow up." He said this less than twenty-four hours after he had left McComb and after a wild chase given by carloads of armed whites up the highway to Jackson.

Again, in a church in Meridian, I witnessed a similar display of courage in a young Negro member of the Congress of Racial Equality (CORE), who was planning to go back into Neshoba County, a death trap for civil rights workers and the place where the bodies of the three young volunteers, James Chaney, Andrew Goodman, and Michael Schwerner, who "disappeared" in June [1964], have now been found: "I will go up there on Saturday with Lilly (a local volunteer) and stay the weekend. Then on Monday we'll move in." They would go there armed only with pencils and sample registration forms and a deep commitment to non-violence. "God help this boy," a

---

SOURCE: Reprinted from *The Progressive* magazine, Madison, Wisconsin, September, 1964, 19–22, by permission of the publisher.

woman jumped up and cried, "He's going there for you and me and I haven't the nerve to go with him. He is going up there to die for us just like James Chaney and the other boys did."

Courage such as this is already legendary in the young movement of nearly 1,000 volunteers recruited by the Student Non-violent Coordinating Committee, CORE, and other civil rights groups. There is hardly an SNCC staff member around who hasn't been clubbed, beaten, and drenched in his own blood by the police and the young hoods that serve them. What is over-powering about the Summer Project and the COFO organization is not the program, which is startling enough, but the people in it. They reveal the passion that is their youth, and they are armed with the ideals of Christ and Patrick Henry and Jefferson and Gandhi. The righteous raging at the "student volunteers—the beatniks, the wild-eyed, left-wing nuts, the unshaven and unwashed trash . . ." reveals a desperate need among the local racists to create as much social distance from the students as possible, lest they see too closely the broken promise of their own youth.

Thus, while the white citizens don their sheets and tough sheriffs go around looking for someone to "knock the fire out of," COFO has been nailing its message to the door of Mississippi. Biracial teams have fanned out daily into Negro neighborhoods to plead with the people there to "go down and register." They have met the apathy and resignation that constitute the Mississippi Negro, and they have read the fear that has been laminated into his hide.

This work is discouraging, often infuriat-ing, but mostly humbling, because on those fearful black faces is the searing truth about tyranny: So many of the subjects have collapsed before the king and are cooperat-ing in their own beheading. "And when," puzzled one Project youth, "they ask us, 'What you goin' to do when they knock my head off, if I go down to register?' what can we say?" There is nothing that can be said, but the Negroes do see these COFO workers risking life and limb, and they, like the whites, cannot help but be im-pressed. The Summer Project is moving a civilization just by its very existence and the paltry returns from the voter registrar's office do not detract from this.

If Negroes cannot be placed on the regular voting rolls then COFO will register them on its own freedom rolls. Thousands are being registered this way, allowing them to vote, even if it is not legally recognized. What cannot be done within the racist political structure of Mississippi is being done outside it and within the structure of the new Freedom Democratic Party (FDP). This political move has an uncertain future, but as an experiment in political education it is already a stunning success.

At a church meeting one night the breathtaking truth of this was revealed when a young Negro COFO worker staged a mock election. With the sensitivity and finesse of King Solomon, he drew shy and retiring people into a contrived precinct meeting and assigned them participating roles. He explained to them the meaning of an election and what a precinct was and told them of the coming county FDP convention. He explained how they were to elect a chairman for their group.

Then they tried it. A woman nominated herself for chairman. Someone had to second the nomination, and the COFO worker showed them how. They did it over again. They squirmed, and someone stood up and complained that she didn't know what was going on. The worker patiently went through the process again, and you could feel the tension and the impatience and the frustration they felt in their ignorance, in front of white people who were in the audience.

These Mississippians were enacting fundamental democratic roles which the caste system has forced them to ignore. They were full grown adults who were participating, for the first time in their restricted lives, in the basic process of a free society. The light of pride in their faces showed through their embarrassment. Moreover, as they became absorbed in this process, they began to function on a new level. They elected a committee to seek the use of the courthouse for the FDP county convention. The subjects of the king had declared themselves citizens of the republic.

It is difficult for a subjugated people to take advantage of such an opportunity merely by having it presented to them. The cost of political interest is so high for the Mississippi Negro, and he has learned so well to avoid it, that in many ways citizenship is not yet a psychological possibility. Education, here, is thus not the mere acquisition of skills but also the process of developing an awareness of self and learning the significance of one's own life experience.

The crushing effects of the caste system in Mississippi, as elsewhere, have left the Negro so severely depressed that he walks in a haze, never knowing who he is and never understanding the real meaning of his trying life. His education has been a preparation for an adjustment to a white world that does not recognize him. It is an education—what there is of it—for a life of servitude, turning him away from opportunities that are not his and teaching him not to see them. COFO is trying to

supplement this thin diet with its voter registration drive, with its encompassing mass-meeting workshops, and, more pointedly, in the establishment of freedom schools with their enriched curriculum of Negro history and contemporary problems.

These schools have functioned all over Mississippi this summer in the hope of providing Negro teen-agers with some awareness of their past and its significance in terms of their present life situation. The courses in Negro history, English language expression, art, and other subjects are all designed to encourage these young people to get into the freedom movement and to work for social change. The social renewal of a broken people is a complex task and cannot rest solely on voting. In Mississippi an enlightened local leadership needs to be developed, and people need to be awakened.

For similar reasons, community centers are being established not only as a resource for recreational, educational, and welfare activities but also to validate the need for people to express varied aims in life so that they can advance beyond working and bearing slave children. As with the freedom schools, these centers also provide Negro children with an opportunity to see the possibilities of an integrated world and to learn something about people beyond their being dangerous or safe. The program is undermining some of the intense hatreds that otherwise would inevitably consume these children when they grow up, and is providing them with some new meanings about freedom that have to do with an inner sense of belonging to this world.

All this has sparked the summer outrage of white Mississippi, and the violence of its reprisals has left its people spent of their energy for cooperation. White Mississippi lacks heart and courage, but most of all it lacks perspective. It is choking on its own lynch-rope and pulling the knot tighter and tighter around its own neck. Here are the *white* victims of the caste system and its racial mythology that keeps them entranced in a state of dysphoric excitement.

The COFO program in its entirety is open to white Mississippi on a segregated basis if need be. The response from whites has been less than enthusiastic, and the rare inquiries that are made make COFO news. On July 5 in Ruleville a local white man came into the community center to inquire of the activities there and to engage in a critical but friendly dialogue (the beginning of enlightenment). He was arrested. More often such dialogues with COFO take place from the window of a pick-up truck, guns blazing with buckshot to scatter "them nigger lovers."

This is Mississippi's ruthless reply to the COFO peace corps. To date, this state has an almost unblemished record of lawlessness, which is supported by the limitless patience of the Justice Department. The present restraint of official violence against the COFO volunteers, however encouraging, is misleading, because local Negroes suffer the reprisals. Bombings, burnings, whippings, shootings, and job dismissals continue to occur with unfaltering regularity. It is appalling to find them appearing in the Northern press as "scattered incidents."

To the Negroes of Mississippi and to the COFO staff, these incidents are a nightmare reality that faces them daily. I cannot recall an instant of my visit in Mississippi that I was not afraid. And you don't have to be a civil rights worker or a COFO supporter to get hurt. If you are black, you might still get killed in a night's "funnin'," and be dumped half and half into the river.

Those who catch the worst of this terror are the Negro civil rights workers, especially those from SNCC who are frequently faced with being beaten by the police in the jailhouse while "resisting arrest." Somehow personal dignity and nonviolence combine to terrorize the authorities and sorely try their already limited capacity for restraint. The record is full of incidents such as this one:

On June 8, five SNCC workers were passing through Columbus, Mississippi, enroute to a staff meeting in Atlanta. They were stopped by the state highway patrol. (Governor Paul Johnson relies heavily on the patrol in his struggle with the county sheriffs for the control of Mississippi.) The patrolman walked up to the car and said, "You goddamn niggers want to change our way of life." (This to my knowledge is not a traffic problem.) He then ordered the five out of the car and searched it, finding Summer Project literature and Fanny Lou Hamer (a Negro candidate for Congress sponsored by COFO) campaign posters. He called the sheriff of Lowndes County and searched each one of the five young men. The sheriff arrived and took four of them, handcuffed, to jail. The fifth went with the highway patrolman to a spot about a mile from where the car had been stopped. The affidavit dated June 8, 1964, and signed by James Black, age seventeen, reads:

"He told me to get out of the car; I refused to get out. So he pulled me out. He started hitting me with his fists, and after about twenty blows he got out his blackjack and hit me one time with it and knocked me down. Then he told me to get back in the car. While he was beating me, he asked if any white folks had ever treated me bad; I told him yes, and he hit me again. He asked me again had any white folks in Mississippi treated me bad, and I told him no. At that point he helped me back into the car.

"Then he took me to the county jail [Lowndes] where I was questioned by the sheriff. The sheriff asked for my driver's license and to take everything out of my pockets . . . I had a friend's I.D. card in my pocket and he asked me if my friend was a Negro or a nigger. I told him a Negro. The same highway patrolman was there, and took out his blackjack and again asked if my friend was a Negro or a nigger. He started to hit me with the blackjack, and I told him my friend was a nigger."

The four other young men were questioned similarly throughout the night and finally charged with reckless driving. James Black was tried, convicted, and fined the following day in court. All were released, after paying $4 each for their night in jail.

This is a common occurrence in Mississippi. In it the cry of "Jew! Jew! Jew!" echoes from the Nazi past amid the thumping cadence of blows to the head and groin, only to be thinly covered up by the barest formalities of the judicial process. And people say, as they once said, "We didn't know."

In its deep commitment to the safety of its volunteers, COFO has covered Mississippi with a security network that would make the Central Intelligence Agency envious. COFO knows when you are out and where you will be and the route you will take and your time of arrival. If at any point in this process a person "disappears," the Federal Bureau of Investigation is notified, and search parties set out immediately. Sometimes the sheriffs get coy and start shifting a prisoner around in order to foul up the search. In one case the sheriff's wife took the jailhouse telephone off the hook to prevent the location of a COFO prisoner. None of this has so far succeeded.

The three young students who "disappeared" in June were not "sacrificed," as was cynically claimed, to bring Federal pressure on Mississippi. Federal attention to the constitutional rights of the student volunteers is what it was from the start —minimal. In a statement to the press July 10 in Jackson, J. Edgar Hoover stated that the FBI does not "and will not give protection to the civil rights workers . . ." And, indeed, the FBI has not. The opening of a permanent FBI office in Jackson and the addition of fifty agents in Mississippi were not very encouraging to the civil rights workers, since the existing contingent of one hundred did not allow itself to become overworked.

The catalogue of official and unofficial violations of Federal law, especially interference with voter registration work in the first month of the Summer Project, covers eight legal-size pages of single spaced type. The FBI arrested three people in one case. It has been called repeatedly for help and has done little if anything. When Chaney, Goodman, and Schwerner disappeared on June 21, the FBI was notified at 10 p.m. It entered the case twenty hours later, after sixteen calls had been made to the FBI and to the Justice Department. This is usual. It leaves the impression that the FBI, this summer in Mississippi, had been little more than a telephone answering service for the Federal government.

The FBI is not entirely to blame, however. Its activity depends on Federal policy. Hoover's televised gesture of solidarity with Mississippi officials was a *tour de force*. They looked as if they were getting married as they upheld the rule of law and order and exchanged vows of allegiance to it. But of the flagrant and systematic violations of the state and Federal constitutions in the denial of due process to U.S. citizens in Mississippi, nothing was said.

The problem of anarchy—the lawlessness of Mississippi law enforcement—seems to have been referred once again to the local authorities. The Federal government is not enforcing the law. Its failure to do so has encouraged local indifference to it in Mississippi. If a Federal judge, hearing a voter registration case in the name of the United States, refers from the bench to the applicants as "a bunch of niggers who are acting like a bunch of chimpanzees," then what can be expected from a county sheriff in the discharge of his duties?

Here is the alarming frustration of the civil rights movement. You fight your way past the bottles and curses to the courthouse. Then you fight your way through a gauntlet of billy clubs up the steps to the registrar's office only to find that you cannot exercise your birthright as an American citizen. Then you fight your way back home again through the same mob. That night your house is bombed, and you stumble dazed and deaf into the front yard where a policeman stands spitting on your grass, trying to conceal his glee. Mississippi, 1964, is Germany, 1936, revisited.

PART NINE Population

Of the major social problems existing today, overpopulation, in the long run, is perhaps the most important. In man's history it has usually been functional for groups of people to reproduce to their full capacity. In the early days of man, perhaps a high birth rate was needed to insure that the tribe would survive the environmental dangers. At a later time in man's history, a nation's power was at least partially dependent upon the gross number of humans in its population. In terms of settling new lands and pushing back the frontier, such as the American west, more and more people were an asset. With undeveloped land and a farm economy, children were useful in developing the land. In modern society, however, these reasons for a high birth rate are no longer relevant. We are no longer in great danger from the environment, except for the dangers we are creating. Secondly, a na-tion's power is much more related today to technology rather than population size. And finally, our economy is no longer of such a nature that children are necessary as a labor force.

Traditional values with great emotional content, such as those surrounding repro-duction, are slow to change; particularly a value which has been so useful in the past. Will we find some ways of controlling our rising population? The authors in this section are among many who have directed their attention to this problem.

The first essay, from Paul Ehrlich's book The Population Bomb, *attempts to delineate the magnitude of the population problem. The second article, "Population Policy: Will Current Programs Succeed?" by Kingsley Davis, is an analysis of the effectiveness of current programs in dealing with the problem of overpopulation.*

23

Too Many People

PAUL EHRLICH

Americans are beginning to realize that the undeveloped countries of the world face an inevitable population-food crisis. Each year food production in undeveloped countries falls a bit further behind burgeoning population growth, and people go to bed a little bit hungrier. While there are temporary or local reversals of this trend, it now seems inevitable that it will continue to its logical conclusion: mass starvation. The rich are going to get richer, but the more numerous poor are going to get poorer. Of these poor, a minimum of three and one-half million will starve to death this year, mostly children. But this is a mere handful compared to the numbers that will be starving in a decade or so. And it is now too late to take action to save many of those people.

In a book about population there is a temptation to stun the reader with an avalanche of statistics. I'll spare you most, but not all, of that. After all, no matter how you slice it, population is a numbers game. Perhaps the best way to impress you with numbers is to tell you about the "doubling time"—the time necessary for the population to double in size.

It has been estimated that the human population of 6000 B.C. was about five million people, taking perhaps one million years to get there from two and a half million. The population did not reach 500 million until almost 8,000 years later—about 1650 A.D. This means it doubled roughly once every thousand years or so. It reached a billion people around 1850, doubling in some 200 years. It took only 80 years or so for the next doubling, as the population reached two billion around 1930. We have not completed the next doubling to four billion yet, but we now have well over three billion people. The doubling time at present seems to be about 37 years.[1] Quite a reduction in doubling times: 1,000,000 years, 1,000 years, 200 years, 80 years, 37 years. Perhaps the meaning of a doubling time of around 37 years is best brought home by a theoretical exercise. Let's examine what might happen on the absurd assumption that the population continued to double every 37 years into the indefinite future.

If growth continued at that rate for about 900 years, there would be some 60,000, 000,000,000,000 people on the face of the earth. Sixty million billion people. This is about 100 persons for each square yard of the Earth's surface, land and sea. A British physicist, J. H. Fremlin,[2] guessed that such a multitude might be housed in a continuous 2,000-story building covering our entire planet. The upper 1,000 stories would contain only the apparatus for running this gigantic warren. Ducts, pipes, wires, elevator shafts, etc., would occupy about half of the space in the bottom 1,000 stories. This would leave three or four yards of floor space for each person. I will leave to your imagination the physical

SOURCE: Reprinted from *The Population Bomb,* by Paul Ehrlich, New York: Ballantine Books, Inc., 1968, pp. 17–35, by permission of the publisher. Copyright © 1968 by Paul R. Ehrlich.

details of existence in this ant heap, except to point out that all would not be black. Probably each person would be limited in his travel. Perhaps he could take elevators through all 1,000 residential stories but could travel only within a circle of a few hundred yards' radius on any floor. This would permit, however, each person to choose his friends from among some ten million people! And, as Fremlin points out, entertainment on the worldwide TV should be excellent, for at any time "one could expect some ten million Shakespeares and rather more Beatles to be alive."

Could growth of the human population of the Earth continue beyond that point? Not according to Fremlin. We would have reached a "heat limit." People themselves, as well as their activities, convert other forms of energy into heat which must be dissipated. In order to permit this excess heat to radiate directly from the top of the "world building" directly into space, the atmosphere would have been pumped into flasks under the sea well before the limiting population size was reached. The precise limit would depend on the technology of the day. At a population size of one billion billion people, the temperature of the "world roof" would be kept around the melting point of iron to radiate away the human heat generated.

But, you say, surely Science (with a capital "S") will find a way for us to occupy the other planets of our solar system and eventually of other stars before we get all that crowded. Skip for a moment the virtual certainty that those planets are uninhabitable. Forget also the insurmountable logistic problems of moving billions of people off the Earth. Fremlin has made some interesting calculations on how much time we could buy by occupying the planets of the solar system. For instance, at

any given time it would take only about 50 years to populate Venus, Mercury, Mars, the moon, and the moons of Jupiter and Saturn to the same population density as Earth.[3]

What if the fantastic problems of reaching and colonizing the other planets of the solar system, such as Jupiter and Uranus, can be solved? It would take only about 200 years to fill them "Earth-full." So we could perhaps gain 250 years of time for population growth in the solar system after we had reached an absolute limit on Earth. What then? We can't ship our surplus to the stars. Professor Garrett Hardin[4] of the University of California at Santa Barbara has dealt effectively with this fantasy. Using extremely optimistic assumptions, he has calculated that Americans, by cutting their standard of living down to 18% of its present level, could in *one year* set aside enough capital to finance the exportation to the stars of *one day's* increase in the population of the world.

Interstellar transport for surplus people presents an amusing prospect. Since the ships would take generations to reach most stars, the only people who could be transported would be those willing to exercise strict birth control. Population explosions on space ships would be disastrous. Thus we would have to export our responsible people, leaving the irresponsible at home on Earth to breed.

Enough of fantasy. Hopefully, you are convinced that the population will have to stop growing sooner or later and that the extremely remote possibility of expanding into outer space offers no escape from the laws of population growth. If you still want to hope for the stars, just remember that, at the current growth rate, in a few thousand years everything in the visible universe would be converted into people, and the ball of people would be expanding with the speed of light! [5] Unfortunately, even 900 years is much too far in the future for those of us concerned with the population explosion. As you shall see, the next *nine* years will probably tell the story.

Of course, population growth is not occurring uniformly over the face of the Earth. Indeed, countries are divided rather neatly into two groups: those with rapid growth rates, and those with relatively slow growth rates. The first group, making up about two-thirds of the world population, coincides closely with what are known as the "undeveloped countries" (UDC's). The UDC's are not industrialized, tend to have inefficient agriculture, very small gross national products, high illiteracy rates and related problems. That's what UDC's are technically, but a short definition of undeveloped is "starving." Most Latin American, African, and Asian countries fall into this category. The second group consists, in essence, of the "developed countries" (DC's). DC's are modern, industrial nations, such as the United States, Canada, most European countries, Israel, Russia, Japan, and Australia. Most people in these countries are adequately nourished.

Doubling times in the UDC's range around 20 to 35 years. Examples of these times (from the 1968 figures just released by the Population Reference Bureau) are Kenya, 24 years; Nigeria, 28; Turkey, 24; Indonesia, 31; Philippines, 20; Brazil, 22; Costa Rica, 20; and El Salvador, 19. Think of what it means for the population of a country to double in 25 years. In order just to keep living standards at the present inadequate level, the food available for the people must be doubled. Every structure and road must be duplicated. The amount of power must be doubled. The capacity of

the transport system must be doubled. The number of trained doctors, nurses, teachers, and administrators must be doubled. This would be a fantastically difficult job in the United States—a rich country with a fine agricultural system, immense industries, and rich natural resources. Think of what it means to a country with none of these.

Remember also that in virtually all UDC's, people have gotten the word about the better life it is possible to have. They have seen colored pictures in magazines of the miracles of Western technology. They have seen automobiles and airplanes. They have seen American and European movies. Many have seen refrigerators, tractors, and even TV sets. Almost all have heard transistor radios. They *know* that a better life is possible. They have what we like to call "rising expectations." If twice as many people are to be happy, the miracle of doubling what they now have will not be enough. It will only maintain today's standard of living. There will have to be a tripling or better. Needless to say, they are not going to be happy.

Doubling times for the populations of the DC's tend to be in the 50-to-200-year range. Examples of 1968 doubling times are the United States, 63 years; Austria, 175; Denmark, 88; Norway, 88; United Kingdom, 140; Poland, 88; Russia, 63; Italy, 117; Spain, 88; and Japan, 63. These are industrialized countries that have undergone the so-called demographic transition—a transition from high to low growth rate. As industrialization progressed, children became less important to parents as extra hands to work on the farm and as support in old age. At the same time they became a financial drag—expensive to raise and educate. Presumably these are the reasons for a slowing of population growth after industrialization. They boil down to a simple fact—people just want to have fewer children.

This is not to say, however, that population is not a problem for the DC's. First of all, most of them are overpopulated. They are overpopulated by the simple criterion that they are not able to produce enough food to feed their populations. It is true that they have the money to buy food, but when food is no longer available for sale, they will find the money rather indigestible. Then, too, they share with the UDC's a serious problem of population distribution. Their urban centers are getting more and more crowded relative to the countryside. This problem is not as severe as it is in the UDC's (if current trends should continue, which they cannot, Calcutta could have 66 million inhabitants in the year 2000). As you are well aware, however, urban concentrations are creating serious problems even in America. In the United States, one of the more rapidly growing DC's, we hear constantly of the headaches caused by growing population: not just garbage in our environment, but overcrowded highways, burgeoning slums, deteriorating school systems, rising crime rates, riots, and other related problems.

From the point of view of a demographer, the whole problem is quite simple. A population will continue to grow as long as the birth rate exceeds the death rate—if immigration and emigration are not occurring. It is, of course, the balance between birth rate and death rate that is critical. The birth rate is the number of births per thousand people per year in the population. The death rate is the number of deaths per thousand people per year.[6] Subtracting the death rate from the birth rate, and ignoring migration, gives the rate of increase. If the birth rate is 30 per thousand per year, and the death rate

is 10 per thousand per year, then the rate of increase is 20 per thousand per year $(30 - 10 = 20)$. Expressed as a percent (rate per hundred people), the rate of 20 per thousand becomes 2%. If the rate of increase is 2%, then the doubling time will be 35 years. Note that if you simply added 20 people per thousand per year to the population, it would take 50 years to add a second thousand people $(20 \times 50 = 1,000)$. But the doubling time is actually much less because populations grow at compound interest rates. Just as interest dollars themselves earn interest, so people added to populations produce more people. It's growing at compound interest that makes populations double so much more rapidly than seems possible. Look at the relationship between the annual percent increase (interest rate) and the doubling time of the population (time for your money to double):

Annual Percent Increase	Doubling Time
1.0	70
2.0	35
3.0	24
4.0	17

Those are all the calculations—I promise. If you are interested in more details on how demographic figuring is done, you may enjoy reading Thompson and Lewis' excellent book, *Population Problems*.[7]

There are some professional optimists around who like to greet every sign of dropping birth rates with wild pronouncements about the end of the population explosion. They are a little like a person who, after a low temperature of five below zero on December 21, interprets a low of only three below zero on December 22 as a cheery sign of approaching spring. First of all, birth rates, along with all demographic statistics, show short-term fluctuations caused by many factors. For instance, the birth rate depends rather heavily on the number of women at reproductive age. In the United States, the current low birth rates soon will be replaced by higher rates as more post World War II "baby boom" children move into their reproductive years. In Japan, 1966, the Year of the Fire Horse, was a year of very low birth rates. There is widespread belief that girls born in the Year of the Fire Horse make poor wives, and Japanese couples try to avoid giving birth in that year because they are afraid of having daughters.

But, I repeat, it is the relationship between birth rate and death rate that is most critical. Indonesia, Laos, and Haiti all had birth rates around 46 per thousand in 1966. Costa Rica's birth rate was 41 per thousand. Good for Costa Rica? Unfortunately, not very. Costa Rica's death rate was less than nine per thousand, while the other countries all had death rates above 20 per thousand. The population of Costa Rica in 1966 was doubling every 17 years, while the doubling times of Indonesia, Laos, and Haiti were all above 30 years. Ah, but, you say, it was good for Costa Rica—fewer people per thousand were dying each year. Fine for a few years perhaps, but what then? Some 50% of the people in Costa Rica are under 15 years old. As they get older, they will need more and more food in a world with less and less. In 1983 they will have twice as many mouths to feed as they had in 1966, if the 1966 trend continues. Where will the food come from? Today the death rate in Costa Rica is low in part because they have a large number of physicians in proportion to their population. How do you suppose those physicians will keep the death rate down when there's not enough food to keep people alive?

One of the most ominous facts of the current situation is that roughly 40% of the population of the undeveloped world is made up of people *under 15 years old*. As that mass of young people moves into its reproductive years during the next decade, we're going to see the greatest baby boom of all time. Those youngsters are the reason for all the ominous predictions for the year 2000. They are the gunpowder for the population explosion.

How did we get into this bind? It all happened a long time ago, and the story involves the process of natural selection, the development of culture, and man's swollen head. The essence of success in evolution is reproduction. Indeed, natural selection is simply defined as differential reproduction of genetic types. That is, if people with blue eyes have more children on the average than those with brown eyes, natural selection is occurring. More genes for blue eyes will be passed on to the next generation than will genes for brown eyes. Should this continue, the population will have progressively larger and larger proportions of blue-eyed people. This differential reproduction of genetic types is the driving force of evolution; it has been driving evolution for billions of years. Whatever types produced more offspring became the common types. Virtually all populations contain very many different genetic types (for reasons that need not concern us), and some are always outreproducing others. As I said, reproduction is the key to winning the evolutionary game. Any structure, physiological process, or pattern of behavior that leads to greater reproductive success will tend to be perpetuated. The entire process by which man developed involves thousands of millennia of our ancestors being more successful breeders than their relatives. Facet number one of our bind—the urge to reproduce has been fixed in us by billions of years of evolution.

Of course through all those years of evolution, our ancestors were fighting a continual battle to keep the birth rate ahead of the death rate. That they were successful is attested to by our very existence, for, if the death rate had overtaken the birth rate for any substantial period of time, the evolutionary line leading to man would have gone extinct. Among our ape-like ancestors, a few million years ago, it was still very difficult for a mother to rear her children successfully. Most of the offspring died before they reached reproductive age. The death rate was near the birth rate. Then another factor entered the picture—cultural evolution was added to biological evolution.

Culture can be loosely defined as the body of nongenetic information which people pass from generation to generation. It is the accumulated knowledge that, in the old days, was passed on entirely by word of mouth, painting, and demonstration. Several thousand years ago the written word was added to the means of cultural transmission. Today culture is passed on in these ways, and also through television, computer tapes, motion pictures, records, blueprints, and other media. Culture is all the information man possesses except for that which is stored in the chemical language of his genes.

The large size of the human brain evolved in response to the development of cultural information. A big brain is an advantage when dealing with such information. Big-brained individuals were able to deal more successfully with the culture of their group. They were thus more successful reproductively than their smaller-brained relatives. They passed on their genes

for big brains to their numerous offspring. They also added to the accumulating store of cultural information, increasing slightly the premium placed on brain size in the next generation. A self-reinforcing selective trend developed—a trend toward increased brain size.[8]

But there was, quite literally, a rub. Babies had bigger and bigger heads. There were limits to how large a woman's pelvis could conveniently become. To make a long story short, the strategy of evolution was not to make a woman bell-shaped and relatively immobile, but to accept the problem of having babies who were helpless for a long period while their brains grew after birth.[9] How could the mother defend and care for her infant during its unusually long period of helplessness? She couldn't, unless Papa hung around. The girls are still working on that problem, but an essential step was to get rid of the short, well-defined breeding season characteristic of most mammals. The year-round sexuality of the human female, the long period of infant dependence on the female, the evolution of the family group, all are at the roots of our present problem. They are essential ingredients in the vast social phenomenon that we call sex. Sex is not simply an act leading to the production of offspring. It is a varied and complex cultural phenomenon penetrating into all aspects of our lives—one involving our self-esteem, our choice of friends, cars, and leaders. It is tightly interwoven with our mythologies and history. Sex in man is necessary for the production of young, but it also evolved to ensure their successful rearing. Facet number two of our bind— our urge to reproduce is hopelessly entwined with most of our other urges.

Of course, in the early days the whole system did not prevent a very high mortality among the young, as well as among the older members of the group. Hunting and food-gathering is a risky business. Cavemen had to throw very impressive cave bears out of their caves before the men could move in. Witch doctors and shamans had a less than perfect record at treating wounds and curing disease. Life was short, if not sweet. Man's total population size doubtless increased slowly but steadily as human populations expanded out of the African cradle of our species.

Then about 8,000 years ago a major change occurred—the agricultural revolution. People began to give up hunting food and settled down to grow it. Suddenly some of the risk was removed from life. The chances of dying of starvation diminished greatly in some human groups. Other threats associated with the nomadic life were also reduced, perhaps balanced by new threats of disease and large-scale warfare associated with the development of cities. But the overall result was a more secure existence than before, and the human population grew more rapidly. Around 1800, when the standard of living in what are today the DC's was dramatically increasing due to industrialization, population growth really began to accelerate. The development of medical science was the straw that broke the camel's back. While lowering death rates in the DC's was due in part to other factors, there is no question that "instant death control," exported by the DC's, has been responsible for the drastic lowering of death rates in the UDC's. Medical science, with its efficient public health programs, has been able to depress the death rate with astonishing rapidity and at the same time drastically increase the birth rate; healthier people have more babies.

The power of exported death control

can best be seen by an examination of the classic case of Ceylon's assault on malaria after World War II. Between 1933 and 1942 the death rate due directly to malaria was *reported* as almost two per thousand. This rate, however, represented only a portion of the malaria deaths, as many were reported as being due to "pyrexia." [10] Indeed, in 1934–1935 a malaria epidemic may have been directly responsible for fully half of the deaths on the island. In addition, malaria, which infected a large portion of the population, made people susceptible to many other diseases. It thus contributed to the death rate indirectly as well as directly.

The introduction of DDT in 1946 brought rapid control over the mosquitoes which carry malaria. As a result, the death rate on the island was halved in less than a decade. The death rate in Ceylon in 1945 was 22. It dropped 34% between 1946 and 1947 and moved down to ten in 1954. Since the sharp postwar drop it has continued to decline and now stands at eight. Although part of the drop is doubtless due to the killing of other insects which carry disease and to other public health measures, most of it can be accounted for by the control of malaria.

Victory over malaria, yellow fever, smallpox, cholera, and other infectious diseases has been responsible for similar plunges in death rate throughout most of the UDC's. In the decade 1940–1950, the death rate declined 46% in Puerto Rico, 43% in Formosa, and 23% in Jamaica. In a sample of 18 undeveloped areas, the average decline in death rate between 1945 and 1950 was 24%.

It is, of course, socially very acceptable to reduce the death rate. Billions of years of evolution have given us all a powerful will to live. Intervening in the birth rate goes against our evolutionary values. During all those centuries of our evolutionary past, the individuals who had the most children passed on their genetic endowment in greater quantities than those who reproduced less. Their genes dominate our heredity today. All our biological urges are for more reproduction, and they are all too often reinforced by our culture. In brief, death control goes with the grain, birth control against it.

In summary, the world's population will continue to grow as long as the birth rate exceeds the death rate; it's as simple as that. When it stops growing or starts to shrink, it will mean that either the birth rate has gone down or the death rate has gone up or a combination of the two. Basically, then, there are only two kinds of solutions to the population problem. One is a "birth rate solution," in which we find ways to lower the birth rate. The other is a "death rate solution," in which ways to raise the death rate—war, famine, pestilence —*find us*. The problem could have been avoided by *population control,* in which mankind consciously adjusted the birth rate so that a "death rate solution" did not have to occur.

Footnotes

[1] Since this was written, 1968 figures have appeared, showing that the doubling time is now 35 years.

[2] J. H. Fremlin, "How Many People Can the World Support?" *New Scientist,* October 29, 1964.

[3] To understand this, simply consider what would happen if we held the population constant at three billion people by exporting all the surplus people. If this were done for 37 years (the time it now takes for one doubling) we would have exported three billion people—enough to populate a twin planet of the Earth to the same density. In two doubling times (74 years), we would reach a total human population for the solar system

of 12 billion people, enough to populate the Earth and three similar planets to the density found on Earth today. Since the areas of the planets and moons mentioned above are not three times that of the Earth, they can be populated to equal density in much less than two doubling times.

[4] "Interstellar Migration and the Population Problem." *Heredity* 50:68–70, 1959.

[5] I. J. Cook, *New Scientist,* September 8, 1966.

[6] The birth rate is more precisely the total number of births in a country during a year, divided by the total population at the midpoint of the year, multiplied by 1,000. Suppose that there were 80 births in Lower Slobbovia during 1967, and that the population of lower Slobbovia was 2,000 on July 1, 1967. Then the birth rate would be:

$$\text{Birth rate} = \frac{80 \text{ (total births in L. Slobbovia in 1967)}}{2,000 \text{ (total population, July 1, 1967)}} \times 1,000$$

$$= .04 \times 1,000 = 40$$

Similarly if there were 40 deaths in Lower Slobbovia during 1967, the death rate would be:

$$\text{Death rate} = \frac{40 \text{ (total deaths in L. Slobbovia in 1967)}}{2,000 \text{ (total population, July 1, 1967)}} \times 1,000$$

$$= .02 \times 1,000 = 20$$

Then the Lower Slobbovian birth rate would be 40 per thousand, and the death rate would be 20 per thousand. For every 1,000 Lower Slobbovians alive on July 1, 1967, 40 babies were born and 20 people died. Subtracting the death rate from the birth rate gives us the rate of natural increase of Lower Slobbovia for the year 1967. That is, $40 - 20 = 20$; during 1967 the population grew at a rate of 20 people per thousand per year. Dividing that rate by ten expresses the increase as a percent (the increase per hundred per year). The increase in 1967 in Lower Slobbovia was two percent. Remember that this rate of increase ignores any movement of people into and out of Lower Slobbovia.

[7] McGraw-Hill Book Company, Inc., New York, 1965.

[8] Human brain size increased from an apelike capacity of about 500 cubic centimeters (cc) in *Australopithecus* to about 1,500 cc in modern *Homo sapiens.* Among modern men, small variations in brain size do not seem to be related to significant differences in the ability to use cultural information, and there is no particular reason

to believe that our brain size will continue to increase. Further evolution may occur more readily in a direction of increased efficiency rather than increased size.

[9] This is, of course, an oversimplified explanation. For more detail see Ehrlich and Holm, *The Process of Evolution,* McGraw-Hill Book Company, Inc., New York, 1963.

[10] These data on the decline of death rates are from Kingsley Davis' "The Amazing Decline of Mortality in Underdeveloped Areas," *The American Economic Review,* Vol. 46, pp. 305–318.

24

Population Policy: Will Current Programs Succeed?

KINGSLEY DAVIS

Throughout history, the growth of population has been identified with prosperity and strength. If today an increasing number of nations are seeking to curb rapid population growth by reducing their birth rates, they must be driven to do so by an urgent crisis. My purpose here is not to discuss the crisis itself but rather to assess the present and prospective measures used to meet it. Most observers are surprised by the swiftness with which concern over the population problem has turned from intellectual analysis and debate to policy and action. Such action is a welcome relief from the long opposition, or timidity, which seemed to block forever any governmental attempt to restrain population growth, but relief that "at last something is being done" is no guarantee that what is being done is adequate. On the face of it, one could hardly expect such a fundamental reorientation to be quickly and successfully implemented. I therefore propose to review the nature and (as I see them) limitations of the present policies and to suggest lines of possible improvement.

The Nature of Current Policies

With more than 30 nations now trying or planning to reduce population growth, and with numerous private and international organizations helping, the degree of unanimity as to the kind of measures needed is impressive. The consensus can be summed up in the phrase "family planning." President Johnson declared in 1965 that the United States will "assist family planning programs in nations which request such help." The Prime Minister of India said a year later, "We must press forward with family planning. This is a programme of the highest importance." The Republic of Singapore created in 1966 the Singapore Family Planning and Population Board "to initiate and undertake population control programmes." [1]

As is well known, "family planning" is a euphemism for contraception. The family-planning approach to population limitation, therefore, concentrates on providing new and efficient contraceptives on a national basis through mass programs under public health auspices. The nature of these programs is shown by the following enthusiastic report from the Population Council:

No single year has seen so many forward steps in population control as 1965. Effective national programs have at last emerged, international organizations have decided to become engaged, a new contraceptive has proved its value in mass application, . . . and surveys have confirmed a popular desire for family limitation. . . .

An accounting of notable events must begin with Korea and Taiwan . . . Taiwan's program is not yet two years old, and

SOURCE: Reprinted from *Science*, November 10, 1967, 158:730–739. Copyright © 1967 by the American Association for the Advancement of Science, by permission of the author and the publisher.

already it has inserted one IUD [intrauterine device] for every 4–6 target women (those who are not pregnant, lactating, already sterile, already using contraceptives effectively, or desirous of more children). Korea has done almost as well . . . has put 2,200 full-time workers into the field, . . . has reached operational levels for a network of IUD quotas, supply lines, local manufacture of contraceptives, training of hundreds of M.D.'s and nurses and mass propaganda. . . .[2]

Here one can see the implication that "population control" is being achieved through the dissemination of new contraceptives, and the fact that the "target women" exclude those who want more children. One can also note the technological emphasis and the medical orientation.

What is wrong with such programs? The answer is, "Nothing at all, if they work." Whether or not they work depends on what they are expected to do as well as on how they try to do it. Let us discuss the goal first, then the means.

Goals

Curiously, it is hard to find in the population-policy movement any explicit discussion of long-range goals. By implication, the policies seem to promise a great deal. This is shown by the use of expressions like *population control* and *population planning* (as in the passages quoted above). It is also shown by the characteristic style of reasoning. Expositions of current policy usually start off by lamenting the speed and the consequences of runaway population growth. This growth, it is then stated, must be curbed—by pursuing a vigorous family-planning program. That family planning can solve the problem of

population growth seems to be taken as self-evident.

For instance, the much-heralded statement by 12 heads of state, issued by Secretary-General U Thant on December 10, 1966 (a statement initiated by John D. Rockefeller III, Chairman of the Board of the Population Council), devotes half its space to discussing the harmfulness of population growth and the other half to recommending family planning.[3] A more succinct example of the typical reasoning is given in the Provisional Scheme for a Nationwide Family Planning Programme in Ceylon:

The population of Ceylon is fast increasing. . . . [The] figures reveal that a serious situation will be created within a few years. In order to cope with it a Family Planning programme on a nationwide scale should be launched by the Government.[4]

The promised goal—to limit population growth so as to solve population problems —is a large order. One would expect it to be carefully analyzed, but it is left imprecise and taken for granted, as is the way in which family planning will achieve it.

When the terms *population control* and *population planning* are used, as they frequently are, as synonyms for current family-planning programs, they are misleading. Technically, they would mean deliberate influence over all attributes of a population, including its age-sex structure, geographical distribution, racial composition, genetic quality, and total size. No government attempts such full control. By tacit understanding, current population policies are concerned with only the *growth* and *size* of populations. These attributes, however, result from the death rate and migration as well as from the birth rate; their control would require deliberate influence over the factors giving rise to all three determinants. Actually, current policies labeled population control do not deal with mortality and migration, but deal only with the birth input. This is why another term, *fertility control,* is frequently used to describe current policies. But, as I show below, family planning (and hence current policy) does not undertake to influence most of the determinants of human reproduction. Thus the programs should not be referred to as population control or planning, because they do not attempt to influence the factors responsible for the attributes of human populations, taken generally; nor should they be called fertility control, because they do not try to affect most of the determinants of reproductive performance.

The ambiguity does not stop here, however. When one speaks of controlling population size, any inquiring person naturally asks, What is "control"? Who is to control whom? Precisely what population size, or what rate of population growth, is to be achieved? Do the policies aim to produce a growth rate that is nil, one that is very slight, or one that is like that of the industrial nations? Unless such questions are dealt with and clarified, it is impossible to evaluate current population policies.

The actual programs seem to be aiming simply to achieve a reduction in the birth rate. Success is therefore interpreted as the accomplishment of such a reduction, on the assumption that the reduction will lessen population growth. In those rare cases where a specific demographic aim is stated, the goal is said to be a short-run decline within a given period. The Pakistan plan adopted in 1966 [5] aims to reduce the birth rate from 50 to 40 per thousand by 1970; the Indian plan[6] aims to reduce the

rate from 40 to 25 "as soon as possible"; and the Korean aim[7] is to cut population growth from 2.9 to 1.2 percent by 1980. A significant feature of such stated aims is the rapid population growth they would permit. Under conditions of modern mortality, a crude birth rate of 25 to 30 per thousand will represent such a multiplication of people as to make use of the term *population control* ironic. A rate of increase of 1.2 percent per year would allow South Korea's already dense population to double in less than 60 years.

One can of course defend the programs by saying that the present goals and measures are merely interim ones. A start must be made somewhere. But we do not find this answer in the population-policy literature. Such a defense, if convincing, would require a presentation of the *next* steps, and these are not considered. One suspects that the entire question of goals is instinctively left vague because thorough limitation of population growth would run counter to national and group aspirations. A consideration of hypothetical goals throws further light on the matter.

Industrialized nations as the model. Since current policies are confined to family planning, their maximum demographic effect would be to give the underdeveloped countries the same level of reproductive performance that the industrial nations now have. The latter, long oriented toward family planning, provide a good yardstick for determining what the availability of contraceptives can do to population growth. Indeed, they provide more than a yardstick; they are actually the model which inspired the present population policies.

What does this goal mean in practice? Among the advanced nations there is considerable diversity in the level of fertility.[8]

At one extreme are countries such as New Zealand, with an average gross reproduction rate (GRR) of 1.91 during the period 1960–64; at the other extreme are countries such as Hungary, with a rate of 0.91 during the same period. To a considerable extent, however, such divergencies are matters of timing. The birth rates of most industrial nations have shown, since about 1940, a wavelike movement, with no secular trend. The average level of reproduction during this long period has been high enough to give these countries, with their low mortality, an extremely rapid population growth. If this level is maintained, their population will double in just over 50 years —a rate higher than that of world population growth at any time prior to 1950, at which time the growth in numbers of human beings was already considered fantastic. The advanced nations are suffering acutely from the effects of rapid population growth in combination with the production of ever more goods per person.[9] A rising share of their supposedly high per capita income, which itself draws increasingly upon the resources of the underdeveloped countries (who fall farther behind in relative economic position), is spent simply to meet the costs, and alleviate the nuisances, of the unrelenting production of more and more goods by more people. Such facts indicate that the industrial nations provide neither a suitable demographic model for the nonindustrial peoples to follow nor the leadership to plan and organize effective population-control policies for them.

Zero population growth as a goal. Most discussions of the population crisis lead logically to zero population growth as the ultimate goal, because *any* growth rate, if continued, will eventually use up the earth. Yet hardly ever do arguments for popu-

lation policy consider such a goal, and current policies do not dream of it. Why not? The answer is evidently that zero population growth is unacceptable to most nations and to most religious and ethnic communities. To argue for this goal would be to alienate possible support for action programs.

Goal peculiarities inherent in family planning. Turning to the actual measures taken, we see that the very use of family planning as the means for implementing population policy poses serious but unacknowleged limits on the intended reduction in fertility. The family-planning movement, clearly devoted to the improvement and dissemination of contraceptive devices, states again and again that its purpose is that of enabling couples to have the number of children they want. "The opportunity to decide the number and spacing of children is a basic human right," say the 12 heads of state in the United Nations declaration. The 1965 Turkish Law Concerning Population Planning declares:

Article 1. Population Planning means that individuals can have as many children as they wish, whenever they want to. This can be ensured through preventive measures taken against pregnancy. . . .[10]

Logically, it does not make sense to use *family* planning to provide *national* population control or planning. The "planning" in family planning is that of each separate couple. The only control they exercise is control over the size of *their* family. Obviously, couples do not plan the size of the nation's population, any more than they plan the growth of the national income or the form of the highway network. There is no reason to expect that the millions of decisions about family size made by couples in their own interest will automatically control population for the benefit of society. On the contrary, there are good reasons to think they will not do so. At most, family planning can reduce reproduction to the extent that unwanted births exceed wanted births. In industrial countries, the balance is often negative—that is, people have fewer children as a rule than they would like to have. In underdeveloped countries, the reverse is normally true, but the elimination of unwanted births would still leave an extremely high rate of multiplication.

Actually, the family-planning movement does not pursue even the limited goals it professes. It does not fully empower couples to have only the number of offspring they want because it either condemns or disregards certain tabooed but nevertheless effective means to this goal. One of its tenets is that "there shall be freedom of choice of method so that individuals can choose in accordance with the dictates of their consciences," [11] but in practice this amounts to limiting the individual's choice, because the "conscience" dictating the method is usually not his but that of religious and governmental officials. Moreover, not every individual may choose: even the so-called recommended methods are ordinarily not offered to single women, or not all offered to women professing a given religious faith.

Thus, despite its emphasis on technology, current policy does not utilize all available means of contraception, much less all birth-control measures. The Indian government wasted valuable years in the early stages of its population-control program by experimenting exclusively with the "rhythm" method, long after this technique had been demonstrated to be one of the least effective. A greater limitation on means is the exclusive emphasis on contraception itself. Induced abortion, for example, is one of the surest means of controlling reproduction, and one that has been proved capable of reducing birth rates rapidly. It seems peculiarly suited to the threshold stage of a population-control program—the stage when new conditions of life first make large families disadvantageous. It was the principal factor in the halving of the Japanese birth rate, a major factor in the declines in birth rate of East-European satellite countries after legalization of abortions in the early 1950's, and an important factor in the reduction of fertility in industrializing nations from 1870 to the 1930's.[12] Today, according to *Studies in Family Planning,*[13] "abortion is probably the foremost method of birth control throughout Latin America." Yet this method is rejected in nearly all national and international population-control programs. American foreign aid is used to help *stop* abortion.[14] The United Nations excludes abortion from family planning, and in fact justifies the latter by presenting it as a means of combating abortion.[15] Studies of abortion are being made in Latin America under the presumed auspices of population-control groups, not with the intention of legalizing it and thus making it safe, cheap, available, and hence more effective for population control, but with the avowed purpose of reducing it.[16]

Although few would prefer abortion to efficient contraception (other things being equal), the fact is that both permit a woman to control the size of her family. The main drawbacks to abortion arise from its illegality. When performed, as a legal procedure, by a skilled physician, it is safer than childbirth. It does not compete with contraception but serves as a backstop when the latter fails or when contraceptive devices or information are not available. As contraception becomes customary, the incidence of abortion recedes even without its being banned. If, therefore, abortions enable women to have only the number of children they want, and if family planners do not advocate—in fact decry—legalization of abortion, they are to that extent denying the central tenet of their own movement. The irony of anti-abortionism in family-planning circles is seen particularly in hair-splitting arguments over whether or not some contraceptive agent (for example, the IUD) is in reality an abortifacient. A Mexican leader in family planning writes:

One of the chief objectives of our program in Mexico is to prevent abortions. If we could be sure that the mode of action [of the IUD] was not interference with nidation, we could easily use the method in Mexico.[17]

The questions of sterilization and unnatural forms of sexual intercourse usually meet with similar silent treatment or disapproval, although nobody doubts the effectiveness of these measures in avoiding conception. Sterilization has proved popular in Puerto Rico and has had some vogue in India (where the new health minister hopes to make it compulsory for those with a certain number of children), but in both these areas it has been for the most part ignored or condemned by the family-planning movement.

On the side of goals, then, we see that a family-planning orientation limits the aims of current population policy. Despite reference to "population control" and "fertility control," which presumably mean determination of demographic results by and for the nation as a whole, the move-

ment gives control only to couples, and does this only if they use "respectable" contraceptives.

The Neglect of Motivation

By sanctifying the doctrine that each woman should have the number of children she wants, and by assuming that if she has only that number this will automatically curb population growth to the necessary degree, the leaders of current policies escape the necessity of asking why women desire so many children and how this desire can be influenced.[18] Instead, they claim that satisfactory motivation is shown by the popular desire (shown by opinion surveys in all countries) to have the means of family limitation, and that therefore the problem is one of inventing and distributing the best possible contraceptive devices. Overlooked is the fact that a desire for availability of contraceptives is compatible with *high* fertility.

Given the best of means, there remain the questions of how many children couples want and of whether this is the requisite number from the standpoint of population size. That it is not is indicated by continued rapid population growth in industrial countries, and by the very surveys showing that people want contraception—for these show, too, that people also want numerous children.

The family planners do not ignore motivation. They are forever talking about "attitudes" and "needs." But they pose the issue in terms of the "acceptance" of birth control devices. At the most naive level, they assume that lack of acceptance is a function of the contraceptive device itself. This reduces the motive problem to a technological question. The task of population control then becomes simply the invention of a device that *will* be acceptable.[19] The plastic IUD is acclaimed because, once in place, it does not depend on repeated *acceptance* by the woman, and thus it "solves" the problem of motivation.[20]

But suppose a woman does not want to use *any* contraceptive until after she has had four children. This is the type of question that is seldom raised in the family-planning literature. In that literature, wanting a specific number of children is taken as complete motivation, for it implies a wish to control the size of one's family. The problem woman, from the standpoint of family planners, is the one who wants "as many as come," or "as many as God sends." Her attitude is construed as due to ignorance and "cultural values," and the policy deemed necessary to change it is "education." No compulsion can be used, because the movement is committed to free choice, but movie strips, posters, comic books, public lectures, interviews, and discussions are in order. These supply information and supposedly change values by discounting superstitions and showing that unrestrained procreation is harmful to both mother and children. The effort is considered successful when the woman decides she wants only a certain number of children and uses an effective contraceptive.

In viewing negative attitudes toward birth control as due to ignorance, apathy, and outworn tradition, and "mass-communication" as the solution to the motivation problem,[21] family planners tend to ignore the power and complexity of social life. If it were admitted that the creation and care of new human beings is socially motivated, like other forms of behavior, by being a part of the system of rewards and punishments that is built into human relationships, and thus is bound up with the individual's economic and personal interests, it would be apparent that the social structure and economy must be changed before a deliberate reduction in the birth rate can be achieved. As it is, reliance on family planning allows people to feel that "something is being done about the population problem" without the need for painful social changes.

Designation of population control as a medical or public health task leads to a similar evasion. This categorization assures popular support because it puts population policy in the hands of respected medical personnel, but, by the same token, it gives responsibility for leadership to people who think in terms of clinics and patients, of pills and IUD's, and who bring to the handling of economic and social phenomena a self-confident naiveté. The study of social organization is a technical field; an action program based on intuition is no more apt to succeed in the control of human beings than it is in the area of bacterial or viral control. Moreover, to alter a social system, by deliberate policy, so as to regulate births in accord with the demands of the collective welfare would require political power, and this is not likely to inhere in public health officials, nurses, midwives, and social workers. To entrust population policy to them is "to take action," but not dangerous "effective action."

Similarly, the Janus-faced position on birth-control technology represents an escape from the necessity, and onus, of grappling with the social and economic determinants of reproductive behavior. On the one side, the rejection or avoidance of religiously tabooed but otherwise effective means of birth prevention enables the family-planning movement to avoid official condemnation. On the other side, an intense preoccupation with contraceptive technology (apart from the tabooed means) also helps the family planners to avoid censure. By implying that the only need is the invention and distribution of effective contraceptive devices, they allay fears, on the part of religious and governmental officials, that fundamental changes in social organization are contemplated. Changes basic enough to affect motivation for having children would be changes in the structure of the family, in the position of women, and in the sexual mores. Far from proposing such radicalism, spokesmen for family planning frequently state their purpose as "protection" of the family—that is, closer observance of family norms. In addition, by concentrating on *new* and *scientific* contraceptives, the movement escapes taboos attached to old ones (the Pope will hardly authorize the condom, but may sanction the pill) and allows family planning to be regarded as a branch of medicine: overpopulation becomes a disease, to be treated by a pill or a coil.

We thus see that the inadequacy of current population policies with respect to motivation is inherent in their overwhelmingly family-planning character. Since family planning is by definition private planning, it eschews any societal control over motivation. It merely furnishes the means, and, among possible means, only the most respectable. Its leaders, in avoiding social complexities and seeking official favor, are obviously activated not solely by expediency, but also by their own sentiments as members of society and by their background as persons attracted to the family-planning movement. Unacquainted for the most part with technical economics, sociology, and demography, they tend honestly and instinctively to believe

that something they vaguely call population control can be achieved by making better contraceptives available.

The Evidence of Ineffectiveness

If this characterization is accurate, we can conclude that current programs will not enable a government to control population size. In countries where couples have numerous offspring that they do not want, such programs may possibly accelerate a birth-rate decline that would occur anyway, but the conditions that cause births to be wanted or unwanted are beyond the control of family planning, hence beyond the control of any nation which relies on family planning alone as its population policy.

This conclusion is confirmed by demographic facts. As I have noted above, the widespread use of family planning in industrial countries has not given their governments control over the birth rate. In backward countries today, taken as a whole, birth rates are rising, not falling; in those with population policies, there is no indication that the government is controlling the rate of reproduction. The main "successes" cited in the well-publicized policy literature are cases where a large number of contraceptives have been distributed or where the program has been accompanied by some decline in the birth rate. Popular enthusiasm for family planning is found mainly in the cities, or in advanced countries such as Japan and Taiwan, where the people would adopt contraception in any case, program or no program. It is difficult to prove that present population policies have even speeded up a lowering of the birth rate (the least that could have been expected), much less that they have provided national "fertility control."

Let us next briefly review the facts concerning the level and trend of population in underdeveloped nations generally, in order to understand the magnitude of the task of genuine control.

Rising Birth Rates in Underdeveloped Countries

In ten Latin-American countries, between 1940 and 1959,[22] the average birth rates (age-standardized), as estimated by our research office at the University of California, rose as follows: 1940–44, 43.4 annual births per 1000 population; 1945–49, 44.6; 1950–54, 46.4; 1955–59, 47.7.

In another study made in our office, in which estimating methods derived from the theory of quasi-stable populations were used, the recent trend was found to be upward in 27 underdeveloped countries, downward in six, and unchanged in one.[23] Some of the rises have been substantial, and most have occurred where the birth rate was already extremely high. For instance, the gross reproduction rate rose in Jamaica from 1.8 per thousand in 1947 to 2.7 in 1960; among the natives of Fiji, from 2.0 in 1951 to 2.4 in 1964; and in Albania, from 3.0 in the period 1950–54 to 3.4 in 1960.

The general rise in fertility in backward regions is evidently not due to failure of population-control efforts, because most of the countries either have no such effort or have programs too new to show much effect. Instead, the rise is due, ironically, to the very circumstance that brought on the population crisis in the first place—to improved health and lowered mortality. Better health increases the probability that a woman will conceive and retain the fetus

to term; lowered mortality raises the proportion of babies who survive to the age of reproduction and reduces the probability of widowhood during that age.[24] The significance of the general rise in fertility, in the context of this discussion, is that it is giving would-be population planners a harder task than many of them realize. Some of the upward pressure on birth rates is independent of what couples do about family planning, for it arises from the fact that, with lowered mortality, there are simply more couples.

Underdeveloped Countries with Population Policies

In discussions of population policy there is often confusion as to which cases are relevant. Japan, for instance, has been widely praised for the effectiveness of its measures, but it is a very advanced industrial nation and, besides, its government policy had little or nothing to do with the decline in the birth rate, except unintentionally. It therefore offers no test of population policy under peasant-agrarian conditions. Another case of questionable relevance is that of Taiwan, because Taiwan is sufficiently developed to be placed in the urban-industrial class of nations. However, since Taiwan is offered as the main showpiece by the sponsors of current policies in underdeveloped areas, and since the data are excellent, it merits examination.

Taiwan is acclaimed as a showpiece because it has responded favorably to a highly organized program for distributing up-to-date contraceptives and has also had a rapidly dropping birth rate. Some observers have carelessly attributed the decline in the birth rate—from 50.0 in 1951 to 32.7 in 1965—to the family-planning campaign,[25] but the campaign began only in 1963 and could have affected only the end of the trend. Rather, the decline represents a response to modernization similar to that

TABLE 1. *Decline in Taiwan's Fertility Rate, 1951 through 1966*

Year	Registered Births per 1000 Women Aged 15–49	Change in Rate (Percent)*
1951	211	
1952	198	−5.6
1953	194	−2.2
1954	193	−0.5
1955	197	+2.1
1956	196	−0.4
1957	182	−7.1
1958	185	+1.3
1959	184	−0.1
1960	180	−2.5
1961	177	−1.5
1962	174	−1.5
1963	170	−2.6
1964	162	−4.9
1965	152	−6.0
1966	149	−2.1

* The percentages were calculated on unrounded figures. Source of data through 1965, *Taiwan Demographic Fact Book* (1964, 1965); for 1966, *Monthly Bulletin of Population Registration Statistics of Taiwan* (1966, 1967).

made by all countries that have become industrialized.[26] By 1950 over half of Taiwan's population was urban, and by 1964 nearly two-thirds were urban, with 29 percent of the population living in cities of 100,000 or more. The pace of economic development has been extremely rapid. Between 1951 and 1963, per capita income increased by 4.05 percent per year. Yet the island is closely packed, having 870 persons per square mile (a population density higher than that of Belgium). The combination of fast economic growth and rapid population increase in limited space has put parents of large families at a relative disadvantage and has created a brisk de-

mand for abortions and contraceptives. Thus the favorable response to the current campaign to encourage use of the IUD is not a good example of what birth-control technology can do for a genuinely backward country. In fact, when the program was started, one reason for expecting receptivity was that the island was already on its way to modernization and family planning.[27]

At most, the recent family-planning campaign—which reached significant proportions only in 1964, when some 46,000 IUD's were inserted (in 1965 the number was 99,253, and in 1966, 111,242)[28]— could have caused the increase observable after 1963 in the rate of decline. Between 1951 and 1963 the average drop in the birth rate per 1000 women (see Table 1) was 1.73 percent per year; in the period 1964–66 it was 4.35 percent. But one hesitates to assign all of the acceleration in decline since 1963 to the family-planning campaign. The rapid economic development has been precisely of a type likely to accelerate a drop in reproduction. The rise in manufacturing has been much greater than the rise in either agriculture or construction. The agricultural labor force has thus been squeezed, and migration to the cities has skyrocketed.[29] Since housing has not kept pace, urban families have had to restrict reproduction in order to take advantage of career opportunities and avoid domestic inconvenience. Such conditions have historically tended to accelerate a decline in birth rate. The most rapid decline came late in the United States (1921–33) and in Japan (1947–55). A plot of the Japanese and Taiwanese birth rates (Fig. 1) shows marked similarity of the two curves, despite a difference in level. All told, one should not attribute all of the post-1963 acceleration in the decline of

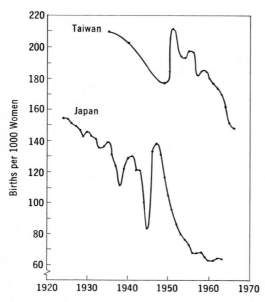

Births per 1000 women aged 15 through 49 in Japan and Taiwan.

Taiwan's birth rate to the family-planning campaign.

The main evidence that *some* of this acceleration is due to the campaign comes from the fact that Taichung, the city in which the family-planning effort was first concentrated, showed subsequently a much faster drop in fertility than other cities.[30] But the campaign has not reached throughout the island. By the end of 1966, only 260,745 women had been fitted with an IUD under auspices of the campaign, whereas the women of reproductive age on the island numbered 2.86 million. Most of the reduction in fertility has therefore been a matter of individual initiative. To some extent the campaign may be simply substituting sponsored (and cheaper) services for those that would otherwise come through private and commercial channels.

An island-wide survey in 1964 showed that over 150,000 women were already using the traditional Ota ring (a metallic intrauterine device popular in Japan); almost as many had been sterilized; about 40,000 were using foam tablets; some 50,000 admitted to having had at least one abortion; and many were using other methods of birth control.[31]

The important question, however, is not whether the present campaign is somewhat hastening the downward trend in the birth rate but whether, even if it is, it will provide population control for the nation. Actually, the campaign is not designed to provide such control and shows no sign of doing so. It takes for granted existing reproductive goals. Its aim is "to integrate, through education and information, the idea of family limitation *within the existing attitudes, values, and goals* of the people." [32] Its target is *married* women who do not want any more children; it ignores girls not yet married, and women married and wanting more children.

With such an approach, what is the maximum impact possible? It is the difference between the number of children women have been having and the number they want to have. A study in 1957 found a median figure of 3.75 for the number of children wanted by women aged 15 to 29 in Taipei, Taiwan's largest city; the corresponding figure for women from a satellite town was 3.93; for women from a fishing village, 4.90; and for women from a farming village, 5.03. Over 60 percent of the women in Taipei and over 90 percent of those in the farming village wanted 4 or more children.[33] In a sample of wives aged 25 to 29 in Taichung, a city of over 300,000, Freedman and his co-workers found the average number of children wanted was 4; only 9 percent wanted less than 3, 20 percent wanted 5 or more.[34] If, therefore, Taiwanese women used contraceptives that were 100-percent effective and had the number of children they desire, they would have about 4.5 each. The goal of the family-planning effort would be achieved. In the past the Taiwanese woman who married and lived through the reproductive period had, on the average, approximately 6.5 children; thus a figure of 4.5 would represent a substantial decline in fertility. Since mortality would continue to decline, the population growth rate would decline somewhat less than individual reproduction would. With 4.5 births per woman and a life expectancy of 70 years, the rate of natural increase would be close to 3 percent per year.[35]

In the future, Taiwanese views concerning reproduction will doubtless change, in response to social change and economic modernization. But how far will they change? A good indication is the number of children desired by couples in an already modernized country long oriented toward family planning. In the United States in 1966, an average of 3.4 children was considered ideal by white women aged 21 or over.[36] This average number of births would give Taiwan, with only a slight decrease in mortality, a long-run rate of natural increase of 1.7 percent per year and a doubling of population in 41 years.

Detailed data confirm the interpretation that Taiwanese women are in the process of shifting from a "peasant-agrarian" to an "industrial" level of reproduction. They are, in typical fashion, cutting off higher-order births at age 30 and beyond.[37] Among young wives, fertility has risen, not fallen. In sum, the widely acclaimed family-planning program in Taiwan may, at most, have somewhat speeded the later phase of fertility decline which would have occurred anyway because of modernization.

Moving down the scale of modernization, to countries most in need of population control, one finds the family-planning approach even more inadequate. In South Korea, second only to Taiwan in the frequency with which it is cited as a model of current policy, a recent birth-rate decline of unknown extent is assumed by leaders to be due overwhelmingly to the government's family-planning program. However, it is just as plausible to say that the net effect of government involvement in population control has been, so far, to delay rather than hasten a decline in reproduction made inevitable by social and economic changes. Although the government is advocating vasectomies and providing IUD's and pills, it refuses to legalize abortions, despite the rapid rise in the rate of illegal abortions and despite the fact that, in a recent survey, 72 percent of the people who stated an opinion favored legalization. Also, the program is presented in the context of maternal and child health; it thus emphasizes motherhood and the family rather than alternative roles for women. Much is made of the fact that opinion surveys show an overwhelming majority of Koreans (89 percent in 1965) favoring contraception, but this means only that Koreans are like other people in wishing to have the means to get what they want. Unfortunately, they want sizable families: "The records indicate that the program appeals mainly to women in the 30–39 year age bracket who have four or more children, including at least two sons. . . ."[38]

In areas less developed than Korea, the degree of acceptance of contraception tends to be disappointing, especially among the rural majority. Faced with this discouragement, the leaders of current policy, instead of reexamining their assumptions, tend to redouble their effort to find a contraceptive that will appeal to the most illiterate peasant, forgetting that he wans a good-sized family. In the rural Punjab, for example, "a disturbing feature . . . is that the females start to seek advice and adopt family planning techniques at the fag end of their reproductive period." [39] Among 5196 women coming to rural Punjabi family-planning centers, 38 percent were over 35 years old, 67 percent over 30. These women had married early, nearly a third of them before the age of 15;[40] some 14 percent had eight or more *living* children when they reached the clinic, 51 percent six or more.

A survey in Tunisia showed that 68 percent of the married couples were willing to use birth-control measures, but the average number of children they considered ideal was 4.3.[41] The corresponding averages for a village in eastern Java, a village near New Delhi, and a village in Mysore were 4.3, 4.0, and 4.2, respectively.[42] In the cities of these regions women are more ready to accept birth control and they want fewer children than village women do, but the number they consider desirable is still wholly unsatisfactory from the standpoint of population control. In an urban family-planning center in Tunisia, more than 600 of 900 women accepting contraceptives had four living children already.[43] In Bangalore, a city of nearly a million at the time (1952), the number of offspring desired by married women was 3.7 on the average; by married men, 4.1.[44] In the metropolitan area of San Salvador (350,000 inhabitants) a 1964 survey[45] showed the number desired by women of reproductive age to be 3.9, and in seven other capital cities of Latin America the number ranged from 2.7 to 4.2. If women

in the cities of underdeveloped countries used birth-control measures with 100-percent efficiency, they still would have enough babies to expand city populations senselessly, quite apart from the added contribution of rural-urban migration. In many of the cities the difference between actual and ideal number of children is not great; for instance, in the seven Latin-American capitals mentioned above, the ideal was 3.4 whereas the actual births per women in the age range 35 to 39 was 3.7.[46] Bombay City has had birth-control clinics for many years, yet its birth rate (standardized for age, sex, and marital distribution) is still 34 per 1000 inhabitants and is tending to rise rather than fall. Although this rate is about 13 percent lower than that for India generally, it has been about that much lower since at least 1951.[47]

Is Family Planning the "First Step" in Population Control?

To acknowledge that family planning does not achieve population control is not to impugn its value for other purposes. Freeing women from the need to have more children than they want is of great benefit to them and their children and to society at large. My argument is therefore directed not against family-planning programs as such but against the assumption that they are an effective means of controlling population growth.

But what difference does it make? Why not go along for a while with family planning as an initial approach to the problem of population control? The answer is that any policy on which millions of dollars are being spent should be designed to achieve the goal it purports to achieve. If it is only a first step, it should be so labeled, and its connection with the next step (and the nature of that next step) should be carefully examined. In the present case, since no "next step" seems ever to be mentioned, the question arises, Is reliance on family planning in fact a basis for dangerous postponement of effective steps? To continue to offer a remedy as a cure long after it has been shown merely to ameliorate the disease is either quackery or wishful thinking, and it thrives most where the need is greatest. Today the desire to solve the population problem is so intense that we are all ready to embrace any "action program" that promises relief. But postponement of effective measures allows the situation to worsen.

Unfortunately, the issue is confused by a matter of semantics. "Family *planning*" and "fertility *control*" suggest that reproduction is being regulated according to some rational plan. And so it is, but only from the standpoint of the individual couple, not from that of the community. What is rational in the light of a couple's situation may be totally irrational from the standpoint of society's welfare.

The need for societal regulation of individual behavior is readily recognized in other spheres—those of explosives, dangerous drugs, public property, natural resources. But in the sphere of reproduction, complete individual initiative is generally favored even by those liberal intellectuals who, in other spheres, most favor economic and social planning. Social reformers who would not hesitate to force all owners of rental property to rent to anyone who can pay, or to force all workers in an industry to join a union, balk at any suggestion that couples be permitted to have only a certain number of offspring. Invariably they interpret societal control of reproduction as meaning direct police supervision of individual behavior. Put the word *compulsory* in front of any term describing a means of limiting births—*compulsory sterilization, compulsory abortion, compulsory contraception*—and you guarantee violent opposition. Fortunately, such direct controls need not be invoked, but conservatives and radicals alike overlook this in their blind opposition to the idea of collective determination of a society's birth rate.

That the exclusive emphasis on family planning in current population policies is not a "first step" but an escape from the real issues is suggested by two facts: (1) No country has taken the "next step." The industrialized countries have had family planning for half a century without acquiring control over either the birth rate or population increase. (2) Support and encouragement of research on population policy other than family planning is negligible. It is precisely this blocking of alternative thinking and experimentation that makes the emphasis on family planning a major obstacle to population control. The need is not to abandon family-planning programs but to put equal or greater resources into other approaches.

New Directions in Population Policy

In thinking about other approaches, one can start with known facts. In the past, all surviving societies had institutional incentives for marriage, procreation, and child care which were powerful enough to keep the birth rate equal to or in excess of a high death rate. Despite the drop in death rates during the last century and a half, the incentives tended to remain intact because the social structure (especially in regard to the family) changed little. At most, particularly in industrial societies, children became less productive and more expensive.[48] In present-day agrarian societies, where the drop in death rate has been more recent, precipitate, and independent of social change,[49] motivation for having children has changed little. Here, even more than in industrialized nations, the family has kept on producing abundant offspring, even though only a fraction of these children are now needed.

If excessive population growth is to be prevented, the obvious requirement is somehow to impose restraints on the family. However, because family roles are reinforced by society's system of rewards, punishments, sentiments, and norms, any proposal to demote the family is viewed as a threat by conservatives and liberals alike, and certainly by people with enough social responsibility to work for population control. One is charged with trying to "abolish" the family, but what is required is selective restructuring of the family in relation to the rest of society.

The lines of such restructuring are suggested by two existing limitations on fertility: (1) Nearly all societies succeed in drastically discouraging reproduction among unmarried women. (2) Advanced societies unintentionally reduce reproduction among married women when conditions worsen in such a way as to penalize childbearing more severely than it was penalized before. In both cases, the causes are motivational and economic rather than technological.

It follows that population-control policy can de-emphasize the family in two ways: (1) by keeping present controls over illegitimate childbirth, yet making the most of factors that lead people to postpone or avoid marriage, and (2) by instituting conditions that motivate those who do marry to keep their families small.

Postponement of Marriage

Since the female reproductive span is short and generally more fecund in its first than in its second half, postponement of marriage to ages beyond 20 tends biologically to reduce births. Sociologically, it gives women time to get a better education, acquire interests unrelated to the family, and develop a cautious attitude toward pregnancy.[50] Individuals who have not married by the time they are in their late twenties often do not marry at all. For these reasons, for the world as a whole, the average age at marriage for women is negatively associated with the birth rate: a rising age at marriage is a frequent cause of declining fertility during the middle phase of the demographic transition; and, in the late phase, the "baby boom" is usually associated with a return to younger marriages.

Any suggestion that age at marriage be raised as a part of population policy is usually met with the argument that "even if a law were passed, it would not be obeyed." Interestingly, this objection implies that the only way to control the age at marriage is by direct legislation, but other factors govern the actual age. Roman Catholic countries generally follow canon law in stipulating 12 years as the minimum *legal* age at which girls may marry, but the actual average age at marriage in these countries (at least in Europe) is characteristically more like 25 to 28 years. The actual age is determined, not by law, but by social and economic conditions. In agrarian societies, postponement of marriage (when postponement occurs) is apparently caused by difficulties in meeting the economic prerequisites for matrimony, as stipulated by custom and opinion. In industrial societies it is caused by housing shortages, unemployment, the requirement for overseas military service, high costs of education, and inadequacy of consumer services. Since almost no research has been devoted to the subject, it is difficult to assess the relative weight of the factors that govern the age at marriage.

Encouraging Limitation of Births within Marriages

As a means of encouraging the limitation of reproduction within marriage, as well as postponement of marriage, a greater rewarding of nonfamilial than of familial roles would probably help. A simple way of accomplishing this would be to allow economic advantages to accrue to the single as opposed to the married individual, and to the small as opposed to the large family. For instance, the government could pay people to permit themselves to be sterilized;[51] all costs of abortion could be paid by the government; a substantial fee could be charged for a marriage license; a "child-tax" [52] could be levied; and there could be a requirement that illegitimate pregnancies be aborted. Less sensationally, governments could simply reverse some existing policies that encourage childbearing. They could, for example, cease taxing single persons more than married ones; stop giving parents special tax exemptions; abandon income-tax policy that discriminates against couples when the wife works; reduce paid maternity leaves; reduce family allowances;[53] stop awarding public housing on the basis of family size; stop granting fellowships and other educational aids (including special allowances for wives and children) to married students; cease outlawing abortions and sterilizations; and relax rules that allow use of harmless contraceptives only with medical permission. Some of these policy reversals would be

beneficial in other than demographic respects and some would be harmful unless special precautions were taken. The aim would be to reduce the number, not the quality, of the next generation.

A closely related method of de-emphasizing the family would be modification of the complementarity of the roles of men and women. Men are now able to participate in the wider world yet enjoy the satisfaction of having several children because the housework and childcare fall mainly on their wives. Women are impelled to seek this role by their idealized view of marriage and motherhood and by either the scarcity of alternative roles or the difficulty of combining them with family roles. To change this situation, women could be required to work outside the home, or compelled by circumstances to do so. If, at the same time, women were paid as well as men and given equal educational and occupational opportunities, and if social life were organized around the place of work rather than around the home or neighborhood, many women would develop interests that would compete with family interests. Approximately this policy is now followed in several Communist countries, and even the less developed of these currently have extremely low birth rates.[54]

That inclusion of women in the labor force has a negative effect on reproduction is indicated by regional comparisons.[55] But in most countries the wife's employment is subordinate, economically and emotionally, to her family role, and is readily sacrificed for the latter. No society has restructured both the occupational system and the domestic establishment to the point of permanently modifying the old division of labor by sex.

In any deliberate effort to control the

birth rate along these lines, a government has two powerful instruments—its command over economic planning and its authority (real or potential) over education. The first determines (as far as policy can) the economic conditions and circumstances affecting the lives of all citizens; the second provides the knowledge and attitudes necessary to implement the plans. The economic system largely determines who shall work, what can be bought, what rearing children will cost, how much individuals can spend. The schools define family roles and develop vocational and recreational interests; they could, if it were desired, redefine the sex roles, develop interests that transcend the home, and transmit realistic (as opposed to moralistic) knowledge concerning marriage, sexual behavior, and population problems. When the problem is viewed in this light, it is clear that the ministries of economics and education, not the ministry of health, should be the source of population policy.

The Dilemma of Population Policy

It should now be apparent why, despite strong anxiety over runaway population growth, the actual programs purporting to control it are limited to family planning and are therefore ineffective: (1) The goal of zero, or even slight, population growth is one that nations and groups find difficult to accept. (2) The measures that would be required to implement such a goal, though not so revolutionary as a Brave New World or a Communist Utopia, nevertheless tend to offend most people reared in existing societies. As a consequence, the goal of so-called population control is implicit and vague; the method is only family planning. This method, far from de-emphasizing the family, is familistic. One of its stated goals

is that of helping sterile couples to *have* children. It stresses parental aspirations and responsibilities. It goes along with most aspects of conventional morality, such as condemnation of abortion, disapproval of premarital intercourse, respect for religious teachings and cultural taboos, and obeisance to medical and clerical authority. It deflects hostility by refusing to recommend any change other than the one it stands for: availability of contraceptives.

The things that make family planning acceptable are the very things that make it ineffective for population control. By stressing the right of parents to have the number of children they want, it evades the basic question of population policy, which is how to give societies the number of children they need. By offering only the means for *couples* to control fertility, it neglects the means for societies to do so.

Because of the predominantly pro-family character of existing societies, individual interest ordinarily leads to the production of enough offspring to constitute rapid population growth under conditions of low mortality. Childless or single-child homes are considered indicative of personal failure, whereas having three to five living children gives a family a sense of continuity and substantiality.[56]

Given the existing desire to have moderate-sized rather than small families, the only countries in which fertility has been reduced to match reduction in mortality are advanced ones temporarily experiencing worsened economic conditions. In Sweden, for instance, the net reproduction rate (NRR) has been below replacement for 34 years (1930–63), if the period is taken as a whole, but this is because of the economic depression. The average replacement rate was below unity (NRR = 0.81) for the period 1930–42, but from 1942 through 1963 it was above unity (NRR = 1.08). Hardships that seem particularly conducive to deliberate lowering of the birth rate are (in managed economies) scarcity of housing and other consumer goods despite full employment, and required high participation of women in the labor force, or (in freer economies) a great deal of unemployment and economic insecurity. When conditions are good, any nation tends to have a growing population.

It follows that, in countries where contraception is used, a realistic proposal for a government policy of lowering the birth rate reads like a catalogue of horrors: squeeze consumers through taxation and inflation; make housing very scarce by limiting construction; force wives and mothers to work outside the home to offset the inadequacy of male wages, yet provide few childcare facilities; encourage migration to the city by paying low wages in the country and providing few rural jobs; increase congestion in cities by starving the transit system; increase personal insecurity by encouraging conditions that produce unemployment and by haphazard political arrests. No government will institute such hardships simply for the purpose of controlling population growth. Clearly, therefore, the task of contemporary population policy is to develop attractive substitutes for family interests, so as to avoid having to turn to hardship as a corrective. The specific measures required for developing such substitutes are not easy to determine in the absence of research on the question.

In short, the world's population problem cannot be solved by pretense and wishful thinking. The unthinking identification of family planning with population control is an ostrich-like approach in that it permits people to hide from themselves the enor-

mity and unconventionality of the task. There is no reason to abandon family-planning programs; contraception is a valuable technological instrument. But such programs must be supplemented with equal or greater investments in research and experimentation to determine the required socioeconomic measures.

Footnotes

[1] *Studies in Family Planning*, No. 16, 1967.

[2] *Ibid.*, No. 9, 1966, p. 1.

[3] The statement is given in *Studies in Family Planning*, No. 1, p. 1, and in *Population Bulletin* No. 23, 6, 1967.

[4] *Studies in Family Planning*, No. 1, p. 2.

[5] *Hearings on S. 1676, U.S. Senate, Subcommittee on Foreign Aid Expenditures*, 89th Congress, Second Session, April 7, 8, 11, 1966, pt. 4, p. 889.

[6] B. L. Raina, in *Family Planning and Population Programs*, ed. B. Berelson *et al.*, Chicago: University of Chicago Press, 1966.

[7] D. Kirk, *Ann. Amer. Acad. Polit. Soc. Sci.*, 369, 53, 1967.

[8] As used by English-speaking demographers, the word *fertility* designates actual reproductive performance, not a theoretical capacity

[9] K. Davis, *Rotarian*, 94, 10, 1959; *Health Education Monographs* 9, 2, 1960; L. Day and A. Day, *Too Many Americans*, Boston: Houghton Mifflin, 1964; R. A. Piddington, *Limits of Mankind*, Bristol, England: Wright, 1956.

[10] *Official Gazette*, April 15, 1965; quoted in *Studies in Family Planning*, No. 1, p. 7.

[11] J. W. Gardner, Secretary of Health, Education, and Welfare, "Memorandum to Heads of Operating Agencies," January 1966; reproduced in *Hearings on S. 1676*, p. 862.

[12] C. Tietze, *Demography*, 1, 119, 1964; M. Muramatsu, *Milbank Memorial Fund Quarterly*, 38, 153, 1960; K. Davis, *Population Index*, 29, 345, 1963; R. Armijo and T. Monreal, *J. Sex Res.*, 1964, 143, 1964; Proceedings World Population Conference, Belgrade, 1965; Proceedings International Planned Parenthood Federation.

[13] *Studies in Family Planning*, No. 4, 1964, p. 3.

[14] D. Bell (then administrator for Agency for International Development), in *Hearings on S. 1676*, p. 862.

[15] Asian Population Conference, New York: United Nations, 1964, p. 30.

[16] R. Armijo and T. Monreal, in Components of Population Change in Latin America, New York: Milbank Fund, 1965, p. 272; E. Rice-Wray, Amer. J. Public Health, 54, 313, 1964.

[17] E. Rice-Wray, in "Intra-Uterine Contraceptive Devices," Excerpta Med. Intern. Congr. Ser. No. 54, 1962, p. 135.

[18] J. Blake, in Public Health and Population Change, ed. M. C. Sheps et al., Pittsburgh: University of Pittsburgh Press, 1965, p. 41; J. Blake and K. Davis, American Behavioral Scientist, 5, 24, 1963.

[19] See "Panel discussion on comparative acceptability of different methods of contraception," in Research in Family Planning, ed. C. V. Kiser, Princeton: Princeton University Press, 1962, pp. 373–386.

[20] "From the point of view of the woman concerned, the whole problem of continuing motivation disappears. . . ." (D. Kirk, in Population Dynamics, ed. M. Muramatsu et al., Baltimore: Johns Hopkins Press, 1965.)

[21] "For influencing family size norms, certainly the examples and statements of public figures are of great significance . . . also . . . use of mass-communication methods which help to legitimize the small-family style, to provoke conversation, and to establish a vocabulary for discussion of family planning." (M. W. Freyman, in Population Dynamics.)

[22] O. A. Collver, Birth Rates in Latin America, Berkeley: International Population and Urban Research, 1965, pp. 27–28. The ten countries were Colombia, Costa Rica, El Salvador, Ecuador, Guatemala, Honduras, Mexico, Panama, Peru, and Venezuela.

[23] J. R. Rele, Fertility Analysis through Extension of Stable Population Concepts, Berkeley: International Population and Urban Research, 1967.

[24] J. C. Ridley et al., Milbank Memorial Fund Quarterly, 45, 77, 1967; E. Arriaga, unpublished paper.

[25] "South Korea and Taiwan appear successfully to have checked population growth by the use of intrauterine contraceptive devices." (U. Borell, Hearings on S. 1676, p. 556.)

[26] K. Davis, Population Index, 29, 345, 1963.

[27] R. Freedman, ibid., 31, 421, 1965.

[28] Before 1964 the Family Planning Association had given advice to fewer than 60,000 wives in 10 years and a Pre-Pregnancy Health Program had reached some 10,000, and, in the current campaign, 3650 IUD's were inserted in 1965, in a total population of 2½ million women of reproductive age. Studies in Family Planning, No. 19, 1967, p. 4, and R. Freedman et al., Population Studies, 16, 231, 1963. See also R. W. Gillespie, Family Planning in Taiwan, Taichung, Taiwan: Population Council, 1965, p. 45.

[29] During the period 1950–60, the ratio of growth of the city to growth of the noncity population was 5:2; during the period 1960–64, the ratio was 5:2; these ratios are based on data of Shaohsing Chen, J. Sociol. Taiwan, 1, 74, 1963, and data in the United Nations Demographic Yearbooks.

[30] R. W. Gillespie, Family Planning in Taiwan, p. 69; R. Freedman, Population Index, 31, 434, 1965. Taichung's rate of decline in 1963–64 was roughly double the average in four other cities, whereas just prior to the campaign its rate of decline had been much less than theirs.

[31] R. W. Gillespie, Family Planning in Taiwan, pp. 18, 31.

[32] R. W. Gillespie, ibid., p. 8. (italics mine)

[33] S. H. Chen, J. Soc. Sci. Taipei, 13, 72, 1963.

[34] R. Freedman et al., Population Studies, 16, 227, 1963; ibid., p. 232.

[35] In 1964 the life expectancy at birth was already 66 years in Taiwan, as compared to 70 for the United States.

[36] J. Blake, Eugenics Quarterly, 14, 68, 1967.

[37] Women accepting IUD's in the family-planning program are typically 30 to 34 years old and have already had four children. (Studies in Family Planning, No. 19, 1967, p. 5.)

[38] Y. K. Cha, in Family Planning and Population Programs, ed. B. Berelson et al., Chicago: University of Chicago Press, 1966, p. 25.

[39] H. S. Ayalvi et al., J. Family Welfare, 12, 60, 1965.

[40] Sixty percent of the women had borne their first child before age 19. Early marriage is strongly supported by public opinion. Of couples polled in the Punjab, 48 percent said that girls should marry before age 16, and 94 percent said they should marry before age 20. (H. S. Ayalvi, ibid., p. 57.) A study of 2,380 couples in 69 villages of Uttar Pradesh found that the women had consummated their marriage at an average age of 14.6 years. (J. R. Rele, Population Studies, 15, 268, 1962.

[41] J. Morsa, in Family Planning and Population Programs, ed. B. Berelson et al., Chicago: University of Chicago Press, 1966.

[42] H. Gille and R. J. Pardoko, ibid., p. 515; S. N. Agarwala, Med. Dig. Bombay, 4, 653, 1961;

Mysore Population Study, New York: United Nations, 1961, p. 140.

[43] A. Daly, in *Family Planning and Population Programs,* ed. B. Berelson *et al.,* Chicago: University of Chicago Press, 1966.

[44] *Mysore Population Study,* p. 140.

[45] C. J. Gomez, paper presented at the World Population Conference, Belgrade, 1965.

[46] C. Miro, in *Family Planning and Population Programs,* ed. B. Berelson *et al.,* Chicago: University of Chicago Press, 1966.

[47] *Demographic Training and Research Centre* (India) *Newsletter,* 20, 4, August 1966.

[48] K. Davis, *Population Index,* 29, 345, 1963.

[49] K. Davis, *American Economic Review,* 46, 305, 1956; *Scientific American,* 209, 68, 1963.

[50] J. Blake, *World Population Conference, Belgrade, 1965,* New York: United Nations, 1967, Vol. 2, pp. 132–136.

[51] S. Enke, *Rev. Economics Statistics,* 42, 175, 1960; S. Enke, *Econ. Develop. Cult. Change,* 8, 339, 1960; S. Enke, *ibid.,* 10, 427, 1962; A. O. Krueger and L. A. Sjaastad, *ibid.,* p. 423.

[52] T. J. Samuel, *J. Family Welfare India,* 13, 12, 1966.

[53] Sixty-two countries, including 27 in Europe, give cash payments to people for having children. (U.S. Social Security Administration, *Social Security Programs Throughout the World, 1967,* Government Printing Office, 1967, pp. xxvii–xxviii.)

[54] Average gross reproduction rates in the early 1960's were as follows: Hungary, 0.91; Bulgaria, 1.09; Romania, 1.15; Yugoslavia, 1.32.

[55] O. A. Collver and E. Langlois, *Econ. Develop. Cult. Change,* 10, 367, 1962; J. Weeks, Berkeley: University of California, unpublished paper; J. Blake, in *Public Health and Population Change,* ed. M. C. Sheps *et al.,* Pittsburgh: University of Pittsburgh Press, 1965, p. 1195.

[56] Roman Catholic textbooks condemn the "small" family (one with fewer than four children) as being abnormal. (J. Blake, *Population Studies,* 20, 27, 1966.)

PART TEN Deviance and Crime

Although this section is titled deviance and crime, criminal behavior is generally considered by sociologists to fall under the general heading of deviance. Deviance is a loosely defined area of study which typically includes such topics as crime, delinquency, mental illness, sex deviations, drug addiction, and other types of behavior which are essentially in violation of societal norms. It should be kept in mind, however, that our definitions of deviance are, to some extent, relevant only to our own society. What is considered deviant in one society may not be considered so in another. From the above list of topics, it becomes obvious that deviance is closely aligned with traditional morality. Homosexuality, for example, is not necessarily deviant in all societies. Evidence suggests that in many societies there is high tolerance, and in some cases high esteem, for this type of behavior.

Deviance is also dependent upon the part of a social system in which the individual is located. Different subcultures have various expectations and tolerances for different types of behavior. Drug usage may be deviant in terms of the general culture, but is it deviant in terms of certain segments of the ghetto or youth subcultures? The point is that deviance must always be analyzed relative to a particular normative structure.

This section begins with an article by Richard Quinney, entitled "Is Criminal Behavior Deviant Behavior?," which analyzes the relationship between crime and deviance. The second article, by Russell Dynes and E. L. Quarantelli, discusses looting as a form of criminal behavior. The authors examine this "modern" violation in relation to the dominant conception of property rights in American society. The final article, by Werner Einstadter, looks at the form and organization of a most common criminal offense in contemporary America, armed robbery.

25

Is Criminal Behavior Deviant Behavior?

RICHARD QUINNEY

One of the basic assumptions in the study of criminal behavior is that behavior in violation of the criminal law also represents deviation from other norms. The criminologist in his research usually proceeds on the premise that the criminal law embodies important social norms and that these norms are held by most persons in society. While these assumptions are rarely questioned in most studies of criminal behavior, a few criminologists have nevertheless recognised that the relationship between the criminal law and social norms is problematic. Some time ago, for example, Fuller observed that the criminal statute is the formal embodiment of someone's moral values and that, depending upon the particular law, all persons may not regard the law as valid according to their own values and group norms.[1] Sellin, touching upon similar matters even at an earlier time, noted that the criminal code is only one set of conduct norms, but one which is binding upon all who live within the boundaries of a political unit.[2]

These and other writers, then, have questioned the degree of correspondence between criminal law and social norms. They have provided enough discussion to caution the criminologist, in his research, that care must be taken in inferring that legal violations are also deviations from other norms. The fact remains, however, that criminologists continue to ignore the problematic relation between legal and extra-legal norms. The result is that much of the behavior that is studied as criminal behavior is not actually deviant behavior from the standpoint of the norms of the groups and subcultures that are being investigated. It is likely that some violations are nothing more than the breaking of a formal rule, a rule which has little or no support in any group.

This paper, then, will explore, on the one hand, the relation between criminal law and social norms and, on the other, the relation between crime and deviation. It is suggested that these relationships may be taken as objects of study in their own right. The strategy becomes one of exploring the relationships rather than taking them for granted. The degree of correspondence between criminal violation and normative deviation poses significant problems for study. Likewise, the relation between criminal law and social norms presents a number of important research problems.

Criminal Law and Social Norms

Criminal law may be regarded as an instrument of formal social control whereby an organized effort is made to regulate certain areas of behavior.[3] As a particular type of formal social control, criminal law is characterized by (1) explicit rules of conduct created by political authority, (2) provisions for punishment, (3) designated officials to make, interpret and

SOURCE: Reprinted from "Is Criminal Behavior Deviant Behavior?" by Richard Quinney, *The British Journal of Criminology,* April, 1965, 5:132–140, by permission of the publisher.

enforce the rules, and (4) uniform administration of the codes for all persons within a given territory.

Law has grown increasingly important as a means of social control as societies have grown in complexity. In preliterate and peasant societies where norms are relatively uniform, stable, and consistent, intimate personal relationships exist to such an extent to control human interaction. The more modern societies, on the other hand, have become highly differentiated in terms of values and norms. Various social groupings have arisen with their own sets of values and norms. In these heterogeneous societies, there are many values and norms which are agreed upon by most members, but there are many values and norms which are unique to the diverse groups. As Sellin has noted: "The more complex a culture becomes, the more likely it is that the number of normative groups which affect a person will be large, and the greater the chance that the norms of these groups will fail to agree, no matter how much they may overlap as a result of a common acceptance of certain norms." [4]

Criminal law, therefore, has emerged as a formal system of maintaining social order in differentiated societies. Other means of social control have proved inadequate in the uniform regulation of many areas of behavior. Where correct conduct cannot be agreed upon, the criminal law serves to control the behavior of all persons within a given political jurisdiction.

It is unlikely, then, that all criminal law incorporates the most cherished values and norms of all persons in a society. There are values and norms supported by some or possibly all persons which are not part of the law, and the law includes values and norms which are not important to some persons. It is going too far to argue,

as have some, that "there is no surer way of ascertaining what kinds of behavior are generally regarded as immoral or anti-social by the people of any community than by reference to their criminal code, for in theory, at least, the criminal code embodies social judgments with respect to behavior, and perhaps, more often than not, fact conforms to theory," or that "most of the people in any community would probably agree that most of the behavior which is proscribed by their criminal law is socially undesirable." [5] Such thinking on the similarity between criminal law and other social norms ignores (1) social differentiation in modern society, (2) processes in the formulation of criminal law, and (3) the relation of social change to criminal law and social norms.

Social Differentiaton

Some legal norms forbidding certain behaviors are supported by nearly all segments of a society, while others find little support. Many of our recent laws do not have the support of the majority of the people. There is little question that the traditional laws regarding such conventional crimes as murder, larceny, and robbery find support in public opinion. However, it is unlikely that laws which define such behaviors as restraint of trade, false advertising and misuse of trademarks as criminal are supported by most persons.[6] These latter laws are unrelated to the social norms of the vast majority of the population.

Due to the heterogeneity of modern society, with varied and often opposing subcultures, there cannot be complete agreement on all norms. "To a large number of persons who live in such a culture, certain life situations are governed

by such conflicting norms that no matter
what the response of the person in such
a situation will be, it will violate the norms
of some social group concerned." [7] Thus,
many people in modern society, depending
upon their particular attachments, do not
regard the official, legal norms as legitimate.
The criminal law may not overlap the
social norms of some groups and thus
may not be supported by some individuals.
The result is that there is selective obedi-
ence to the law for most persons. Some
laws are obeyed and others are not according
to a person's own values and the norms
of his groups.[8]

Formulaton of Criminal Law

Another reason for the lack of agreement
between criminal law and other social
norms is due to the particular processes
that operate in the formulation of the law.
Cultural diversity creates special groups,
and certain of these groups become organized to an extent that they are in a
position to exert influence at strategic
points in the formulation of criminal law.[9]
The values and norms for some groups
become a part of the criminal law, while
other groups are not represented in the law
which is binding upon all persons and
groups.

The content of the criminal law, then,
including the kind of conduct prohibited
and the nature of sanctions attached, depends upon the norms of those groups in
society which influence legislation, court
decisions, and administrative rulings. In
addition, these influential groups may not
be in the majority in numbers or even
represent the interests of the majority in
the population. Indeed, as noted by Fuller,
"Our parliamentary democracy is so constituted that much of our legislation is, in

fact, the legislation of well-organized,
articulate and powerful minorities." [10] The
social values and norms, then, "which
receive the protection of the criminal law
are ultimately those which are treasured
by dominant interest groups." [11]

The ability of groups to influence the
formulation of law is related to the power
positions of the particular groups. A group
that can get in a strategic power position
can determine the content of criminal law.
Furthermore, the criminal law changes as
the values and norms of the dominant
groups are modified and as the place of
these groups is altered in the power structure itself. Therefore, what is defined as
criminal behavior in a society is related to
the success of certain groups in influencing
legislation, the values and norms of these
groups, the compromises of these groups,
and shifts in the power structure of the
society. In addition, the determination of
what is criminal extends into the interpretation and enforcement of the law. The
values and norms of groups in positions of
power can enter at any point in establishing
the criminality of any behavior.[12]

Social Change

The degree of correspondence between
criminal law and social norms is also
affected by the changes in a society. For
instance, many criminal laws lag behind
the changing societal norms. The well-
known "blue laws" are an example of
criminal laws which were once related to
the norms of several groups or segments
of society but have since become dated
and obsolete because of normative modifications and changes.

It is also the case that some laws precede
the norms that will some day become
established for a large portion of the

society. In fact, law can serve as a device to induce social change.[13] The recent civil rights legislation in the United States in reference to Negro-white relations is forcing a change in social norms in some segments of the population. As has been noted by Segerstedt, social codes—or imperatives—create social customs.[14] Thus, in a number of ways, criminal law is related to social change. Social change and changes in the law are constant and interacting processes.[15]

It can therefore be seen that the relationship between criminal law and social norms is a function of a number of factors, of which the most important appear to be social differentiation, processes in the formulation of criminal law, and social change. It is clear that the relationship between criminal law and social norms is a problematic one. Criminologists cannot take the relationship—in terms of complete correspondence—for granted. The nature of the relation of any criminal law to other social norms is far from certain.

Crime and Deviation

Much of what is called criminal behavior may thus be viewed as behavior that is oriented to norms other than those embodied in the criminal law. Such illegal behavior is, of course, in a sense deviant behavior in that there is deviation from a norm, the legal norm. However, in keeping with recent conceptualization, deviant behavior represents "behavior which violates institutionalized expectations—that is, expectations which are shared and recognized as legitimate within a social system."[16] Similarly, deviant behavior consists of "only those situations in which behavior is in a disapproved direction, and of sufficient degree to ex-

ceed the tolerance limit of the community."[17] While behaviors in violation of many of a society's legal norms deviate from institutionalized expectations and exceed the tolerance limit of the community, it is also true that some crimes are not in violation of expectations (or social norms) and are not disapproved to such a degree as to exceed the tolerance limit of the community. Criminal behavior and deviant behavior can thus be treated as two separate orders of behavior.

It follows that the formulation of hypotheses for research in criminology must take into consideration the deviant nature of the behavior as well as its criminality. Behavior that does not deviate from the group norm, but which is nevertheless illegal, will require an explanation different from behavior which represents both normative deviation and criminal violation.

The problem of the correspondence between deviant behavior and criminal behavior becomes particularly crucial in the study of white collar crime—or occupational crime.[18] The question arises whether or not the behaviors which have been defined as criminal—many of them only recently—are also deviations from the normative structure of the occupation. If it can be established that the behaviors are regarded as deviant, as well as criminal, by the occupational members, the criminal violations can truly be studied as deviations from occupational norms, thus eliminating the cumbersome problem—usually not resolved—that criminal behavior may not be normative deviation from the standpoint of the group being studied.

Methods must be developed to determine the correspondence between deviant and criminal behavior. One procedure which appears to have promise involves the measurement of the attitudes of group members towards criminal cases. In a study of prescription violation by retail pharmacists, the author[19] was able to determine the deviant nature of certain illegal behaviors by presenting the respondents with several cases of criminal violations. Through an analysis of forced choice responses, it was possible to establish whether or not the specific behaviors were regarded as criminal, deviant, or both.

The otherwise confusing problem that some criminal violations are not regarded as criminal by the group members becomes clear when it is found that these behaviors are not actually deviant. The eventual explanation of these behaviors cannot be based on a theory of deviant behavior. On the other hand, behaviors that are deviant as well as criminal are subject to an explanation in terms of deviant behavior. An understanding of the deviant nature of the criminal behavior must precede any attempt to explain the behavior.

The Study of Criminal Law and Social Norms in Criminology

To the criminologist, scientific interest in crime emerges when the important norms by which certain behaviors are defined as crime are themselves subjected to analysis rather than taken for granted. All too often the facile solution that the criminal behavior under study is behavior in deviation from social norms has been relied upon. Future studies must explore the relation between legal norms and extra-legal norms instead of resorting to the inference that the two are the same. An investigation which considers both the criminal law and social norms will provide valuable insights concerning the conditions under which behavior becomes defined as crime. In addition, information regarding the process of law-making will be obtained. Such a study will be likely to produce knowledge regarding the structure of society itself.

The importance of criminal law to the study of criminal behavior was forcefully noted some time ago by Michael and Adler, when they stated that criminal law is the formal cause of crime: "If crime is merely an instance of conduct which is proscribed by the criminal code it follows that the criminal law is the formal cause of crime." [20] It is the criminal law that gives behavior its quality of criminality. One might go on so far as to say, then, as did Michael and Adler, that "all of the problems of crime, practical and theoretical, have their roots in the criminal code." [21]

The idea that criminal law should be given serious attention by criminologists has been suggested on several occasions. Vold pointed out that in criminology there is "always a dual problem of explanation —that of accounting for the behavior *as behavior,* and equally important, accounting *for the definitions* by which specific behavior comes to be considered as crime or non-crime." [22] In a series of articles, Jeffery has strongly stated that criminologists have over-emphasised the study of the behavior of criminals to the neglect of the study of the way in which the behaviors become defined as crime.[23] Moreover, he states: "Criminologists need a theory of crime, a theory which explains the origin and development of criminal law in terms of the institutional structure of society." [24]

Likewise, Mannheim has suggested a sociology of criminal law which examines the structure of society, the groups, values and attitudes in relation to the content of the criminal law;[25] but actual research in the sociology of criminal law has been sparse. Some exceptions are Segerstedt's report on the attitudes towards the law and towards lawbreakers,[26] Hall's study of the relationship between social structure and the development of criminal law on theft,[27] Rusche and Kirchheimer's recent observations on the use of legal procedures for political ends.[28] In addition, there has been some research on the prosecution and adjudication of criminal cases.[29]

The importance of the relation between criminal law and social norms has been acutely drawn to the attention of criminologists particularly through the study of white collar crime. As Aubert has noted: "The unexpected and somehow deviant nature of many recent laws defining white collar crimes has made it natural to ask for an explanation of the norms themselves and not only of their infringements. As soon as this happens new theoretical vistas are immediately opened." [30] It is not altogether unlikely that the study of the process of law-making, the groups influencing legislation, and the social norms behind the criminal law may provide a level of analysis for the actual explanation of the behaviors that occur in violation of the law.

Administration of Criminal Justice

The relation between legal norms and other norms has consequences for violation and enforcement of the criminal law. In general, those laws which are in accord with the important extra-legal norms of most of the population are realized in actual behavior.[31] Enforcement becomes a problem when there is a lack of agreement on the norms embodied in the criminal law. Sutherland and Cressey have summarized the problem of the correspondence between

criminal law and the important norms as it relates to enforcement: "Laws have accumulated because the mores have been weak and inconsistent; and because the laws have not had the support of the mores they have been relatively ineffective as a means of control. When mores are adequate, laws are unnecessary; when the mores are inadequate, the laws are ineffective."

Finally, in reference to the relation between criminal law and social norms, it may be suggested that much criminal behavior in modern, heterogeneous society represents a normal response to the accumulation of criminal laws. There is a tendency in modern societies to make laws as a first reaction to situations which are defined by some as difficult and unpleasant. The result is that today our criminal codes consist of many laws which contradict one another and many which are antiquated.[32] Each year there are thousands of new laws added to the statute books, creating many new crimes. It has been estimated, for example, that since 1900 in the United States the number of offenses for which a person can be arrested has doubled.[33] Many of the laws no longer incorporate the social norms on which they were once based. Changes both in norms and scientific knowledge have made many laws obsolete. Such laws are likely to meet with resistance. Violation may occur where the usefulness of the proscribed action is doubtful. Violation of these laws may be the only possible solution to present-day problems and situations.

Several undesirable consequences result from such an unwieldy accumulation of criminal law. A genuine disrespect and disregard for the particular laws may be created and, what is more, even for law in general. This may be furthered when law enforcement agencies must often ignore the offense when the law is obsolete but still exists on the statute books. Enforcement and administrative procedures in general tend to break down. Furthermore, there may be an outright attempt by the public to outwit the law enforcement agencies in violation of these laws and others. Thus, as stated by Michael and Adler, "Laws which make certain types of behavior criminal may be more undesirable in their consequences than the behavior itself." [34]

When criminal laws no longer receive social support, or the laws become obsolete because of scientific knowledge, the laws should be changed, with old and inefficient ones repealed and, if necessary, new ones enacted. It may also be desirable to bring within the scope of the criminal law behaviors which deviate from the basic values of the society.[35] Thus, as has been suggested by several writers, the study of criminal law by criminologists could provide the necessary knowledge for rational legislation.[36] Further investigation of the relation between criminal behavior and deviant behavior could contribute to this purpose.

Footnotes

[1] R. C. Fuller, "Morals and the Criminal Law," *Journal of Criminal Law, Criminology and Political Science*, 32, 1942, pp. 624–630.

[2] S. Sellin, *Culture, Conflict and Crime*, New York: Social Science Research Council, 1938.

[3] See: F. J. Davis, "Law as a Type of Social Control," *Society and the Law*, ed. F. J. Davis *et al.*, New York: The Free Press of Glencoe, 1962, Chapter 2; R. R. Korn and L. W. McCorkle, *Criminology and Penology*, New York: Holt, Rinehart & Winston, 1959, Chapter 4; T. Parsons, "The Law and Social Control," *Law And Sociology*, ed. W. M. Evan, New York: The Free Press of Glencoe, 1962, pp. 56–72.

[4] Sellin, p. 29.

[5] J. Michael and M. J. Adler, *Crime, Law, and Social Science*, New York: Harcourt, Brace, 1933, pp. 2–3.

[6] See: M. B. Clinard, *Sociology of Deviant Behavior*, New York: Holt, Rinehart & Winston, 1963, pp. 152–153; E. H. Sutherland, "White Collar Criminality," *American Sociological Review*, 5, 1940, pp. 1–12.

[7] Sellin, p. 60.

[8] Clinard, pp. 172–174.

[9] See: R. M. Williams, Jr., *American Society*, New York: Alfred A. Knopf, 1960, pp. 270–279; V. O. Key, Jr., *Politics, Parties and Pressure Groups*, New York: Thomas Y. Crowell, 1958; D. Truman, *The Governmental Process*, New York: Alfred A. Knopf, 1951.

[10] Fuller, p. 627.

[11] Sellin, p. 21.

[12] J. F. Cuber, R. A. Harper, and W. F. Kenkel, *Problems in American Society: Values in Conflict*, New York: Henry Holt, 1956, pp. 160–163.

[13] A. M. Rose, "The Use of Law to Induce Social Change," *Transactions of the Third World Congress of Sociology*, 6, 1956, pp. 52–63.

[14] T. T. Segerstedt, "Customs and Codes," *Theorica*, 8, 1942, pp. 3–22 (Part I), 126–153 (Part II).

[15] See: Y. Dror, "Law and Social Change," *Tulane Law Review*, 35, 1959, pp. 787–802; F. Friedman, *Law in a Changing Society*, London: Stevens & Sons, 1959.

[16] A. K. Cohen, "The Study of Social Disorganization and Deviant Behavior," *Sociology Today*, ed. R. K. Merton, *et al.*, New York: Basic Books, 1959, pp. 461–484, p. 462.

[17] Clinard, p. 22.

[18] E. R. Quinney, "The Study of White Collar Crime: Toward a Reorientation in Theory and Research," *Journal of Criminal Law, Criminology and Police Science*, 55, 1964, pp. 208–214.

[19] Quinney, *Retail Pharmacy as a Marginal Occupation: A Study of Prescription Violation*, unpub. Ph.D. dissertation, University of Wisconsin, 1962, Chapter 9. See also: Quinney, "Occupational Structure and Criminal Behavior Prescription Violation by Retail Pharmacists," *Social Problems*, 11, 1963, pp. 179–185.

[20] Michael and Adler, p. 5.

[21] Michael and Adler, p. 20.

[22] G. B. Vold, *Theoretical Criminology*, New York: Oxford University Press, 1958, p. 202.

[23] See: C. R. Jeffery, "The Structure of American Criminological Thinking," *Journal of Criminal Law, Criminology and Police Science*, 46, 1956,

pp. 658–672; Jeffery, "Crime, Law and Social Structure," *Journal of Criminal Law, Criminology and Police Science*, 47, 1956, pp. 423–435; Jeffery, "An Integrated Theory of Crime and Criminal Behavior," *Journal of Criminal Law, Criminology and Police Science*, 49, 1959, pp. 533–552.

[24] Jeffery (1959), p. 534.

[25] H. Mannheim, *Group Problems in Crime and Punishment*, London: Routledge & Kegan Paul, 1955. See especially Chapter 12.

[26] See: T. T. Segerstedt, "A Research in the General Sense of Justice," *Theorica*, 15, 1949, pp. 323–338; E. O. Smigel, "Public Attitudes Toward 'Chiseling' with Reference to Unemployment Compensation," *American Sociological Review*, 18, 1953, pp. 59–67.

[27] J. Hall, *Theft, Law and Society*, 2nd ed., Indianapolis: Bobbs-Merrill, 1952.

[28] O. Kirchheimer, *Political Justice: The Use of Legal Procedure for Political Ends*, Princeton: Princeton University Press, 1961.

[29] See: C. Foote, "Vagrancy-Type Law and its Administration," *University of Pa. Law Review*, 104, 1956, pp. 603–650; S. S. Nagel, "Judicial Backgrounds and Criminal Cases," *Journal of Criminal Law, Criminology and Police Science*, 53, 1962, pp. 333–339; D. J. Newman, "Pleading Guilty for Consideration: A Study of Bargain Justice," *Journal of Criminal Law, Criminology and Police Science*, 46, 1956, pp. 780–790.

[30] V. Aubert, "White Collar Crime and Social Structure," *American Journal of Sociology*, 58, 1952, pp. 263–271, p. 264.

[31] See: Davis, pp. 58–60; Y. Dror, "Values and the Law," *The Antioch Review*, 17, 1957–58, pp. 440–454.

[32] See: H. E. Barnes and N. K. Teeters, *New Horizons in Criminology*, Englewood Cliffs: Prentice-Hall, 1959, pp. 70–75; H. A. Bloch and G. Geis, *Man, Crime, and Society*, New York: Random House, 1962, pp. 63–64.

[33] C. R. Jeffery, "Criminal Justice and Social Change," *Society and the Law*, ed. F. J. Davis, *et al.*, New York: The Free Press of Glencoe, 1962, Chapter 8, p. 300.

[34] Michael and Adler, p. 353.

[35] H. Mannheim, *Criminal Justice and Social Reconstruction*, New York: Oxford University Press, 1946.

[36] See: F. Beutel, *Some Potentialities of Experimental Jurisprudence as a New Branch of Social Science*, Lincoln: University of Nebraska Press, 1957; Mannheim (1946), Chapter 11; Michael and Adler.

26

What Looting in Civil Disturbances Really Means

RUSSELL DYNES AND E. L. QUARANTELLI

In March and April of this year [1968], there were civil disturbances in Memphis, Tenn., Washington, D.C., Chicago, Pittsburgh, and Baltimore. Many films and photographs were taken of people looting other people's property. These looting incidents conformed to the pattern, for according to many reports, people may be found looting when a community is having certain kinds of crises. One of these crises is caused by a natural disaster—a flood, hurricane, and so forth. And the other is caused by a civil disturbance, like the ones that have hit American cities every summer since the Watts outbreak of August 1965.

Natural disasters and civil disturbances give people a chance to help themselves to other people's goods. Yet there are important, fascinating differences between what happens in these two crisis situations. For example, looting is far more common in civil disturbances than in disasters. Then too, the *kinds* of goods taken during these two crises are different. And public disdain for the act varies. Sometimes taking other people's property during a community crisis is not even considered looting!

In order to examine the differences between the two crisis situations, let us analyze what happens to private property during natural disasters, and then contrast this with the transfers of property that take place during civil disorders.

The word "looting" has military roots.

It implies that invading armies take property by force, generally when the rightful owner cannot protect it. Similarly, in civil disturbances "invading armies" plunder property left unguarded when the owner is forced out by violence or the threat of violence. During disasters, according to common belief, "invading armies" of opportunists take property left unguarded when the owner is forced out by the disaster.

The looting that takes place in these situations is usually interpreted as evidence of human depravity. In periods of natural or civil chaos, goes the explanation, the human animal is stripped of his usual social controls. Without them, he is not a noble savage, but an ignoble one. For the general public, reports of looting are easy to incorporate into their images of the "criminal elements" who clean out the corner grocery during a racial disturbance, or the fiends and ghouls who roam distaster-stricken areas.

After the Galveston hurricane of 1900, published accounts told of people being summarily shot when they were caught with pocketsful of severed fingers with rings on them. In 1906, after the San Francisco earthquake and fire, the *Los Angeles Times* reported that "looting by fiends incarnate made a hell broth of the center of the ruined district. Sixteen looters were shot out of hand on April 19, while robbing the dead." In his reconstruction of events after the earthquake, reporter Q.

SOURCE: Reprinted from *Trans-action*, May, 1968, 5:9–14, by permission of the publisher. Copyright © May, 1968, by Trans-action, Inc., New Brunswick, New Jersey.

A. Bronson noted "reports . . . of . . . looters wantonly shot in their tracks by Federal troops, miscreants hanged in public squares, and ghouls found cutting off the fingers and ears of corpses for rings and earrings attached."

Today, most radio and television accounts of disasters are less dramatic, but looting is still a major theme. After a tornado hit some suburbs of Chicago in April 1967, a county sheriff reportedly announced that "orders had gone out that beginning at 10 p. m. Friday, any looters . . . were to be shot on sight." After a power failure blacked out the Cincinnati area in May 1967, a wire-service story told of the smashing of store windows and looting in Cincinnati and in neighboring Newport and Covington, Ky.

Public officials, expecting certain kinds of community emergencies to activate human depravity, often request additional law enforcement. They mobilize National Guard units and take extra security measures. These steps are often upon the first reports of a civil disturbance or a natural disaster. Frequently, before the situation has even developed, television and radio will report what *is expected to happen*—the fear of looting and the steps being taken to prevent it.

That most people are concerned about looting in civil disorders and disasters is beyond dispute. Reliable evidence, however, points to a surprising fact: while looting clearly does occur in civil disturbances, in disaster situations it is very rare.

Many studies of disasters mention *reports* of looting, but very few cite authenticated cases. One study that did inquire into actual cases of looting was the National Opinion Research Center (N.O.R.C.) study of White County, Ark., after it was ravaged by a tornado in 1952. In the community

that suffered the greatest damage, about 1000 of the 1200 residents were left homeless. A random sample of people from this town and adjacent areas were asked whether they had lost any property by looting. Only 9 percent reported that they, or members of their immediate household, had lost property that they even *felt* had been taken by looters. And fully one-third of these people were uncertain whether the loss was really due to looters, or whether the missing items had been blown away or buried in the debris. Finally, most of the articles were of little value.

In contrast, 58 percent of the people questioned said they had heard of *others'* property being stolen. In fact, 9 percent claimed that they had even seen looting in progress or had seen looters being arrested. The N.O.R.C. study team on the scene, however, could verify the theft of only two major items—a cash register and a piano.

Other disaster research confirms the rarity of looting. A study made after the 1953 floods in the Netherlands found that, although there were many reports of looting, law enforcement agencies could discover not a single verified case. The Dutch researchers attributed many of the reports of looting to memory lapses in the immediate post-flood period, and pointed out that a number of people who reported thefts later found the missing items. Charles Fritz and J. H. Mathewson, in a review of disaster studies published up to 1956, concluded that "the number of verified cases of actual looting in peacetime disasters, in the United States and in foreign countries, is small."

More recent studies point in the same direction. The Disaster Research Center at Ohio State University, in field studies of more than 40 disasters both in the United

States and abroad, has found extremely few verified cases of looting. Actual police records support these findings. For example, in September 1965, the month Hurricane Betsy struck New Orleans, major crimes in the city fell 26.6 percent below the rate for the same month in the previous year. Burglaries reported to the police fell from 617 to 425. Thefts of over $50 dropped from 303 to 264, and those under $50 fell from 516 to 366.

Misinterpreted Motives

Since all evidence is that looting is rare or nonexistent in natural disasters, why do reports of looting in disaster situations occur over and over again? And why are these reports persistently believed, even when there is no clear evidence to back them up?

To answer these questions, we need to look at four conditions that usually prevail in the immediate post-impact period: misinterpretations of observed behavior; misunderstandings over property ownership; inflated reports of looting; and sensational coverage of disaster situations by the news media.

Reports of looting are often based on misinterpretation of people's motives. After a disaster, masses of people—often numbering in the thousands—converge on the impact area. Local officials, particularly those with little experience in large-scale emergencies, frequently regard these convergers as sightseers—and, by extension, as potential looters. However, Fritz and Mathewson have shown that there are at least five different types of convergers: the returnees—the disaster survivors who want to go back to the impact area; the anxious —those concerned with the safety of kin and friends; the helpers—those who want to donate their services; the curious—those

attempting to make some sense out of the unusual events that have occurred; and the exploiters—those seeking private gain from public misfortune. The number in this last category is small and includes, in addition to potential looters, souvenir hunters, relief stealers, and profiteers.

The important point is that those who converge on a disaster area have a variety of motives. Community officials often do not seem to recognize this. For example, a property owner whose house has been destroyed may return to the area to sift through the debris of his own home in the hope of recovering lost articles. To a casual observer, his behavior may look like looting. Out-of-town relatives may come into a disaster area with a truck to help their kin collect and store their remaining possessions. People engaged in informal search-and-rescue activities of this sort may also appear to be looters. The souvenir hunter is looking for something that has symbolic rather than material value. But in the disaster context, his behavior too becomes suspect.

Another source of false looting reports is the fact that, although little or no property is stolen in disaster situations, goods are frequently given away. Sometimes there is confusion about which items are free, and who is entitled to them.

In one disaster, the report began circulating that a grocery store had been looted. Investigation revealed that the owner had placed damaged goods outside on the sidewalk, announcing that anyone was welcome to take them. Since his store front had been demolished, however, the line between the free goods and the owner's undamaged stock was vague—and some people who came to get the free goods inadvertently took items from the undamaged stock instead. This misunderstanding was soon cleared up. But an early report of the incident, given to the military authorities in the area, quickly spread throughout the community as an authentic case of looting. And what's more, the looting report was later accepted as valid even by members of the military who had established that it was false.

Overblown estimates of disaster losses are the third source of unfounded looting reports. Officials in a disaster area frequently tend to overestimate the seriousness of the situation. Messages about either the quantity of aid needed or the extent of the damage tend to mushroom as they pass from one person to another. If one official asks another for 100 cots, the second official may relay a request to a third official for 150 cots, and so on. In much the same way, reports of looting get blown out of proportion.

The following incident occurred at a communications center in a major metropolitan area that had been bit by a hurricane: a patrolman in the field, talking over his radio, made a casual comment that, since some store fronts were open and could easily be entered, perhaps a policeman might be dispatched to that location. The patrolman who received this call was busy for a few minutes with other queries. Then he made a call to the state police requesting that a force be rushed to that location— since, he said, "a hell of a lot of looting is going on there."

Sensational news accounts round out the picture. Naturally, the mass media emphasize the dramatic. The atypical and the unique are what catch the newsman's attention. Photographs of disaster areas depict the buildings that are destroyed, not the ones that are still intact. And in press accounts, any stories about looting—including stories that are inaccurate and inflated— are quickly seized upon and highlighted.

These accounts are often accepted as reasonable descriptions of what is occurring even by community officials themselves. In the absence of up-to-date and direct information, what happened or what is happening is not easy to determine. The phone system may be disrupted, preventing direct feedback of information from field points. Movement may be severely restricted. Direct observation is often impossible. And the pressure for immediate action may prevent anyone from keeping accurate records. Since few people in any community have much first-hand experience with large-scale disasters, journalistic accounts become a major means of defining reality. As one police chief said in reply to a question about his knowledge of looting, "Well, I'm not sure. All I know right now is the reports I've heard over the radio."

The upshot of all this is that many reported cases of post-disaster "looting," based on misinterpretation or misunderstanding and publicized by exaggerated or sensational accounts, are not really cases of looting at all. They involve no unlawful appropriations of property.

Still, the fact remains that certain "illegal" appropriations of property *do* occur in disaster situations. For example, people sometimes break into stores and warehouses without the owner's consent and take medical supplies, cots, generators, and flashlights. Now, is this looting? And if not, why not?

Here we come to the critical element of "property redefinition." Incidents of this sort are *not* looting. The notion of "property" involves a shared understanding about who can do what with the valued resources within a community. When a disaster strikes, property rights are temporarily redefined: There is general agreement

among community members that the resources of individuals become *community
property*. Individual property rights are
suspended, so appropriation of private
resources—which would normally be considered looting—is temporarily condoned.
Before these resources can be given back to
private use, the needs of the disoriented
larger community have to be met.

When a natural crisis occurs, the usual
plurality of individual goals gives way to
the single, overriding goal of the community
—the goal of saving as many lives as possible. Any way of achieving this becomes
legitimate. People who are trapped have to
be rescued; people who are in dangerous
areas have to be evacuated; people who
have been injured have to be given medical
attention; people who are missing, and
perhaps injured, must be found. If this
means community appropriation of private
search equipment, medical material, and
even vehicles, it is implicitly viewed as
necessary. In one case, a city attorney even
made it official: he announced that people
were to disregard any laws that would
interfere with the search-and-rescue efforts
going forward in the central part of the
city. This meant formally sanctioning
breaking into and entering private stores
and offices in the city.

The redefinition of property that occurs
during natural disasters, then, almost
defines looting out of existence. Almost,
but not quite. For implicit in the redefinition is the idea that access to the redefined
property is limited to community members,
and for community ends. If outsiders enter
the disaster area and begin appropriating
private property for their own use, it is
still looting. And in fact, evidence indicates
that the few verified instances of looting
that do occur in natural disasters are almost

always of this sort—that is, they are committed by outsiders.

Occasionally there are authenticated reports that seem to contradict our finding
that looting in natural disasters is very rare.
One example is the looting that occurred
during the very heavy snowstorms that
paralyzed Chicago in late January and
early February 1967. A few of the incidents
reported were probably routine burglaries,
but others were clearly looting. They were
not randomly distributed by location, and
most of the cases occurred in the same
neighborhoods—and sometimes on exactly
the same streets—where looting had taken
place in the civil disturbances during the
summer months of 1966. Along Chicago's
Roosevelt Road, for example, looting took
place on some of the very same blocks.

This suggests that the looting that occurred in Chicago during the snowstorm
was actually a continuation, or perhaps a
resurgence, of the earlier civil disturbance.
For the general public, the habit of viewing
civil disturbances as exclusively summer
events probably obscured the true nature
of the snowstorm looting. But some local
policemen clearly interpreted the looting as
a winter recurrence of the summer's civil
disorders.

In contrast to what happens in a disaster
situation, looting in civil disturbances is
widespread, and the looters are usually
members of the immediate community.
During the past few summers, films and
photographs have shown looting actually
in progress. The McCone Commission
reported that about 600 stores were looted
or burned in Watts. In Newark, around
1300 people were arrested, mostly for taking
goods. In the July 1967 holocaust in Detroit,
unofficial estimates were that about 2700
stores were ransacked.

Redefinition of Property

Disasters and civil disturbances are alike in that the normal order and organization of the community is disrupted. In addition, there is, in both situations, a temporary redefinition of property rights. But the two situations differ in other respects. In a disaster, there is general agreement among community members about community goals, especially about saving lives. As a result, by general agreement, all the resources are put at the disposal of the total community until emergency needs are met. A civil disturbance, on the other hand, represents conflict—not consensus—on community goals. The outbreak itself represents disagreement over property rights within the community. Access to existing resources is questionable, and often there is open challenge to prior ownership.

The critical role of attitudes toward property in determining the nature of looting is best seen by contrasting the looting that occurs in civil disturbances with that found in disasters. There are three significant differences. As already noted, widespread looting *does* occur in civil disturbances, while it is infrequent in disasters. Further, the looting in civil disturbances is selective, focusing on particular types of goods or possessions, often symbolic of other values. And, while out-and-out looting is strongly condemned in disaster situations, looters in civil disturbances receive, from certain segments of the local community, strong social support for their actions.

The occurrence of looting in civil disturbances needs no further documentation. And selectivity can be seen in the fact that, in racial outbreaks, looters have concentrated overwhelmingly on certain kinds of stores. In Watts, Newark, and Detroit, the main business affected were groceries, supermarkets, and furniture and liquor stores. In contrast, banks, utility stations, industrial plants, and private residences have been generally ignored. Apartments and homes have been damaged, but only because they were in or near burned business establishments. Public installations such as schools and Office of Economic Opportunity centers have also been spared. There has not been indiscriminate looting. Certain kinds of consumer goods have been almost the only targets.

Looters in civil disturbances are also likely to receive support from many people in their community. Spiraling support coincides with shifts in property redefinitions, and these shifts occur in three stages. Initial looting is often a symbolic act of defiance. The second phase, in which more conscious and deliberate plundering develops, is possibly spurred on by the presence of delinquent gangs that loot more from need or for profit than for ideological reasons. Finally, in the third stage, there is widespread seizure of goods. At this point, looting becomes the socially expected thing to do. For example, a sociological survey at U.C.L.A. found that nearly one-fourth of the population participated in the Watts outbreak (although all of these participants probably did not engage in the looting).

If looting means strictly the taking of goods, little of it occurs in the first phase of civil disturbances. Instead, destructive attacks are most frequently directed against symbols of authority in the community. Police cars and fire trucks are pillaged and burned. What is involved here is perhaps illustrated most clearly in other kinds of civil disturbances, such as some of those created by college students. One of the authors once watched a crowd of students determinedly attack, for over an hour, an overhead traffic light. It conveniently symbolized the city administration and police—the actual target of the demonstrators' wrath. In racial civil disturbances, the police and their equipment are also seen as obvious symbols of the larger community toward which the outbreak is directed. How intense this focus can be was shown in the Watts disturbance. About 168 police cars and 100 pieces of fire-fighting equipment were damaged or destroyed.

The full redefinition of certain property rights occurs next. The "carnival spirit" observed in the Newark and Detroit disturbances did not represent anarchy. It represented widespread social support for the new definition of property. In this phase, there is little competition for goods. In fact, in contrast to the stealthy looting that occasionally occurs in disaster situations, looting in civil disturbances is quite open and frequently collective. The looters often work together in pairs, as family units, or in small groups. Bystanders are frequently told about potential loot. And in some instances, as in the Watts outbreak, looters coming out of stores hand strangers goods as "gifts."

Looting in civil disturbances is by insiders —by local community members. These looters apparently come not only from the low socioeconomic levels and from delinquent gangs, but from all segments of the population. During disturbances in Toledo, 91 percent of the 126 adults arrested for taking goods had jobs. A random sample in Detroit found that participants in the outbreak came more or less equally from all income brackets.

In both disasters and civil disturbances, there is a redefinition of property rights within the community. The community authorities, however, respond very differently to the two situations. In disasters, responsible officials tolerate, accept, and encourage the transition from private to community property. In civil disturbances, community authorities see looting as essentially criminal behavior—as a legal problem to be handled forcefully by the police. And many segments of the larger community, especially middle-class people, with their almost sacred conception of private property, tend to hold the same view. This view of looting in civil disturbances fits in neatly with the ideas they already have about the criminal propensities of certain ethnic groups, notably Negroes.

Looting as a Mass Protest

At one level, there is no question that looting in civil disturbances is criminal behavior. But the laws that make it so are themselves based on dominant conceptions of property rights. Widespread looting, then, may perhaps be interpreted as a kind of mass protest against our dominant conceptions of property.

Mass protest is not new in history. According to George Rudé's analysis, in his book *The Crowd in History,* demonstrating mobs from 1730 to 1848 in England and France were typically composed of local, respectable, employed people rather than the pauperized, the unemployed, or the "rabble" of the slums. The privileged classes naturally regarded these popular agitations as criminal—as fundamentally and unconditionally illegitimate. Rudé notes, however, that such protest effectively communicated the desires of a segment of the urban population to the élite. E. J. Hobsbawm, in his analysis of the preindustrial "city mob," takes the same position: "The classical mob did not merely riot as a protest, but because it expected to achieve something by its riot. It assumed that the authorities would be sensitive to its movements, and probably also that they would make some immediate concession. . . . This mechanism was perfectly understood by both sides."

In current civil disturbances, a similar mechanism and a similar message may be evolving. An attack against property rights is not necessarily "irrational," "criminal," or "pointless" if it leads to a clearer system of demands and responses, in which the needs and obligations of the contending parties are reasonably clear to themselves and to one another. The scope and intensity of current attacks indicate the presence of large numbers of outsiders living within most American cities. If property is seen as a shared understanding about the allocation of resources, and if a greater consensus can be reached on the proper allocation of these resources, many of these outsiders will become insiders, with an established stake in the communities in which they live.

This, then, is the most fundamental way in which looting in civil disturbances differs from looting after natural disasters: The looting that has occurred in recent racial outbreaks is a bid for the redistribution of property. It is a message that certain deprived sectors of the population want what they consider their fair share—and that they will resort to violence to get it. The fact that looting in riots is more widespread than in disasters, that it concentrates on the prestige items that symbolize the good life, and that it receives the support and approval of many within the deprived sectors who do not participate themselves, merely indicates the true nature and intention of looting under conditions of mass protest.

The basic question now is whether American community leaders can or will recognize that such looting is more than "pointless" or "criminal" behavior. If they do, it may mark the beginning of a new political dialogue, in which the outsiders in our urban communities can express their desires nonviolently to the insiders—insiders who will have finally learned to listen. If not, then in the summers to come, and perhaps in the winters as well, many men and women from the growing urban population may continue to demand a redefinition of property rights through disorder and violence.

27

The Social Organization of Armed Robbery

WERNER J. EINSTADTER

In most criminological studies, when the group life of adult professional criminals is discussed a single theoretical model is employed. It is usually assumed that the adult professional criminal operates within the structural context of the *mob*. The model of the mob has been variously described in the literature, but was most clearly formulated by Sutherland.[1]

A body of literature on professional crime has centered largely on an extension or modification of Sutherland's conception of the essential social characteristics of professional theft and his unifying theoretical statement of differential association.[2] As Clinard and Quinney have pointed out, however, empirical research concerning various types of professional crime has been sparse; this is especially true with regard to the social organization of various professional criminal groups.[3] No studies appear to have been concerned specifically with a reexamination of Sutherland's conception of the social organization of the professional criminal.

The concept of the mob implies that professional criminal collectivities operate according to a number of common understandings, rules of conduct, or working relationships which are considered binding on all its members. These modes of conduct found among groups of professional thieves are presumed to have universal applicability to all professional criminal groups.

The purpose of this paper is two-fold; first, it is an attempt to relate Sutherland's conception of the mob to professional robbery and to reassess its utility and relevance as a generic explanatory model; secondly, it is an effort to describe a specific type of criminal behavior system.

Methodology

Twenty-five convicted robbers on parole in California were studied. In addition to interview material, data gathered over several years from an equal number of convicted robbers who were confined were used. Official records were employed as supplementary material, to check the official criminal record, prior commitments, and offense statements.

The respondents selected represent robbers who were considered to be professional or career robbers in that they all met the following criteria:

a) Each subject in company with others committed more than a single robbery prior to detection. Each subject either committed a series of robberies or several series of robberies separated by prison terms. In a number of instances there were robberies unknown to officials.

b) All were armed robbers. All employed weapons that were operative. None simulated weapons. Each instance of robbery was calculated and the subject fully intended to carry the act to its completion.

SOURCE: Reprinted from *Social Problems,* Summer, 1969, 17:64–83, by permission of the author and The Society for the Study of Social Problems.

c) Each subject considered himself a robber and for various periods had spent a considerable portion of his time in the engagement of robbery.

d) In all instances the subject's sole stated interest was robbery. In no case was the robbery incidental to some other form of crime (e.g., rape, drug addiction).

The subjects, therefore, may be considered as representing more than just casual robbers, but individuals who engaged in this form of criminal conduct on a purposive, rational and sustained basis over various periods of time.

Findings

Sutherland describes a number of signficant features that emerge in the group life of professional thieves which he considers the binding rules of the mob. As such, these rules develop into a formal code of ethics subscribed to by the professional thief much like other codes of conduct among legitimate professional groups.[4]

A comparison of the type of organization that develops among professional robbers with the type of organization that develops among professional thieves reveals little similarity as the following discussion will make clear. Whereas the professional thief finds his organizational counterpart in the legitimate professions, the professional or career robber may be compared more accurately with the legitimate businessman in the organizational form of the partnership.

Sutherland's thief is quite explicit in his description of the norms that develop in the mob. A review of the rules of the mob should prove revealing in highlighting the differences between the type of structure that is characteristic of groups of profes-

sional thieves and that of groups of armed robbers:

1. Gains are equally shared. A percentage is given to outsiders who assist the mob.

In general, robbers share equally with their associates whatever is taken. However, there is no sharing with outsiders as they do not exist for the robber. If someone has helpful knowledge about sites to rob or assist in some way in the robbery even if only tangentially, from the robber's point of view, he is not an outsider, but a member of the group and receives his share of the gain. Once robbery is discussed by a group with any amount of seriousness, all become full partners and all consider themselves equally involved and have a stake in the success of the planned enterprise. Planning need not be extensive in order for this involvement to occur; there merely needs to be some discussion of robbery amongst a group that intends to carry it to completion.[5] Hence no one is ever considered an outsider to the group after preliminary discussions have taken place. The statement of one robber is illustrative:

[If] you compare notes with somebody, you are going to join them. In other words, my crime partner and I were talking to you and another fellow, and we were comparing notes, eventually the four of us are going to do something together, whether it be tonight, tomorrow night or the next night, regardless. By openly admitting to one another our situation, I think we find a binding point, where we, you say, I know a spot over there, let's go get it. And you say let's go get it, why, the four of you go instead of one or two.

2. Expenses of the mob come off the top.

The robber's expenses are minimal and are usually paid out of pocket by the individual concerned. Such outlays are in the nature of small business expenses and are managed quite informally from one robbery to the next. One respondent stated it simply:

> I paid the gas and oil on the first job, the second time around somebody else got it. Usually it was just a couple of bucks and nobody expected anything back . . . .

Large expenses, such as the purchase of an automobile or the purchase of weapons are usually paid on a share-and-share-alike basis. Each contributes his amount to the total. In some instances, expenses are taken off the top, but this is not by any means a regular procedure. There is nothing formal about any of these arrangements, rather like any other informal group undertaking where there are expenses, there is a tacit agreement that each member contributes his share.

3. All loans are repaid out of the first sum of stolen money.

A number of robbers who were asked about this provision seemed perplexed and had no knowledge regarding this type of arrangement. These loans refer to an organized mob that needs capital to carry out its illegal enterprises. This rarely occurs in the sense that there are financial backers for the robber. When large sums of monetary outlays are necessary that cannot readily be managed by the group, other methods than seeking a backer are employed. A group that generally commits the more sophisticated variety of robbery —(e.g., banks, large grocery chains)— where such outlays sometimes become necessary, may commit a number of small preliminary minor robberies before venturing to tackle a more formidable victim. Often such a group may rob a few smaller establishments to fund a contemplated large robbery which may require some additional equipment. Frequently such items are stolen directly.

4. A fourth rule described by Sutherland is concerned with a number of general understandings about the mob's action when a member is arrested. Basically, the understanding is that the mob helps the apprehended member by sharing the expenses of court costs if he is arrested "on business." Furthermore, a share of the *take* is saved for him and money is regularly set aside for bail to be used by any member.

The reply of one informant when queried about this procedure is graphically illustrative and provides a good summary:

> Hell, no, the guy went into this with his eyes wide open, oh, sure, we'd feel sorry for the guy, but, hell, he'd be on his own. If he were arrested we'd split to save our own necks. He'd be expected to keep his mouth shut, but that can only last for a little while. Whatever dough there was would be split amongst the guys out; if we get caught we'd come to an understanding later, but if he ratted he'd have nothing coming.

Robbers give little thought to being arrested while actively engaging in robbery. That such occurrence is an eventuality is recognized, but is given little weight. Should an arrest be made, the arrestee expects no assistance from his partners. Conversely, the group expects the member arrested to remain silent but is realistic enough to realize that this cannot be a permanent situation; nevertheless, it may apply sanctions if the arrested member gives information too readily.[6] In view of the seriousness of the offense, robbers are rarely released on bail once arrested. When bail is set, it is usually a high amount which the arrested member has difficulty in obtaining. Were a fund established by a robbery group to meet this need, it would have to be a considerable sum, something prohibitive for most groups of robbers. Both the nature of the robbery venture and the type of group that emerges precludes this kind of foresight.

Hence there is little evidence in the social organization of robbers of group cohesion during periods of stress in the manner described by Sutherland. The robber's organization is a more fluid arrangement taking into account existing conditions; it is not conceived by those involved as a permanent group but more or less a loose confederation of individuals joined together for a specific purpose on a short-term basis. Among certain types of robbers, specific role relationships do develop; however, these always are assumed to be temporary by the robbery participants even though the association is of some duration. When this type of social organization exists, no provision need be made for incapacitated members; each member considers himself on his own.

5. Members of the mob are to deal honestly with each other.

This rule generally applies to armed robber groups. As was pointed out under rule one, participants are expected to make even division of the stolen money, and are required to deal honestly in matters of robbery. But this expectation applies only to matters of the immediate present; hence robbers are not expected, for example, to reveal all their background or even be completely honest when they do. Most robbers anticipate that their partners will exaggerate about their past exploits as robbers, other criminal activities, prision experiences, dealings with women, etc., and openly tolerate a certain amount of these exaggerations when such information is supplied. Furthermore, robbers, as a rule, do not reveal too much about themselves to

each other with the exception of current pressing problems, the stated reasons, which bring them into robbery. This lack of candor is respected. But there are "understandings" and cues which reveal much to the robber about his associates.

. . . And, well, I don't know it's just kind of a thing, you meet some guy and you say, I like him, and he likes you, and so you start horsing around, well, you don't know each other, really, you don't know anything about each other, but eventually, it comes out, you know. You let it slip, you ask him about something,—how do you like what you're doing,—and he says,—it's whole lot better than doing time. Then I knew, and I told him yeah, and you finally out on your backgrounds. So, we got to talking and talking about an easier way to make money . . . He says "I know a couple of guys, and we all got guns, and we can go out and hit a few places, now and then. If we don't hit it heavy, we won't get caught." So, we started doing this stuff.

. . . .

. . . You are not exactly hanging around in a place for a long period of time, which we were. We were there, oh hell, six out of the seven nights a week. And, quite naturally, you learn to know somebody by their conversation, at least outwardly, you know them. And eventually, the money is going to drain out, then a suggestion is going to come up, provided you feel that the person you are talking to is of your same caliber, and evidently when I met him at this particular time I felt that I could trust him, and I think there was, at my suggestion, if I remember correctly, that he come in with me. And between the two of us, why, we did a series of robberies.

Unless the robbers are acquaintances of long standing or are related and aware of each other's backgrounds, these understandings play a significant part in the trust relationship that becomes established.

6. Members voluntarily leaving the mob may ask to be taken back in, but it would not be proper for the leader of the mob to request they return.

This is another rule which is not applicable to armed robbers, indeed; there is serious question as to leadership in the first place. Any member is privileged to leave the group any time. He may also "sit one out" if he feels a particular robbery will be too dangerous for him, although this is not a frequent practice. Leaving robbery voluntarily is a rare occurrence; when it does occur it is temporary and returning presents no problems. There are no particular rules of etiquette that govern robbery group conduct, as the group is not a tightly knit organization with fixed personnel and standards of behavior. The needs of the moment dictate the method of operation; there are few subtleties or niceties among robbers and, in this respect also, a group of robbers bears little resemblance to the mob described by Sutherland's thief.[7]

7. Members of the mob are not held responsible for events which they cannot control.

This is the only rule that seems relevant; robbers as well as thieves do not appreciably blame each other too severely for certain blunders that are made.

. . . We planned to get around $30,000 to $40,000 or $80,000 out of this bank; as it turned out, this one who was spending the money, he's quite a nervous fellow, anyhow, he went into the vault, had the assistant manager go into the vault, and there was a big sack. It must have been as big as a mail sack, and he picked it up and said, "What's in this?" It was locked, and the guy said it was non-negotiable securities,

so the kid let it down. Turned out it was $40,000 . . . Anyhow he went out and cleaned out two or three of the cages and he got $10,000 out of that but . . . he thought he had more . . . we found out we had missed $40,000 so we were kinda grumbling at him for overlooking it but we figured he didn't have any experience and he wouldn't know how much paper would weigh anyhow . . .

Here a loss of $40,000 was rationalized away as insufficient experience. At a later time this same individual again made a costly error and again he was excused:

So that time we got $16,500 and $17,000 . . . . again we passed up $80,000, I think it was, I forget the reason why they missed it. But again it was the same guy who goofed it up . . .

The fates enter heavily into robbers' lives in general, and this is merely an instance of the common tendency among robbers to use "fate" as a rationale of life. It's the "breaks" that count; you either have them or not. Fate is deemed to control the robber's destiny;[8] when the cards are right, when the dice are right, when the *setup* is perfect, nothing can go wrong, but if luck is against you, "you haven't got a chance." It, therefore, becomes easy to excuse what would under ordinary circumstances be considered an unforgivable error. Also with this rationale the occasional violence that occurs may be explained away as an accidental twist of fate. The fate motif is probably more responsible for the group attitude of not holding members responsible for uncontrollable events than any other aspect in the robber's group life. This seeming reversion to magic on the part of the robber is difficult to explain. One would expect a lessening of this motif as the robber becomes more proficient, i.e., as he has learned to reduce the hazards and is more in control of the situation; however, such is not the case.[9] The fate motif is discernible in all levels of robbers' groups. It may be that robbery, no matter how well planned, in view of its direct personal interaction, always presents the possibility of uncontrollable hazards and hence uncertainty.

8. No member of a mob should cut in on another member. This is another etiquette rule which forbids any mob member from "cramping the style" of another. The exception being an emergency or an inexperienced member who has only been given a minor role to perform.

Robbers, when necessary, help each other out in the performance of a robbery in the event of an "emergency." The rule appears to refer to mobs of pickpockets or shoplifters, and only in a very general way would be applicable to a group of robbers.[10]

9. The last mob maxim refers to the mob member's responsibility to do everything possible to fix a case for any other member of the mob who may have been arrested as a result of mob activities.

This raises the entire question of regarding the practice of "fixing" cases, bribes, etc., as it exists today and would go beyond the confines of this paper. It is quite clear that the *fix* as described by Sutherland with reference to thieves is not practiced by contemporary armed robbers.

Arrest Strategy

If arrested, the strategy is to obtain the best "deal" with the prosecutor on the basis of the amount of information and evidence known to him. The "fixer" as described in the *Professional Thief* is unknown to the informants. Members of robber troupes also express no feelings of obligation to help out a member arrested; the main concern is with maintaining their own individual anonymity.

The practice of obtaining the best "bargain" possible often requires the revelation of the crime partners' identities in exchange for a more favorable disposition; knowledge of the possibility of this occurrence creates considerable anxiety on the part of a group when one of its members is arrested. The result, therefore, is for all members to "split" and attempt to "ride it out" if possible, but it is a well known fact among robbers that the arrest of one usually spells the end for all. Hence, under present circumstances, the last thing a robber would think about is to attempt a "fix" even were it possible, for not only would he reveal his identity and suffer the likelihood of arrest, but he would also defeat a possible bargaining position of his associates.

Discussion

From the foregoing comparison it becomes obvious that the group of careerist robbers seems to bear only slight resemblance to the mob that Sutherland describes. How can one account for this difference? One obvious answer is simply that times have changed and so has the complexity of relationships in society. What was possible during the first quarter or more of this century is no longer feasible under present circumstances. The entire scope and function of law enforcement has changed, making certain criminal styles obsolete. One need only mention the revolutionary developments in systems of identification of criminals, modern communication, transportation methods, and methods of scientific investigation to stress the point.

The mob as an organized form of criminal activity must be related to a particular point in historical experience, a point where it served a purpose—a point where it was functional. During the first few decades of this century, the "mob style" was particularly adapted to the social conditions of the day; the "fix" was possible because personal relationships were simpler and more direct.[11] Criminals, as well as others, knew each other personally with the resultant development of congeniality and rules of behavioral etiquette which guided the criminal mob both in its relationship among its own members and with outsiders. With the increasing complexity of society, these relationships were no longer possible and the mob was due to change. To paraphrase Bell, as the style of society changed, so did, in lagging fashion, its style of crime.[12]

There is, however, another reason why the robber's group differs from the mob. The mob, in general, referred to the organization of professional theft, which Sutherland distinguishes from robbery on the basis of style. Whereas the thief relies chiefly on wits, front, and talking ability, Sutherland declares, ". . . robbers, kidnappers and others who engage in the 'heavy rackets' are generally not regarded as professional thieves for they depend primarily on *manual dexterity or force*." [13] However, there are those robbers who "use their wits, 'front,' and talking ability, and these are regarded by the professional thieves as belonging to the profession." [14] The robber's group also reflects the peculiar style of the robber; the elements of robbery require a different type of organization in order for the crime to be carried to completion. Furthermore, the robber's group reflects the life style of persons not concerned with the etiquette of relationships, nor the reciprocals inherent in group life,

but chiefly concerned with accomplishing a specific goal—the rapid accumulation of money.

The armed robber's entire engagement in robbery differs from the professional thief's engagement in theft, even when the former possesses "wit, front, and talking ability." Both the quality and the nature of the commitment itself differ, with the robber being more compelled in his action in the sense of feeling restricted as to the alternative courses of action open to him.[15] He is in a "get-rich-quick enterprise" and as such needs to move quickly and strike swiftly when the opportunity presents itself. In his scheme of action, he simply does not have time for the amenities of the professional thief, nor can he appreciate the latter's moderate approach to profit.[16] The formal relationships of the mob are not functional for his needs; more adaptable to the style necessary for the accomplishment of his goal is the social organization represented by the partnership.[17] Much as the professional thief resembled other professionals, the careerist robber resembles the businessman who conducts his business through the tutelage of a partnership. The robber similarly works through a group of partners with whom he shares equally in what risks there are and invests his services to the total enterprise. As a partner he shares in the profits and losses of the operation. The partnership also provides opportunity for differentiation of various tasks necessary to carry out a robbery and to plan its strategy. Career robbery is conducted in and through partnerships; the lone systematic robber is rare.[18]

Armed career robbers then develop a form of social organization that is essentially dissimilar to the model originally proposed by Sutherland for professional thieves, which by extension has been applied to all professional criminal activities. A closer examination of career armed robbery will serve to further distinguish this form of deviant action from other criminal behavior systems.

Functional Differentiation and Group Structure in Career Robbery

From the beginning, the strategy or engineering of a *job* is a group product and must be viewed in an interaction context. An individual may present a solid robbery plan to his associates which is eventually acted upon; however, there is always deliberation by the group. Thus, partnership consensus must be reached prior to the commission of any act of robbery.

Although there is little discernible evidence of distinctive leadership roles, previous experiences of members are given due recognition. Where leaders are recognizable, they become most apparent in adroit partnerships, in the less definitive form of what might more appropriately be titled *planning consultants*. The role behavior is one of guiding rather than directing and in this sense fully meets the role expectations of the members of the partnership. Some members may become more persuasive than others, but dicta from partners are frowned upon and do not constitute the basis of action. When there is divergence of opinion, there is majority rule of sorts, but as has been implied, there is no enforcement of majority rule on dissident members, rather the partners make accommodations.

It may be argued that in terms of the explicit goals of the partnership, these types of arrangements are functional since to force an unwilling or dissident member to join in a robbery would only endanger the whole group. The success of the partnership depends on cooperative effort. The group then is a partnership of equals, each with a voice; what leadership arises comes out of mutual recognition of the expertise of an individual member which serve the group's goals.

These deliberations are informally structured, vary in duration of time, and are likely to occur anywhere the potential participants happen to be congregated—an automobile, a bar, a motel room—throughout, it is a rational and deliberative, albeit at times haphazard process of decision making. Once the decision is reached that a particular robbery or series of robberies is to be performed, there does not appear to exist a specific pattern of planning the robbery encounter. The planning of a robbery may vary from a simple drive around a neighborhood to "case a joint" to a series of complex maneuvers; the strategy employed depends on the type of robbery and the sophistication of those involved.

Prior to any robbery, however, no matter what the level of potential complexity, assignments are made as to the role each partner is to play in the encounter. In this effort the strengths and weaknesses of various members may be assessed and conclusions reached as to the roles best fitted to each participant.[19] Again this decision is reached through group interaction; no single individual gives orders or assigns positions without group and individual consensus.

The account of one respondent who preferred not to participate directly in holdups but was a competent driver describes the process of how one such decision was reached.

For one reason, I wasn't going in, that was the first reason. I told them that, but they wanted me to go in. Then they got talking about that he [another partner] was going to drive the car because one of them couldn't see good, and the second one, he's so damn nervous he'd probably take the key out and put it in his pocket and then couldn't find the key. We didn't think he would keep his head cool enough to stay in the car listening to the radio calls come in, especially if one came in that said there was a robbery in progress. Then we didn't know how to trust the fourth guy that just came in; we didn't know whether he might run off and leave all of us, if all three of us went in. He probably wasn't going to do it, but they were considering it. Well, anyway, it all boiled down to that I should be driving the car because I don't get excited and I drive well.

At other times a more flexible arrangement is used with assignments shifting from robbery to robbery. The functional differentiation depends chiefly on what talents are available; however, the temperament of individual partners also may enter as a determinant.

We switched around one time I went in with . . . at other times . . . went in. We sorta decided on the spur of the moment. All of us were pretty good, so it didn't matter. It sorta depended on how we felt at the time, you know, the mood we were in so we usually sorta decided beforehand; we agreed on who would go in . . .

A loose type of specialization results which is flexible and adaptable according to circumstances. In this way partnerships conform to fluctuations of member's moods and the possible eccentricities of various individuals. Individuality is never completely relinquished by the careerist. He cooperates but he is never subjugated. He fits himself into the allocated roles of the partnership to accomplish certain purposes but tries whenever possible to carry them

out on his own terms. In so doing, he attempts to use the partnership as a vehicle to reach his goal—nothing more.

The Minimum Essentials—The Actor's Role

The successful completion of a robbery depends mainly on the coordination of various tasks that must be completed. Through coordination and specialization of roles of participants in the robbery, the robbery group not only assures more protection to itself but adds a measure of efficiency and shock in quickly overtaking the victim by a show of disciplined force. A well operating partnership need only have three men and successfully carry out profitable robberies. Sometimes the same results may be obtained by a dyad, but generally a group of three men appears to be the most tactically effective unit.[20]

The typical career robbery triad consists of two men who enter the establishment armed; the third remains outside in the vicinity in an automobile, is usually armed but need not be.[21] Of the two men who perform the actual robbery, one is considered the "back-up." It is his function to watch any customers in the establishment, prevent any from leaving, and "cover" those that might enter while his partner gathers the cash. At times he assists also in gathering the *take* if there are no customers or other conditions that need his attention. The "wheel" or "wheelman" in addition to driving the get-away car also acts as lookout or "pointman," and at times is given added responsibilities of a variety of sorts.

An example of a wheelman's role in a series of bank robberies is informative both of his role obligation and the rather sophisticated planning that may take place in some partnerships. Not all robberies committed by the careerist robber are this well planned and executed, but the interview excerpt describes the extent to which the systematic robber may go to assure his goal:

I: So then you had the place cased and then did you commit the robbery?

S: No. We decided against it for some reason. I think we might have kept refining our plans as we went along and what we had done was decided, well we found that there were a number of characteristics the bank had to have before it was acceptable into our situation; one, it had to have a nice getaway, so we could abandon one car if a police car or some citizen chased us; we didn't want to shoot anyone, you know, or shoot at them or be shot at, so we could leave this car and either jump over a fence or go through a culvert or through a walkway so no car could follow us and report it. Then we could go over and pick up another car and then take off. So not all banks would fit into this sort of category . . . Anyhow, my job was to go up the telephone pole and cut the telephone wires so they couldn't call the cops. And then as soon as I cut the wires then these two walk in the bank and then I would go down the pole and get in the car. We had a police radio so we could tell if the cops got a signal, I could drive up to the bank and honk; otherwise I could get into the car and give them one minute exactly to go clean out the bank.

I: How did you decide on the one minute?

S: Well, we figured how long it would take, if everyone cooperated, and we decided that one minute would probably be safe. So anyway they went in. They had the stocking caps up under these men's hats, snap brim hats, and then they had masks that dropped down, I think one of them had a stocking cap that pulled over and the other one had a mask that just dropped down. So as soon as they walked in the door they just dropped it;

customers walked in and noticed it; they just walked out; they didn't believe there was a bank robbery going on. So I sat there and watched all of that. I was just sitting there listening to the radio and watching my watch. So anyhow, as soon as one minute was up, I left the parking place, looking carefully to see that there were no cops, and I drove up to the bank and just as I did, the guy inside, one was holding at bay and the other was getting the money, he got nervous or something. Anyway, he gathered up all he could and ran out the door just at the very minute I got to the door, just as we had rehearsed it, and I had the doors open for him. They jumped in the car and off we went. And all the customers and people out on the sidewalk just going like this and I don't think anybody chased us, although later we heard somebody did. It was some three blocks back. So we got about $10,000 out of that. We pulled the car up near a school and went down a little ravine and jumped into another car, drove it to one of the fellow's house and drove it right into his garage, pulled the garage door down, went out the back door and went into his cottage and got in there and stayed in there listening to the police radio . . .

Additional men may be added depending on the size of the robbery and its felt complexity; however, these men perform no different roles from the basic triad. They assist those engaged in the holdup, that is, they become extra personnel.

The "wheelman" does not have assistants but often has additional responsibilities such as planning the escape route, obtaining the get-away car, arranging lodging, and acting as lookout. There is general agreement among career robbers that the "wheel" has the greatest responsibility at the critical period of escape; as such, he is required to be the most "mature" of the group.

No matter how many robbers participate

in a robbery and no matter how functionally differentiated the partnership might be, the element of surprise and momentary domination of the scene must be maximized if the robbery is to be successfully completed.

Robberies are foiled if either a) the victim is not surprised, b) the coordination of the partnership is poor, c) the robbers do not completely dominate the scene. Violence is also likely to occur if any one or combinations of these conditions exist. The aim, therefore, is to so structure the situation that the victim is rendered helpless to resist and "cooperates" toward the successful completion of the crime. In the words of one robber, "It has to be a smooth operation or else someone is likely to get hurt." To accomplish this goal, robbers employ a number of tactics or styles with varying degrees of "smoothness" which reveal different levels of planning and proficiency depending in part on the type of partnership and in part on the situation.

Styles of Career Robbery

These robbery tactics may for purposes of discussion be divided into three categories and labeled according to style of approach.

1. *The Ambush*—This type of robbery is the least planned of all and depends almost entirely on the element of surprise. All participants literally attack an establishment guerrilla fashion and attempt to obtain whatever might be found in cash or other items of value. There is no sophistication in this style of robbery and it is considered the *lowest* form of robbery from the viewpoint of the careerist. There is almost randomness in the selection of the victim, with no thought as to what conditions might be present in the situation that may affect the outcome of the robbery. It is also the type of robbery where the chances of violence

are high. As a rule it is a style employed by less systematic robbers.

2. *The Selective Raid*—In this form there is a minimum of planning. Sites are tentatively selected and *cased* even though very briefly. Site conditions are analyzed to some degree before the robbery is attempted. There is a tentative plan of approach; however, the planning may be accomplished very casually and several robberies may be committed in rapid succession.

3. *The Planned Operation*—Robberies that fall into this category are well planned and well structured crimes where all aspects are carefully delineated in the group and each partner knows his part well. At times there may be rehearsals or "dry runs" so that all possible conditions are taken into account. Risks are held at a minimum.

It would be ideal, for purposes of analysis, if partnerships practiced one style during the life of the group. Such, however, is not the case. Each individual partnership practices different styles of robbery during its existence. Thus, for example, one partnership that is in the planning stages of a *planned operation* may commit a few *selective raids* to finance what is thought to be a more lucrative robbery. On the other hand, certain groups may practice only one style and become quite proficient in it. Generally, however, the *ambush* is a desperation measure for careerists and is resorted to only when an emergency occurs such as the threatened capture of the group where money for flight must be raised quickly.

Robbery Skills

This raises the issue of skills required to engage in robbery. Obviously the three robbery styles require different levels of planning ability and creative potential. A *planned operation* may be a highly sophisticated crime requiring unique creative capacities, whereas an *ambush* can be attempted by anyone. A number of skills, therefore, are necessary to plan the more resourceful types of robberies that are committed by the careerist. In order to engage in robberies other than the ambush, the robber must have a sense of organization, timing, ability to take into account unforeseen events, etc. But these are skills or capacities of planning which bring structure to the robbery; the robbery itself requires little skill or ability. The synthesizing of robbery requires talent; its commission does not. This is not the case with certain other professional crimes, the variety of which Sutherland speaks. Compare the pickpocket, who must learn intricate sets of muscular movements, learn to perfect the art of misdirection in order to become successful in his endeavor, or the booster who must learn techniques of concealment and misdirection to avoid detection as a shoplifter. The confidence man has to develop a high degree of front, wit, and talking ability, before he can carry out his swindle. All the robber needs, in the final analysis, is a revolver. This one attribute can make him the master of the situation. The skill involved in robbery pertains to the style employed and to the amount of planning of which the individual partnership is capable. These skills may be brought to robbery and need not necessarily be learned exclusively through interaction with other robbers.[22] They may, however, be modified and shaped to meet the conditions of the robbery situation. Noncriminal learning structures may provide the necessary qualifications which may easily be converted to robbery.

Military experience of a certain variety, for example, lends itself readily to robbery:

. . . And I thought, well, with four of us—I can start running out squad training techniques—another of those I learned in the military and that possibly we could start . . . doing some fairly large things—One thing I had sort of in mind—I thought of taking . . . the golf prizes from the . . . Lodge which usually involves a couple hundred thousand dollars—and—doing it around the point by water—and we had actually run an intelligence project on this . . . My partner had made it a point to become acquainted with and questioned fairly thoroughly, if indirectly, a fellow that worked in the office there—the assistant to the accountant—and so we actually knew much of the scheduling around the handling of this money and the operation of the Lodge and we were going to make our approach by water—and with four of us operating as a commando unit, it would have gone quite smoothly. I approached the thing as I would approach a military problem. I ran general intelligence rather than just the sort of thing that usually in the criminal profession is called "casing." I had hoped to train my men to the . . . disguise that didn't bear the earmarks of camouflage—whistles and so forth.

Business acumen may also be turned to robbery:

I planned it just like I've seen businesses operate and what I did in my own "front" business. We checked out details just like anybody running a firm. I didn't want anybody getting hurt or getting too excited, so I checked to see whether anybody had heart trouble in the bank through channels I knew about, that are open to employers . . .

These planning capacities may, of course, come from previous criminal experiences or indeed through association with robbers, but need not be limited to these sources.

The skills of robbery, therefore, center mainly around planning ability. The greater the organization aptitudes of the members of the partnership, the greater the number of *planned operations* in the career of the partnership. The greater the number of *planned operations*, the more successful the partnership becomes, the more likely the pattern will continue.

It is as a consequence of planning ability being brought to robbery that relatively newly formed partnerships may adopt more sophisticated styles from the beginning and are thus able to prolong their careers because of their expertise. Furthermore, during the initial period they may be unknown robbers, a characteristic which tends to lessen the probability of detection.[23] Thus one bank robber states:

It was really a well planned job and we knew exactly what to do. It was perfect . . . Now I'm known. I've been mugged and printed. I wouldn't think of trying anything. Hell, every time somebody pulls something around here and even faintly resembles me, I better have a good alibi.

Patterns of Activity

Related to the particular styles of the robber partnership is the choice of victim. Although among careerists there is a definite victim preference, there is much divergence among partnerships as to the type of victim preferred; hence, few generalizations can be made; nevertheless, careerists would consider banks, loan companies, supermarkets, drug stores, bars, liquor stores, gas stations, corner groceries, a fair ranking of victims in descending order of profit but not necessarily in terms of preference. Intervening variables, i.e., the conditions sought or avoided in the robbery setting, are the important determinants in the selection of robbery victims. The victim is always viewed as part of a larger configuration; his profit-

potential is never the sole consideration for the armed robber. These variables, however, become different objects of concern depending on the partnership. Identical sets of conditions may be perceived in completely opposite terms by different groups of armed robbers, and distinctive, nevertheless contradictory, rationales concerning these differential perceptions develop.

Thus, for example, contrast the different victim perception of supermarkets and the antithetical rationales concerning the optimum time that robberies should be perpetrated:

There's usually quite a bit of money and there is usually quite a bit of disorganized activity. There is very little danger of being shot in the store. Many stores will have a look-out arrangement and an armed person at the look-out arrangement from say a walled mezzanine or something. A robber is very apt to be shot from concealment. There are enough people moving about in a supermarket that this is not very apt to happen. Your safest bet is probably a supermarket . . . .

Yes, we preferred to take an action either when there were other people in the store, which would be during operating hours, or before they would have occasion to expect anyone to be able to enter and set up a defense . . . .

We didn't ever develop any real pattern relative to that [best time of day]. We took one early in the morning when they were unloading supply trucks in the back—shortly after the time that we felt the safe would be open on its time lock. We've taken others in the late evening. Really there was—so far as we determined by operating it—no reason for taking it at one time of the day rather than at another . . . .

. . . the biggest factor was—was the place crowded? And we never did anything in the day time. So the biggest factor was how many people would be in—that was how many people would be in that place about the time we wanted to walk in. And this is why we cruised the streets. We may just stop at a place and walk right in and rob it, because there was no one in there . . . .

Say an average of three or four people in there, which is detrimental, you can't watch all of them at the same time. Banks, well, that's like a race track. You've always got people. So, in my thinking the less people the better. And even the supermarket there is always too many people in there, until absolute closing time, let them lock me in, and then I knew just where the two people were . . . .

As a consequence of these differing patterns of social perception of optimum robbery conditions and diverse interpretations as to the impact of these conditions, no unitary model of what robbers consider the ideal robbery setting is possible. Individual armed robbers all have varying opinions and rationales to such degree that the "perfect set-up" may be spoken about, but there is little commonality in its explication among robbery partnerships.

The potential *take* thus never is the single criterion of victim choice, but the contingencies, as interpreted by each partnership, enter as important variables of victim selection. For this reason, few careerists become bank robbers, although the lure of the vast sums to be had and the excitement involved are attractive. Generally, banks present a multiplicity of conditions to take into account; as a result they are considered only by the more accomplished partnerships as potential victims. Contrary to some accounts, banks fall prey more often to the amateur than the committed robber. Indeed those careerists who do specialize in bank robberies, tend to fear the amateur bank robber as a potential source of difficulty.

The guy who sticks up a bank who doesn't know what he is doing makes it tough all around. He's never in control and somebody is liable to take advantage—some hero—then there is violence. This makes it hard for when some dude comes in who really means business they think he's just another amateur and things get out of control and somebody is liable to get hurt . . . .

Quantitatively, careerists tend to prefer what might be termed victims of the middle range: liquor stores, drug stores, and supermarkets.

Retail liquor establishments play a peculiar role as careerists' victims; they are popular yet not necessarily preferred. Their very prevalence in urban communities and ready availability most hours of the day and night, however, make them easy if not choice victims, lending themselves readily to serial robbery. A series of liquor store holdups can yield a handsome sum, even though the single store may only give small reward:

We hit nothing but liquor stores, sometimes two or three a night. We'd make 20, 50, 100 bucks a store—that's at the most 300 split three ways—you'd have to hustle to make it . . . .

Although it is difficult to point to any single victim preference, among armed robbers there are a number of themes of victim choice on which there is some unanimity.

Rationales, Myths and Values

Perhaps it is imprecise to speak of a victim from the point of view of the robber, for to him a victim in the usual sense of the term is rarely present in the crime situation.[24] Careerist partnerships make conscious efforts to choose as sites for robberies locales that are either parts of corporations or large organizations. The employee with whom the robbery encounter is made is considered to have nothing at stake since there is no personal loss for him, at most he is conceived of as an agent-victim. It is quite clear in the career robber's rationale that for an employee to worry about a sum of money that does not belong to him in the first place is foolish. He views the actual robbery encounter as an impersonal matter, for in so doing he is not robbing a person but some amorphous mass—a bank, a supermarket, a loan company. In the actual robbery confrontation he may be dealing with a role incumbent but the role is only in the vaguest sense representative of the impersonal company which is the object of his attack. Hence it is inconceivable to the carrer robber that an agent-victim should resist, since there is no cause for resistance; no one loses personally. Careerists rarely rob the patrons who happen to be in an establishment at the time of the robbery, precisely because the encounter is deemed too personal.

The careerist robber frowns on other robbers who rob individuals, considers them amateur "hot heads" and "bums who make it hot for everybody." Small neighborhood grocery stores and gas stations are the domain not of the careerist but of the latter type of robber:

No, we'd only hit big markets. They're insured anyway. Nobody is out of pocket . . . Why should some small clerk put up a fuss? It isn't his money. They're not hurting . . .

The careerists' ambivalence about robbing liquor stores becomes clearer when one realizes that often these businesses are owner-operated. Under such circumstances it is difficult to avoid a person who may have "something at stake," but even in these circumstances there is always the insurance rationale.

I try to make sure the owner isn't around by knocking the place over late at night, figuring he'll have somebody working for him then who wouldn't care.

I: And if the owner is around?

S: The insurance would cover him anyway, but it's riskier. The employee doesn't care; the owner does, and he might be concerned . . .

Whenever possible, the careerist robber attempts to avoid the "human" in the situation; where it is unavoidable, he overcomes it by the rationale of recovery. Not unlike the soldier who makes a different object out of a human being by calling him the "enemy," the robber makes redefinitions in the very process of becoming a careerist. His victims are already depersonalized objects to him; robbing an impersonal business or company only makes it simpler, and as we shall see subsequently, more acceptable.

Next to the denial of the victims, the conception of honesty has an important place in the robber's rationale system. Sweeping aside the inherent paradox, the career robber views his form of acquisition as a not-too-dishonest enterprise. This appears at first glance as a peculiar stance, but becomes more intelligible when the behavioral elements that make up the robbery situation are examined. Robbery is an open, direct, face-to-face encounter coupled with a non-disguised coercive demand; there is no stealth or furtiveness as with a thief but a confrontation of unabashed power. It is this quality of candor that the robber equates with honesty, an apologia which in his own self-reflexive action makes the robbery career an object of worth, if not noble.

No, I never thought of committing other kinds of crime. It just never occurred to me. I never thought about writing checks or stealing, somehow, I don't know—this will sound funny, but it just never seemed honest. It's funny. I can't really explain it . . .

I: What do you mean, it wasn't *honest*?

S: Well I just—I couldn't steal anything. You know—behind someone's back. When I took something I'd make no bones about it. I didn't hide or make out phony papers. I don't know, I guess it's just sorta being yourself—you just take it in front of the guy; you don't pussyfoot it around and do a lot of pretending . . .
And something else—it's a lot cleaner. You feel better about it. You're a pretty big man standing there with your gun. Makes you feel oh—kinda important—big, somebody people don't mess with . . .

To the robber, then, the career gives importance and is a noncontrived means of gaining a goal from a "faceless" victim in a situation in which, if all "play their cards right," no one suffers.

A considerable attraction of robbery is its challenge and its call to action—qualities which are savored by the careerist and discussed in the partnership. The review and *post-mortem* of each robbery adds further excitement and stimulation to the career. With each completed robbery a victory is achieved. In the *post-mortem* interaction each success binds the partnership further and provides the motive for continued involvement. In this fashion, each robbery serves to stimulate the next where there is always the chance of richer rewards. Thus

the career continues, and with continued success there is the ever-present proof that "nothing can go wrong." A myth of invincibility gradually develops and takes shape, and often is the precursor to the dissolution of the partnership through capture.

As already pointed out, careerists do not think in terms of capture; although they are aware of the possibility, it is always a remote awareness. As the career unfolds for the individual robber confidence grows that no one can break his pattern—as long as he is careful. Continued interaction with his crime partners serves to reify the myth.

Yeah, we thought we'd go on indefinitely, and not get caught. I think this is everybody's feeling—that they'll never get caught. I think everything that somebody does, that they are conscious of, they think they have this feeling that they'll never get caught. I heard it time after time. "Shit, I had such a thing going for me that I thought I'd never get caught." I really don't think that the consequences are really thought about at all.

Akin to the invincibility myth is the myth of the *utopian heist*. This refers to what most careerists call the "big job," the most lucrative robbery. It is to be the final event which leads to retirement—the robbery that promises to end robbery. It is the ever-alluring pot of gold at the end of the rainbow—the solution to all the careerist's ills. In this connection, one must remember that the careerist's commitment to robbery is viewed by him as a temporary affair. To him robbery is a career escalator to more conventional endeavors.[25] He hopes to return triumphantly where he has previously failed. The "pot of gold" could lead him there quickly. Partnerships discuss the "big job," sometimes with fervor, as a realistic possibility. In the loosely knit group of the partnership the *utopian heist* has a coalescing function. Moreover, it serves to focus the robbers' attention toward continued involvement.

When the rare "big job" is accomplished, events do not change for the rewards are dissipated only to start the cycle anew.

> . . . he and I took off and got us a couple of girls, and we went down to Mexico. Well, we had a heck of a time getting across the border, because we had to go cash it all into small bills. Part of it we left buried up around our homes. And we stayed down there about a week horsing around. Came back and decided we didn't want to go back to work, because it was too easy. And we started getting a little bit too rambunctious and almost every night we'd look for a place to rob. We weren't satisfied with what we had. Good clothes, the leisurely hours and the girls you could spend a lot of money on, and check into the biggest hotels, the nicest motels, all of this stuff kinda went to make us go out every night for some more.

The Career Armed Robber as a Type

Viewed as a type, the individual careerist assumes the posture of a man whose round of life never quite seems to meet the standards of middle-class convention. He need not have a delinquent background nor have committed serious crimes prior to his career, but the rhythm of his existence has never been in tune with the conventional.

Typically, the careerist represents one who lives on the fringes, more a "night" dweller than a "day" dweller. In his circle of intimate acquaintances are the hustler, the bookie, the gambler, and the pimp; the bartender, the taxidriver, and the bellhop. Involvement in robbery does not remove him from this life arena but locks him more securely in it. The career, however, promises upward social mobility; thus the robbery

ostensibly to finance a legitimate business, to open a motel, to enable a trip to start anew, but the style of life does not permit it. As the careerist reveals, he "blows it" and thus remains true to the "easy come, easy go" style of his social surroundings. Whereas the racketeer or organized criminal may achieve respectability for himself and his family, the career robber never translates his economic gain into objects of legitimate social worth or more conventional style of life. Hence, the career does not change the existing life style; rather, it is an extreme expression of it and functions for the careerist as a transitory, if illusive, transcendent experience.

On those infrequent occasions when the careerist terminates the career on his own volition, the previous life cycle is usually resumed with reasonably appropriate accommodations as to costs and risks. The involuntary termination of the career, however, often leads to even further estrangement, for as Lemert has suggested, ". . . [when] the exconvict advances economically to the point where better positions become open to him, he may be rejected because of inability to obtain a bond or because his past criminal record comes to light. If the man's aspirational roles are low, he may adjust successfully as, say, a laborer or casual worker; otherwise, he nearly always shows the marks of his difficult struggle." [26]

The careerist thus eventually returns to his former milieu after the career is ended, whether he leaves it voluntarily or is forced to relinquish it by being caught and confined. In the latter instance, however, the stigmatic burden of the identified criminal makes it extremely difficult for him ever to lift himself above his circle:

> I did a lot of time for a few robberies. I'm not complaining, I shoulda known better . . .

when you come out you're right back where you started only worse, nobody knows you and times have changed. So you knuckle under—you can make it—but you sure have to change your way of thinking. You can't be afraid of carrying a lunch bucket—if you don't you're sunk or you go back to capering and the same old shit starts over again.

The brief triumph leads to defeat or accommodation that must ultimately involve a reorganization of the self toward acceptance of a modified role as an actor on the social stage.

Footnotes

[1] Edwin H. Sutherland, *The Professional Thief*, University of Chicago Press, 1937, pp. 27–42.

[2] Edwin H. Sutherland and Donald R. Cressey, *Principles of Criminology*, 7th ed., Philadelphia: J. B. Lippincott Co., 1966.

[3] Marshall B. Clinard and Richard Quinney, *Criminal Behavior Systems—A Typology*, New York: Holt, Rinehart and Winston, Inc., 1967, p. 429. See their listing of the few representative studies in this area.

[4] Sutherland, *The Professional Thief*, pp. 35–42, 215 ff.

[5] For a fuller discussion of the process of commitment involved in becoming a professional robber see Einstadter, *op. cit.*, pp. 31–66.

[6] An interesting parallel is found in military life. During war time, a soldier is expected to give only his name, rank, and serial number if captured. It is recognized that he might "break" due to "brainwashing" and torture but he is still considered a traitor by his side if he does and is sanctioned accordingly. As one informer put it, "He should do his own time and number."
Sanctions may be applied in prison to the informing robber in the form of ostracism or violence. But often a curious reversal of intentions occurs. Since prison authorities usually are aware of the informing robber's "enemies," those who intend harm are placed in the ironic position of having to protect the informer since they would receive the blame in case any injury befalls him.

[7] This has been recognized for criminal relationships in general. ". . . The social relationships of criminals are quite tenuous and much more likely to take the form of transient combination . . ."

See Edwin M. Lemert, *Social Pathology*, New York: McGraw-Hill, 1951, p. 48.

[8] See Walter B. Miller, "Lower Class Culture as a Generating Milieu of Gang Delinquency," *Journal of Social Issues*, XIV, 1958, 5–19. Fate discussed as one of the focal concerns of the lower class.

[9] Primitive practices at least follow this pattern. Malinowski has noted in his study of Trobrianders that when they fished using the reliable method of poisoning and a rich catch was a certainty, magic was not practiced. On the other hand, when they fished in the open sea with its dangers, magical rituals were abundantly employed. See Robert K. Merton, *Social Theory and Social Structure*, 2d ed. rev., New York: Free Press of Glencoe, 1957, p. 108.

[10] A recent study of department store shoplifting would indicate that this form of theft is no longer primarily a group phenomenon. See Mary Owen Cameron, *The Booster and the Snitch*, New York: Free Press of Glencoe, 1964, p. 58.

[11] The fix still seems to be pervasive and widespread but in subtler form in relationship to organized crime. See Report by the President's Commission on Law Enforcement and Administration of Justice. *The Challenge of Crime in a Free Society 1967*, Chapter 7 passim.

[12] Daniel Bell, "Crime as an American Way of Life," *Antioch Review*, XIII, Summer 1953, 131–157.

[13] Sutherland, *Professional Thief*, p. 198 (emphasis supplied).

[14] *Ibid.*

[15] Einstadter, *op. cit.*, Chapter 12 passim.

[16] It is perhaps also imprecise to refer to the robber who engages in robbery on a persistent basis as professional in the sense that Sutherland refers to a thief as professional. More descriptive are the terms *career robber* or *careerist*. Others have found difficulty in applying Sutherland's professional criteria to criminal groups other than thieves. Cf. Edwin M. Lemert, "The Behavior of the Systematic Check Forger," *The Other Side*, ed. Howard S. Becker, New York: Free Press of Glencoe, 1964, pp. 211–224.

[17] Webster defines partnership as "a relationship . . . involving close cooperation between parties having specified and joint rights and responsibilities (as in a common enterprise)." Robbers tend to refer to their associates as *crime partners*.

[18] Although robberies may be performed by a single person, careerists feel that a profitable robbery is rarely completed successfully alone. Groups have also been found to have greater probability

of accuracy in solving problems, since groups of individuals have greater resources for ideas and capacity for dealing with error—hence the possibility for the robber to better plan his crimes. See generally D. C. Barnlund, "A Comparative Study of Individual, Majority and Group Judgment," *Journal of Abnormal and Social Psychology*, LVIII, January, 1959, 55–60; J. F. Dashiell, "Experimental Studies of the Influence of Social Situations on the Behavior of Individual Human Adults," *A Handbook of Social Psychology*, ed. C. Murchinson, Worcester: Clark University Press, 1935, pp. 1097–1158; H. V. Perlmutter and Germaine de Montmollin, "Group Learning of Nonsense Syllables," *Journal of Abnormal and Social Psychology*, XLVII, October, 1952, 762–769; R. C. Ziller, "Group Size: A Determinant of the Quality and Stability of Group Decisions," *Sociometry*, XX, June, 1957, 165–173.

[19] Robber partnerships confirm previous findings about group structure. Thus, for example, the fact that individuals vary in the ability to assume a given role has been shown by T. R. Sarbin and D. S. Jones, "An Experimental Analysis of Role Behavior," *Journal of Abnormal and Social Psychology*, LI, September, 1955, 236–241, and that particular traits are needed to meet certain role expectations, as shown by E. F. Borgatta, "Role-Playing Specification, Personality, and Performance," *Sociometry*, XXIV, September, 1961, 218–233; R. Rapoport and I. Rosow, "An Approach to Family Relationships and Role Performance," *Human Relations*, X, September, 1957, 209–221.

[20] Hare has pointed out that "in general, when the size of the group decreases, the strength of the affectional ties between members increases, with the dyad allowing the possibilities for the greatest degree of intimacy," A. Paul Hare, "Interpersonal Relations in the Small Group," *Handbook of Modern Sociology*, ed. Robert E. L. Faris, Chicago: Rand McNally, 1964, p. 252. When a dyad exists the partners as a rule are either close friends or are related.

[21] It has also been shown that where there is a need for fine coordination there is a tendency to restrict the size of the group. *Ibid.*, p. 253.

[22] These findings are at variance with the "differential association tradition" which purports that criminal techniques are learned in association with other criminals. See Edwin H. Sutherland and Donald R. Cressey, *Principles of Criminology*, 5th edition rev., New York: Lippincott, 1955, pp. 74–81. What is being maintained here is that the planning skills required in robbery are generic skills which are adaptable from a variety of noncriminal experiences and need not necessarily be learned *only* in association with other robbers. These capacities may be brought into the partnership from the outside. They may, however, be modified to meet specific requirements of robbery. See also Cressey's critique in Donald R. Cressey, *Other People's Money*, New York: The Free Press of Glencoe, 1953, and his review of the theory and criticism of literature in Donald R. Cressey, "Epidemiology and Individual Conduct: A Case from Criminology," *The Pacific Sociological Review*, Fall 1960, III, 47–54.

[23] This is also contrary to the professional thief whose professionalism depended on being accepted, tutored and recognized by other thieves. To the careerist robber, planning ability combined with anonymity are important factors in a successful career. See Sutherland, *Professional Thief*, p. 207.

[24] Cf. with Sykes' and Matza's discussion of the denial of the victim by delinquents. Gresham M. Sykes and David Matza, "Techniques of Neutralization: A Theory of Delinquency," *American Sociological Review*, Vol. XXII, December, 1957, 664–670.

[25] Howard S. Becker and Anselm C. Strauss, "Careers, Personality, and Adult Socialization," *American Journal of Sociology*, LXII, November, 1956, pp. 253–263.

[26] Lemert, *Social Pathology*, p. 331.

Further Readings

The potentially pertinent literature on the sociological areas covered in this book is so vast that no brief bibliography can be considered representative. The titles below are a sampling of some of the recent research and commentary on issues in contemporary American society. Many additional selections may be found in these social science journals: *Trans-action, Psychology Today, Social Prolems, The Journal of Social Issues, The Annals,* and *The Public Interest.*

BAKER, LUTHER G., JR. "The Personal and Social Adjustment of the Never-Married Woman," *Journal of Marriage and the Family,* 30, August, 1968, 473–479.

BITTNER, EGON. "The Police on Skid-Row: A Study of Peace Keeping," *American Sociological Review,* 32, October, 1967, 699–715.

BLUM, RICHARD H., *et al. Students and Drugs. Drugs II: College and High School Observations.* San Francisco: Jossey Bass Inc., Publishers, 1969.

BORDUA, DAVID (ed.). *The Police: Six Sociological Essays.* New York: John Wiley and Sons, Inc., 1967.

BOSKIN, JOSEPH. "The Revolt of the Urban Ghettos," *Annals of the American Academy of Political and Social Science,* 382, March, 1969, 1–14.

BROWN, MICHAEL E. "The Condemnation and Persecution of Hippies," *Trans-action,* 6, September, 1969, 33–46.

BUCHANAN, JAMES M. "Student Revolts, Academic Liberalism and Constitutional Attitudes," *Social Research,* 35, Winter, 1968, 666–680.

CAHNMAN, WERNER J. "The Stigma of Obesity," *Sociological Quarterly,* 9, Summer, 1968, 283–299.

CAREY, JAMES T. *The College Drug Scene.* Englewood Cliffs, N.J.: Prentice-Hall, Inc., 1968.

COONEY, JOHN AND DANA SPITZER. " 'Hell, No, We Won't Go!' American Deserters in Sweden and Canada," *Trans-action,* 6, September, 1969, 53–62.

COSER, LEWIS A. "The Sociology of Poverty," *Social Problems,* 13, Fall, 1965, 140–148.

COX, HARVEY. "The 'New Breed' in American Churches: Sources of Social Activism in American Religion," *Daedalus,* 96, Winter, 1967, 135–150.

DEANE, PAUL C. "The Persistence of Uncle Tom: An Examination of the Image of the Negro in Children's Fiction Series," *Journal of Negro Education,* 37, Spring, 1968, 140–145.

DEGLER, CARL N. "Revolution Without Ideology: The Changing Place of Women in America," *Daedalus,* 93, Spring, 1964, 653–670.

ECKLAND, BRUCE K. "Genetics and Sociology: A Reconsideration," *American Sociological Review,* 32, April, 1967, 173–194.

EISEN, JONATHAN AND DAVID STEINBERG. "The Student Revolt Against Liberals," *Annals of the American Academy of Political and Social Science,* 382, March, 1969, 83–94.

ESSELSTYN, T. C. "Prostitution in the United States," *The Annals of the American Academy of Political and Social Science,* 376, March, 1968, 123–135.

FRIEDENBERG, EDGAR Z. "The Generation Gap," *Annals of the American Academy of Political and Social Science,* 382, March, 1969, 32–42.

GAGNON, JOHN H. AND WILLIAM SIMON. "Sexual Deviance in Contemporary America," *The Annals of the American Academy of Political and Social Science,* 376, March, 1968, 106–122.

GOODE, ERICH (ed.). *Marijuana.* New York: Atherton Press, 1969.

GOULD, LEROY C. "The Changing Structure of Property Crime in an Affluent Society," *Social Forces,* 48, September, 1969, 50–59.

GUTTMANN, ALLEN. "Protest Against the War in Vietnam," *Annals of the American Academy of Political and Social Science,* 382, March, 1969, 56–63.

HADDEN, JEFFREY K. "Clergy Involvement in Civil Rights," *Annals of the American Academy of Political and Social Science*, 387, January, 1970, 118–127.

HAMBLIN, ROBERT L. AND ROBERT O. BLOOD, JR. "Pre-Marital Experience and the Wife's Sexual Adjustment," *Social Problems*, 4, October, 1956, 122–130.

HARP, JOHN AND PHILIP TAIETZ, "Academic Integrity and Social Structure: A Study of Cheating Among College Students," *Social Problems*, 13, Spring, 1966, 365–373.

HEISE, DAVID R. "Norms and Individual Patterns in Student Deviancy," *Social Problems*, 16, Summer, 1968, 78–92.

HERSEY, JOHN. *The Algiers Motel Incident*. New York: Alfred A. Knopf, 1968.

HOROWITZ, IRVING L. "The Life and Death of Project Camelot," *Trans-action*, 3, November–December, 1965, 3–7, 44–47.

HORTON, JOHN. "Time and Cool People," *Trans-action*, 4, April, 1967, 5–12.

HOWARD, JOHN R. "The Making of a Black Muslim," *Trans-action*, 4, December, 1966, 15–21.

HUMPHREYS, LAUD. *Tearoom Trade: Impersonal Sex in Public Places*. Chicago: Aldine Publishing Company, 1970.

KNOPF, TERRY ANN. "Sniping—A New Pattern of Violence?" *Trans-action*, 6, July–August, 1969, 22–29.

KRADER, LAWRENCE. "Environmental Threat and Social Organization," *Annals of the American Academy of Political and Social Sciences*, 389, May, 1970, 11–18.

KRUEGER, CYNTHIA. "Do 'Bad Girls' Become Good Nurses?" *Trans-action*, 5, July–August, 1968, 31–36.

LIEBERSON, STANLEY AND ARNOLD R. SILVERMAN. "The Precipitants and Underlying Conditions of Race Riots," *American Sociological Review*, 30, December, 1965, 887–898.

LIEBOW, ELLIOTT. *Tally's Corner*. Boston: Little, Brown and Company, Inc., 1967.

LOPATA, HELENA ZNANIECKI. "Loneliness: Forms and Components," *Social Problems*, 17, Fall, 1969, 248–262.

LOPATA, HELENA ZNANIECKI AND JOSEPH R. NOEL. "The Dance Studio—Style Without Sex," *Trans-action*, 4, January–February, 1967, 10–17.

McCAGHY, CHARLES H. AND JAMES K. SKIPPER, JR. "Lesbian Behavior as an Adaptation to the Occupation of Stripping," *Social Problems*, 17, Fall, 1969, 262–270.

McDOWELL, SOPHIA. "Research Note on a Serendepitous Experiment: The Racial Identification of Strangers," *The American Sociologist*, 3, August, 1968, 245–246.

MARX, GARY T. *Protest and Prejudice: A Study of Belief in the Black Community*. New York: Harper and Row Publishers, 1967.

MASOTTI, LOUIS (ed.). *Riots, Violence and Disorder: Civil Turbulence in Urban Communities*. Beverly Hills, Calif.: Sage Publications, 1968.

MAZUR, ALLAN. "The Littlest Science," *The American Sociologist*, 3, August, 1968, 195–200.

MEYER, MARSHALL W. "Automation and Bureaucratic Structure," *American Journal of Sociology*, 74, November, 1968, 256–264.

MOSKOS, CHARLES C. "Racial Integration in the Armed Forces," *American Journal of Sociology*, 72, September, 1966, 132–148.

NELKIN, DOROTHY. "Unpredictability and Life Styles in a Migrant Labor Camp," *Social Problems*, 17, Spring, 1970, 472–487.

NELSON, JOEL I. "Anomie: Comparisons Between the Old and New Middle Class," *American Journal of Sociology*, 74, September, 1968, 184–192.

NISBET, ROBERT A. "The Year 2000 and All That," *Commentary*, 45, June, 1968, 60–66.

PETER, LAWRENCE J. AND RAYMOND HULL. *The Peter Principle*. New York: Bantam Books, 1969.

POLSKY, NED. "Poolrooms: End of the Male Sanctuary," *Trans-action*, 4, March, 1967, 33–40.

QUARANTELLI, E. L. AND RUSSELL R. DYNES. "Looting in Civil Disorders: An Index of Social Change," *American Behavioral Scientist*, 11, March–April, 1968, 7–10.

REISS, IRA L. *Premarital Sexual Standards in America*. Glencoe, Ill.: The Free Press of Glencoe, 1960.

REX, JOHN. "Students and Revolution," *New Society*, 11, May 30, 1968, 791–793.

ROBINSON, JOHN P. "Public Reaction to Political Protest: Chicago, 1968," *Public Opinion Quarterly*, 34, Spring, 1970, 1–9.

ROHTER, IRA S. "The Righteous Rightists," *Trans-action*, 4, May, 1967, 27–35.

ROSSI, ALICE. "Abortion Laws and Their Victims," *Trans-action,* 3, September–October, 1966, 7–12.

SCHIFF, LAWRENCE F. "Dynamic Young Fogies —Rebels on the Right," *Trans-action,* 4, November, 1966, 31–36.

SCHWARTZ, DAVID C. "On the Ecology of Political Violence: 'The Long Hot Summer' as a Hypothesis," *American Behavioral Scientist,* 11, July–August, 1968, 24–28.

SKIPPER, JAMES K., JR. AND CHARLES H. MC-CAGHY. "Stripteasers: The Anatomy and Career Contingencies of a Deviant Occupation," *Social Problems,* 17, Winter, 1970, 391–405.

SLATER, MARIAM K. "My Son the Doctor: Aspects of Mobility Among American Jews," *American Sociological Review,* 34, June, 1969, 359–373.

SOLOMON, DAVID (ed.). *The Marihuana Papers.* Indianapolis, Ind.: The Bobbs-Merrill Company, Inc., 1966.

SPIEGEL, JOHN P. "Campus Conflict and Professional Egos," *Trans-action,* 6, October, 1969, 41–50.

SPRADLEY, JAMES P. *You Owe Yourself a Drunk: An Ethnography of Urban Nomads.* Boston: Little, Brown and Company, Inc., 1970.

STRAUSS, ANSELM. "Medical Ghettos," *Transaction,* 4, May, 1967, 7–15, 62.

SUTTLES, GERALD D. *The Social Order of the Slum: Ethnicity and Territorality in the Inner City.* Chicago: The University of Chicago Press, 1968.

TAVISS, IRENE. "Changes in the Form of Alienation: The 1900's vs. The 1950's," *American Sociological Review,* 34, February, 1969, 46–57.

TOCH, HANS H. *Violent Men.* Chicago: Aldine Publishing Company, 1969.

WRONG, DENNIS H. "The Oversocialized Conception of Man in Modern Sociology," *American Sociological Review,* 26, April, 1961, 183–193.

YABLONSKY, LEWIS. *The Hippie Trip.* New York: Pegasus, 1968.

A B C D E F G H I J   9 8 7 6 5 4 3 2 1